Objectivity and Insight

MARK SACKS

CLARENDON PRESS · OXFORD
2000

OXFORD
UNIVERSITY PRESS

Great Clarendon Street, Oxford OX2 6DP

Oxford University Press is a department of the University of Oxford.
It furthers the University's objective of excellence in research, scholarship,
and education by publishing worldwide in

Oxford New York

Athens Auckland Bangkok Bogotá Buenos Aires Calcutta
Cape Town Chennai Dar es Salaam Delhi Florence Hong Kong Istanbul
Karachi Kuala Lumpur Madrid Melbourne Mexico City Mumbai
Nairobi Paris São Paulo Shanghai Singapore Taipei Tokyo Toronto Warsaw
and associated companies in Berlin Ibadan

Oxford is a registered trade mark of Oxford University Press
in the UK and certain other countries

Published in the United States
by Oxford University Press Inc., New York

© Mark Sacks 2000

The moral rights of the author have been asserted
Database right Oxford University Press (maker)

First published 2000

All rights reserved. No part of this publication may be reproduced,
stored in a retrieval system, or transmitted, in any form or by any means,
without the prior permission in writing of Oxford University Press,
or as expressly permitted by law, or under terms agreed with the appropriate
reprographics rights organizations. Enquiries concerning reproduction
outside the scope of the above should be sent to the Rights Department,
Oxford University Press, at the address above

You must not circulate this book in any other binding or cover
and you must impose the same condition on any acquirer

British Library Cataloguing in Publication Data

Data available

Library of Congress Cataloging-in-Publication Data
Sacks, Mark.
Objectivity and insight / Mark Sacks.
p. cm.
Includes bibliographical references and index.
1. Objectivity. I. Title.
BD220.S18 2000 121'.4—dc21 00–057114
ISBN 0–19–825058–4

1 3 5 7 9 10 8 6 4 2

Typeset by Graphicraft Limited, Hong Kong
Printed in Great Britain
on acid-free paper by
T.J. International Ltd
Padstow, Cornwall

Preface

MOST of this book was written during a year in Berlin made possible by the award of a Humboldt Fellowship. I am indebted to the Alexander von Humboldt Foundation for their support; and to the University of Essex for approving a generous leave of absence that enabled me to take up the fellowship, and for subsequently offering further relief from teaching to assist in completion of the book.

The year in Berlin was significantly enriched by several people who, individually and collectively, opened a social and intellectual space that was far beyond anything that a visitor to a country can reasonably expect. In particular, I would like to record thanks to Christoph Menke, Beate Rössler and Albrecht Wellmer.

While most of the writing was done during that year, the project was in the pipeline for very much longer than that. I would like to express my gratitude to those who over a period of years offered an enabling combination of philosophical interaction and friendship. I am deeply indebted to Jay Bernstein, Peter Bieri (whose hospitality during my stay in Berlin was extraordinary), Sebastian Gardner, Axel Honneth, Gideon Makin and the late Tony Tanner. Similarly, to Adrian Moore and Peter Sullivan, who in addition read the completed manuscript and provided very helpful comments. I am especially grateful to David Bell, for his comments on some of the early material, and for many conversations, most notably on Kant and transcendental idealism during the year we were by chance both in Berlin.

My thanks too to Peter Momtchiloff, Philosophy Editor at Oxford University Press, for his positive and conscientious attitude throughout; to Charlotte Jenkins, who oversaw production of the book; and to Laurien Berkeley for her sympathetic copy-editing. I am also very grateful to two anonymous readers for their generous and helpful comments.

My deepest debt is to Lucy O'Brien, for her philosophical input, and for so much else.

Acknowledgements

Two of the chapters here appeared, in earlier forms, as papers. A version of Chapter 4 was published in A. Biletzki and A. Matar (eds.), *The Story of the Analytic Tradition* (London: Routledge, 1998); and a version of Chapter 6 appeared in the *International Journal of Philosophical Studies*, 5 (1997). (A part of Chapter 8, Section 1 appeared in R. Stern (ed.), *Transcendental Arguments* (Oxford: Oxford University Press, 1999).)

Contents

Introduction   1

PART I. SUBJECT-DRIVEN SCEPTICISM

1. Empiricist Theories of the Mind: Locke and Hume   7
2. Kant   43
3. James and Bergson: The Neglected Alternative   94

PART II. WORLD-DRIVEN SCEPTICISM

4. From the Egological Subject to the Domestication of Reason   145
5. The Scope of Objectivity   169
6. Transcendental Constraints and Transcendental Features   198

PART III. CONCEPTIONS OF OBJECTIVITY

7. A Compulsion to Objectivity in Experience   221
8. A Defence of Transcendental Arguments   273
9. Conclusion: Objectivity, Insight, and the Place of Fictional Force   312

References   329
Index   339

Introduction

THIS book is concerned, primarily, with insight into the nature and scope of objectivity. This concern is addressed directly in Part III. The issue is set in relation to two forms of scepticism, in Parts I and II. While these serve to bring out the nature and costs of our standard conception of objectivity, to which the final part aims to be a corrective, the intention has been to present the discussion in such a way that all three parts can be read separately.

Part I (Chapters 1–3) develops what can be called the subject-driven threat to the possibility of securing knowledge of such objective order as there might be. The concern is primarily with objectivity as that which is not merely subjective, which is not indexed to first-personal experience. On the understanding that different philosophical construals of the mind are possible, and that these stand to have differing ramifications for the prospect of securing access to the objective world, central philosophical models of the mind are examined. In doing this Part I also offers something of the relevant, and in part neglected, setting of the issue in the history of modern philosophy. Progressing from discussion of Locke and Hume in Chapter 1, to Kant in Chapter 2, and through William James and Bergson in Chapter 3, different models are examined primarily in the light of the extent to which they enable the Cartesian gap between subject and object to be bridged effectively. The discussion throughout brings out the central, but insufficiently noted, role that the assumption of psychological atomism plays in the standard empiricist and Kantian framework.

Objectivity can be contrasted in this way with what is local in the sense of being merely subjective. However, it can also be contrasted with what is local in the sense of being indexed to the lie of the land in one place, in one context, as opposed to what is universally or absolutely valid. The concern of Part II (Chapters 4–6) is to show that even if we are able to set aside the subject–object gap of subject-driven scepticism, we are still open to the worry of what may be called world-driven scepticism. Here the concern departs from the epistemological question of whether we could have knowledge that captured the way of the independent external world. It turns to the question of whether, taking our beginning now from a naturalistically conceived world with which a subject is conceived as interacting unproblematically, there is room for objective normative or classificatory structures that will hold universally. Of course, there is room for structures to be presented as having universal validity. The normative structures and belief contents of most religions, for example, are—or at least in certain times and places have been—regarded as comprising universal truths. The question is whether all such claims to universality are illusory, such that reflection on them will result in scepticism, or whether there might be scope for some claims to objectivity to be upheld even in the context of critical reflection and insight into their pedigree. The import and impact of the question is perhaps most salient when it comes to ethics and politics, but it is significantly wider than that. And the wider question is central enough for it to face, and in places draw upon, disparate philosophical developments.

Chapter 4 addresses the pressure, which has arisen in various quarters, on the idea of the individual subject, taken on its own, as the source of universal normative and classificatory structure. With that pressure taken on board, universality would have to be grounded in the wider context in which the individual is nested, and Chapter 5 addresses the prospects of that as a source of stability. An epistemological duality characteristic of transcendental idealism is identified, and it is seen how in a naturalized framework that same duality leads to unrestricted relativism. The possibility of an attenuated form of transcendental idealism which would suffice to block such relativism is examined in Chapter 6, and found wanting.

The distinctly non-metaphysical setting of the discussion throughout is important: the assumption is that there is no licence to appeal to any ontological system or order that transcends the empirical world towards which the natural sciences are directed. That critical orientation is prevalent today across a range of philosophical orientations, and the concern is to bring out the extent of the relativist threat it might pose. Given that the post-metaphysical orientation seems appropriate, the challenge to the naturalist outlook is all the more demanding of our attention, and the scope for meeting it all the more restricted.

Parts I and II, in their different ways, jointly explore the prospects for objectivity on the standard conception of objectivity. Those prospects, on this conception, turn out not to be good.

Part III (Chapters 7–9) addresses these worries. Chapter 7 turns back to the subject-driven scepticism of Part I. In presenting arguments which attempt to establish the interdependence between subjectivity and objectivity, without reliance on transcendental psychology, the chapter aims to meet, to some extent, the challenge of subject-driven scepticism. The arguments offered have the character of transcendental arguments, and Part II provided us with grounds for casting doubt on the credibility of such arguments. The possibility of such arguments is taken up in Chapter 8, which is concerned to address the world-driven scepticism of Part II. In that chapter grounds are offered for thinking that the relativist pressure on objectivity identified in Part II may to an appropriate extent be resisted. In particular, grounds are offered for thinking that arguments of the kind developed in Chapter 7 may not succumb to such pressure and in fact provide a way of resisting it.

In the course of these chapters we are led to rethink the theoretical status of the subject–object dichotomy, and consequently to reject (at the level of philosophical explanation) the standard conception of objectivity. This conception, which is identified as the ontological conception, emerges as inherently bound up with illusory force and self-deception, which, far from being eliminable, are fundamental to our natural orientation in the world. Yet this does not lead to relativism: on the contrary, recognition of this is precisely what leads on to the more resilient conception of objectivity that we need when it comes to philosophical reflection. The result is a conception of objectivity that does not face either of the dual problems confronting the standard conception: neither problems regarding the inference to reality (subject-driven scepticism), nor the problem of universality (world-driven scepticism).

Thus by the end of the book two different conceptions have been identified, each of which serves to underpin a distinct understanding of what is involved in claims regarding an objective order. Both conceptions are compatible with a non-metaphysical orientation. They differ, however, in terms of their relation to reflection. The standard conception, which leads to scepticism about the prospects for objectivity, turns out to be insufficiently critical to have been doing philosophical duty. The other is sufficiently critical, but is more revisionary of our standing theoretical assumptions than the first.

The former, ontological construal, which has also been the default in metaphysical treatments, is seemingly indispensable at one level, and is germane to the explanatory stance of the natural sciences. The other conception turns on, and brings out, a truth in transcendental idealism. Put in this way, the contrast may be misleading. While the project is Kantian, in both inspiration and orientation, it is—for all the usual reasons—not meant as a defence of transcendental idealism. Once incoherences and uncritical elements are expunged, it is not clear that there is anything acceptable left over that still counts as transcendental idealism. Rather, the attempt is to identify an insight, one that seems to underlie Kant's transcendental idealism, but which is readily distorted beyond recognition in the context of the various metaphysical excesses that comprise that position and render it unacceptable. The play-off then, in coming to terms with our entitlement to claims to objectivity, is between the conception at work in philosophical naturalism on the one hand, and a central (equally non-metaphysical) insight intimated in transcendental idealism on the other. The aim is not, and cannot be, to discard the one conception in favour of the other, but rather to accord to each its proper remit.

It is worth noting that an important element in the discussion, namely, the unseating of the subject–object dichotomy from the status traditionally accorded to it, and subsequently of a complacent endorsement of naturalism, is closely related to a theme running through much of 'continental' philosophy (as it is still called). It is a concern that can be traced from Fichte to Hegel, Husserl, Heidegger, and others. (That this has largely been ignored within the analytical tradition is of interest, although the various reasons for it can be left aside for present purposes.) Taking the primary import of this displacement, as identified in Part III, and setting it on a trajectory that runs through the work of these philosophers, would clearly be of interest. I have not attempted this here, primarily for reasons to do with limitations of space, and competence. Consequently, the precise relation between the line of thought developed in Part III and that literature will have to remain implicit in what follows. But space and caution aside, this omission might also have distinctly philosophical, and perhaps strategic, advantages.

A general comment on the implicit strategy of the discussion throughout is appropriate. Underlying the entire discussion is what may be presented as a certain disrespect for the sceptic's expectation that his case either be met with a head-on refutation, or else be accepted. The guiding thought is that the relevant response to recalcitrant sceptical problems is to diagnose an alternative to the one the sceptic is addressing, an alternative on which the problems raised can be sidestepped, thereby explaining why the sceptic is most properly ignored from that turning-point on. This is a further respect in which the present work is broadly Kantian. Kant essentially adopts this strategy with scepticism about the external world, conceding defeat to the sceptic as far as transcendental realism goes, but pointing out that empirical realism is all we actually require. In fact, however, the argument here does not adhere to this minimal strategy all the way. In the end it does not merely identify a way of avoiding the sceptical claim *while still being committed to its validity*. And the resulting distance from Kant is precisely such that the insight identified in transcendental idealism, for better or for worse, can no longer be said to constitute a form of transcendental idealism.

I

Subject-Driven Scepticism

Subject-Driven Scepticism

1
Empiricist Theories of the Mind: Locke and Hume

THE concern in this and the next two chapters is with the question of objectivity as it emerges in the traditional epistemological framework. This question is perhaps best seen as a form of subject-driven scepticism. The present chapter draws selectively on largely familiar material in order to set up the discussion of such scepticism here. As we will see, at issue is the relation between conceptions of the subject and epistemological yield: the guiding question is whether we can find an adequate model of the mind that is also adequate to the task of securing objectivity.

It is difficult to avoid the impression that for a long time philosophical models of the mind were, to a significant extent, adopted with a certain amount of inattentiveness, certainly without sufficient argument. It is as if a sense of familiarity with the mind's workings obscured the extent to which a description of those workings would nevertheless be theory-laden. And in so far as it was not a salient fact that any choice of a theoretical model of the mind was involved, there was also little attention to the fact that alternative models were possible. Given that this is so, and that different models of the mind might have different epistemological ramifications, it follows that at least some of the epistemological results that philosophers ended up with stood to be revealed as having been determined before the philosophical pursuit had started in earnest, just in virtue of the model of the mind they adopted more or less uncritically.

To exemplify the way in which this interplay works we need only set out a reminder of Descartes. The rehearsal is particularly appropriate, given that the general orientation involved here—the basic chasm between knowing subject and known object-world—was crystallized for early modern philosophy by Descartes, and is within his thought largely a consequence of his particular view of the mind. One can, as we will see in what follows, set oneself apart from the details of Descartes's conception, while still retaining enough to share the basic dichotomy that he did so much to entrench.

There are several distinct theses that combine in Descartes to constitute his more or less uncritically endorsed conception of the mind. It is assumed that the individual has direct and privileged access to the contents of his or her own mind, and that the determination of meaning, in two senses, does not stand in need of any external support. The individual can both have his or her thoughts autonomously, and know them perspicuously. 'I can see clearly', Descartes states, thereby making himself a hostage to fortune, 'that there is nothing which is easier for me to know than my mind.'[1]

Moreover, it is the received view of Cartesian individualism that the individual is authoritative about the contents of the mind in the strong sense that there is no possibility of his or her being wrong about them. It is not clear that Descartes is in fact essentially committed to anything so strong. He says that 'as to what concerns ideas, if we consider them only in themselves and do not relate them to anything else beyond themselves, they cannot properly speaking be false'.[2] His thinking is that in themselves ideas are not the sorts of thing that can be true or false; only judgements employing those ideas can be, and so the possibility of error comes in only when we make judgements. What this leaves open, and what the contemporary externalist critique of Cartesian individualism alerts us to, is that while ideas may not be truth-evaluable, knowing what my ideas are seems to involve a judgement, namely the judgement that such-and-such is the content of my thought. And so even if it is granted that error comes in only where judgement is involved, it does not follow that the individual thinker cannot be wrong about the contents of his or her mind.[3] What deflects Descartes from the recognition of this possibility is perhaps the way in which he readily runs together the notion that making a judgement involves relating ideas to something beyond them (in some sense of 'beyond') with the notion of relating ideas to something outside the individual. Thus he says:

the principal error and the commonest which we may meet with in them [i.e. in those judgements], consists in my judging that the ideas which are in me are similar or conformable to the things which are outside me; for without doubt if I considered the ideas only as certain modes of my thoughts, without trying to relate them to anything beyond, they could scarcely give me material for error.[4]

---

[1] Descartes, Second Meditation (Descartes 1975: 157).

[2] Descartes, Third Meditation (1975: 159).

[3] In the context of a discussion of Cartesian individualism, the way in which the individual might be wrong about the content of his thought is by not having access to certain determinants of meaning that are external to the individual and so might lie beyond his knowledge. But it is worth pointing out another respect in which later developments allow us to recognize that Descartes's assumption of the person's transparency to his own meanings is too hasty. Descartes does not allow for the possibility of unconscious goings-on, such that it might be the case that internal to the individual there are goings-on that preclude an easy assumption of transparency.   [4] Descartes, Third Meditation (1975: 160).

What this obscures is the possibility of not merely entertaining ideas but using them to make a judgement that goes beyond them, but only in the sense of applying them to other ideas or mental contents.

The result is a picture of the individual at home with his thoughts, immune from error as long as he remains confined to his own mental contents and does not engage in epistemic forays into the world beyond him. Moreover, there are some mental contents that the mind has innately, such that possession of them is not dependent on any interaction with the natural world external to the mind. But the autonomy thus claimed for the Cartesian individual has notorious epistemological costs. Just setting the subject up as the autonomous bearer of meaning already juxtaposes the subject to the rest of the world, so that some significant work will be involved if the subject is to be assured of epistemic contact with the world beyond his ideas.

There are, of course, other tenets to the Cartesian position, which are not so exclusively to do with his conception of the mind, but which further contribute to these epistemic problems. Descartes's trust in innate ideas *over* others is one such further exacerbating tenet;[5] another is his substance dualism.[6] However, although various such extraneous theses do make their exacerbating contribution, the basic conception of the mind involved is sufficient on its own to produce the epistemic challenge.

Now if such problems were consequent upon a conception of mind that was unassailable, as Descartes took it to be, there would be little option other than to allow them to set the agenda for us in just the way that they did for Descartes. But precisely because his view of the mind is not unassailable, we need to reconsider it in the wider context of the interplay between alternative philosophical models of the mind and their further ramifications. There remains hope that a different model of the mind will have less troubling ramifications, so that whether or not it sustains unpalatable consequences becomes one of the tests for an adequate conception of the mind.

---

[5] Only judgements can be true or false, but judgements for Descartes are operations on ideas: to judge that *p* is to assert that there is a fact corresponding to the idea of *p*, such that that idea is similar or conforms to that fact. So the question is, when it comes to judgements about the external world, which ideas are more reliably used as the basis of judgement? Descartes notoriously puts his primary trust squarely with innate ideas. But given that these ideas are innate, and are not causally grounded in the world, relying on them only further widens the epistemic gulf between us and that world. Why should any ideas with which we are pre-programmed in any way constitute a guide to the way of the independent world? Clearly a range of answers is in principle available, from pre-established harmony set up by a benevolent God, to a subsequently established harmony set up by natural selection. The relevant point here is that the more independent those basic ideas are from the world they are about, to the point that they would persist as they are regardless of the way of the world they purport to describe, the more work such explanations will have to do.

[6] The resulting difficulty in explaining how there could be any causal interaction between subject and world would be relevant, since that causal relation would seem to be required if we were *not* to rely on innate ideas.

1. LOCKE

Given that the Cartesian model of the mind drives us to scepticism about the external world, consideration of alternative models was bound to be welcome. Locke, famously, set out to repudiate the rationalist conception of the mind, starting with his attack on the idea that there are any such things as innate ideas.[7] He articulated, although did not strictly follow through with, the empiricist model of the mind. The starting-point of this conception is that the mind is at birth a *tabula rasa*; the rudiments of the story of how it then comes to be furnished with content are well known.

All the materials of reason and knowledge come from *experience*, which for Locke covers two primary sources: sensation and reflection. Ideas of *sensation* are those distinct perceptions conveyed by the five senses from external objects. These include all sensible qualities.[8] Ideas of *reflection* are those acquired not by the influence of external objects via the senses, but by the mind reflecting on its own operations. By the mind's operations he means the powers, capacities, and activities of the mind. Locke suggests that we might think of this as an internal sense. By means of it we gain a set of ideas that could not have been derived from without the mind, such as the ideas of 'perception, thinking, doubting, believing, reasoning, knowing, willing'.[9] Locke regards these two sources, inner and outer senses, as the two 'fountains of knowledge' from which alone experience furnishes the mind with ideas.[10]

As long as the mind is confined to these two sources of ideas, it is passive.[11] The mind thereby comes to be furnished with its stock of *simple* ideas. Ideas, having entered the mind in this way, can then be 'compounded and enlarged'.[12] The result is a variety of *complex* ideas. The production of such complex ideas calls for activity of the mind: it involves various operations on those original ideas, combining them in various ways. Locke conceives of the simple ideas as the basic building-blocks. These can enter the mind only through sensation or reflection; they cannot be invented; nor once in the mind can they be broken down or destroyed.[13] It is out of this given stock of simple ideas that all complex ideas are constructed. He emphasizes that the combinatorial possibilities are vast, just as out of '24 letters' an infinite number of words can be constructed.[14] The combination of simple ideas into complex ones is not restricted to the original order of reception. The mind can, 'by its

---

[7] Locke, *An Essay concerning Human Understanding*, bk. I.   [8] Ibid. II. i. 3.
[9] Ibid. II. i. 4.   [10] Ibid. II. i. 2, 5.   [11] Ibid. II. i. 25.   [12] Ibid. II. i. 5.
[13] Ibid. II. ii. 2.   [14] Ibid. II. vii. 10.

own power, put together those ideas it has and make new complex ones, which it never received so united'.[15]

It is important to note that in itself the mere distinction between simple and complex ideas, and the claim that all simple ideas are passively received through sensation or reflection, and that complex ideas are composed of them, leaves open a central question about the *genesis* of our ideas. Is it merely the bare simple ideas that are passively received in experience, or might complexes of them be received in this way too? That is, do all ideas register *as* simple ideas, which we must then combine to form complexes, or do we (at least in some cases) passively receive from the world wholes, complex ideas, which we then subsequently break down, through analysis, into the constituent simple ideas? This seems to be a real theoretical choice, between two psychological models: holist (Gestalt) and strictly atomist. It is interesting—and, as we will see later, is also of some consequence—that Locke clearly, but without argument, goes for psychological atomism. Thus, for example, he writes:

Though the qualities that affect our sense are, in the things themselves, so united and blended that there is no separation, no distance between them, yet it is plain the *ideas* they produce in the mind enter by the senses simple and unmixed. For, though the sight and touch often take in from the same object, at the same time, different *ideas*, as a man sees at once motion and colour, the hand feels softness and warmth in the same piece of wax; yet the simple *ideas* thus united in the same subject are as perfectly distinct as those that come in by different senses. The coldness and hardness which a man feels in a piece of *ice* being as distinct *ideas* in the mind as the smell and whiteness of a lily, or as the taste of sugar, and smell of a rose; and there is nothing can be plainer to a man than the clear and distinct perception he has of those simple *ideas*; which, being each in itself uncompounded, contains in it nothing but *one uniform appearance* or conception in the mind, and is not distinguishable into different *ideas*.[16]

The psychological atomism that is so clearly in evidence here and elsewhere in the writings of empiricists on the workings of the mind seems to have been a more or less uncritical importation, motivated perhaps by the success of such atomism in physics. The assumption seems to have been that what worked so well in explaining the workings of the material world should work equally well in explaining the mental world.[17] Why this should be so is unclear, and it seems that more critical attention to the importation might have made it seem less obviously right. There is certainly room to sustain a distinction between

---

[15] Ibid. II. xii. 2. The powers with which the mind can operate on simple ideas, or indeed on complex ideas, to produce novel complex ideas, include retention (II. x. 1–2), discerning (II. xi. 1–3), comparing (II. xi. 4), composition (and enlarging) (II. xi. 6), and abstraction (II. xi. 9) of ideas. [16] Ibid. II. ii. 1.
[17] Ibid. II. ii. 2, for example. But see also Ayers (1993: 17–18).

simple and complex ideas without endorsing psychological atomism. One might indeed hold on to the priority of simple over complex ideas, constituting something like logical atomism, and still not be committed to psychological atomism.

We have here, in outline, the rudiments of the empiricist story of the workings of the mind. It is important to recognize that it is only a story. However well argued the retreat from the rationalist acceptance of innate ideas might have been, it did not suffice to lead all the way to this alternative story about the mind.[18] But that it *is* a story, rather than the result of an argument, means only that it will be that much more vulnerable to any weaknesses in its performance. It will have to be judged by how well it does the job, since there is no clear independent consideration constraining us to accept it.

We can, accordingly, turn to some of the specific difficulties facing Locke's employment of this model. It is convenient to divide the question of the adequacy of the proposed model into two. The first constitutes an internal criterion of adequacy: is the proposed model sufficient as an account of the workings of the mind? The second constitutes an external criterion: is the proposed model satisfactory when viewed in the larger context of the philosophical system of which it is a part? Turning first to the internal criterion, it would seem that as an account of the mind and its capacities Locke's story is less adequate than he fully takes on board. There are certain ideas—such as solidity, extension, space—which Locke classifies as simple ideas.[19] He in fact has no other option: it is difficult to see how they could be construed as complexes constructed out of prior simple ideas, for reasons that I will turn to below. But they equally, given the psychological atomism, cannot have first entered the mind as complex structures. So they must have been received as simple ideas. But it is not clear how any of them could count as simple ideas, given that it is simply not true to say of them that they are 'uncompounded', or not 'distinguishable into different ideas'.[20] The idea of space, or of extension, can and indeed must be distinguished into different ideas, such as ideas of differently located points—possibly construed by the empiricist as sensible points (*minima sensibilia*), but alternatively simply coordinate points—all adjacent to one another. We cannot have an idea of space until we have at least two such adjacent points.[21]

Other ideas are also classified as simple ideas: e.g. existence, power, and succession.[22] Again, it is not clear that Locke is not here helping himself to more

---

[18] I will return to this issue in particular in Ch. 7, where the viability of a strictly atomistic view will come under pressure.   [19] *Essay*, II. iv–v, viii. 9.
[20] Ibid. II. ii. 1.
[21] For Locke's apparent concession that our ideas of extension and space must contain parts, see e.g. ibid. II. xiii. 7, xxi. 3. See also discussion in Ayers (1993: 41–2).
[22] *Essay*, II. vii. 7–9.

than he legitimately should. That something exists, or has existence, is taken to involve it 'being actually there', whether within or without the mind. Clearly, the idea is supposed to be of an *independent* or real existence. But, as Hume was to point out, it is difficult to see how there could be any experience that would impart to us the idea of independent existence. Similar Humean considerations count against there being a suitable simple idea (or impression) of power—the power between cause and effect.[23] Perhaps more interesting here is the case of succession, since here Hume offers no corrective, but simply repeats the same mistake. This is something that I will turn to in more detail in the discussion of Hume below.[24] For now, the case can be put briefly. The claim is that we have a simple idea of succession, because 'if we look immediately into our selves, and reflect on what is observable there, we shall find our *Ideas* always, whilst we are awake, or have any thought, passing in train, one going, and another coming, without intermission'.[25] From this experience we are supposed to glean our concept of succession, and ultimately of time.[26] But it would seem clear that the mind could not first be equipped with temporal structure by observing the train of ideas, since to observe that passage already presupposes the ability to operate and detect a temporal structure. Apart from this circularity, to which I will return, there is here also the assumption of a unity of consciousness across different atoms of experience, and yet there is nothing about Locke's empiricist model of the mind that can account for this unity. The conclusion from this brief sample of problems would seem to be that there are central conceptions (including space, time, and existence) and essential characteristics of our mental life (namely, unity of consciousness) which we obviously can have, and which Locke does not notice that we could not in fact come to have, or at least cannot readily explain how we might, on his empiricist model of the mind.

Turning now to the second, external criterion: it is well known that Locke's empiricism about the mind has some startling wider epistemic ramifications, which Locke himself saw, or half-saw, but did not in fact fully endorse. But

---

[23] There might be room for a simple new impression of reflection, one that arises in the mind from the experience of the *expectation* that results from the previous constant conjunction of certain event types. Hume offers such an account as the only possible source of an idea of causation (*Treatise*, I. iii. 14; 1978: 155, 165–6). This clearly is not what Locke has in mind (at least at II. vii. 8—the matter is less obviously clear at II. xxi. 1, which perhaps shifts vaguely towards the Humean account). But in any event, as Hume makes plain, such a source leaves the idea of causation as a fiction of the mind whose application to the world cannot be licensed by either reason or experience. In fact, as we will see below, there are reasons for doubting that the empiricist mind could come by the notion of causality in this way. For now the point is that the simple idea of causality that is suited to our epistemic task is one that we cannot come by on the empiricist account of the mind, whereas the one that we might be able to possess is unsuitable to those tasks. The empiricist account of the mind thus cannot, in its explanation of the origin of our notion of causality, meet both the internal and external tests of adequacy.

[24] See below, Sect. 2.   [25] *Essay*, II. vii. 9.   [26] See also ibid. II. xiv. 3 ff.

it is important, and interesting, to understand that although it is true that he is less rigorous in the application of empiricism than, say, Hume, this is not necessarily the result of philosophical faint-heartedness or a failing on Locke's part.

The mind, on the Lockean model, is restricted to simple ideas, and complexes constructed out of them, and we notice that certain of these ideas are constantly clustered together. The colour, the shape, the texture, and the smell of an apple by and large stick together. We are inclined to conclude that they inhere in one and the same thing, as so many properties of some one underlying and unifying substrate. We are encouraged by the fact that we use one name to refer to the whole cluster, and come to think of it as naming a single thing that owns the various properties, and so think of there being a simple idea of that thing, when in fact there is only a complex of simple ideas that somehow belong together.[27] '... not imagining how these simple *ideas* can subsist by themselves, we accustom ourselves to suppose some *substratum* wherein they do subsist, and from which they do result; which therefore we call *substance*.'[28] Masquerading as a simple idea—and as such there could be no doubting it[29]—is a complex construct of which we in fact have no clear idea, and for which there is no good evidence. And having reached an 'obscure and relative idea of substance in general', we come to entertain the idea of particular sorts of substances—man, horse, gold, water—as the support for the various qualities that cluster together in our experience of these particular items, 'though it be certain, we have no clear, or distinct *idea* of that *thing* we suppose a support'.[30] For Locke, the appeal to substance is as vacuous as the appeal in mythology to some thing, we know not what, that supports the tortoise that supports the elephant that supports the world.[31] On the Lockean model of the mind there is really no licence for this postulation of an underlying substance as the bearer of the various material qualities of which we have simple ideas. The mind is so set up that the way in which the concept of substance must arise leaves no justification for applying it to the world.

Moreover, Locke recognizes that the same holds true of the mind. We assume that all the various operations of the mind—thinking, reasoning, fearing, etc.—are operations carried out by some thing other than the body, some mental substance.[32] But we have no more an idea of this thinking substance, as distinct from its properties, than we do of material substance: 'the one being supposed to be (without knowing what it is) the *substratum* to those simple ideas we have from without; and the other supposed (with a like ignorance of what it

---

[27] *Essay*, II. xxiii. 3. See also II. xxiii. 14: 'I say our specific ideas of substances are nothing else but a collection of a certain number of simple ideas considered as united in one thing.'
[28] Ibid. II. xxiii. 1.   [29] Ibid. II. ii. 2.   [30] Ibid. II. xxiii. 4. See also II. xxiii. 6.
[31] Ibid. II. xxiii. 2.   [32] Ibid. II. xxiii. 5.

is) to be the *substratum* to those operations which we experiment in ourselves within'.³³ Having earlier distinguished ideas in us from external qualities that give rise to them,³⁴ now Locke addresses the way in which we tend to underpin those polarities with the notion of substances underlying each: material substances underlying qualities, and a spiritual substance underlying the ideas those qualities give rise to in us.

But notoriously, and contrary to what we might have expected at this stage, Locke does not withdraw from any such recognition of substances—whether spiritual or material—and recognize the sceptical impasse into which he has been led. In a rather surprising continuation of the passage just quoted he writes:

> It is plain then that the idea of corporeal substance in matter is as remote from our conceptions and apprehensions as that of spiritual substance, or spirit; and therefore, from our not having any notion of the substance of spirit, we can no more conclude its non-existence than we can, for the same reason, deny the existence of body: it being as rational to affirm there is no body, because we have no clear and distinct idea of the substance of matter, as to say there is no spirit, because we have no clear and distinct ideas of the substance of a spirit.³⁵

Rather than drawing the sceptical conclusion to which his own theory of mind would seem to have led him, Locke goes on to talk of substances, both material and spiritual.³⁶ And it is here that we need to be charitable in trying to understand why it is that he does not consistently follow through to the consequences of his empiricist model. The question then is, how does Locke come to terms with this refusal of his to endorse the sceptical conclusion to which his model of the mind in fact leads him?

The root of an answer lies, I would suggest, in his conviction that there are things that transcend human cognitive powers, aspects of the world to which we are not well equipped to attend. He elaborates on this in the sections that immediately precede his conclusions regarding substance,³⁷ talking of the fact that there are most likely 'things that our philosophy cannot account for'.³⁸ These sections seem to be so placed as to soften up the reader for those of his conclusions regarding substance that seem to extend beyond the limits of his official empiricist model of the mind.

He talks here of the limitations that are built into our mental apparatus, such that the mechanisms involved are well suited to our needs in coping with

---

³³ Ibid.   ³⁴ Ibid. II. viii. 8.   ³⁵ Ibid. II. xxiii. 5.

³⁶ His peculiar stance comes out well in the following passages: *Essay*, II. xxiii. 15, 19, 20, 22, 29–32, 37. It is interesting to juxtapose the above passage from Locke with the following from Hume: 'Philosophers begin to be reconcil'd to the principle, *that we have no idea of external substance, distinct from the ideas of particular qualities*. This must pave the way for a like principle with regard to the mind, *that we have no notion of it, distinct from the particular perceptions*' (*Treatise*, App.; 1978: 635).   ³⁷ *Essay*, II. xxiii. 11–13.

³⁸ Ibid. II. xxiii. 13.

the world in which we are situated, but they might well involve missing out on certain truths about the world. Indeed, it might be that a certain cognitive blindness is actually required if we are to survive in this world.

The infinite wise Contriver of us and all things about us hath fitted our senses, faculties, and organs to the conveniences of life, and the business we have to do here.... We are furnished with faculties (dull and weak as they are) to discover enough in the creatures to lead us to knowledge of the Creator and the knowledge of our duty, and we are fitted well enough with abilities to provide for the conveniences of living: these are our business in this world. But were our sense altered and made much quicker and acuter, the appearance and outward scheme of things would have quite another face to us and, I am apt to think, would be inconsistent with our being, or at least well-being in this part of the universe we inhabit.[39]

Locke goes on to provide examples of this. He talks, for example, of a being whose vision was so acute that it could, unaided, observe the minutest workings of a clock—could observe the micro-structure of the spring, and see how its macroscopic elasticity depended on certain atomic structures.[40] Someone with those capacities

would no doubt discover something very admirable; but if eyes so framed could not view at once the hand and the characters of the hour-plate, and thereby at a distance see what o'clock it was, their owner could not be much benefited by that acuteness, which, whilst it discovered the secret contrivance of the parts of the machine, made him lose its use.

The idea is that our sensory and cognitive capacities are well suited to the task of coping with the environment—'this globe of earth allotted for our mansion'[41] —such that a certain blindness on our part is essential for our survival. If we were cognitively and perceptually altogether open, so that no fact passed by unnoticed, simple survival tasks such as crossing the road would become impossible: every atom buzzing in the air around us would be seen, and heard, and would be as much part of our foreground of attention as the bus bearing down on us.[42] It is vital to our survival that we do not register all features of our environment, but rather attend selectively only to those that are relevant, and are so constructed as to ignore, or be blind to, certain other features.

... if by the help of such microscopical eyes (if I may so call them), a man could penetrate further than ordinary into the secret composition and radical texture of

---

[39] *Essay*, II. xxiii. 12.   [40] Ibid.   [41] Ibid.

[42] Locke seems to be identifying here the sort of phenomenon that came to the fore more recently in philosophical discussions of 'the frame problem' in artificial intelligence, which addresses the difficulty of giving robots the kind of flexible framing capacities we humans have at our disposal. See e.g. Dennett (1987) and other papers in Pylyshyn (1987). It is interesting to note that Locke speaks repeatedly of 'framing' and 'frames' in the course of this discussion.

bodies, he would not make any great advantage by the change, if such an acute sight would not serve to conduct him to the market and exchange, if he could not see things he was to avoid at a convenient distance, nor distinguish things he had to do with, by those sensible qualities others do.[43]

To hear the sounds that matter—a person talking, a car hooting, an avalanche rumbling—it is vital that we do not drown all that out by registering the sound made by the constant swirling of atoms around us, and indeed within us. Similarly for the case of sight. Locke's thought here is reminiscent of Russell's reminder that if we could see *everything*, if nothing was invisible to us, we would see photons too, and if that were the case, we would effectively be blind.

Locke thus recognizes the sense in which our survival requires epistemic shortfall. He recognizes—'an extravagant conjecture'[44]—that there could be beings with what we might think of as case-sensitive perceptual lenses, such that they could zoom in and out, selecting their attention level relative to the task at hand. That would surely be epistemically valuable, but it is not the sort of flexibility we ourselves have. And given that we must make do with a relatively fixed perceptual and cognitive apparatus, survival requires that that apparatus have a degree of blindness, a set of built-in limitations, adjusted to produce those patterns of salience that will minimally safeguard survival in the environment. For us today, post-Darwinian, the idea might most naturally be that this match is produced non-mysteriously by natural selection. For Locke, however, this uncanny match between the environment's constraints and those constraints that our cognitive limitations make salient for us is secured by God.

God has, no doubt, made us so as is best for us in our present condition. He hath fitted us for the neighbourhood of the bodies that surround us and we have to do with; and though we cannot, by the faculties we have, attain to a perfect knowledge of things, yet they will serve us well enough for those ends above-mentioned, which are our great concernment.[45]

The relevance of this in the present discussion is that Locke introduces here a distinction between the optimal way in which we can experience the world to be, and the way it is in itself. This is in effect a form of the distinction between transcendental appearance and transcendent reality that is more standardly recognized in Leibniz and Kant than in an empiricist like Locke. The distinction Locke is making is not merely between appearance and reality in the empirical sense. The idea is that there is a gap between *the best that our epistemic structure can deliver* and the way the world is in itself. In virtue of our cognitive and perceptual structure we inhabit a particular empirical world, perspectivally individuated, which is not isomorphic with the way the world is in itself. Moreover, other creatures differently constituted would inhabit different and possibly contradicting empirical worlds:

---

[43] *Essay*, II. xxiii. 12.   [44] Ibid. II. xxiii. 13.   [45] Ibid.

were our senses altered and made much quicker and acuter, the appearance and outward scheme of things would have quite another face to us . . . Nay, if that most instructive of our senses, seeing, were in any man 1,000 or 100,000 times more acute than it is now by the best microscope, things, several millions of times less than the smallest objects of his sight now would then be visible to his naked eyes, and so he would come nearer the discovery of the texture and motion of the minute parts of corporeal things. . . . but then he would be in a quite different world from other people: nothing would appear the same to him and others . . .[46]

It remains true, of course, that for Locke any of these empirical realities we inhabit might not distort reality at the level of primary qualities (contra Kant and Leibniz); but nevertheless these 'worlds' are (*a*) a consequence of our cognitive structure, and (*b*) do fall short as a matter of principle of capturing the full story about the way the world is in itself. And this kind of necessary confinement to an empirical reality of our own making which in principle cannot limn the structure of the transcendent reality can be seen as the beginning of a Kantian distinction between empirical realism and transcendental idealism.

Now this curtailment of the pretensions of knowledge might serve, for one thing, to explain why it is that Locke need not be that bothered by the question of how we can know that those ideas produced in the mind capture the way of those external things that are thought to give rise to them. Although Locke is not clear about it, there seem to be the rudiments of an insight that Kant was to develop more fully: essentially that we have no need to be certain that our perception delivers the world as it is, only that it delivers the world-view that is appropriate for beings like ourselves. The latter, but not the former, can be assured by the proper workings of the mind.

But, more directly relevant to the present point, this distinction between the world as we have the capacity to know it, and the world as it is in itself, might also help to explain the tolerance Locke manifests towards the fact that it is a consequence of his empiricist theory of the mind that we are in principle unable to know substances. On this modest view of the optimal world-view attainable by human beings like ourselves, there should be no assumption that our faculties are guaranteed to be able to plumb the depths and reach to the far corners of reality. Consequently, the mere fact of a principled shortfall in a model of mind will not be thought to count against that model. Moreover, Locke's willingness to help himself to the notion of substance, despite there being no direct justification for it on his own terms, can also be seen as a result of an awareness that experience and empirical enquiry impose limits on our knowledge, beyond which it is none the less legitimate to move on faith, so long as there is no contradiction involved.[47] Again, the

---

[46] *Essay*, II. xxiii. 12.   [47] Cf. ibid. II. xxiii. 29–32, and IV. xviii. 10.

proto-Kantian tone here should be evident. But the position is still distinctly pre-critical—the proper place of appeals to faith is here not yet located firmly beyond the boundaries of critical philosophy, as it came to be first in Hume and then in Kant.

We have seen how Locke has softened us up for a curtailment of knowledge, beyond which only faith can carry us,[48] and that with this in place he proceeds to the rather limp statements that he makes about substances.[49] It is worth noticing that this should not be thought of so much as a weakening of Locke's empiricism: he still accepts that all our knowledge in the strict sense is confined to that which we can learn through sensory input and reflection upon it. Rather, it is that while adhering to this empiricist theory, he here manifests a reserved or non-doctrinaire endorsement of the Enlightenment ideals. He seemingly accepts that the epistemic yield of the empiricist mind leaves a remainder of epistemically dark areas into which the philosopher must progress on the basis of faith. Philosophy involves endorsing propositions expressive not only of knowledge and certainty, but also of mere 'judgement and opinion', such that Locke is driven to conclude 'that natural philosophy is not capable of being made a science'.[50] As long as this curtailment of the Enlightenment ideal is held in place, the shortcoming of the empiricist theory of mind in delivering knowledge can be accommodated readily. It is only as the Enlightenment tradition builds up momentum, and the conviction spreads that the sleep of reason (the restriction of rational enquiry) brings forth monsters, that the shortfall of the Lockean model of the mind comes to represent a problem: a gap that constitutes either an untenable scepticism, or—worse—an invitation to dogmatism.

Hume, adhering to a model of the mind essentially similar to Locke's, is commonly thought of as being more consistent in following up its sceptical consequences. This readily promotes the view of Locke as somehow too

---

[48] Ibid. II. xxiii. 11–13.   [49] Ibid. II. xxiii. 14–37.

[50] Ibid. IV. xii. 10. Throughout bk. IV Locke returns to the theme that there are various degrees of what passes as knowledge, supplemented by and shading into faith (= mere opinion and judgement). The existence of external things without us, of substances, of unobserved existence, and of other minds, for example, are all cases where claims to knowledge rest on a degree of faith. On this, see ibid. IV. ii. 14, iii. 6 (Locke 1975: 541–2), iii. 21, 22–3, 26, vi. 13–14, xi. 3, 8–12, xii. 9–10, 12. Locke's general demarcation of the provinces of faith and reason (IV. xviii) explicitly leaves room for relying on faith on issues into which we can have an approach by 'natural faculties' (cf. IV. xviii. 8). It is, however, important to note in the context of that demarcation that characterizing faith as belief based merely on probability or opinion (IV. ii. 14, xv. 2–3, and *passim*) is one thing; regarding that belief as having its source in *revelation* is another (IV. xvi. 14, xviii. 2 ff.). It is primarily in the former sense that faith is allowed to supplement philosophical knowledge. (But see, for example, IV. xi. 3, 12, or IV. xii. 12.)

The discussion of Locke in this section has been concentrated more on bk. II (in which Locke's empiricist conception of the mind is developed) than on bk. IV (with its more narrowly epistemic concerns), since it better fits with the central theme of exploring the interplay between conceptions of the mind and epistemic adequacy.

faint-hearted to admit, or too feeble-minded to see, where his own theories lead. A more reasonable view may be that between the publication of Locke's *Essay* and Hume's *Treatise* the Enlightenment had become more of a force, so that consequences of the Lockean model of the mind that were not yet problematic in the one context had already become so some fifty years later.[51]

2. HUME

So far I have considered some of the specific features of Locke's endorsement of an empiricist of the mind. Now although the details of the model differ between early empiricists, and in particular between Locke and Hume, the story remains essentially the same in virtue of three primary philosophical strands that retain their salience across the different versions:

1. the *tabula rasa* thesis, perhaps the cornerstone of empiricism, that all mental contents are gleaned from experience;[52]
2. psychological atomism;
3. the commitment, necessitated in consequence of the first two, to there being principles of association, combinatorial powers of the mind in virtue of which it can still be allowed that the isolated atoms of experience that enter the mind can manifest a constancy in the way they are ordered.

The appraisal of the generic empiricist model of the mind embodied in these three commitments is appropriately centred within a discussion of Hume, since he distilled and adhered to this model with much more rigour than Locke did. Consequently, in looking at Hume's treatment a much clearer picture is gained of the shortcomings of that model.

My concern in this appraisal is, again, not only with the assessment of the internal adequacy of this model of the mind as such, but also with its wider philosophical, and in particular epistemological, ramifications. Hume's more or less unargued endorsement of this model in the first few pages of the *Treatise* can be seen to have made inevitable many of the disturbing philosophical conclusions that he was subsequently so much more rigorous than Locke in pursuing. I concentrate, however, on the question of the internal adequacy of this model.

---

[51] i.e. roughly between 1689 (Locke's *Essay*) and 1739 (Hume's *Treatise*).

[52] The term 'mental contents' is meant to cover particular and general ideas, concepts, representations, or sortal structures, but not mere powers and dispositions (such as the power to acquire concepts or the disposition to do mathematics when suitably endowed with concepts).

2.1. The Passive Tabula Rasa of Empiricism

Hume starts with the division of mental contents, perceptions in the human mind, into impressions and ideas.

The difference betwixt these consists in the degrees of force and liveliness, with which they strike upon the mind, and make their way into our thought or consciousness. Those perceptions, which enter with most force and violence, we may name *impressions*; and under this name I comprehend all our sensations, passions and emotions, as they make their first appearance in the soul. By *ideas* I mean the faint images of these in thinking and reasoning; such as, for instance, are all those perceptions excited by the present discourse, excepting only, those which arise from the sight and touch, and excepting the immediate pleasure or uneasiness it may occasion.[53]

He assumes, conveniently, that this distinction is clear: 'I believe it will not be very necessary to employ many words in explaining this distinction. Every one of himself will readily perceive the difference betwixt feeling and thinking.'[54]

Impressions themselves are divided into two kinds: those of *sensation* and those of *reflection*. Here Hume is following Locke, who also held simple ideas to be of one or other of these two sources. But unlike Locke,[55] who just helps himself to the notion that those arising from sensation are caused by outside objects—the existence of which he has no right to help himself to—Hume is more cautious, and says of impressions of sensation that they arise 'from unknown causes'.[56] Of impressions of reflection he follows Locke, in essence, but sees them as the result of the mind reflecting on its own contents, rather than powers.

He then draws another distinction which cuts across the previous one: the division of perceptions (both impressions and ideas) into simple and complex ones:

Simple perceptions or impressions and ideas are such as admit of no distinction nor separation. The complex are the contrary to these, and may be distinguished into parts. Tho' a particular colour, taste, and smell are qualities all united together in this apple, 'tis easy to perceive they are not the same, but are at least distinguishable from each other.[57]

At first it seems right to say that corresponding to every impression is an idea, which resembles it in all except the degree of vivacity. But Hume points out that complex impressions do not always have corresponding complex ideas precisely resembling them. Thus the complex impression of, say, Paris might

---
[53] *Treatise*, I. i. 1 (1978: 1).
[54] Ibid. On the notorious problems thereby passed over, see e.g. Stroud (1977: 27–33).
[55] *Essay*, II. i. 5.   [56] *Treatise*, I. i. 2 (1978: 7).   [57] Ibid. I. i. 1 (1978: 2).

not be one of which I can form an accurate corresponding complex idea. And the other way round: I have many complex ideas—such as the idea of a golden mountain, or of a garden party for Homeric gods—of which I have no corresponding and resembling complex impression.[58] 'I perceive, therefore, that tho' there is in general a great resemblance betwixt our *complex* impressions and ideas, yet the rule is not universally true, that they are exact copies of each other.'[59]

With regard to simple perceptions, however, he concludes that the rule holds almost without exception, 'that every simple idea has a simple impression, which resembles it; and every simple impression a correspondent idea. That the idea of red, which we form in the dark, and that impression, which strikes our eyes in sun-shine, differ only in degree, not in nature.'[60] He contends that while it cannot be proved that this is the case for all simple perceptions, everyone ought to be persuaded of it by their sheer inability to come up with exceptions to the generalization.[61] He then promptly does just that, identifying an exception himself—the case of the missing shade of blue.[62] But Hume's own view, notoriously, is that this case is 'so particular and singular, that 'tis scarce worth our observing, and does not merit that for it alone we should alter our general maxim.'[63]

Hume then notes that the fact that simple impressions and simple ideas are always paired cannot be attributed to mere coincidence, and must rather indicate a dependence of the one on the other, and so raises the question of which member of the pair causes the other. He concludes that it is the simple impressions that have priority, and that the simple ideas arise from them: 'all our simple ideas in their first appearance are deriv'd from simple impressions, which are correspondent to them, and which they exactly represent'.[64]

Hume goes on to claim that this principle 'of the priority of impressions to ideas', despite 'the simplicity of its appearance', is nothing other than a refutation of the claim that there are innate ideas.[65] His thought is that if 'all our ideas proceed either mediately or immediately, from their correspondent impressions',[66] then obviously there are no ideas already waiting in the mind, prior to the opening of the sensory channels. The mind remains a *tabula rasa*, empty of ideas, until the first impressions are received.

---

[58] Hume's example here is that he can imagine to himself a city as the New Jerusalem (Ibid., I. i. 1; 1978: 3). [59] Ibid.
[60] Ibid. [61] See ibid. (1978: 3–4).
[62] Ibid. (1978: 5–6). The idea is that a person who has never seen a particular shade of, say, blue (and so has no impression of it) would nevertheless readily detect its absence if faced with an array of shades of blue, ordered from darkest to lightest, from which only that one shade was missing. From the evident gap, Hume admits, the person would be able to form the idea of that particular shade, even though it had never been conveyed to him by his senses. For a window onto the discussion of the missing shade of blue, see Stroud (1977: 33–5); Cummins (1978); Russow (1980); Morreall (1982); Fogelin (1984); W. H. Williams (1992).
[63] *Treatise*, I. i. 1 (1978: 6). [64] Ibid. (1978: 4). [65] Ibid. (1978: 6–7).
[66] Ibid.

In fact there is a problem in the move from the principle of the priority of impressions to ideas, to the refutation of innateness, if we take strictly Hume's definition of the distinction between impressions and ideas. That distinction is drawn intrinsically: in terms of the difference in degrees of vivacity between impressions, which are the more lively, and ideas, which are less so. Nothing is said in this about the origin of either. It may happen that sensory experiences by and large present us with our liveliest perceptions, and so with our impressions, but there is nothing in the definition to preclude there being perceptions lively enough to count as impressions, but which are not sensory. Consequently, the mere priority of impressions to ideas, or the dependence of ideas on impressions, does not establish that there are no innate perceptions; only that if there are any, they will be so vivacious as to count as innate impressions rather than innate ideas, which would hardly count as a refutation of the rationalist's innateness doctrine. The trouble here, of course, is with the fact that Hume starts with a minimalist intrinsic characterization of a distinction between impressions and ideas. He then introduces claims about a causal connection between them (which is already a scientific hypothesis for which he has no strict licence according to his empiricism) and, further, adds that impressions first arise via the senses, simple ideas (and impressions of reflection) being subsequently based upon them.[67] Now to the extent that Hume is being rigorous in his adherence to empiricism, he says of these initial impressions of *sensation* only that they arise 'in the soul originally, from unknown causes';[68] and to that extent giving those impressions priority—as the first furnishings of the mind—does not amount to a refutation of innatism. But at the same time he also talks of those impressions that first strike upon the senses,[69] or which are conveyed by the senses,[70] and that suggests the more usual view of sensory impressions as those that impinge on the mind from 'outside'. This view of the origin of sensory contents, along with the relegation of all other impressions as posterior to them, obviously *does* count against there being innate ideas; but it does so simply by introducing a philosophical story that directly legislates against innate ideas, and to which he is not strictly entitled anyway. This is after all just where his original intrinsic characterizations promised to be more strictly empiricist than Locke's characterization of ideas of sensation as those that come to us from external objects.

There is a further problem. If we grant the more doctrinal construal of the principle of the priority of impressions to ideas (as we are in fact likely to do

---

[67] Ibid. I. i. 2 (1978: 7–8).

[68] Ibid. (1978: 7). Similarly, elsewhere, in passing, he says: 'As to those *impressions*, which arise from the *senses*, their ultimate cause is, in my opinion, perfectly inexplicable by human reason, and 'twill always be impossible to decide with certainty, whether they arise immediately from the object, or are produc'd by the creative power of the mind, or are deriv'd from the author of our being' (ibid. I. iii. 5; 1978: 84). [69] Ibid. I. i. 2 (1978: 8).

[70] Ibid. I. i. 1 (1978: 7).

if we grant it at all), then the conclusion that there are no innate ideas would indeed seem to follow. Since that would still be a significant result, it is worth looking carefully at the way in which Hume establishes that principle in the first place. The grounds for this principle are set out rather briefly: (*a*) that the simple impressions always appear before the mind first—we never find the idea followed by the impression; and (*b*) that where the senses are damaged such that the simple impressions do not arise, there the corresponding simple ideas are also missing.[71] From these observations Hume concludes 'that our impressions are the causes of our ideas, not our ideas of our impressions'.[72]

This argument is too quick. In the first place, 'that the simple impressions always take the precedence of their correspondent ideas, but never appear in the contrary order' seems to be counter-instanced in the case of that 'one contradictory phenomenon',[73] the missing shade of blue, where the simple idea certainly appears in the mind first; but I will return to this shortly. Leaving that aside, Hume is appealing to a temporal precedence of our awareness of simple impressions to that of their corresponding simple ideas. But that cannot on its own establish that those 'simple ideas in their first appearance [in the mind] are deriv'd from the simple impressions',[74] except in an importantly qualified sense. The order of appearance to us of impressions and ideas does not determine the order of dependence between them, without an implicit extra premiss. Hume's argument would be sound only if he were entitled to the Lockean thought that there is no unconscious content, no unconscious ideas.[75] Because if there are, then the conclusion does not follow. It is then not necessarily the case that what first enters consciousness is what first enters the mind. This is relevant, for example, to any Fodorian claim that the mind is not a *tabula rasa*, but rather comes already equipped with ideas, which therefore precede the vivid impressions in the mind, although not in consciousness. Of course there could still be a reformulated claim, to the effect that the simple impressions precede and cause the *emergence* of corresponding simple ideas—which might have been resident in the mind all along—*into the conscious mind*. But that would be a far cry from underpinning the empiricist view of the mind. There is thus a premiss missing from Hume's argument for the principle of the priority of impressions over ideas, without which that principle cannot be established in a way that counts against there being innate ideas. Bringing out this implicit premiss also enables us to appreciate the importance for the classical empiricist model of the mind of denying that there is or can be an unconscious mind.

---

[71] Ibid., I. i. 1 (1978: 4–5).   [72] Ibid. (1978: 5).   [73] Ibid.   [74] Ibid. (1978: 4).
[75] Locke, *Essay*, II. i. 10: 'I do not say that there is no soul in a man, because he is not sensible of it in his sleep; but I do say he cannot think at any time waking or sleeping without being sensible of it. Our being sensible of it is not necessary to anything but to our thoughts; and to them it is and to them it will always be necessary, until we can think without being conscious of it.'

The same problem pertains to (*b*) as grounds for thinking that impressions causally underpin ideas. It might well be true that where the senses are inoperative ('entirely destroyed'), or simply have not been activated, certain ideas are not activated either.[76] The point is that this would not show that, in the absence of the stimulus provided by the simple impressions, there are none of the corresponding simple ideas in the mind. It might well be that the stimulus provided by the simple impressions is needed not to originate, but only to activate, consciousness of ideas that have in fact been resident in the unconscious mind all along. Indeed it can be argued (as it is by Fodor[77]) that without such ideas the mind would not have been able to process the impression that then triggers conscious access to the underlying simple idea that corresponds to the impression.

So much by way of comment on the first strand of Hume's model of the mind. Let us now turn to the second central tenet of the view of the mind he endorses.

2.2. Psychological Atomism

Hume, like Locke, assumed, more or less in passing, that 'complex [ideas and impressions] are formed from [simple ideas and impressions]'.[78] He does not in fact attempt to defend this claim, nor even make it very saliently. Yet prior to that, in first introducing the distinction between complex and simple ideas, he did not discuss the claim that the one is constructed out of the other at all. He there mentions the case of the apple, in which various impressions are united into a complex, but there is no discussion of whether we register them as a complex and later abstract the simple from that whole, or the other way round. That simple ideas have priority, and complex ones are constructed out of them, is simply assumed in passing in the course of the subsequent discussion.[79]

Thus we find the commitment to psychological atomism slipping into Hume's theory of mind at the outset, even though his own example of the missing shade of blue might have raised doubts in someone more attentive to the issue.

---

[76] *Treatise*, I. i. 1 (1978: 5). It is in this context that Hume raises 'the one contradictory phenomenon of the missing shade of blue'.   [77] The *locus classicus* is Fodor (1979).

[78] *Treatise*, I. i. 1 (1978: 4).

[79] Ibid. Hume says of the sense in which his impressions are simple that they 'are indivisible to the eye or feeling' (I. ii. 3; 1978: 38), which seems aimed at a psychological–phenomenological criterion, as distinct from a mathematical one: 'Here therefore I must ask, *What is our idea of a simple and indivisible point?* No wonder if my answer appear somewhat new, since the question itself has scarce ever been thought of. We are wont to dispute concerning the nature of mathematical points, but seldom concerning the nature of their ideas.' It is important not to ridicule his atomism by conflating psychological and mathematical simplicity.

Indeed, the significance of the example, as Hume sets it up, is perhaps not so much that it constitutes a counter-example to Hume's contention that simple ideas are always derived from simple impressions that preceded them —we might accept that the example 'is so particular and singular, that 'tis scarce worth our observing' it.[80] Rather, it is significant because it can serve to bring out a deep tension between Hume's non-reflective commitment to atomism on the one hand, and strict empiricism on the other. It is worth trying to bring this out.

Hume assumes that our impressions and ideas of colour are simple.[81] If he did not assume this, there would not be any problem in accounting for the presence of an idea without a corresponding impression in the case of the missing shade of blue. But of simple ideas and impressions Hume says that they are 'such as admit of no distinction nor separation'.[82] This means that it cannot be that we come up with the idea of the missing shade of blue by comparing other shades of blue on the continuum, and recognizing that while, say, A and B and D are all the same colour, D is lighter than B by much more than B is lighter than A, such that there is room for a shade C between B and D which will be lighter than B by just as much as B is lighter than A. After all, if this were the right story, then we would in the case of all these colours be distinguishing, separating out, the colour from the lightness, such that we can say that they have the same colour, but differ in degrees of lightness. Now we might consider this to be the only way of coming up with an idea of the missing shade of blue—namely, by denying that the impressions and ideas of colour are simple.[83] But that would in effect be to give up on atomism. It would be to assert, at least in this one case, that what the mind first registers are structures, complexes, which are subsequently broken down, analysed. But if this is the result in the case of colours, a category which seems to offer paradigm cases of simple impressions, what reason is there for insisting on atomism in other cases?[84]

In the appendix Hume seems to reject this line of thought, and so in effect to defend his atomism, by holding that the comparability of ideas need not

---

[80] *Treatise*, I. i. 1 (1978: 6).

[81] This is clear from the following, for example: 'I venture to affirm, that the rule here holds without any exception, and that every simple idea has a simple impression, which resembles it; and every simple impression a correspondent idea. That idea of red, which we form in the dark, and that impression, which strikes our eyes in sun-shine, differ only in degree, not in nature' (ibid.; 1978: 3).   [82] Ibid. (1978: 2).

[83] Stroud (1977: 253 n. 9) notes essentially this possible move, and that it will not solve the specific problem as Hume conceives it. He does not bring out the general significance the missing shade has as a threat to Hume's atomism, or to the combination of atomism and the *tabula rasa* thesis.

[84] Particularly given that it might seem that for every candidate category, there could in principle be a missing instance, so that exactly the same argument could be run against atomism with regard to that category.

belie their simplicity.[85] The idea is that there are distinctions of reason[86] between, say, the colour and the degree of lightness, although in the impression and the correlated idea there is no distinction between the two. But the question then is how the mind comes by the classifications implemented by reason in these cases, as between colour and lightness, such as to be able to judge that a range of exemplars has one but not the other in common. The ideas that service these distinctions of reason by hypothesis could not have been derived from the ideas to which they are applied, since the latter are now being said to be simple. The distinctions of reason, in these cases, must be applying classificatory devices that have some other source. Here we see the tension emerging between upholding both atomism and the *tabula rasa* thesis.

Before turning to that, we ought to appreciate first why the threat of wholesale dismissal of atomism is something that Hume is loath to countenance. He has good reason to be reluctant on this score. If what the mind first registers are complexes, then how does it come subsequently to break them down by analysis into simpler ideas?[87] It would seem that it must bring concepts to bear on those complex impressions, concepts which enable us to detect—separate out—distinct aspects of the complex. But then where would those concepts have arisen from? They could themselves be said to have been distilled from other complexes only on pain of an infinite regress: how did that distillation get going? This line of thought can easily lead back to the assumption, then, that if what the mind first registers are complexes, there must be some concepts already waiting, resident in the mind, to do the work of analysis. But this would precisely be a return to innate ideas that Hume is anxious to avoid. Here it might naturally be suggested that while there are some impressions which are registered first as a complex, some are not, and the latter give us the simple ideas that serve in analysing the former, complex impressions. It could be argued that this is in fact not a possibility, but we can leave this aside for the moment.[88] More to the point here is that this is only one way to argue,

---

[85] Thus he says: "'Tis evident, that even different simple ideas may have a similarity or resemblance to each other; nor is it necessary, that the point or circumstance of resemblance shou'd be distinct or separable from that in which they differ. *Blue* and *green* are different simple ideas, but are more resembling than *blue* and *scarlet*; tho' their perfect simplicity excludes all possibility of separation or distinction. . . . 'Tis the same case with all the degrees in any quality. They are all resembling, and yet the quality, in any individual, is not distinct from the degree' (1978: 637). For treatments of the missing shade of blue that pursue this line of thought, see Russow (1980); Fogelin (1984); or W. H. Williams (1992). [86] *Treatise*, I. i. 7 (1978: 24–5).

[87] This question is central to any commitment to a form of non-conceptual holism, of which James and Bergson (cf. Ch. 3) are both early exponents.

[88] The argument is, essentially, that to be integrated into our mental lives, related to other impressions and ideas, and to self-conscious awareness, what we register must be complex. Strictly speaking, a simple impression would shrink to a mathematical point, or a philosophical simple, which would be a mere theoretical posit that could not furnish us with any experienced content as required within the empiricist appeal to simple impressions. I will return to this later, in Ch. 7.

and the other would lead straight back to the endorsement of innate ideas. Given that Hume does not want to compete with, but rather completely to discount, the appeal to innate ideas, he would not go for a view that countenanced unindividuated sensory input, that then required some prior established conceptual activity of the mind to analyse it. That would come too close to inviting a priori contents of the mind. The straightforward insistence that the mind initially takes in impressions only as simple, and then forms complexes out of them, comes much closer to ruling out any need to appeal to innate ideas, and so conforms well to the adherence to the *tabula rasa* thesis. For this reason it can be seen as important to Hume to hold on to the atomistic conception. It seems germane to his case for empiricism. Which is why the tension between the two that is being addressed here is significant.

Let me spell out this tension in relation to the missing shade of blue. If the idea of any particular colour, and so too of the missing shade of blue, is simple, then in virtue of what are we able to see its resemblance to other colours, and to place it so accurately as belonging at a particular place on the blue continuum? Consider the various petals of a flower, all of which are blue, but of slightly different shades. On the atomist conception each is a simple and indivisible experience. But if it is not by comparing various elements that comprise each shade with those of another, how do we detect respects in which they resemble one another, and respects in which they differ? In the face of atomism, taken strictly, it would seem that if the various simple impressions and their corresponding ideas are to be brought into relation with one another, there are in fact only two obvious options.

The one option is to say that at some point we do in fact register a complex, a colour structure with its internal relations, as a whole. That would then give us the relevant ideas with which to analyse such simple colours as come along, leaving scope to extrapolate imaginatively how, say, a colour might remain the same but the lightness differ. But the trouble with this, for Hume, is that it again assumes that some impressions enter the mind as complexes, and this is at odds with his thoroughgoing atomism, to which, as we have seen, he has reason to adhere.

The other option would seem to be to hold on to atomism consistently, and say that the ideas and relations comprising the relevant colour matrix are pre-given, are part of the cognitive apparatus of the working mind, so that simple impressions that then enter the mind can take up their place in relation to it. The same explanation of the missing shade would then run. Or, putting it very schematically, we might say that then once the matrix was filled, simple colours having been placed in the appropriate slot by a relation of identity, empty places would result in ideas for which no impression had been received, such as the missing shade of blue. But of course this direction of solution would be at odds with Hume's empiricism: it would assume that there are specific sortal structures resident in the mind prior to the advent of experience.[89]

In other words, Hume cannot avail himself of a complex structure that is received a posteriori, because that is at odds with his atomism; and he cannot avail himself of such a structure that is present a priori, because that is at odds with his empiricism. Yet it seems that these are the only ways in which we could cope with the missing shade of blue. In this way the analysis of the missing shade of blue puts pressure on Hume's combination of atomism and empiricism in one theory of the mind; and at the same time Hume cannot simply jettison the one, without imperilling his hold on the other: without atomism the empiricism might seem to be threatened, as we have seen, and without empiricism the atomism seems unmotivated. In fact the missing shade of blue suggests a model that is at odds with the combination of psychological atomism and empiricism: a model according to which what we, phenomenologically, trace first awareness back to (simple perceptions) is not necessarily what has priority in psychological explanation (namely, complex structures), whether the latter are then thought to be a posteriori or a priori.

In any event, given Hume's atomism, it follows that all complex perceptions are constructed out of simple ones, and that, within the range of simple perceptions, all simple ideas are caused by simple impressions—so that it is out of simple impressions that our mental contents are constructed. They are the basic building-blocks of our mental contents. Impressions that enter the mind are copied, and so make an appearance in the mind as ideas as well. Hume thinks that there are two different ways in which this process of generating ideas can take place:[90] *memory*, whereby the idea arising from the impression retains a considerable degree of its vivacity, 'and is somewhat intermediate betwixt an impression and an idea', or *imagination*, whereby it entirely loses that vivacity, and is a perfect idea. Apart from the difference in vivacity, there is another difference between the two: 'the imagination is not restrain'd to the same order and form with the original impressions; while the memory is in a manner ty'd down in that respect, without any power of variation'.[91] This is not a difference that Hume considers sufficient to distinguish these two,[92] and for that he ultimately relies on the difference in vivacity between the two. (Of course, how exactly this can work is not at all clear.)

Now, given that imagination can separate impressions, and then put them together again in all sorts of fantastical ways, there must be some principles guiding that faculty

---

[89] The imprecision of the distinction between dispositions and ideas is a problem anyway (see Stroud 1977: 35), but it seems clear that it would collapse altogether if to avoid the problem Hume were to regard the full range of colour sortals as innate dispositions, rather than ideas.
[90] *Treatise*, I. i. 3 (1978: 8).   [91] Ibid. (1978: 9).
[92] For his reasons for this, see ibid. I. iii. 5 (1978: 85).

which render it, in some measure, uniform with itself in all times and places. Were ideas entirely loose and unconnected, chance alone wou'd join them; and 'tis impossible the same simple ideas should fall regularly into complex ones (as they commonly do) without some bond of union among them, some associating quality, by which one idea naturally introduces another.[93]

This points to the general danger facing the atomist theory of ideas, which foreshadows Kant's worries.[94] Essentially the problem with psychological atomism combined with the *tabula rasa* thesis is the threat of incoherence of our mental life, the danger of ideas (and impressions) never being drawn into larger wholes in the same way twice. There need to be some principles governing the way in which atomistic ideas in the mind are clustered and reclustered over time.

2.3. Principles of Association

Hume recognizes this requirement, and to meet it offers three principles which control our manner of associating ideas with one another:

The qualities, from which this association arises, and by which the mind is after this manner convey'd from one idea to another, are three, *viz.* RESEMBLANCE, CONTIGUITY in time or place, and CAUSE and EFFECT.[95]

As he says in the *Enquiry concerning Human Understanding*:

That these principles serve to connect ideas will not, I believe, be much doubted. A picture naturally leads our thoughts to the original [= resemblance]: the mention of one apartment in a building naturally introduces an enquiry or discourse concerning the others [= contiguity]: and if we think of a wound, we can scarcely forbear reflecting on the pain which follows it [= cause and effect].[96]

The idea is that these qualities or relations amongst ideas bring about a rule-governed association of ideas. Any two ideas or impressions will be connected together in the imagination not only if the one either directly resembles, is contiguous with, or is the cause of the other, 'but also when there is interposed betwixt them a third object, which bears to both of them any of these relations. This may be carried on to a great length; tho' at the same time we may observe, that each remove considerably weakens the relation.'[97] These then are taken to be the principles whereby the association of ideas is sustained in a uniform manner, 'the principles of union or cohesion among our simple ideas, and in the imagination supply the place of that inseparable connexion, by which they are united in memory'.[98] Hume concedes that he does not know

---

[93] *Treatise*, I. i. 4 (1978: 10).
[94] See Ch. 2, Sect. 2.
[95] *Treatise*, I. i. 4 (1978: 11).
[96] *Enquiry*, III (Hume 1975: 24).
[97] *Treatise*, I. i. 4 (1978: 11).
[98] Ibid. (1978: 12).

how to show that there are only these three general principles—and can only point out that the more instances we examine, the more confident we might become that this enumeration of principles is indeed complete.[99]

But in fact we need to be careful about these relations or qualities which are supposed to constitute the principles that direct our systematic way of associating ideas. Let us take each in turn, concentrating on the principle of contiguity. The critique of this principle in particular brings out the repercussions of Hume's acceptance of the conjunction of the *tabula rasa* thesis and atomism, and best prepares us for the Kantian appraisal and alternative model of mind discussed in the next chapter.

Resemblance

Notoriously, it is not clear how resemblance can effectively guide association of particular ideas, since any two ideas associated would stand in *some* resemblance relation. There is, after all, a perfectly good sense in which anything resembles any other thing, in some respect. The idea might be that there will be degrees of resemblance, and that the more two ideas resemble one another, the more they will be called to mind together; the mind will recall the one upon encountering the other. But simple degrees of resemblance will not do. For one thing, degrees of resemblance are relative to interest. From the perspective of a footballer, a watermelon will immediately bring to mind a football; to the farmer it might with equal force bring to mind a cucumber. So there is no sense to saying that an idea will always call up those ideas which most resemble it, where that is meant to be taken extensionally, to mean some objective set of ideas. If, on the other hand, it is taken intensionally, then there is nothing here to serve as a helpful principle of association. Any idea will be associated with whatever other idea at the time seems most to resemble it, given the particular perspective onto it at that time. And given that interests change, there is nothing in the notion of resemblance that would make sure that our perceptions had anything like the stability required in the combination of them at different times.

Another, and perhaps more worrying, reason why simple degrees of resemblance will not work can be appreciated by attending to the fact that something will *equally* resemble an indefinite number of disparate things *simultaneously*. Thus a watermelon equally and simultaneously resembles a cucumber, a football, and (consider a sci-fi film director) an alien pod. Mere resemblance cannot in itself determine association of ideas, but requires that the relevant interest be operative. But that means contending that all association of ideas by resemblance relations is dependent on the operation of interests, which is problematic. If the interests in question are cognitively mediated, then

---

[99] *Enquiry*, III (1975: 24); see also *Treatise*, I. iii. 6 (1978: 92–3).

they cannot get off the ground without experience being sufficiently ordered, such that resemblance relations are already operative. Those resemblance relations might in turn be thought to be fixed by further interests, ultimately underpinned by interests that are no more than animal propensities, brute inclinations, which, not being cognitively implemented, do not presuppose any further ordering by resemblance relations. Without the latter claim the association of ideas by resemblance relations that precedes cognitively mediated interests would be a blind pick of resemblance relations, entirely arbitrary, and we would be back where we started. But the claim in question is a substantial empirical hypothesis that cannot be upheld just because it is required for the envisaged principle of association to work. Acceptance of that principle is now linked to the independent corroboration of that hypothesis.

In addition, it is worth noting that there is a particular problem regarding the association of *simple* ideas on the basis of resemblance relations between them. This was already implicit in the preceding discussion of the missing shade of blue. If impressions or ideas are simple, then they 'are such as admit of no distinction nor separation'.[100] But in the absence of any such complexity, there is no room for the distinction between something having one aspect in which it resembles something else, and another in which it does not. And that means that the only relation of resemblance at the level of simple impressions or ideas will be that of identity. (Indeed, for reasons that will emerge immediately below, in the discussion of *contiguity*, the identity must be numerical rather than merely qualitative.) But that will not allow association of *different* simple perceptions. And a principle of association that cannot facilitate association of simple perceptions, impressions and ideas, would not be of much use to Hume, given his atomism.

Contiguity

By 'contiguity' Hume means spatial or temporal contiguity. "Tis likewise evident, that as the senses, in changing their objects, are necessitated to change them regularly and take them as they lie *contiguous* to each other, the imagination must by long custom acquire the same method of thinking, and run along the parts of space and time in conceiving its objects.'[101] The common-sense appeal of Hume's claim here is undeniable. We do believe that experiences that are regularly in close proximity to one another, either in time or in space, will be associated by the mind. Just as 'the mention of one apartment in a building naturally introduces an enquiry or discourse concerning the others', so too the mention of a ball going up naturally introduces the thought of the ball coming down.

[100] *Treatise*, I. i. 1 (1978: 2).   [101] Ibid. I. i. 4 (1978: 11).

The trouble is that here too there is an unrecognized threat to Hume's combination of atomism and the *tabula rasa* thesis. For association of ideas to be regulated by contiguity, we must be able to experience the contiguity of perceptions, and that requires *spatial* and *temporal* structures, or proto-structures, such that we can plot individual perceptions onto them, sufficient to distinguish patterns of contiguity between their contents. This much is surely uncontentious. To associate perceptions by contiguity, we must be able to tell which are contiguous with which. But the question is, how do we come by the requisite experience of spatial and temporal contiguity in the first place?

Hume offers an explanation of how we come by our ideas of space[102] and time.[103] We may start from his explanation regarding time. He says that the idea of time is derived from the succession of our perceptions: 'from the succession of ideas and impressions we form the idea of time'.[104] In this he is again essentially following Locke,[105] as will be clear from the earlier brief discussion. Hume's point is that without the *succession of experiences*, there would be no experience of time. First, time on its own is not an object of experience—it is not 'possible for time alone ever to make its appearance, or be taken notice of by the mind'.[106] This point is one that Kant too makes.[107] Secondly, having just one unchanging perception would equally not be enough for the experience of time.[108] 'A man . . . strongly occupy'd with one thought, is insensible of time.'[109] It takes the passage of perceptions, what Locke calls a *train* of thoughts, to produce the experience of time.

> Wherever we have no successive perceptions, we have no notion of time, even tho' there be a real succession in the objects. From these phænomena, as well as from many others, we may conclude, that time cannot make its appearance to the mind, either alone, or attended with a steady unchangeable object, but is always discover'd by some *perceivable* succession of changeable objects.[110]

---

[102] Ibid. I. ii. 3 (1978: 33–4).   [103] Ibid. (1978: 34–5).   [104] Ibid. (1978: 35).
[105] *Essay*, II. vii. 9 and II. xiv. 3.   [106] *Treatise*, I. ii. 3 (1978: 35).
[107] See e.g. *Critique of Pure Reason* (henceforth: *Critique*), First Analogy (A182–9/B225–32).
[108] While the point is surely right, the argument that Hume provides for it (*Treatise*, I. ii. 3; 1978: 36) is not very well worked out. He argues that the parts of time are not coexistent, but that one unchangeable object will produce only coexistent impressions, and so produces no impressions that can give us the idea of time, 'and consequently that idea must be deriv'd from a succession of changeable objects, and time in its first appearance can never be sever'd from such a succession'. The trouble is that here (as indeed in the passage quoted next in the text) Hume appears to conflate a succession of perceptions with a succession of objects perceived. It is perhaps right that a perception of time requires a perception of succession, and that a perception of succession requires a succession of perceptions; but there is no reason why a succession of perceptions should in turn be predicated on a succession of objects perceived. (Arguably, however, with a suitably wide construal of the notion of an *object* the succession of perceptions just *is* a real succession of objects perceived.)   [109] Ibid. (1978: 35).
[110] Ibid.

Essentially, the experience of time requires the experience of a succession of moments; and that succession of moments can be experienced only if those moments can each impinge distinctly on our consciousness; and that in turn requires that those moments are, so to speak, 'filled', i.e. that they be presented as (containing) distinct perceptions. A perceivable succession of such perceptions then is necessary, and Hume seems to think is also sufficient, to supply us with our idea of time.[111] But there is an important difference between a succession of perceptions and a perception of a succession. Hume's saying that time is discovered 'by some *perceivable* succession of changeable objects' is insufficiently clear on the difference between the two, and so masks the problem. While there is no problem for Hume in accommodating a succession of perceptions, it is a perception of succession that is required here.

While the 'appearance in the mind' of the idea of time is derived from the experience of a succession of perceptions, it still remains to be explained how the atomist mind is able to experience a succession of perceptions as a succession in the first place. No number of simple impressions impinging sequentially on the blank page of the mind—say, to use Hume's example, five consecutive notes on a flute[112]—will give rise to the impression and/or idea of succession, just in virtue of having been successively received. Imagine, first, a blank slate registering a particular note. A moment later the same note is sounded, and that is registered on the slate again. Without any further story, each note enters in its own right, and that they are in succession goes by unnoticed. For all that this kind of mind would notice, it might as well be a new mind each time that it registers each new note.[113] There is nothing here to register the sequentiality, the succession. There is, in other words, only the succession of perceptions, not the perception of succession.

Now we can complicate the story a little, by imagining that each impression leaves its trace, and is somehow still lurking in the mind when the new impression impinges. Indeed, this is something that Hume assumes. That would mean that when the second impression registers, it shares the stage with a trace of another impression of that note (a trace which, being less vivid than the impression that occasioned it, might count as an *idea* for Hume). So the total content of the mind would be different on the two consecutive occasions on which the same note registers. (Indeed, something like this seems right, as we will see when I turn later to discuss William James's notion of traces and fringes.[114])

---

[111] In this gloss of Hume's text I have tried to avoid his apparent conflation of the distinction between a succession of perceptions and a succession of objects perceived, alluded to in n. 108 above. (That distinction is, of course, quite different from the one introduced next.)

[112] *Treatise*, I. ii. 3 (1978: 36).

[113] Of course, it is a separate problem for empiricists that they have no explanation to give concerning why it is *not* a new mind at every new moment. This is something that I will return to shortly. [114] See Ch. 3, Sect. 2.

But all that these traces give us is difference in mental content at two different times: there is nothing about this difference that would in itself give rise to the experience of succession. Nothing so far would equip the mind in question with the ability to register that it had had two consecutive impressions. The experience of this mind, for all that we have been told about it, would still be no different from the case of one mind experiencing the first note, and then another mind coming into existence to experience an occurrence of the note along with a faint accompanying perception of another such note. Mere difference in content of perceptions cannot sustain a perception of succession, any more than mere identity of content can. What is needed to explain our experience of succession—that is, to get from a succession of perceptions to a perception of succession—is not a difference in the content of the successive perceptions, but an appropriate link between the perceptions.

To provide that link we might now complicate the story of our simple atomistic minds a little further. The mind must not only retain the trace of the first note, but should then be able to recognize that trace (residue) not just as an occurrent quality, but indeed *as* a surviving trace of the first note. It must, that is, be able to recognize that faint presence alongside the second note as a *memory* of the first note. That would give us the required link between the two perceptions. But unfortunately this cannot be an account of the way in which the experience of succession is grounded in the first place. After all, having a *memory* of the first note when experiencing the second note involves, amongst other things, registering that the present experience of the second note just is a *second* experience, that it comes later than, *after*, an earlier experience of the first note. It involves being able to register the trace that accompanies the experience of the second occurrence of the note, *as a trace of an earlier experience*. But the experience of things as being earlier and later, before and after, just is experience as of temporal succession. So a grasp of those relations *as temporal* must be already available for the atomistic mind to be in a position to register a perception of succession in the first place. And it is hard to see how Hume could explain that grasp except in terms of ideas of temporal succession.

It would seem, then, that this explanation of how the Humean mind first comes to be equipped with the notion of temporal succession must be circular: presupposing that the mind already has that the first acquisition of which is supposed to be explained. Yet any more impoverished model of the atomist mind, as we have seen, could not be such as could register a succession of perceptions as a succession. It is thus unclear how the atomistic empiricist model can adequately explain how the mind comes to be equipped with an experience or understanding of the temporal structure.

It might be objected to this line of argument that the fact that we can recognize red things does not show that we have a concept of *red* prior to the encounter with red things, so why should the argument work in the case of time? This objection can be addressed in one of two ways. The heroic way is just to grant that the analogy does hold, and that we should therefore say about observational concepts like *red* exactly what we say about *time*. This is the line that Fodor took in his defence of the Language of Thought hypothesis. The other way of addressing the objection is to point out that the two cases are not analogous. In the case of the concept *red*, the suggestion is that it can be gleaned from occurrent experiences: the direct encounter with red things. In the case of time, at least on an atomistic conception, the concept of time cannot be gleaned from an occurrent experience, since temporal duration is not itself directly perceivable. It must therefore be gleaned from a *relation* between other perceptions. And this is the important difference: to be able to pick out that relation between perceptions, the mind must already be plotting perceptions as temporally structured. If it wasn't, it could not even encounter the relevant phenomenon in the first place. The same is not true of the encounter with red things.

One might think (with Fodor) that it is the same, that in just the same way unless one could already distinguish red things from others, one could not have the encounter with the relevant item, and so could not glean the relevant concept of *red*. But this is in fact not obviously the case. One can in principle attend to a red expanse, and at that point in time not distinguish it from anything other than the possibility of other earlier or later experiences,[115] and from that direct encounter glean the concept *red* with which subsequently to distinguish it from other items. This in fact leads on to a further point of disanalogy between the two cases. The argument in the case of time can be strengthened, in a way that the argument in the case of the colour concept, for example, cannot. It is not merely that we must, on the atomist view of the mind, already be equipped with the notion of time to register that two perceptions are *in succession*. Rather, the argument is that if we are to be in a position even to distinguish that there are two perceptions, we must already be able to place them in a temporal structure. This line of thought will emerge more clearly when I turn to discuss Kant, in the next chapter.[116]

A further objection might be formulated along the following lines. The argument may be taken to show only that the mind must be equipped with some implicit, possibly rudimentary, representation of a temporal order, but that is compatible with its acquiring a well-articulated conscious concept of time only in consequence of the encounter with a succession of perceptions. This is very probably true, but of course it will not help our empiricist. It again invites the notion of an unconscious level of thought (or experience), and as

---

[115] The significance of this caveat will emerge in the course of the discussion in Ch. 7.
[116] See below, Ch. 2, Sect. 1.

we have seen for the Lockean or Humean empiricist there is, for good reason, no unconscious level at which representations can lurk, working wonders, but only later to be brought to the surface of consciousness. For the Humean or Lockean empiricist nothing is hidden. We can put this by saying that, for this empiricist, the order of awareness cannot differ from the order of priority in psychological explanation. But what we see here is precisely that, with regard to the notion of time, the order of awareness is not the same as the order of priority in psychological explanation. It might be that we first become *conscious* of the temporal structure on the basis of a succession of impressions: but we must already have had an implicit representation of temporal structure— it must have been part of our mental framework. Otherwise we would not be able to experience the succession *as a succession*. And how would that prior representation of temporal structure have resulted? There would seem to be only two possibilities: either it is something we brought with us to experience (contra the *tabula rasa* tenet of empiricism) or it is something that we acquired whole (contra the atomist tenet of classical empiricism). Either way, a deep tension emerges in Hume's model of the mind.[117]

Now essentially the same point as has been made with regard to time can be made with regard to spatial contiguity. Hume distinguishes interestingly between the perceptions that give rise to spatial experience and those that give rise to temporal experience. In the latter case any perceptions would do ('perceptions of every kind, ideas as well as impressions, and impressions of reflection as well as of sensation'[118]), whereas when it comes to space it is only impressions of sensation that will serve as 'the model, from which the idea of space is deriv'd'.[119] The 'passions, emotions, desires and aversions' offer no support for the idea of extension in space. This observation parallels Kant's point that while all appearances are in time, only those of outer sense are presented in space.[120]

With regard to the idea of space, Hume suggests that 'The table before me is alone sufficient by its view to give me the idea of extension.'[121] The question then arises, in virtue of what impression received from the table does the idea of spatial extension arise? The basic claim is that it is from the composition of coloured or tactile points that we first receive the idea of spatial extension. Since it would seem that the only impressions conveyed by the senses in this case are those of coloured points arranged in a certain way, 'we may conclude with certainty, that the idea of extension is nothing but a copy of these colour'd points, and of the manner of their appearance'.[122] At first we might have learned the concept from an array of points that were all of a

---

[117] The problem with the empiricist (Lockean) derivation of time is briefly alluded to by Allison (1983: 84).   [118] *Treatise*, I. ii. 3 (1978: 35).
[119] Ibid. (1978: 33).   [120] *Critique*, A34/B50.   [121] *Treatise*, I. ii. 3 (1978: 34).
[122] Ibid.

certain colour, and so the idea of space in so far as it was gleaned from that initial impression would always have called to mind not just the particular configuration of points, but also their being of that particular colour. But subsequent impressions of such configurations teach us that the colour can vary from one configuration to another, and indeed within one configuration, and so we learn to abstract the idea of the spatially extended configuration from any question of its colour. Indeed, we learn to abstract from their visual appearance altogether, recognizing that the idea of space is conveyed equally by the sense of touch as by the sense of sight.

The problem with this derivation should now be clear. If the mind is a *tabula rasa*, with no pre-given representation of a spatial structure, then the atomistic encounter with so many coloured, or tactile, points should amount to just so many distinct impressions, each attended to in complete isolation from the others. There would be nothing to enable us to register that they were in fact spatially contiguous with one another. If, say, they were registered serially, one after the other, then (as in the case of temporal points) each new coloured point would be registered in isolation, 'in a mind of its own', so to speak. (Talk of them being registered serially is a mere convenience; exactly the same would apply if they were not.) There would be nothing in such a mind that could count as the emergence of an idea of spatial contiguity. To form an idea of spatial contiguity, the mind would have not only to register the individual impressions, but also to combine several such points as distinct from and yet simultaneous with one another. But for that the mind would already have to have some sort of spatial grid onto which to plot the individual colour or tactile points.[123]

So it would seem that if the mind registers individual colour points atomistically, as the Humean empiricist would have it, then either for that mind there would be no recognition of spatiality, or the spatial structure must be presupposed. It would then seem that, as in the case of time, the Humean explanation of how the mind first comes to have the notion of spatial structure must be circular. The story would work only for a mind that already had the capacity, with regard to the impressions that were to occasion the idea of space, to represent them as being collected together in a particular way; and that way turns out to mean that such an account presupposes as a feature of the mind precisely that—the representation of spatial structure—the original emergence of which the account was supposed to explain. Circularity aside, that presupposition is in direct contradiction to the *tabula rasa* thesis of the traditional empiricist model.

An alternative would be to deny that the perception of those coloured or spatial points was atomistic. That is, it might be that what is taken in as a

---

[123] On this, see below, Ch. 7, Sect. 4.

whole is the impression of those points as coexisting alongside one another, so that the spatial structure is learned directly from an impression of that structure.[124] There is, then, no need for there to be a prior spatial structure in the mind, enabling it to combine in the appropriate way the isolated, individually registered, impressions of points. But, of course, this option is not open to Hume, in so far as it clashes directly with his endorsement of psychological atomism.

It is worth noting here, again, that on either of these two alternatives, the ability to identify two different spatial locations in fact also presupposes being able to perceive the temporal ordering of perceptions. We must be able to attend first to the one, and then to be aware that a moment later we are attending to another. Without that temporal structure there would be no coming to an awareness that there were two perceptions here. And we must also be aware that we could have surveyed them in any order—first point A and then point B, or the other way round. Without that there would be no coming to an awareness that the two perceptions were coexisting. This is the sense in which Kant insists that not only succession, but also coexistence, is a relation we cannot identify without a perception of time. This dependence of any identification of spatial contiguity on temporal structure further strengthens the case against the empiricist derivation of the notion of time. I will have occasion to return to this point below.

For now the point is that with regard to the ability to detect spatial contiguity, as in the case of temporal contiguity, there would seem to be only these two possibilities: either the conception of space is something we brought with us to experience (contra the *tabula rasa* tenet of empiricism) or it is something that we acquired whole (contra the atomist tenet of empiricism). Either way, again, Hume's model of the mind seems unworkable.[125]

We can conclude that it looks as though in the case of both time and space, something is assumed, as prior to any simple impressions that enter the mind; there is, so to speak, the grid onto which subsequent impressions can be plotted so as to tell which are spatially and/or temporally contiguous with which. And this assumption is at odds with *either* the official atomism *or* the official *tabula rasa* thesis of empiricism.

Cause and Effect

Just as the acquisition of the powers required for association of ideas in accordance with principles of spatial and temporal contiguity is problematic on the Humean model of the mind, so too is the explanation of how we come

---

[124] This would perhaps seem independently plausible when we think of the minimal yield of a tactile sensation, say of a fingertip print.

[125] Again, there are various objections to consider, some of which will be addressed when I turn to discuss the Kantian form of these arguments.

by the idea of cause and effect that is operative in the third and final general principle for the association of ideas. This is, of course, in large part because the relation of cause and effect is not independent of those of spatial and temporal contiguity. For the purposes of this discussion we need probe no further—this is problem enough. It is worth reminding ourselves, however, that even given no problem with spatial and temporal contiguity, there are further problems. In particular, Hume's construal of causation involves some notion of necessity over and above succession, contiguity, and constant conjunction. Hume attempts to explain the idea of a necessary connection as the result of an impression of reflection brought about by the experience of events in constant conjunction. But it is difficult to see how that could in fact yield anything more than anticipation, or an idea of anticipation. The idea of a necessary connection seems to involve more than could be delivered on the basis offered.

So far we have seen some of the internal prima-facie problems that face Hume's model, inherited from Locke in essence, which result from combining the *tabula rasa* thesis, psychological atomism, and the principles of the association of ideas. But, as was mentioned above, the concern here is not only to evaluate the adequacy of a given model in accounting for the operations of the mind, but also—and, in the long run, primarily—to assess these models in the light of their wider philosophical ramifications. In fact the wider philosophical problems relevant to the question of the external adequacy of Hume's model of the mind are well known enough not to need detailed rehearsing here. The problems of causality, the problem of external existence, the existence of substance, whether material or immaterial (soul), and of personal identity are all famously elaborated without compromise by Hume.[126] It is also amply clear (not least to Hume himself), and so again is in no need of elaboration here, that these philosophical problems are indeed largely ramifications of his uncompromisingly adhered-to empiricist model of the mind. The question is, where does this leave us with regard to the acceptability of the model in question?

It should, of course, be borne in mind here that for Hume the above is a list of philosophical insolubles, but not of sceptical problems. This is where Hume's naturalism comes into play.[127] Critical enquiry cannot validate the fundamental beliefs identified, for example belief in the external world, in causality, in

[126] The following indicates loci of central discussions of these problems in the *Treatise*. Causation: I. iii. 14 (1978: 73–7, 87–94); I. xiv, 'Of the idea of a necessary connection' (1978: 162–5). External existence: I. ii. 6 (1978: 67–8); I. iv. 2–4. Substance: I. i. 6 (1978: 15–16). Soul and personal identity: I. iv. 5–6; App. (1978: 633–6). See also *Enquiry concerning Human Understanding*, esp. sects. IV–V, VII, XII.   [127] For discussion of this, see e.g. Stroud (1977).

personal identity. That is, there remains a gap between what critical enquiry can validate and what we need to believe in. But scepticism would threaten here only if we thought that this gap had to be covered by philosophical proof, by steps answerable to critical reasoning. Hume's naturalism involves precisely giving up on this article of philosophical faith. The remaining distance is covered by natural propensities to believe, on a par with other natural functions and propensities, and it would be irrational to think there was anything wrong with that naturalistic source of validation. That a belief is ultimately sustained by habit, or a natural impetus, and cannot be seen to rest squarely on reason, is perhaps a disappointment to the hopes and aspirations of philosophy, but it is not detrimental to our entitlement to the belief.[128] This naturalistic nesting concedes that the fabric of our beliefs and judgements perhaps cannot be validated in the way that our Enlightenment ideals dictate. To a committed upholder of Enlightenment ideals such naturalism will therefore look, as indeed it did to Kant, like defeatism. But it nevertheless remains strictly committed to an Enlightenment conception of philosophy in that the limits of critical enquiry are the limits of philosophy, the shortfall of the one is the shortfall of the other, and there is no room for philosophy to blur the line between critical and naturalistic validation of belief, or to lay claim to grounding any beliefs for which there is no evidence or proof. Such beliefs fall clearly outside the remit of philosophy, coming into play only when we have made a break with that study. It is here that Hume's commitment to Enlightenment ideals is more resolute than Locke's, resulting in a clearer portrayal of the shortfall involved in consistent adherence to empiricism.[129]

Whether we see the epistemic shortfall identified as constituting sceptical conclusions, sceptical problems,[130] or merely as naturalistically nested philosophical insolubles, the fact surely remains that they are in principle unwelcome philosophical limitations. And as such, they must plainly militate against any philosophical orientation, and in particular any model of the mind, of which they are consequences, and to which there are in principle alternatives. This is just the point of strategy identified above: that any model of the mind must be assessed in terms not only of internal but also of external adequacy.

Hume might, however, have responded that this is indeed the case, but that as it happens there are no acceptable alternatives to this model of the mind. More precisely, it might be contended that if we are going to respect the line

---

[128] Thus Hume famously says, 'Nature, by an absolute and uncontroulable necessity has determin'd us to judge as well as to breathe and feel...' (*Treatise*, I. iv. 1; 1978: 183). And later: 'Thus the sceptic still continues to reason and believe, even tho' he asserts that he cannot defend his reason by reason... Nature has not left this to his choice, and has doubtless esteem'd it an affair of too great importance to be trusted to our uncertain reasonings and speculations' (I. iv. 2; 1978: 187). [129] See pp. 19–20 above.
[130] The two are clearly not the same, but Hume does not see it as either.

between critical licence and mere fancy, and make sure that our philosophical account of the mind is strictly streamlined to avoid illegitimate furnishings (e.g. innate ideas), then this is just the sort of model of the mind we end up with. And if the shortfall in yield resulting from this appropriately streamlined model is unwelcome, so be it: what we have is nothing other than the yield proper to a fully critical philosophical model of the mind.

It is at this point that it becomes important to have made the case that it is not only external inadequacy that the Humean model of the mind must contend with. If it were, then Hume's envisaged response might have been appropriate. But we have seen, in the course of the discussion above, some of the central reasons for thinking that it is not even internally adequate. If the streamlined construal of the mind cannot even account for the undeniable workings of the mind, then there cannot be any denying that the minimalism was carried too far. And the search must then be on for a different model, one that it is hoped might prove to be both internally and externally adequate in a way that Hume's was not. The hope is that a model that is rich enough to be internally adequate as an account of the mind might also prove to be externally adequate. And certainly, among such internally adequate models of the mind as we might formulate, external adequacy would be a criterion for selection.

Implicit in this last comment is the acknowledgement, which should be noted, that even if the Humean model of the mind had turned out to be internally adequate, the strategy here would be to regard its external inadequacy as counting against it, just as long as alternative models of the mind are theoretically possible. The case then would have been less easy to make than it has been, of course. It would have been necessary to show that other competing models might be on a par with Hume's in requisite minimalism, and until we had done so, we could not expect the Humean to entertain doubts about Hume's model, or to join the search for a better one. As it stands, however, he would at this point appear to have no other option.

2

Kant

WHILE Hume himself is a naturalist, rather than a sceptic, his conclusions are clearly significant for anyone committed to finding more than just the natural drive of nature with which to explain and underpin our belief that there are laws of nature (such as the causal law), or that there are objects that exist independently of us, or indeed that there is anything to me beyond the fleeting string of perceptions, something in virtue of which it will make sense to say that all these perceptions are mine. While Hume was prepared to close the door to his study and acquiesce in beliefs that could not be supported by critical reflection, this can look—and to philosophers like Kant did look—like defeatism, or unacceptable quietude. Thus from the easy admixture of faith and rational enquiry within the bounds of philosophy that we still find in Locke, via the reliance on faith only in response to the clear sceptical deliverance of what is meant to be pure rational enquiry, we reach the determination to respond to the deliverances of rational enquiry without any reliance on mere faith, which is now firmly excluded as a fitting response to central philosophical problems. The transition from Locke, via Hume, to Kant can thus be seen to manifest the increasing separation of rational enquiry and faith that is characteristic of the Enlightenment.

Kant's response to the challenge left by Hume embodies the conviction that rational enquiry does not itself lead straight to a scepticism from which escape is possible only by turning away from such enquiry. If things seem that way, then the problem might be not one of the principled shortfall of rational enquiry, but of the fact that it started from the wrong presuppositions. Having come to see that rationalism could not explain our knowledge of an objective world, but rather ended up courting scepticism, and that the empiricists were in just as much of a sceptical bind, Kant realized fully that grounding objectivity, the possibility of knowing the external world and objective laws pertaining to its workings, would require a reworking of certain presuppositions, in particular of the model of the epistemic subject, towards a new model that would not commit rational enquiry to sceptical conclusions.

But it is not simply that Kant searched around for a different model of mind and opted for the one that would most conveniently solve the problems into which Hume was forced. Although we could so structure the exposition that from the solutions to the wider problems we moved to see the structure of mind that Kant has to adopt to sustain them, one can equally reverse the direction of explanation, and proceed from the internal constraints on an acceptable philosophical psychology to its wider philosophical ramifications. Seen in this way, what Kant shows is that once the problems with Hume's theory of *mind* are put right, those other wider metaphysical problems are in fact solved as well. This is the essence of Kant's Refutation of Idealism: we undoubtedly do have a unified stream of consciousness, and once you work out what constraints there are on the working of the mind that enables us to have this, it is too late to doubt still whether there is an external world.

This kind of strategy with the sceptic can be generalized. It is essentially an instance of the strategy that gives rise to transcendental arguments. The idea is that the sceptic who makes the accusation that others are naïve in accepting certain beliefs as true without sufficient reflection in fact stands guilty of just that naïve lack of insight themselves. They prematurely assume that they can doubt something, A, without realizing that in fact A is a necessary presupposition of something else which they cannot doubt. The sceptic is like someone cognitively myopic who, while pleasantly going up and down on one side of the see-saw, thinks that he can genuinely doubt that the other side exists. His doubt trades on his epistemic blindness to the presuppositions of his own location and activity. The 'see-saw strategy' thus aims to show that the sceptic's effort is contradictory, and that it is only his own cognitive short-sightedness that masks the fact from him.[1]

The reconstruction below will, then, pursue those problems pertaining to the Locke–Hume model of the mind to which Kant seems to have responded, and show how this led Kant to a different model of the mind. Given this central axis of explanation, it will be helpful to identify at the outset some of those features of the empiricist model of the mind from which the Kantian conception was to depart. The ground for this identification has already been prepared by the preceding discussions of some of the problems facing the empiricist view of the mind. There are at least three central assumptions of the empiricist conception from which Kant distanced himself:

1. The mind is a *tabula rasa* that registers atomistic impressions (from which it is then capable of constructing spatio-temporal structures).
2. The mind first *passively* registers impressions, which are subsequently combined into coherent complexes by means of principles of association (these being, in Hume's case, contiguity, resemblance, cause and effect).

---

[1] Other applications of this strategy with the sceptic can be found in more recent philosophy, some of which is not specifically concerned with scepticism or with Kant. A salient example is externalism about meaning, and Burge clearly notes this strategic significance in passing (1982: 116–17).

3. We take the fact of our unified consciousness over time as given, without further explanation of it.

We will see how, and to what effect, Kant is motivated to modify his account of the subject on each of these points.[2]

1. SPACE AND TIME

We can start with the first tenet that Kant found problematic, that the mind is a *tabula rasa* that registers atomistic impressions and is capable of constructing spatio-temporal structures from that. We have already seen in the case of Locke and Hume that it is not at all clear how we could derive our conception of either spatial or temporal structures from 'atoms' of experience. The Kantian modification of this first tenet of the empiricist conception of the mind can be seen to result from what is essentially the same perception of the problems facing the empiricist derivations. Kant concludes that far from gleaning our concept of space and time from particular perceptions, whether of outer objects or of inner (mental) states, in fact we must already be equipped, a priori, with the spatial and temporal structure if we are to make sense of registering particular experiences as following one after the other, or as coexisting alongside one another.

Put formulaically, the difficulty for the empiricist account, in the case of temporal structure, is to explain how we get from a *succession of perceptions*, to a *perception of succession*. The parallel difficulty in the case of space is to explain how we get from the *spatial contiguity of perceptions* (or, more strictly, of perceptual contents) to the *perception of spatial contiguity*. In both cases, we have seen that once the distinction is made, it becomes clear that all the empiricist mind can register is the former (a succession of perceptions or spatially contiguous perceptions), whereas to acquire the notion of time and space we would need a mind that could have the latter too (a perception of the succession itself or of the spatial contiguity). We have also seen that what makes it impossible for the empiricist theory of the mind to pass from the former to the latter is the insistence on adhering to both psychological atomism and the *tabula rasa* thesis. It is this combination that blocks explanation of how a conception of spatio-temporal structures is reached on the basis of sensory input. This suggested that there might be two strategies for modifying the empiricist model of the mind to eliminate the problem.

---

[2] The reconstructive licence taken with Kant throughout this discussion should be clearly emphasized. Nevertheless it is, I believe, recognizable that these are moves that Kant implicitly endorses, or would endorse.

The one was to give up on psychological atomism. That would mean that the mind was not confined to registering only simple—indivisible—contents in the first instance, but rather that whole structures could be what first imprinted on the mind, the parts of which only later came to be distinguished by a process of analysis, if at all. On this view, we could be said to have immediate sensuous awareness of, say, the flow of time, a holistic impression of temporal extension. It could consequently readily be acknowledged that there is no way that merely from the succession of so many isolated perceptions we could come up with the perception of a succession. That impossibility would no longer be a problem, because we need no longer construct the idea of temporality in that way: it is rather derived directly, and holistically. In this way, giving up on psychological atomism would enable us to retain the view of the mind as a *tabula rasa*, with the commitment that the mind could acquire the conception of time only through sensory experience. And, of course, the same story, *mutatis mutandis*, can be told for spatial contiguity. This strategy is arguably implemented by William James, and so can be left aside until we turn to discuss James in the next chapter.

The other strategy goes the other way. It upholds the commitment to a form of psychological atomism, but gives up on the commitment to the mind being a *tabula rasa*. This is essentially the strategy that Kant takes. Some care, however, needs to be taken in attributing psychological atomism to Kant, and in allocating it to its appropriate place in his arguments. Although there is no doubt that Kant says things that seem to indicate acceptance of psychological atomism, many would dispute whether a charitable interpretation should hold him to it. Certainly the atomism cannot be simply the sensory atomism of the empiricists. For the moment let it be taken on trust that Kant is nevertheless committed to a form of psychological atomism. The specification of what that atomism involves, and so a clear view of what the rejection of it amounts to, will emerge only later, as it is in fact a consequence of Kant's model of the mind rather than an unmotivated premiss of it.[3]

On this approach, we do not question that sensory perceptions are first apprehended atomistically, and must subsequently be combined with other 'atoms' to form complexes. And the problem of how then we could ever pass from a succession of such perceptions, each atomistically registered in isolation from the others, to a perception of succession is acknowledged. But the

---

[3] It is important to distinguish two questions: the one is what form of psychological atomism Kant's general view of the mind entails, the other is what form of psychological atomism might be required for some of his specific arguments to run. Specifically, regarding space and time there is reason to think that his arguments require a form of atomism stronger than he is otherwise committed to. For now we can ignore this, since all that matters is that those arguments do rest on a form of such atomism; but see n. 65 below.

claim is that again we need not solve that problem. We would need to solve it, if it were the case that our conceptions of space and time had to be derived from that sensory input. But, the claim is, that problem simply shows that it cannot be on the basis of that input that we learn about space and time. The Kantian concludes that since the conceptions of time and space could not possibly have been constructed a posteriori along empiricist lines, and yet we do undeniably have such conceptions, it can only be that they were resident in the mind a priori.

What we have here, in considering these two strategies, is an important junction. The traditional empiricist claim that passively received impressions give rise to ideas of space and time puts pressure on either psychological atomism or the *tabula rasa* thesis. The Jamesian approach can be seen as the result of holding on to the *tabula rasa* thesis and rejecting atomism, whereas the Kantian keeps atomism and rejects the *tabula rasa* thesis. It is worth noting that, of the two, the Kantian strategy constitutes a much more radical departure from empiricism than the alternative Jamesian strategy. Indeed, James is free to consider himself a radical empiricist. Both options will be seen in what follows to have bearing on more than just our preferred model of the mind: specifically, they bear on the possible grounding of objectivity. We begin with the case that can be made in accordance with the second, Kantian strategy.[4]

Contrary to the empiricist *tabula rasa*, Kant's model involves identifying structures that constitute the fundamental features of the mind.[5] Such structures are not ordinary empirical facts discoverable in experience. Rather, they are taken to be structural features without which we would not have experience at all: they are conditions of the possibility of experience. Such presuppositional structures are said to be transcendental. Kant takes this to mean that they cannot be merely empirical items that enter the mind on the basis of sensory experience. He considers them to be a priori structures that we must, so to speak, bring with us to that experience, since without them such experience would not be possible. In fact, of course, there is some distance between identifying something as a transcendental condition of experience, and hence as something that can be known a priori to obtain, and identifying

---

[4] It is worth pointing out that Kant himself does not notice that there is an alternative strategy. He seems unaware that someone might avoid his conclusion that the forms of space and time are inbuilt (even if allowing that they are a priori), simply by denying psychological atomism and so avoiding the choice of either denying the *tabula rasa* thesis or not being able to explain how space and time are available to us at all.

[5] Thus Kant talks readily of the forms of space and time that 'lie ready for sensations *a priori* in the mind' (*Critique*, A20/B34). For Kant these structures are paradigms of non-conceptual representational structures.

it as an a priori subjective furnishing of the mind. This distance makes it possible in principle to accept the former and deny the latter.[6] Kant, however, for reasons that we will turn to below, does not recognize this possibility.[7]

Kant distinguishes more sharply than the empiricists between two faculties, sensibility and understanding, and with regard to each is led to identify a priori transcendental structures. In the first part of the *Critique of Pure Reason*, the Transcendental Aesthetic, Kant is concerned to identify those elements with which the faculty of sensibility is furnished a priori, as a precondition of experience. In the Transcendental Analytic he is concerned to identify the a priori elements of the faculty of understanding. For now, we are concerned with the former, with the identification of the a priori elements of the faculty of sensibility, since with regard to this faculty Kant argues that those fundamental transcendental structures—forms—that we bring with us to experience are space and time. Let us look at the argument for this conclusion.

I will focus here on the arguments presented in the metaphysical exposition of the representation of space and time[8] rather than on the transcendental exposition,[9] since suitably reconstructed those arguments are significantly stronger and more persuasive than the transcendental exposition.[10] With regard to the metaphysical exposition of both representations, space and time, Kant provides four numbered arguments; I will attend in each case primarily to the first two, which are designed to establish that the representation in question is a priori, rather than a posteriori.

The following are the central paragraphs from the metaphysical exposition of the 'concept' of space:

1. Space is not an empirical concept which has been derived from outer experiences. For in order that certain sensations be referred to something outside me (that is, to something in another region of space from that in which I find myself), and similarly in order that I may be able to represent them as outside and alongside one another, and accordingly as not only different but as in different places, the representation of space must be presupposed (*die Vorstellung des Raumes schon zum Grunde liegen*). The representations of space cannot, therefore, be empirically obtained from the relations of outer appearance. On the contrary, this outer experience is itself possible at all only through that representation.

2. Space is a necessary *a priori* representation, which underlies all outer intuitions. We can never represent to ourselves the absence of space, though we can quite well think it as empty of objects. It must therefore be regarded as the condition of the

---

[6] There is a question—which I will not pursue now—whether this possibility would suffice to account for the assumed *synthetic* a priori nature of geometrical knowledge. The possibility of pure *intuition* that Kant wants to uphold would seem to be undermined by it.
[7] The reasons for Kant not noticing this distance are, as we will see, closely linked to his acceptance of atomism. [8] Space: *Critique*, A22–5/B37–40; time: A30–2/B46–8.
[9] Space: ibid., A25/B40–1; time A31 (§4, no. 3)/B48–9. [10] See Allison (1983: 81–2).

possibility of appearances, and not as a determination dependent upon them. It is an *a priori* representation, which necessarily underlies outer appearances.[11]

Similarly, we find the parallel argument in the case of time:

1. Time is not an empirical concept that has been derived from any experience. For neither coexistence nor succession would ever come within our perception, if the representation of time were not presupposed as underlying them *a priori*. Only on the presupposition of time can we represent to ourselves a number of things as existing at one and the same time (simultaneously) or at different times (successively).

2. Time is a necessary representation that underlies all intuitions. We cannot, in respect of appearances in general, remove time itself, though we can quite well think time as void of appearances. Time is, therefore, given *a priori*. In it alone is actuality of appearances possible at all. Appearances may, one and all, vanish; but time (as the universal condition of their possibility) cannot itself be removed.[12]

The gist of these arguments should be familiar, if only on the basis of what has already been said above. I will concentrate here on the arguments concerning space, for the most part leaving aside the exposition of the arguments concerning time where the parallel is close enough for this not to matter. The first argument concerning space might at first seem rather uninteresting, indeed tautological. Kant might seem to be saying only that in an awareness of things as arranged in space there must be an underlying representation of space. And on the assumption that the argument at any rate does not suffice to make anything more than this of the presupposition claim, some have thought that we might well ignore this argument, in the hope that Kant has more to say elsewhere in defence of the apriority of space.[13] However, it is possible to reconstruct the argument charitably, to reveal what Kant might have been getting at.[14]

The idea is not that to recognize spatial structures we must have the concept of space, akin to the claim that to recognize things as red we must have the concept of redness. Kant does talk about the representation of space being presupposed by our being able to refer to something 'outside me . . . in another region of space from that in which I find myself. . . . and similarly . . . as outside and alongside one another . . . in different places'. But the reconstructive idea is that we should charitably take this talk of representing objects as 'outside me' and 'outside and alongside one another' to mean something like 'set apart from me, distinct from me, and from one another'. The argument then becomes that, for beings like ourselves, the only way in which we can represent objects as distinct from us, and from one another, is by locating them in space, so that they are identifiable as being in different places. In other words, rather than a logical condition, what we have here is the

---

[11] *Critique*, A23–4/B38–9.   [12] Ibid., A30–1/B46.   [13] See Strawson (1966: 58–9).
[14] This interpretation follows Allison (1983: 82–90).

identification of what Allison refers to as an epistemic condition. There might well be other beings that can distinguish objects as distinct from themselves, and from one another, by some other means. But we cannot conceive of what those other means would be. And for beings like ourselves, the only way of coming to experience objects as distinct from us and from one another is by locating them in space.

The case is not difficult to make. Consider two qualitatively identical water drops. If they were not plotted onto a spatial matrix, such that one was, say, just to the left of the other, there would be nothing to keep them apart. We would not be able to experience them as being distinct, unless we could so locate them in space. The assumption of qualitative identity made here serves to bring out in a particularly salient way the importance of space for the recognition of numerical distinctness. But it would not do to say that this necessity of spatial location arises only for qualitatively identical objects. It should be clear that qualitative diversity alone cannot sustain numerical diversity.

To bring this out we might consider two water drops that are *not* qualitatively identical; the one, say, reflects a spark of red light, the other a spark of blue light. In virtue of what could this diversity of qualities on its own sustain recognition of the numerical distinctness of the two drops? There is in fact nothing in the qualities ascribed to distinguish between there being two drops, one with a red sparkle and the other with a blue sparkle, and there being only one drop, with both a red and a blue sparkle. Again, without first locating the two drops in different places or locations within one spatial structure, there would be no way of establishing their numerical distinctness.

It might be thought that there is nevertheless a way in which qualitative diversity can, *all on its own*, necessitate numerical distinctness, without there being any need to appeal to spatial structure. The idea might be that the qualities in question might clash in such a way as to preclude their combination within the representation of a single drop of water, thereby forcing recognition of the numerical distinctness of two drops. In fact, what is right here is that there can be a specification of qualities that defies their combination within a representation of a single object; but that is not to say that that is enough on its own to sustain the recognition of there being two numerically distinct objects.

To bring this out, imagine that the quality of twinkling red and that of twinkling blue are rendered incompatible, such that they cannot possibly characterize one and the same object, say by insisting that the red twinkle and the blue twinkle occur at exactly the same point. Since an object cannot be both blue and red at one and the same point, we are invited to conclude that such qualitative diversity, on pain of incompatibility, necessitates recognition of there being numerical diversity. An obvious objection here would be that just to conceive of the coloured twinkle either being or not being *at the same point* is already to introduce implicit appeal to a spatial dimension, so we do not have a case of qualitative diversity establishing numerical diversity all on its own, without appeal to spatial structure. But this is perhaps only the fault of the example. Consider instead the simple properties of *emitting a sound $A^{\#}$* and *emitting a sound $C^{\#}$*. The two are incompatible in the relevant sense: a drop of water hitting a taut surface might make one sound, or the other, but not both at once. Surely, then, if we know that both qualities are attributable at the same time, we know that we are dealing with more than one drop. Of course in setting up the story here we are talking of water drops, surfaces, one falling onto the other, all of which presuppose spatial extension. But that is seemingly irrelevant: it is, for one thing, merely a feature of a supporting story, which could be discarded. More significantly, that introduction of spatial structure does not yet show that spatial structure is specifically needed to sustain a representation of the numerical distinctness of qualitatively distinct objects, which is what is at issue here.

What does show this, however, is the following consideration. We might well have two qualities—say, emitting $A^{\#}$ and emitting $C^{\#}$—pertaining to some kind of object that is simple enough for it to be impossible to attribute both qualities to one and the same object of that kind. The two qualities are mutually exclusive. Knowing that both qualities nevertheless apply, we then readily assume that they each inhere in a numerically distinct object of that kind. A move is made then from qualitative diversity to numerical diversity. But *that* move is itself possible only in so far as we can resort to a spatial structure, so as to represent one object of that kind as being in one place, and another as elsewhere. Without that spatial structure, we would be left simply with the impossibility of representing the given combination of properties. That it is not rendered an impossible representation is the result of our appeal to spatial structure, so as to make sense of two different objects, one for each of the two mutually exclusive qualities. This is what was meant by saying that qualitative diversity might be such as to render a certain representation impossible without numerical diversity, but is not sufficient *on its own* to sustain a representation of numerical diversity. We might put the point by saying that the representation of qualitative diversity might on its own be such as to *require* the representation of numerical diversity, but it is not enough on its own to *sustain* it. It is sustaining that representation that essentially involves resorting to a spatial structure.

So much, then, for the necessity of spatial structure to sustain the representation of objects as numerically distinct from one another. Of course, there is an air of artifice about the discussion, since it seems to suggest, wrongly, that without the representation of space (and barring contradictory qualities) the example would leave room to distinguish only one drop of water, rather than two. But, of course, there would not even be room to distinguish one drop, if by that is meant one drop that is distinct from me, the observer. This brings us to the other part of Kant's claim, namely that without the representation of space one would not be able to identify objects as distinct from the self and its mental states. Of course, the argument for this is no different from the one I have just gone through. It is just that here we have the special case in which one of the two numerically distinct objects, for the distinction of which space is required, is the experiencing subject. Given the way we are,[15] without the representation of a spatial structure no one would be able to recognize objects as numerically distinct from him- or herself. If an experienced quality was such that it could not be attributed to an object in a different spatial location from my own, then it would not be possible to represent it as a property of an object other than myself. It would become a quality of experience—strictly speaking, not even of *my* experience—rather than it being possible to regard it as a quality inhering in something else of which I have experience.

Consider, for example, the perception of a table. It is represented as an object distinct from me. But for this it is essential that I can take it to be *there* while I am *here*. Where we cannot resort to that spatial indexing, the epistemic conditions of making that distinction between myself and another object and its properties are absent. This is the case, typically, with mental states. A feeling of, say, anxiety cannot be located in space, and just for that reason it becomes difficult to consider anxiety as an object of experience that is distinct from the experiencing subject. (I can readily make sense of anxiety that is not mine, but that is only by locating it in someone else, say you, who is in another place from me.) Not all mental states are of that sort. Between experiences of anxiety or depression and experiences of tables and chairs are other mental states, such as pains. These (headaches, toothaches, etc.) are unlike feelings of anxiety or depression, in that they are presented as having a spatial location (in the head, tooth, etc.) and yet are unlike tables and chairs in that they are *not to be met with publicly* in space.[16] Whatever philosophical model we ultimately would want to endorse regarding pains and other such located sensations, it seems clear—and this is the only point relevant here—that it is only in so far as they are experienced as spatially located that it is relatively easy (even if unlikely) to use a perceptual model in thinking of them: thinking of the pain in my arm, say, as residing in, or as a property of, my arm, and to which I am perceptually related. In the case of love, or anxiety, which do not have that spatial location, the possibility of using the perceptual model is correspondingly tenuous.

---

[15] Again, it is important to bear in mind that the claim is not that this is a logical truth: there might well be beings who are able to represent objects as distinct from themselves without locating them in space. [16] Cf. G. E. Moore (1939: 276 ff.).

The case of pain highlights the fact that talking here of an object being distinct from the subject is not necessarily to talk of it as being ontologically independent of it: a pain might be *ontologically distinct* from the subject, without being *ontologically independent* of it. It would seem that spatial structure, as construed by Kant, is being said to be a condition of ontological distinctness, and not only of ontological independence. But we should note also that this cannot hold without qualification; there is an important oversimplification in the above. It applies only where the notion of an object is construed narrowly enough for there to be a difference between *A* being an object distinct from *B*, and *A* being a distinct property of *B*. Once we work with a broader notion of object that no longer upholds that difference, we might say of a perceived colour, for example, that it is an object ontologically distinct from the expanse it fills, although not ontologically independent of it. It is clear that there is here no difference in spatial location that will serve to maintain the distinctness between the colour and its spatial expanse. In fact, however, on a more generic conception of spatial structure, spatiality could be shown to be necessary for the representation of ontological distinctness even in such cases (including mental phenomena such as anxiety that are not presented as having a location in physical space). This will inform the discussion in Chapter 7. The point for now is only to note that physical space is an epistemic condition for the representation of objects as numerically distinct from one another only on a restricted view of what counts as an object.[17]

In this way, then, we can see the grounds on which Kant contends, in the first argument (of the metaphysical exposition of the concept of space), that to become perceptually aware of objects as distinct from myself, and as distinct from one another, there must be resort to a spatial grid, or matrix, in which they can be located. And given that the recognition of distinct items in this way already presupposes the representation of space, it is not possible that it is by means of that recognition that the representation of space is first constructed. The empirical experience of outer objects is itself possible only through the representation of space, so it cannot be that that representation is first obtained, a posteriori, from the encounter with those objects. And so Kant concludes: 'The representation of space cannot, therefore, be empirically obtained from the relations of outer appearance. On the contrary, this outer experience is itself possible at all only through that representation.'[18]

Now while this is right, our earlier discussion enables us to appreciate that it does not so easily suffice in itself to show that the representation of space is given a priori as part of the subjective furnishing of the mind. What it does

---

[17] A further question suggested by the case of pain, but which I leave aside for now, is whether spatiality is only *necessary* for regarding two items as ontologically distinct, or is also sufficient. It is only the former that the Kantian needs. [18] *Critique*, A23/B38.

show is that it cannot be derived a posteriori from the original encounter with distinct (outer) objects *as such*; but that is not to say that it cannot originally be derived a posteriori. The reason this might not initially be clear is that there is a ready tacit assumption of psychological atomism, such that if the representation of space is to be derived a posteriori, it *must* be derived from a series of experiences of distinct objects. And then, when *that* proves impossible as the original source of the representation of space, we conclude that it cannot be derived a posteriori, and so must be given a priori. But that conclusion does not follow without the implicit atomist assumption, for which no argument has been given. Without that commitment, all that follows is that an atomistic a posteriori derivation of space is impossible, but that is only one kind of a posteriori derivation, and so cannot establish that *no such* derivation could work.

In particular, it might be thought that the representation of space is derived a posteriori holistically. That is, that what we register are not individual and discrete items the contiguity of which ushers in our conception of spatial and temporal structure, but rather is a whole structure of ordered parts from which we then abstract, a posteriori, both the representation of pure space and the distinct items that can be plotted in relation to one another as 'nodes' within that holistically received structure. (The identification of distinct objects is then strictly internal to that structure, which is itself not registered as a distinct object from us, thereby avoiding the contradiction inherent in the atomist derivation, as well as being in keeping with our experience.) This acknowledges that a spatial structure is epistemically necessary for us to be able to represent objects as distinct from one another and from ourselves, and to the extent that there can be no experience without the latter kinds of representation, it follows too that the representation of space is a transcendental feature of our experience. That is, we might say that we know a priori that our experience will be spatio-temporally structured, but claim that this does not suffice to show that we possess *an a priori representation of space*.[19] This is because of the sort of a posteriori grounding of the representation of space that the first argument cannot preclude. And so, although that argument does perhaps bring out what is wrong with the kind of derivation of space and time offered by Locke and Hume, there is no short step from that particular failure of a posteriori grounding to Kant's conclusion that the representations of space and time must be *given* a priori.

It should be noted that this conclusion is at odds with Allison, who takes the first argument as a self-contained proof for the apriority of the *representation* of space, and moreover seems to consider it a sound argument.[20] It would

---

[19] For a sympathetic explanation of Kant's slippage from one sense of a priori, 'presupposed for experience', to the other, 'not arising out of experience', see Gardner (1999: 81–4).
[20] Cf. Allison (1983: 81 ff.).

seem instead that the second argument should be seen as having to complement the first, because of the inadequacies of the first taken on its own.[21] Perhaps the lack of clarity on the relation between the two arguments derives at least in part from the implicit commitment to atomism and the unexamined possibility of rejecting that commitment. In so far as some form of psychological atomism is accepted, the first argument suffices to establish that the representation of space is a priori, since it then follows that there is no way that we could have derived it a posteriori in experience. This, as I said earlier, is the direction that Kant takes, upholding atomism and rejecting the empiricist *tabula rasa* thesis. But as long as the atomism involved has not been argued—and Kant does not explicitly argue for it—the argument remains incomplete, apparently leaving scope to reject atomism and so escape the commitment to a priori representations not derivable from experience.[22] The question now is whether the second argument can make good the shortcomings of the first.

The second argument for space being an a priori representation, presupposed by experience of outer objects (= outer appearances) and not derived a posteriori from them, turns on the claim that we 'can never represent to ourselves the absence of space, though we can quite well think it as empty of objects'. Again, on the most charitable construal, the claim here is neither psychological nor logical, but rather epistemic.[23] The first part of the thought is that in the absence of the representation of space, there is nothing left of outer appearances. That in itself does not show that the representation of space is given a priori; it might be something that is an essential feature of outer appearances—which is why in its absence there would be nothing left of those appearances—but which is itself registered a posteriori along with those appearances. That is essentially the possibility that faced the first argument, once atomism was questioned. What supposedly precludes this possibility here is the second half of the claim, namely that we can quite well think of space as empty of objects. Even without the representation of outer objects in space, there is a content and a structure to empty space—pure space—that we can know. So while there can be no outer appearances without spatial structure, there is available to us a representation of spatial structure without outer appearances; this is supposed to show that the representation of spatial structure is both a condition of, *and is given independently of,* outer appearances.

In fact, this second (stage of the) argument for space (and, *mutatis mutandis*, for time) being an a priori representation is not altogether satisfactory. It is

---

[21] For another version of this view of the relation between the two arguments, see Kemp Smith (1962: 99–105); Paton (1936: i. 110–13).

[22] This, I think, can be seen to sustain the sort of objection Allison traces back to Maass (although without commitment to the Leibnizian conception of space), and to reveal why Allison (1983: 84–5) is wrong to conclude quite so quickly that this sort of objection does not apply to the first argument.   [23] See Allison (1983: 86–7).

true that we can think of space as empty of outer objects, and similarly that we can think of time as void of appearances. But it is important to appreciate that this independence of the representation of space and time from appearances in them has to be qualified. Even if we think away all empirical objects that fill space, and all empirical items that fill time, what we are left with still necessarily adverts to appearances in space and time; there might not be any *material* triangles that fill space, or any *concrete events* that succeed one another in time, but there must then be virtual triangles, and the process of moments in succession. Without such virtual, or pure, appearances there would be no scope to say that what we are left with, after eliminating all empirical appearances, would still count as spatial and temporal structures. Now the Kantian would say at this point that while space and time are indeed dependent on such pure appearances, these are not in turn dependent on empirical appearances, so that we can represent space and time independently of empirical appearances (call this claim A). And this, on top of the conclusion that we cannot represent empirical appearances without space and time, amounts to the conclusion that space and time not only are epistemic conditions of empirical appearances, presuppositions of experience, but are also a priori representations—given prior to and independent of those appearances. But for all that, we have seen that there is no reason why claim A should not be disputed. It remains entirely possible for the empiricist to claim that the representations of space and time—and their virtual (or pure) contents—are *originated* wholly a posteriori from the holistically registered structure of empirical appearances. Once derived, it is recognized that those structures are necessary conditions of there being such appearances, and so we know a priori that all appearances will conform to them, but that is not to say that they are a priori in the sense of being inbuilt representations that we bring with us to experience. The latter commitment, which runs counter to empiricism, has thus still not been shown to follow without the commitment to psychological atomism. But it remains true that that, as a generic commitment, is one that Locke and Hume made as well. To that extent the argument should at least work within the framework of Kant's immediate empiricist interlocutors.

Leaving aside, then, the questionable but operative assumption of some form of psychological atomism, we can turn now to address some of the consequences of this Kantian view of the mind as already equipped with the forms of space and time. It might be thought that once such representations are countenanced, the problems with rationalism that initially motivated the empiricist project must once again be threatening. In particular, given that there are such a priori representations, or structures, what guarantees that they are guides to the way of the external world? Why should the a priori structures of our mind have anything to do with the way of the world?

The Kantian response to such questions is that they are ambiguous. The ambiguity resides in what is meant by 'the way of the world'. It emerges that in one sense it is true that those structures are not guides to the way of the world, but that sense is not at all worrying; whereas in another sense, the one that matters, there is every reason to be certain that those structures are good guides to the way of the world. Here the model of the mind introduced by Kant reveals itself to have significant ramifications.

Given that space and time are forms of human sensibility, any contents that beings like us can register will be spatio-temporally structured. Consequently, the world will essentially be presented to us as spatio-temporal. But that is not to say that the world as it is in itself is in space and time. The structures of space and time apply only to *empirical reality*, to the world as it necessarily appears to us, subject to the constraints we impose upon it. Our knowledge is confined to this empirical reality. That is the world that science investigates. As for the world as it is in itself, independent of the structuring we necessarily introduce, we can have no knowledge of it, we can barely make it intelligible to ourselves, precisely because anything we will become aware of will already have taken on the spatio-temporal form required for us to have experience of it in the first place. This position, whereby we can only ever know appearances rather than the way of the world as it is in itself, is Kant's *transcendental idealism*.

Kant takes it that this confinement of knowledge to empirical reality, leaving the world as it is in itself for ever beyond our reach, is an altogether welcome consequence of his model of the mind as essentially imposing spatio-temporal structure on any world it can experience. He sees it as confining knowledge to its proper place, thereby avoiding the problems that traditionally arose when philosophers assumed that the aim was to know the world as it is in itself. For one thing, he thinks that only in this way can the sceptic about the external world be dealt with. This is something to which I will return. He also considered it important to curtail knowledge in this way in order to make room for faith in a manner that makes it clear that the two are not in competition. The empirical world is spatio-temporal, and that is the domain in which causal laws hold, such that everything that happens is caused. Such determinism notoriously leaves little room for an uncaused cause, for God, or for free will. But once it is recognized that that causal network is confined to the spatio-temporal domain, which is mere empirical reality, there is scope for God and free will in the world as it is in itself. With scientific knowledge confined to mere empirical reality, and faith to the world in itself, the age-old clash between faith and reason is potentially resolved.

Faith and knowledge are clearly demarcated. Within the domain that is appropriate for knowledge, there are no cognitive dark spots at which faith is required to complement knowledge. Here we see the extent to which Kant emerges as a paradigmatic Enlightenment thinker. His curtailment of knowledge is systematic, as opposed to Locke's or Hume's willingness simply to make do with less than full knowledge of the way of the world. Kant safeguards *exhaustive* knowledge, albeit of merely empirical reality, rather than ending up with something less than knowledge of the world as it is in itself.

So far we have seen how Kant reverses the empiricist assumption: since it seems impossible that atomistic impressions give rise to our notions of spatial and temporal structure, Kant argues that in fact the spatial and temporal structures are a priori, where that is taken to mean that they are forms that the mind of necessity imposes on the manifold of intuition, so that the manifold of impressions that enters the mind is preceded there, and must conform to, the spatio-temporal form. One result of this is that our confinement to investigation of a spatio-temporal world now seems to be confinement to the world as we necessarily construe it anyway, with no reason to think that this empirical world in which we live our lives is also the way the world is in itself. (Notoriously, Kant in fact contends that we can know that it is not.[24]) As indicated, Kant himself does not think that this is a problem; on the contrary—he thinks it is the solution to a problem. But the point for now is that it is certainly a metaphysical commitment, and seems to be ushered in, or at least facilitated, by his modification of a thoroughgoing empiricism about the mind.

2. COGNITIVE FACULTIES

Having seen how Kant identifies the forms of space and time as the a priori furnishings of the first faculty of the mind, sensibility, let us now see how he identifies the a priori furnishing of the other major faculty, understanding. We can see this by turning to the second tenet of the empiricist theory of mind that Kant saw reason to modify.

According to this tenet we proceed from simple perceptions to coherently ordered complexes of them by means of association according to principles of contiguity, resemblance, cause and effect, etc. For Locke[25] as long as we remain confined to simple ideas of sensation or reflection, as for Hume to impressions based on sensation or reflection, the mind is merely receptive. There is no reason, at least as far as these empiricist thinkers are concerned, why in just apprehending simple impressions or ideas the mind cannot function

---

[24] For attempts to explain why Kant might be entitled to this stronger claim, which seems to contradict his claim about the unknowability of things in themselves, see e.g. Allison (1983: 111–14) or Gardner (1999: 107–11).

[25] *An Essay concerning Human Understanding*, II. i. 25, xii. 1.

passively. It is only when it comes to combining those ideas into complex ones, or at least when operating with complexes already received, that the mind must become active. Kant distances himself from this feature of the mind, for what seem to be good reasons. It is these reasons that will also point us to the particular form of psychological atomism to which Kant is committed.

There is a problem about how the combination of simple impressions or ideas is supposed to work on the empiricist model. Hume himself was aware of these problems, to some extent. He realized that there must be principles governing the ways in which ideas are combined, since in his view the imagination itself could combine any two ideas. It is to this end that he proposes his laws or principles of association. But Kant remains unhappy with this solution, and it is the assumption of the passivity of the mind which the Kantian regards as being at the root of the problem.

There are two main points to be addressed here. First, it is important to understand why it is that Kant considers passive reception and combination of perceptions to be wrong. It is this that introduces us to transcendental characteristics of the faculty of the understanding, counterparts to those of sensibility, and to an important structural difference between the Kantian and the empiricist models of the mind. Secondly, we must see how the Kantian alternative solves the problems with empiricist associationism.

2.1. The Extent of Conceptualization and the Relation between the Faculties

I start with the reasons for departing from passive reception and combination of ideas. The Kantian argues that any association of ideas, if it is not to be entirely haphazard, must be governed by rules. There must be rules that determine which ideas belong with which others, which should be associated, which left alone. If there were no such rule-governed association of ideas, our mental lives would exhibit no order or continuity; it would be entirely a matter of chance whether we ever managed to combine ideas in the same way on two separate occasions. Without such order, there would be no scope in our lives for recognition or memory, for example. Random association of ideas into heaps, haphazard clusters, would not do for the purpose of creating any kind of unity. The association in question must, therefore, be rule-governed. Now such rules, namely that enable us to judge that such-and-such perceptions belong together, are *concepts*; that, after all, is what concepts do. Concepts are rules for sorting particulars, for identifying clusters of properties as belonging together, constituting a particular of a certain kind, as distinct from others which fall under a different rule. To have the concept *dog*, say, just is to be equipped with a rule with which to discriminate between contents of experience, picking out all dog-contents as belonging to the same kind, not leaving out any instances of that kind, and not including anything that is not a dog.[26]

Now this would seem to be compatible with our having learned the rules in question by observing how perceptions are in fact united in the world, equipped only with the powers allowed by the empiricists, to recognize resemblances, contiguities, etc. obtaining between impressions. But the Kantian view is that no such empiricist bootstrapping could work to furnish the mind with its entire repertoire of concepts. Any combination of impressions can be registered by us as a combination, a complex, only by means of an act of judging or somehow recognizing that here such-and-such an impression is combined with some other impression; and that involves the synthesis of the given impressions, holding them together as a complex; and that combination, according to Kant, already requires the employment of concepts. Concepts are required to bind simple impressions into complexes. So it would seem that it cannot be that our first concepts are learned from experience of combinations (complexes) of impressions; they must rather precede them.

We must already have concepts available to us, when the manifold of intuitions impinges upon our senses. Of course this is not to say that all concepts need to be given a priori. Many are merely a posteriori. But to be in a position to glean any of these concepts from our manifold impressions, we must be able to make some initial sense of that manifold, must be able to apprehend some order of combination of sensations, and that is already conceptual activity. Thus, for example, merely being able to detect that there are two impressions, that they are always conjoined, requires the concept of existence, of number, of totality... So there must be some such concepts given prior to the impact on our minds of sensory input. Kant's derivation of what he takes to be the twelve fundamental 'Categories' need not concern us here.[27] It is only the principle of there necessarily being such a priori concepts—presupposed and pre-given—that is of concern in the present context.

Kant thus reaches the conclusion that there are a priori transcendental furnishings not only to the passive faculty of sensibility, but also to the active

---

[26] This use of the concept *concept* is broad, and allows unproblematically for pre- or non-linguistic conceptual activity. Possession of a concept is implicated just when we have a subject taking something (whether consciously or not) to be thus and so. Conceptualization on this view is not limited to conscious content.

[27] Roughly, his strategy, in the Metaphysical Deduction of the Categories, is to identify the most fundamental forms of judgement without which no other judgement is possible, then identify the basic concepts involved in each, and so to come up with his identification of those twelve basic concepts without which no others could be acquired. Few today hold out much hope for Kant's attempted derivation of the Categories. In any event, the failure to derive any such list, even if principled, is hardly important, and preoccupation with the question would be something of a red herring in relation to the current concern.

faculty, understanding (and for very similar reasons). Moreover, and in contrast to the empiricist model of the mind, both of these faculties are required to make their contribution *before experience can get under way*.[28] And this means that the two are required as complementary faculties *all the way down*.

This last claim requires some clarification. It is meant to exclude the possibility of simple impressions, and indeed possibly of haphazard concatenations of them, first being received by the mind quite passively, without any use of concepts, concepts 'kicking in' only later. This kind of initial association might ultimately be insufficient for the regularity required for a unified mental life—hence the dissatisfaction with associationism registered by both Hume and Kant. And it would certainly open the door to external-world scepticism, for reasons that will become clear shortly. But putting these philosophical grounds for worry aside: could it not be that, just as a matter of the workings of the mind, there is nothing to preclude there being a rudimentary stage at which we have non-conceptual impressions, and even non-conceptual combinations of impressions?

Now with a sufficiently narrow concept of *concept* one can certainly sustain the claim that there is non-conceptual content.[29] But at least in the broad sense of *concept* identified above the Kantian view denies that there can be a form of awareness that is entirely non-conceptual, even at the foundational level. Conceptual activity is involved right at the outset, at the ground floor. It is not difficult to see what reasons the Kantian might have for thinking this (although the arguments that follow are not offered explicitly by Kant himself). Let us start with the case of *complex impressions*.

For any complex impression to be registered in the mind *as a complex*, there must be some ability to distinguish between those parts out of which it is made up—say, to take a simple case, colour and texture. Were that distinction not made, the experience would register in the mind as simple, rather than complex, no matter what internal but to us undetectable complexity there was to it. And making that distinction requires being able to separate out in thought the different elements that constitute the complex.[30] If we do not want to go along with the claim that separation in thought is required, we must at least insist on something like the capacity for making that separation in deliberate

---

[28] Thus Kant famously says: 'Without sensibility no object would be given to us, without understanding no object would be thought. Thoughts without content are empty, intuitions without concepts are blind. . . . These two powers or capacities cannot exchange their functions. The understanding can intuit nothing, the senses can think nothing. Only through their union can knowledge arise' (*Critique*, A51/B75).

[29] Many have: see e.g. Evans (1982); Peacocke (1983, 1992).

[30] This is something that Hume recognizes: 'Whatever is distinct, is distinguishable; and whatever is distinguishable, is separable by the thought or imagination' (*Treatise*, App.; 1978: 634; see also p. 36). The distinction between simple and complex impressions makes essential reference to the individuating capacities of the subject.

action. But either way that separation involves being able to judge, if only in a sense as broad as the notion of *concept* in play, that such-and-such (a) part(s) of the experience belong(s) in one category, belong(s) on one side, so to speak, under one sortal, as distinct from the other part(s) which belong(s) in another, separate category, falling under another sortal. An example might help to make this clearer. To tell that the impression I now have of {*a pen on a table*} is a complex impression, I must be able to distinguish more than one kind of component, such that some elements belong together as pertaining to the pen-content, and that excludes the other elements of the experience, which belong in a different constellation, that of the table-content. But to distinguish in this way between kinds of thing just is to have concepts, rules for taxonomizing impressions as being of one kind of thing or another.

In this example neither table-content nor pen-content constitutes a simple impression, but this is clearly irrelevant. Break up those complexes in turn, and the same recurs. If the impression or idea of a pen is complex, then that can only be because we can in turn distinguish within it some elements that belong together, in a way that other elements in it do not. Eventually, say, we reach a complex idea made up out of just two simple impressions. The same still applies. To tell that they are *two* impressions combined, rather than just *one* simple impression, we must be able to separate them, such that we recognize that they are of different sorts: the one is a colour, say, while the other is a texture. Again, this ability to differentiate in thought or in deliberate action between different sorts just is to employ concepts. So just having a complex impression—in the sense of recognizing it *as complex*, and not merely being subject to an undetectable complexity—would require that we already be equipped with some basic concepts, and be able to apply them. Again, of course, this is not to say that we must be equipped with the concept of a pen a priori. It seems likely that the initial recognition of complexes as complexes requires no more than those concepts needed for rudimentary judgements, such as the concept of an object (broadly construed), of plurality, of unity. But without some such basic concepts already up and running, there could be no recognition of impressions as complex.

Let us turn now to the case of *simple impressions*. What of the possibility of having a simple impression without conceptual activity? We can see that while this might, in a sense, be possible, it would be merely an insignificant theoretical nicety, devoid of distinguishing content. Without any conceptual element, there could be no judgement enabling the recognition that the experience was of such-and-such a sort. That would leave us with nothing more than the possibility of something unindividuated occurring within us. The distinctive 'raw feel' that stands to make the impression not just something that happens in us, and that is true *of me*, but something that is true *for me*, would be lost.³¹ For the impression of pain to be something for me, distinct from, say, an impression of heat, I must be able to identify the pain as being distinct from other kinds of impression. Without that recognitional element the raw feel of pain, however distinctive, would not be *registered by me* as distinctive, as different from the raw feel of heat (or a colour, or smell ...). We must be able to identify them *as*, respectively, pain and heat, or at least *as* different kinds of item in some respect, however impoverished (relative to the full-blown concepts of pain and of heat). And that requires applying some concepts.³² So, without basic concepts up and running, there could be no recognition of simple impressions either.³³

It would seem, then, that there is some scope to argue for the mutual dependence of conceptual activity and sensory reception all the way down to the point of initial consciousness; that there can be no experience, however rudimentary, that does not involve the contribution of both faculties. This puts us in a position to appreciate the reasons for Kant's contention that the manifold of intuition, or of representations, would just be a blind disorderly mess if we did not *organize* them, and that what organizes them is the way in which they are 'run through, and held together'³⁴ by the mind, by the application of concepts, and in particular of the categories. And the fact that this happens right from the outset constitutes a significant deviation from the empiricist model of the mind.

We can capture the difference graphically in the following way. On the empiricist model sensibility (which passively receives sensory input) and understanding (which deals with conceptual activity on that input) are, so to speak, *stacked*: the one precedes the other. The blank mind first registers and becomes aware of passively received impressions and combinations of impressions, which subsequently give rise to ideas that the understanding associates by means of

---

[31] Schwyzer (1990: 70) calls on a similar distinction: 'The empiricists' ... is the doctrine ... that for something to be true *for* one it is sufficient that something be sensorily true *of* one. This is the view that Kant is denying; he is claiming that without apperception and the categories the data of sensibility remain mere data and cannot reach the understanding; without the categories nothing can be true for one.' See also, from outside the specifically Kantian literature, Shoemaker (1984).

[32] It might be thought that without concepts one might be in a position to recognize *that* an impression had occurred, although there would be no capacity to recognize *what* it was, to distinguish an impression of pain from one of colour, say. But the state in question not only could not be distinguished from any other qualitative state, it would also not be distinguished qualitatively from the absence of any such state. For that would require recognition of some distinguishing quality, which would reintroduce conceptualization. Taken strictly without concepts, it would seem that the state in question no longer counts as an *impression*, as a *qualitative* state, rather than as a mere event.

[33] It should be noted that the case is even clearer where a simple impression being something for me is not construed in terms of its phenomenal content.

[34] *Critique*, A99.

principles of association. On the Kantian model the two faculties of sensibility and understanding are operative side by side, making complementary contributions, from the outset. There is no stage at which the one is operative and the other not. And, in working side by side, each faculty brings its a priori furnishings to bear: in the case of sensibility it is the forms of space and time, and we have now seen that in the case of the understanding it is some basic concepts without which no others could be acquired, which Kant identifies as the pure concepts of the understanding (the Categories). These two sets of a priori furnishings obviously jointly constitute a marked departure from the empiricist *tabula rasa* thesis addressed earlier (Section 1 above), but it is also important to concentrate on the significance of the further deviation from the empiricist model of the mind that we have just seen, namely the Kantian insistence on the necessity of there being conceptual activity *in tandem* with sensory reception from the outset.

On the Humean model of the mind the contents of sensibility and of understanding are not interdependent, and so it is in principle possible for the two to come apart in experience. It is possible that future sensory contents be registered such as would no longer allow for the application to them of the ideas previously applicable to sensory impressions. Thus there is nothing, on this model, to guarantee that we will not begin at any point to receive impressions that no longer allow for the application to them of the idea of causation, say, or of external existence. In this way, this empiricist model of the mind in virtue of its 'stacked' faculties opens up sceptical possibilities.

On the Kantian model of the mind this kind of deviation of the two faculties is no longer a possibility. Given the way in which understanding (the faculty of concepts) and sensibility (the faculty of contents) are interdependent, it is not possible for us to be in the unfortunate position of registering sensory contents and finding that our basic concepts no longer apply to them. Were those basic concepts to fail in applicability to sensory contents, those contents would themselves be nothing to us. And from this, with a little more work, one might move to the conclusion that there is no sceptical possibility here of basic categories like causation failing to apply *in our experience*. There is only the possibility of experience coming to an end—which of course is neither a new nor a sceptical worry that philosophy must avoid.

In this way the structural difference in Kant's model of the mind already ushers in the promise of anti-sceptical results. But so far it is no more than a promise. We have seen, perhaps, why experience must be conceptual all the way down, but not why the concepts in question must be such that the necessity of their application would constitute an anti-sceptical proof regarding the external world. This is something to which I will return (in Section 3 below). We can also defer until then the development of the precise form of Kant's commitment to psychological atomism, the ground for which is already given in the immediately preceding discussion.

2.2. Synthesis and Association of Ideas

Distinct in principle from that anti-sceptical yield, although Kant does not really see it as distinct, is the second issue identified above, namely, that this Kantian model stands to solve the problems with empiricist associationism.

For Hume, we could start off with just passive receipt of impressions. These might be all that we are aware of. These then give rise to ideas, and different ideas become associated with one another by arising together, and consequently are such that the occurrence of the one immediately brings to mind the recollection of the others. It is the operation of these laws of association that is supposed to explain how ideas cluster together in fixed bundles in the mind. Clearly, such laws, like the problem to which they are a proposed solution, are called for only because of Hume's psychological atomism. Given such atomism, these proposed laws 'are the only bonds that unite our thoughts together, and beget that regular train of reflection or discourse, which, in a greater or lesser degree, takes place among all mankind'.[35] Without these bonds, we would not have sufficient coherence to our experience to facilitate communication, or indeed survival.[36]

Now Hume was not altogether satisfied with his own associationism, and for good reason. He recognized, for example, that laws of association could not in fact explain our belief in abiding objects, as they were supposed to. But also that it was not clear how association could work given that the properties of objects, and hence the impressions to which they give rise, are constantly changing. Moreover, even if the properties of the objects were not changing, the impressions would still be changing constantly. Lighting conditions, subjective constitution, relative location, all mean that it hardly ever happens that we see a given tree or patch of grass in the same way twice. Given the instability of impressions, it is unclear how fixed associations of resembling and contiguous properties could be formed. Kant too was deeply dissatisfied with such associationism. But in so far as he shared with Hume some form of psychological atomism, he accepted that there must be empirical principles of association. Thus he says:

If, however, representations reproduced one another in any order, just as they happened to come together, this would not lead to any determinate connection of them, but only to accidental collocations; and so would not give rise to any knowledge. Their

[35] Hume, *An Enquiry concerning Human Understanding*, v. ii. 41 (1975: 50).
[36] Ibid. (1975: 54–5).

reproduction must, therefore, conform to a rule, in accordance with which a representation connects in the imagination with some one representation in preference to another. This subjective and *empirical* ground of reproduction according to rules is what is called the *association* of representations.[37]

As to the rule in question, he continues:

Now if this unity of association had not also an objective ground which makes it impossible that appearances should be apprehended by the imagination otherwise than under the condition of a possible synthetic unity of this apprehension, it would be entirely accidental that appearances should fit into a connected whole of human knowledge.[38]

Now the question is: what is this objective ground? Kant has two answers available here, and I think that he does not always adequately distinguish them. For Hume there is association by contiguity and resemblance between contents, under the following conditions: (*a*) the sources of those impressions are themselves not known to be rule-governed, and (*b*) those impressions are merely registered as so many passively received sensory parcels. The only resources that we then have to draw on to guide association are the concatenations of individual impressions. It is in consequence of this that it is difficult to explain how there would be sufficient constraints on association to produce one stable pattern of association, contiguity and resemblance themselves being too open to interpretation and to the instability of impressions to fix on just one combination. Given a form of psychological atomism, this is bound to happen wherever both conditions (*a*) and (*b*) are allowed. To improve matters, it is enough in principle to reject either (*a*) or (*b*). Kant, of course, denies both. The particular way in which he does so means that he obscures the two distinct answers to the question of what the objective constraint on association of ideas might be: either knowledge of a rule-governed order of the external world that is the source of those impressions (contra (*a*)), or a model of the mind that allows more than the mere passive receipt of impressions (contra (*b*)).

The point can be brought out well in relation to the following paragraph, in which Kant is clear about the need for some objective constraint that would guide the empirical association of ideas:

It is a merely empirical law, that representations which have often followed or accompanied one another finally become associated, and so are set in a relation whereby,

---

[37] *Critique*, A120. That Kant does accept some form of psychological atomism is, incidentally, evident in the following passage, which immediately precedes the passage quoted in the text: 'Now, since every appearance contains a manifold, and since different perceptions therefore occur in the mind separately and singly, a combination of them, such as they cannot have in sense itself, is demanded. There must therefore exist in us an active faculty for the synthesis of this manifold.'   [38] Ibid., A121.

even in the absence of the object, one of these representations can, in accordance with a fixed rule, bring about a transition of the mind to the other. But this law of reproduction presupposes that appearances are themselves actually subject to such a rule, and that in the manifold of these representations a coexistence or sequence takes place in conformity with certain rules. Otherwise our empirical imagination would never find opportunity for exercise appropriate to its powers, and so would remain concealed within the mind as a dead and to us unknown faculty. If cinnabar were sometimes red, sometimes black, sometimes light, sometimes heavy, if a man changed sometimes into this and sometimes into that animal form . . . my empirical imagination would never find opportunity when representing red colour to bring to mind heavy cinnabar.[39]

Taken on its own this can be read austerely, as saying merely that there must be regularity in the world if association of ideas is to be regulated in turn. But the context makes it entirely clear that the rules governing appearances here are those introduced by the mind through its acts of synthesis. Given this we can see here how Kant should, but does not, distinguish between the way in which his account of the mind suffices to answer the problem with associationism and the way in which it purportedly also delivers an answer to scepticism about the external world. He uses the latter to handle the former. Indeed, given his claims that the rules for synthesis produce nature,[40] it is easy to see that there is hardly any stopping-point between the two. The presuppositions of adequate association of ideas, sufficient to constitute a coherent mental life, just do run straight from the necessity of synthesis according to rules to there being an empirical world that abides by those rules. Thus the success and constancy of empirical association of ideas can readily be said to be underpinned by, and predicated on, rules known to obtain between the phenomena—transcendental phenomena, objective events in the empirical world—that occasion the representations. This resolves the difficulty about coherent patterns for the association of ideas along the lines of contesting (*a*) above. But that trades on Kant's argument to the effect that synthesis is also the lawgiver of nature,[41] or at least on his answer to scepticism about the external world.

In fact Kant's model of the mind already has the materials with which to resolve the problems with empiricist principles of association, along the lines of contesting (*b*) above, without having to appeal to the further anti-sceptical conclusion it might yield. Just in so far as sensory contents are something for us—are subject to what Kant refers to as synthesis of apprehension—the mind must, as we have seen, apply certain concepts to that material. The faculty of understanding thereby orders those contents. What matters is only that that ordering, or synthesis of contents, fixes a rule governing

---

[39] Ibid., A100–1. See Kitcher (1990: 78). [40] *Critique*, A113–14, A125–8.
[41] Ibid.

what contents are initially, and then subsequently in recollection—what Kant refers to as synthesis of reproduction—properly associated with others. Any empirical association of ideas, such as results from habit and custom, is consequently held in place not merely by internal relations between sensory contents, some chance order of occurrence in the mind, or some fluctuating resemblances, but by the fixed conceptual operations of the mind that have already been operative in those contents being registered in the first place. This is enough, in principle, to impose an objective rule on the combination (synthesis) of sensory contents. Constellations of sensations or impressions will be fixed in accordance with rules for their conceptualization, which might remain fixed in the face of the flux of internal relations between the constituent sensations.

Whether that ordering of sensory contents is also such as to synthesize out of them an abiding objective empirical world, an independent law-governed domain, as Kant thought, or perhaps—less extravagantly—at least to presuppose such a world, is a distinct question that can and should be left aside here. What has been said so far is only that the understanding is such as to secure constancy in the way in which sensations are clustered into objects on various occasions, which is not in itself to say that there need be any appeal to those objects being such as persist from one such occasion to the next, that is, to them being independent of those acts of judging which clusters obtain.[42] Whether or not they are thus independent of judgement-acts seems to require further investigation. It is that investigation that also stands to yield a refutation of scepticism about the external world. But it is not necessary to rely on the claim that the synthesis in question constitutes or presupposes some such independent abiding world just in order to explain how the Kantian modification of the empiricist model of the mind affords a solution to the problem with empiricist association of ideas. In principle there is room, on the Kantian model, to conceive of the mind being such as repeatedly to apply the same concepts to the manifold of intuition, thereby resolving the problem of association, regardless of whether it also suffices to deliver to us the experience of an objective abiding world.

It should be noted that the problem regarding the association of sensory contents or perceptions, and so the need for the Kantian solution, again arises only given the commitment to some form of psychological atomism. Kant himself seems clearly both to accept that commitment, and to recognize that it is responsible for the ensuing problem for the ordering of ideas.[43]

---

[42] The distinction here parallels Strawson's. Another way of putting it is to say that objects here can be taken in the thin sense, i.e. as the mere accusatives of judgements, there being nothing yet to ensure that these objects are such as to exist in the weighty sense that concerns ontological independence of the judgement. For Strawson's distinction, see Strawson (1966: 73 ff.). See also Allison (1983: 136).

[43] See *Critique*, A97, A99, A116, A120–1, for example.

But, again, he does not seem to countenance the possibility of rejecting that psychological atomism. This will be of particular consequence in what follows.

3. HOW UNITY OF CONSCIOUSNESS IS POSSIBLE

It is now time to take a look at the kind of anti-sceptical argument regarding our knowledge of the external world that Kant's model of the mind might sustain, and to turn more generally to the wider philosophical ramifications of that model. The prospect of the following kind of argument seems to open up. If all experience involves the application to sensory input of conceptual judgement, then there will be some conceptual content that is a priori. We know, then, that there will be some concepts such that, just in so far as we have experience, that of which we have experience will fall under them, conform to them. The way in which things appear to us will be synthesized according to the basic concepts we apply. That is just to say that the world will be judged to hold together in a certain way. So a certain regularity in the experienced world can be known a priori to obtain, just in so far as it is a world of which we have experience in the first place.

This is just what could not be argued on the Humean or Lockean model of the mind, where in principle there seemed to be scope for our having a play of impressions, without knowing with any certainty that (1) the concepts derived from those impressions would have application to the empirical world beyond them; or indeed without knowing even that (2) there was a rule-governed world independent of those impressions. On the Kantian model we do know this; and we do so precisely because that model blurs the distinction between (1) and (2). The role of conceptualization in our experience is such that it is assured application to an empirical world beyond impressions precisely because it constitutes that rule-governed external world; we know that our concepts will apply to the world because our experience requires the participation of concepts such as to deliver that world. That empirical world is the world as constituted by us, as a condition of our having experience in the first place.

For Hume, as indeed for Descartes, the model of the mind advocated is compatible with, and invites the thought that we are aiming at, knowledge of the world as it is in itself—what Kant calls transcendental realism—and that our experience could be just as it is, and yet we know nothing about the way of that world. Kant's model of the mind, even if it does not quite deny us the notion of the world as it is in itself, is such that it interposes, between us and that world, the empirically real world, knowledge of which is presupposed by our having our subjective experiences. It is in the confinement of that world, which is in part constituted by the mind, that we live our lives; and therein lies the answer Kant provides to scepticism about the external world—the only external world we can experience.

This, in broad and sympathetic outline, indicates how the Kantian model of the mind serves to link our subjective experience with the experience of a rule-abiding object-world, although not perhaps quite the one we might pre-critically have had in mind, and thereby to answer the sceptic, although not perhaps in quite the way that we would have liked. The argument itself[44] can be run through and presented in a variety of reconstructions, adhering more or less attentively to the details of Kant's model of the mind. Before I turn to this, it will help to have the background to the argument in place.

3.1. The Setting

We can see Kant as setting out from the question, what must be the case for all my experiences to be mine, for them to form a single unified consciousness? In this he is turning to address the third tenet of empiricism identified above. Kant obviously does not want to take issue with this; but he does wish to explain how such unity is possible.

Locke and Hume both assume that there is some sort of unified consciousness over time. The problem is that on the empiricist view of the matter it is singularly difficult to see what the explanation might be. The empiricist model of the mind seems too restricted to afford an explanation. Hume, famously, confronts the problem:

For my part, when I enter most intimately into what I call *myself*, I always stumble on some particular perception or other, of heat or cold, light or shade, love or hatred, pain or pleasure. I never catch *myself* at any time without a perception, and never can observe any thing but the perception. . . . I may venture to affirm of the rest of mankind, that they are nothing but a bundle or collection of different perceptions, which succeed each other with an inconceivable rapidity, and are in a perpetual flux and movement.[45]

Unlike the case of those perceptions that give rise to belief in abiding objects located in the external world, there is here no real continuity and persistence of content which would explain the opinion that there is a continuing abiding self. In the case of external objects, 'the opinion of the continu'd existence of body depends on the coherence and constancy of certain impressions'.[46] There is nothing of the sort when it comes to the myriad of changing perceptions that are met with 'when I enter most intimately into what I call *myself*': in the case of the self or person, 'there is no impression constant and invariable.

---

[44] Drawn primarily from the Transcendental Deduction, A95–130/B129–69.
[45] *Treatise*, I. iv. 6 (1978: 252).   [46] Ibid. I. iv. 2 (1978: 195).

Pain and pleasure, grief and joy, passions and sensations succeed each other, and never all exist at the same time.'[47]

The problem here is particularly pressing. Accommodation of common sense aside, it is a presupposition of Hume's own empiricist theory of mind that there is continuity of consciousness from one experience to the next; that our multitude of experiences are unified into a single consciousness—that they are all mine. Without that unity, there would be no explaining how combinations in consciousness of atomistic impressions could be possible; without it we could not observe similarity across diverse experiences, could not observe a train of impressions or ideas, as Locke and Hume both agree that we can. We thus have a feature that is rendered inexplicable by a theory that itself presupposes it. For this reason the fact that Hume is unable to find any such persisting subject of experience constitutes a problem not just for those (like Kant) who are interested in philosophical certainty, but for the working of Hume's own associationist theory of mind. Indifference, or naturalism, which works so well in response to other problems, provides less obvious relief here.

Now Kant accepts that at the empirical level, that which is alone available to phenomenological introspection, Hume is right. Thus he says: 'Consciousness of self according to the determinations of our state in inner perception is merely empirical, and always changing. No fixed and abiding self can present itself in this flux of inner appearances. Such consciousness is usually named *inner sense*, or *empirical apperception*.'[48] The question then is, how is it possible that we nevertheless do not have a fragmented consciousness, with as many candidate unities as there are moments of empirical apperception? Under one possible reconstruction, the notoriously obscure argument of the Transcendental Deduction proceeds from this point as follows.

3.2. One Possible Reconstruction

Although much of the material on which this reconstruction draws is presented in a way that suggests reliance on psychological atomism, the argument here can be prised apart from any such commitment. We begin with the idea of the passively received manifold of intuition as being sufficiently inchoate and inarticulate, as it is given to sensibility, for it not to count as comprising representations at all. We have already seen that for that manifold to be anything for us, rather than merely something happening to us, it must be conceptualized. In this way representations arise, be they initially simple or complex. These representations may be self-consciously self-ascribed. Whether or not they are, it is clear that as yet there is nothing here that

---

[47] Ibid. I. iv. 6 (1978: 251–2). See also ibid., App. (1978: 634, 635–6).
[48] *Critique*, A107.

would unify them all in *one* consciousness. For there to be unity of consciousness across representations, the various representational contents—over which particular representations range—somehow have all to be combined, held together ('compared and connected'[49]), just as contents do within one particular representation. Only so could they all belong to a single, unified, encompassing experience, *my* experience.

Kant's crucial contention, on this reconstruction, is that this combination cannot be secured by sensibility on its own. An additional ability on our part to combine representational contents, and recognize them as combined, is required. Thus, ignoring for now the apparent assertion of atomism in the first sentence, Kant says:

since every appearance contains a manifold, and since different perceptions therefore occur in the mind separately and singly, a combination of them, such as they cannot have in sense, is demanded. There must therefore exist in us an active faculty for the synthesis of this manifold.[50]

The act of combining such representations as there may be requires recognition—however primitive—of all representational contents as falling under sortals; only so can they be recognized as a unified plurality, set in determinate relations *to one another*, and so be something to *me*. The combination or synthesis thus involves acts of conceptualization. And some of these must be a priori:

This synthetic unity [of the manifold in all possible intuition] presupposes or includes a synthesis, and if the former is to be *a priori* necessary, the synthesis must also be *a priori*. The transcendental unity of apperception thus relates to the pure synthesis of imagination, as an *a priori* condition of the possibility of all combination of the manifold in one knowledge.[51]

Since this synthesis, or conceptual organization of the material of sensibility, is in play from the very beginning as a precondition of *my* experience, in so far as nothing can be anything for me without the contribution of this conceptualization, it follows that the synthesis must be done in accordance with some a priori concepts, which are brought to experience, rather than learned from experience. Now we might argue directly for some of the concepts that are thus involved a priori, such as *unity* or *plurality*: they could not have been derived from experience of different representational contents, since their application is required for the combination of those contents in one consciousness in the first place.[52] But this is not how Kant proceeds. He takes himself

---

[49] *Critique*, A97.
[50] Ibid., A120. Cf. also A110: 'There is one single experience . . . in accordance with concepts.'
[51] Ibid., A118.
[52] The parallel between this line of argument and the argument for space and time being a priori forms of intuition should be evident.

to have already established in the Metaphysical Deduction what these a priori concepts are. And so at this point he simply imports that list, and—rather heroically to contemporary eyes—takes the a priori concepts involved in the required synthesis to be fixed and identifiable Categories. So it follows that all representations, if they are to be united within one consciousness, must be united according to the rules embodied in the Categories.

> In the understanding there are then pure *a priori* modes of knowledge which contain the necessary unity of the pure synthesis of imagination in respect of all possible appearances. These are the categories, that is, the pure concepts of understanding.[53]

Like all other concepts with which the understanding operates, the Categories are rules for synthesis: rules for identifying or for bringing 'various representations under one common representation'.[54] The application of such rules consists of making judgements; and judgements are essentially *about something*. Since the synthesis of the manifold is necessarily performed using these rules (the Categories), the same rules that enable the unity of representations within one consciousness are also thereby those that determine the unity of a domain that the rules are applied to, the objects that the judgements made are about.

Now the Categories as Kant identifies them include, aside from unity and plurality, substance, causality, existence . . . So given that the synthesis of the manifold, which is necessary in order for the manifold to belong to a single consciousness in the first place, and without which it would be nothing for me, is done in accordance with the Categories, and given that it follows that the manifold will be combined to constitute a domain that is shaped by those rules for synthesis that the Categories comprise, their application to the manifold will constitute out of it an objective domain that abides by the law of causality, in which substances exist and are distinguished from their accidents, etc.

And so we find Kant saying:

> Thus the understanding is something more than a power of formulating rules through comparison of appearances; it is itself the lawgiver of nature. Save through it, nature, that is, synthetic unity of the manifold of appearances according to rules, would not exist at all . . .

> However exaggerated and absurd it may sound, to say that the understanding is itself the source of the laws of nature, and so of its formal unity, such an assertion is none the less correct, and is in keeping with the object to which it refers, namely, experience.

> Pure understanding is thus in the categories the law of the synthetic unity of all appearances, and thereby first and originally makes experience, as regards its form,

---

[53] *Critique*, A119.   [54] Ibid., A68/B93.

possible. This is all that we were called upon to establish in the transcendental deduction of the categories . . .[55]

To recapitulate in summary what we have seen on this first reconstruction of the argument: the unity of consciousness requires that the diversity of representational content be held together. That combination, and the recognition of it, cannot itself come to us through sensibility, but rather involves an activity on the part of the understanding[56]—synthesis. That synthesis must be rule-governed (otherwise synthesis would result only in haphazard collocations of impressions, which would make recollection and hence unity of consciousness impossible). That rule-governed synthesis amounts to the application of concepts to the representational content.[57] That in turn involves making judgements, since that is just what the application of concepts comes to. But judgements are essentially about objects. Hence, all my experiences can be held together in a single consciousness only by acts of synthesis, which very acts also constitute objects: which brings out the way in which the understanding is the lawgiver of nature.

Now the standard objection to this line of argument is that it entitles us to conclude only that the unity of consciousness necessitates judgements about objects in a 'thin' sense. The objects here are simply the correlates of acts of judgement.[58] As such they do not necessarily carry any connotation of objectivity, of existence independent of the subjective states of awareness. Unity of consciousness entails that we make judgements about objects, but in so far as these objects might be nothing more than intentional objects, there is nothing about this act of object-constitution that will count as a surprising answer to the epistemic sceptic. For that we would need to show not merely that all judgements are about objects, as the accusatives of judgements, but that they are about an objective world in the weighty sense of the term that carries a commitment to an encounter with an ontologically independent world. So far it would seem that the argument outlined here suffices to establish only the former.

It is clear that Kant means the argument to establish the latter as well, given the way in which the faculties of sensation and understanding are related. To the extent that the understanding is thought of as playing an intellectual, theorizing role, one might be tempted by the thought that the Categories constrain how we *think* about the world, but not how the world simply is in our encounter with it. That is, it might seem that they constrain the construal only of objects as the mere accusatives of judgements, as theoretical or intentional entities, not as the items that we bump into in the world. But in fact

---

[55] *Critique*, A126–7, A127, A128.   [56] Ibid., B129–30.
[57] Note that '. . . a concept is always, as regards its form, something universal which serves as a rule' (ibid., A106).   [58] See Allison (1983: 146–8, 159 ff.).

the integration between sensibility and understanding is much too close to allow for the Categories to apply only to that aetiolated sense of an object. The integration of conceptual activity into the process of ordering—in the sense of apprehending, recollecting, and recognizing—the sensory manifold goes all the way down, as I have said; and this makes it impossible to think that the understanding constrains only how we *think* of objects, how we *judge* them to be in some intellectual sense, without being equally involved in the construal of the very objects ('objects' in the weighty sense) which we meet upon leaving the philosophical study. That this is Kant's intention is clear. But it is not clear that the argument of the Transcendental Deduction actually suffices to establish this much. Precisely because the Transcendental Deduction confines itself abstractly to the role of the understanding as a faculty of judgement in unifying representations, in isolation from the question of its function in a subject embedded in the spatio-temporal world, it can seem to take us no further than the necessity of construing objects in the weak sense in accordance with the Categories. But, of course, this means only that the Transcendental Deduction should not be taken to be an altogether self-standing anti-sceptical move.[59]

A more significant weakness of this version of the anti-sceptical move is that it can take us only as far as the conclusion that there must be some a priori concepts that the empirical world in our experience conforms to, but cannot on its own tell us what these are, at least not in any degree of sufficient detail. For that we are asked to rely on the results of the Metaphysical Deduction of the Categories, in which Kant attempts to identify them. But the derivation of the Categories in the Metaphysical Deduction carries far too little conviction for it to be appealed to as the final step of the argument.[60] In particular, it is not clear that because experience requires the a priori application of some concepts, it follows that there is one set of a priori concepts that is required by every form of experience. And without that step the conclusion, that the unity of consciousness presupposes experience of objects, is not strong enough to be of much interest. This again would be a case for not regarding the Transcendental Deduction as constituting a self-standing anti-sceptical move.

It is at this point pertinent to offer a second reconstruction of the Kantian attempt to show that accounting for unity of consciousness at the same time constitutes an anti-sceptical move.

---

[59] We will see how it can be supplemented by the Analogies when I turn to the second reconstruction. Strawson too calls on the post-Schematism chapters in order to make good the shortcomings of the Transcendental Deduction. What he has in mind, however, is to substitute the later results for the reliance in the Transcendental Deduction on the dubious results of the Metaphysical Deduction (and indeed of the doctrine of synthesis). See Strawson (1966: 117–18, 121–2, 125 ff.).   [60] See Bennett (1966: 124); Strawson (1966: 88, 117–18).

3.3. A Second Possible Reconstruction

The opening assumption is, again, that there are constantly changing experiences, and that all my experiences are unified so as to count as one and all *mine*. But that alone would not suffice for the reconstructed argument to go through. Additionally this reconstruction, unlike the previous one, turns on a commitment to a form of psychological atomism. Some of Kant's explicit utterances notwithstanding, it is unclear whether the Transcendental Deduction is in fact best regarded as predicated on some form of psychological atomism. To that extent it is a strength of the previous reconstruction that it did not turn specifically on any such commitment. That being the case is, of course, compatible with the argument resting, as I believe it does, on a model of mind that has such atomism as its consequence. But the present reconstruction, by contrast, rests explicitly on that consequence of the Kantian conception of the mind, in a way that the former does not.

Some care, however, needs to be taken in construing both the form of atomism involved, and the form of its involvement. It is at this point that I turn to the task so far postponed, of specifying the form of psychological atomism to which Kant is committed. Importantly, what is involved is not the form of psychological atomism we find in empiricism, namely sensory atomism. Equally importantly, the atomism that is involved does not serve as a new premiss that Kant helps himself to. I will clarify each of these in turn.

The sensory atomism of the empiricist has it that the sensations (impressions) that first enter the mind do so singly, as indivisible simples, in isolation from one another. In places, as we have seen, Kant certainly seems to commit himself to something of this sort, but in fact it is not such atomism that is germane to his argument, or at least to the present construal of it. I take this to be a strength of the construal, since strictly speaking Kant is not in a position to endorse anything of the sort. For one thing, accepting such atomism would imply that sensations are registered as already individuated, prior to any conceptual operation. And this would seem to render the need for conceptual synthesis far more restricted than it is in Kant—namely, merely to the combination of already registered and individuated sensory contents. Or, to put the problem differently, given the extensive role played by conceptual synthesis, we are not in a position to know anything about the manner in which the preconceptualized sensory content is delivered to sensibility. The assertion of sensory atomism, or its denial, is already a conceptualization of it. Also, while we do, for Kant, know something about the a priori form of intuition, the fact of a spatio-temporal structure imposed on the sensory contents received does not tell one way or another about whether the sensory material is atomistically received: indeed it counts against the intelligibility of that assertion. It would, then, be inappropriate for a reconstruction of the Transcendental Deduction to hold Kant to the endorsement of a form of sensory atomism as a premiss of the argument.

The relevant form of psychological atomism is better understood as an atomism of *perceptions*, rather than of *sensations*. However sensory content is registered, we have seen that, for Kant at least, it becomes something for us only when it is subsumed under a concept, when it is apprehended or recognized as being of one kind or another. Two sensory contents that were by hypothesis different in themselves would nevertheless not amount to different perceptions of ours if there was not a single respect in which they could be distinguished by us—whether consciously or not—as being of different kinds. The difference between them would be nothing to us; it would be perceptually null. Similarly, of course, if a sensory content were supposed to be present but to be such that it was not brought under any concept to the exclusion of others, there would in effect be no difference in perception between an organism having that sensory content and not having it. Again, any such content would be perceptually insignificant.[61] That is just the sense in which Kant contends that intuitions without concepts are blind. Unconceptualized, such sensory contents as there might be do not amount to perceptions. Or, to put it positively, perceptions are conceptualized sensations. Now, at least on Kant's view, the application of concepts, the apprehension that a particular falls under a general rule, can be implemented only by, and so is tantamount to, the making of judgements. So every perception is delivered by a judgement; and judgement-acts are distinct from one another, and discrete. So too, then, are perceptions.[62]

This is in fact sufficient as a starting-point for the Transcendental Deduction, but it is not yet perspicuously tantamount to perceptual atomism. Nothing has been said explicitly by way of delivering a decision on whether the content of each of the perceptions from which we take our cognitive beginnings is simple (i.e. is not further divisible), or instead comprises a complex

---

[61] For a similar thought, although not in the context of Kant but rather of assessing functionalism, see again Shoemaker (1984).

[62] The insistence on conceptualization and judgement for perception is obviously not an uncontestable claim, as we will indeed see later. But it is important that it is not contested for the wrong reasons. To that end it is worth emphasizing how weak the construal of the central contention can be: in particular, the application of concepts, the making of judgements, need not be conscious; nor—for present purposes—need it be thought to occur in a being that is in principle capable of articulating such judgements *verbally*. Non-human animals such as dogs and cats can well be allowed perceptions on this view: all that is needed is that there be some articulated difference for the animal between kinds of experience, sufficient to allow perceptions of type A to be grasped as being of the same general sort, and distinct from perceptions of the not-A type. (This is obviously not to deny that theories of animal perception that do not postulate judgement-acts to sustain that difference might be more attractive.) We should also be wary of taking the contesting claim that a creature with no capacity for conceptualization can perceive objects, to amount to more than the conceded possibility that there could be sensory data that were non-perceptual.

structure. Nevertheless, given what has been said, it is clear why Kant seems to be committed to the former. If the complexity of content is not distinguished by the perceiver, whether consciously or not, then the complexity does not enter into the structure of the perception. So if we are dealing with a perceptual complex, then it must be that the perceiving organism distinguishes between its component parts; or at least distinguishes that there are component parts.[63] But for that the content in question would have to be perceived as comprising at least two different kinds. And for that, at least on Kant's view, they must already be conceptualized, such that one element of the complex falls under one sortal which the rest does not (and for Kant that is tantamount to the exercise of judgement). But such conceptualized sensory contents are already perceptions. A perceptual complex, then, on Kant's view, can only be a complex of cognitively prior perceptions. It cannot consequently be the kind of perception from which we take our cognitive beginnings. To put the point the other way round: any perception which is not regarded as a composite of prior perceptions, and which in that sense can count as basic, must be a simple perception, because any complexity that there might be in its content would be rendered invisible—that is, it could not be perceptually articulated—by the unity of the act of conceptualization that constitutes that perception. Of course, what remains inchoate in the confines of one perception might be individuated in subsequent perceptions. But then they are just that, subsequent perceptions, distinct judgement-acts. It remains the case that what is registered in the initial perception is registered as simple. Any recognition of complexity must result from the way in which different perceptions are combined and brought to bear one on the content of the other. And for that the different perceptions must be combined by a single judgement into a perceptual complex. But far from that being an easy solution, it merely identifies the basic problem addressed by the Transcendental Deduction. The Transcendental Deduction can be seen precisely as the attempt to work out the conditions under which the unification of distinct perceptual contents in a single consciousness is possible.

So much by way of clarifying the kind of psychological atomism to which Kant is committed, an atomism of perceptions rather than of sensations, where perceptions are the product of conceptualized sensations. It should also be clear from the above discussion that this form of psychological atomism should not be regarded as a new premiss that Kant introduces for the purpose of the

[63] It is important to note the modality here. The claim is that the perceiver actually distinguishes, not merely that the complexity is *distinguishable*. Perceptual atomism differs in this respect too from the empiricists' sensory atomism, where the claim was that an impression is complex if it is divisible, leaving scope to consider that it might be so regardless of whether it is so divided by the perceiver. Underlying this difference is the fact that sensory atomism is an ontological (or metaphysical) claim about what is given, whereas underlying perceptual atomism is an epistemological claim about our apprehension. Kant clearly can more readily accommodate the latter kind of claim than the former.

Transcendental Deduction, but rather is a direct consequence of his general view of the mind: given how the Kantian mind works, the commitment to perceptual atomism cannot be avoided.[64] Nevertheless, although not a new premiss, this perceptual atomism does serve as the starting-point for the argument on the present reconstruction of the Transcendental Deduction. (Kant does not attempt to justify the atomism that his discussion seems to advert to, but the above discussion of the content of and licence for that atomism perhaps explains why that is appropriate enough: being a consequence of previous moves, rather than a new premiss, it does not stand in need of further defence.)[65]

We start then from a plurality of discrete perceptual units or moments corresponding to discrete judgement-acts. We can for convenience in what follows symbolize these as P_1, P_2, P_3, etc. Whether these occur strictly seriatim or not is irrelevant: what matters is only that they are discrete from one another. (For the sake of simplicity we can construe the plurality as linear, as Kant himself does: even if this is an oversimplification, nothing relevant is lost by it—it is easy to see how the story would accommodate cotemporaneous and not only successive perceptual moments.) Importantly, this atomistic flux of perceptions is something that Hume, while not sharing Kant's need to distinguish perceptions from raw sensory contents, would accept. From here the setting of the problem is clear: We cannot accept that there is *just* this flux. It cannot be denied that all my perceptions are mine, that they are or can be united into a single consciousness. We must represent the subject as unified, persisting over time. And the question then is, *how* are those various perceptions so united? It would seem that we must have some unifying mechanism that is not itself just another occurrent perception, since the latter would simply take its place alongside all the others, as one more of the perceptions that needed to be united. Rather, we need as a unifying device something that is somehow external to, and ranges over, the whole series of perceptions that are to be unified.

Now we want the minimal construal of that mechanism, so as to be sure that we are identifying conditions for unity of consciousness that are not merely

---

[64] Indeed, it is for that reason that William James, as we will see in the next chapter, could avoid the impetus towards such psychological atomism by rejecting the Kantian model.

[65] A look back at the arguments for space and time being a priori representations may suggest that the perceptual atomism just outlined is weaker than the form of psychological atomism needed for those arguments to run. Here we have an atomism of perceptions which seems to leave open the possibility of pre-perceptual content registering holistically, and so providing a posteriori the material for the subsequent representation of space. A stronger form of atomism, such as the sensory atomism of the empiricists, would suffice to foreclose this possibility, but that is not a form of atomism Kant can properly adopt, as we have seen. This increases pressure on Kant's argument to the effect that in addition to knowing a priori that experience will be spatio-temporally structured, the representation of space and time is given a priori. Obviously, though, it does not decrease its effectiveness against the empiricists' *tabula rasa* thesis.

sufficient but also necessary. To this end it will help to approach gradually the point at which such unity can first emerge. Let us start, then, from consideration of a simple atomistic string of perceptions in which there is consciousness but no self-consciousness. There is, then, a certain awareness of content—on Kant's view this is conceptualized content—but no self-ascription of the perceptual content is possible. In such a set-up, as the perceptual moment P_1 passes, so does the perceptual awareness of it. Another perception, P_2, then comes into existence. It is a new perception, with no access to the previous one. In each perceptual moment consciousness is confined to that perception, and is separate from the awareness of the next. For a being of this sort, viewed sideways on, it will be true that all its perceptual experiences—again barring coexistent perceptions for simplicity—succeed one another in time. But there is no scope for an internal perception of this succession. So for a being like this there is a problem in saying that it forms a single unified consciousness.

Thus, if instead of a single being of this sort we imagine an exchange of minds between each experience, so that each is had by a separate being of the same restricted sort,[66] or indeed, if the whole world goes out of existence for a while between each such perception, it would make no difference in terms of the awareness had at any of the moments involved, or indeed in terms of the cumulative awareness of them all combined. There is no unity between these experiences that would be disrupted by such events. All we have is a sequence of conscious perceptions—which is not the same as those perceptions being unified in one consciousness.

Thus Kant says:

For the empirical consciousness, which accompanies different representations, is in itself diverse and without relation to the identity of the subject. That relation comes about, not simply through my accompanying each representation with consciousness, but only in so far as I *conjoin* one representation with another, and am conscious of the synthesis of them. Only in so far, therefore, as I can unite a manifold of given representations in *one consciousness*, is it possible for me to represent to myself the *identity of the consciousness in [i.e. throughout] these representations*.

In other words, only in so far as I can grasp the manifold of the representations in one consciousness, do I call them one and all *mine*. For otherwise I should have as many-coloured and diverse a self as I have representations of which I am conscious to myself.[67]

---

[66] Assuming, that is, that it would be possible to have a form of experience, a mind, that only ever had one representation, one conceptualized sensory content, such as is perhaps supposed to be had by Hume's thirsty oyster (*Treatise*, App.; 1978: 634). It is in fact doubtful that there could be a mind quite so simple, for reasons which are perhaps obvious, but which will in any event be brought out in Ch. 7.   [67] *Critique*, B133, B134.

To move beyond this fragmented series of perceptions, it is necessary that consciousness can somehow avoid the confinement to an occurrent perception, and range over different perceptual episodes. That would give the space to have not just a succession of conscious states, but also the possibility of being aware that those states are in succession. But there can be said to be unity of consciousness spanning discrete perceptions only if in having one of them, there is room to judge that the others were also had by 'me'. For it to be one and the same consciousness that ranges over the various perceptions it must be that, aside from consciousness of occurrent perceptions, there is consciousness that each of those perceptions is subject to one and the same consciousness. Unity of consciousness thus seems to involve consciousness of consciousness, in the form of *self-consciousness*. There must be the possibility of ascribing each of those perceptions to myself.

Now from here we could simply pick up the thread of the previous argument: to be able to self-ascribe in this way requires judgement that such-and-such a state is mine. And *that* would require the application of concepts, even if conceptualization had not come in at the earlier stage of converting sensory content into perceptions, into being something for me in the first place. Without a conceptual apparatus in operation with which to pick out and combine different perceptions, we would never be able to self-ascribe them all to one consciousness. And Kant would say that he has identified these a priori concepts. Hence we could conclude that the Categories must apply in experience, and must dictate the way in which the various perceptions are held together... But we are trying here to reconstruct the argument without wheeling on from the wings the Categories, as already identified in the Metaphysical Deduction, and without relying on the objectual synthesis and the correlated weaknesses of the conclusion. Instead, we can pursue the present reconstruction further, by noticing the kind of judgement that must be possible for the appropriate kind of self-consciousness to be possible.

If we could make only 'intra-perceptual' judgements, i.e. judgements internal to a given perceptual moment (what we might loosely think of as *present-tense* judgements[68]), we would in fact be back with the confinement of consciousness to occurrent perceptual episodes. We could now get beyond the mere consciousness characteristic of our previous hypothetical beings, but could still not move beyond the confinement to momentary experience. We would seem to have room for self-conscious self-ascription of the contents of the immediate experience, but that would just give us so many

---

[68] Loosely, both because strictly speaking a reconstruction of the Transcendental Deduction should deal with the issue in abstraction from its spatio-temporal situatedness, and also because the assumption of a linear progression of perceptions is, as we mentioned, a simplification: there might, without it, be room for distinct intra-perceptual judgements all of which occurred at the same time.

moments of self-conscious experience, and could not suffice to combine the plurality of such moments into a single consciousness. A series of self-consciously self-ascribed experiences is not the same as the self-conscious self-ascription of the series. The latter is clearly what the unity of consciousness requires.

So, to combine the plurality of momentary experiences into a single consciousness in the relevant sense, that is, to allow self-consciousness to range over different experiences, we need to have the resources to make judgements other than those internal to the perceptual unit. Most significantly, for the present argument, it seems clear that, in addition to such self-ascriptive judgements (at their simplest *present-tense* judgements), we must be able to make ascriptions of experiences across perceptual moments (most simply, *past-tense* self-ascriptions).[69] It must be possible for the self-conscious mind, in addition to self-ascribing a current perception, to look across and self-ascribe other perceptions that it has (or had). Only in that way can the string of isolated perceptions be 'owned', self-ascribed, by one and the same self-consciousness, and thereby be united in a single consciousness.

But for inter-perceptual judgements to be possible there must be an objective order to the world, such that we can make sense of there being some truth about one region of the world to which the subject now, from some other perceptual region, is reaching back. For a genuine inter-perceptual judgement to be made, there must be something at P_1 which is independent of how things seem from P_2 which the subject of P_2 might get wrong. If that were not the case, we would be dealing with no more than the intra-perceptual judgement at P_2. So what we have is the possibility of a self-conscious judgement at P_1, self-ascribing the experience,[70] and then, at some other perceptual moment, P_2, there is (another) self-conscious self-ascription of the experience had at P_1. And this immediately opens the possibility that the inter-perceptual judgement about the experience at P_1 might not agree with the occurrent judgement at P_1 about the experience had at P_1. That is, how things seem from P_n to be at P_m might not be true either to how things are at P_m or to how things seem at P_m. (Lapsing for a moment into allowing the simplification involved in a temporal construal of the point: how things seem to have been might not be true either to how they were in fact, or to how they then seemed.) A gap opens up between subjective appearances and the objective order of things. Importantly, this cannot be merely a matter of

---

[69] See Bennett (1966: 116–17, 119–25; and in relation to what follows, §51).

[70] Note the weakness of the claim. The self-ascription in P_2 of the now remote P_1 is possible only if P_1, when it was current, was something for the subject, which requires there to have been conceptualization and hence judgement; but that is not being construed to mean that at the time of being current there must have been actual self-conscious self-ascription of P_1—only that there was the possibility of it.

reaching across from one region of consciousness to judge about another: given the atomism in question, the various perceptual moments can be set in relation to one another in the first place only if they all take their place as events occurring in a single unified world that itself exists independently of them. The possibility of inter-perceptual judgements (most simply, past-tense judgements) has turned out to entail that the world in our experience of it must have an objective history, which includes the occurrence of some events, such that some descriptions of them might be false and others true, and with regard to which there is room for an appearance–reality distinction. But that means that some of the basic concepts that Kant identified in the Metaphysical Deduction of the Categories (e.g. unity, plurality, reality, negation, possibility, existence) must apply to the world in our experience.

Since the application of those basic concepts turns out to be a precondition of the unity of consciousness, it follows that in so far as we have the latter, we know a priori that those conceptualizations will apply to the world. If they did not, we would not even have a single, unitary consciousness—our experience would become utterly fragmented, with even less coherence to it than a dream. There would be simply as many minds as there are conscious perceptual atoms: each could be self-ascribed, but none could be ascribed to a larger whole. For that to be possible, we need inter-perceptual judgements, over and above intra-perceptual judgements. And that possibility entails that there be an objective order to the world. The objective world is thus a precondition of the unity of consciousness.

To this extent the conclusion of this reconstruction converges with that of the first. The present reconstruction, however, promises to avoid some of the problems pertaining to the other. Apart from bypassing any reliance on the Metaphysical Deduction of the Categories in identifying some of the basic concepts that must apply a priori to the world,[71] it also avoids the other problem identified earlier. In this second reconstruction we have not been looking in isolation at the necessary role played by one faculty, the understanding, in sustaining a unified experience, but rather have been considering in general how the subject embedded in the world must experience the world to be if he is to have unity of consciousness. Consequently, there is not the sense that the necessity of the Categories applying to *objects* might be restricted only to 'objects' in the attenuated sense of correlates of the workings of just one faculty, the accusatives of judgement. Here it is clear that what is in question is the way in which the organism as a whole, the experiencing subject, is of necessity confronted with an objective environment, the very one in which they live their life.

Now in Kant a translation of the abstract conclusions of the Transcendental Deduction into more concrete conclusions applying specifically to the

---

[71] A strategy that both Bennett (1966) and Strawson (1966) follow.

spatio-temporally embedded subject has to await the far side of the Schematism chapter, and the Principles in particular. To the extent that this is seen to result merely from Kant's architectonic structure (treating first sensibility and then understanding in isolation), there would seem to be little point in adhering to this separation in a reconstructive effort. Nevertheless, the second reconstruction offered here has tried to respect this Kantian distinction. The reason for this is that abstraction from the spatio-temporal construal of the argument captures the full generality of the argument. The transposition into spatio-temporal terms results in a simplification which, although essentially harmless, does conceal further complexity that remains to be explored. In particular it is important that the distinct perceptual moments might be distinguished not by temporal location, but by modality. For now it is important only to have flagged this further complexity; the exploration of it can be deferred.[72]

The transposition to spatio-temporal terms does afford an easier handle on the central insight. Thus drawing further on the discussion in the Principles, and in the First Analogy in particular,[73] we can bring out more intuitively the point involved in this second reconstruction of the dependence of the unity of consciousness on there being an objective world.[74] Kant adheres to the assumption that our awareness of particulars in experience is always successive.[75] It might be thought that there is a weak sense in which this claim is defensible: given the distinction flagged above between temporality and modality as that which keeps perceptual atoms apart, we can see that perceptual atomism does not entail that all perceptions occur successively (or are successively apprehended), but it might be allowed that recognition of them as mine will essentially be successive. That is, we can say that perceptual atomism does not entail that all perceptions are successive,[76] but might entail that any

---

[72] See Ch. 7 below.

[73] *Critique*, A182–9/B224–32; cf. also the Refutation of Idealism, B274–9.

[74] A more detailed consideration of the argument of the First Analogy, to the effect that the very possibility of experience presupposes that there be some permanent object (substance) in experience, will not be undertaken here. For further discussion, see Ch. 7.

[75] This claim recurs in all three Analogies (as well as elsewhere in the *Critique*). The assumption does not in fact receive any explicit support, and seems simply to be taken for granted. In Kemp Smith's view it is in fact false: 'an assumption which Kant also employs elsewhere in the *Critique*, but which he nowhere attempts to establish by argument; namely, that it is impossible to apprehend a manifold save in succession. This assumption is, of course, entirely false (at least as applied to our empirical consciousness) . . .' (Kemp Smith 1962: 348; see also 358).

[76] A separate question, of course, is whether there is any entailment the other way, whether experience being successive entails it being atomistically apprehended. It might seem not: as indeed the discussion of William James below will bear out, there is room for combining a commitment to a flow of sequential experiences without accepting atomism. Arguably, however, construed strictly—as the claim that our apprehension of the manifold is *always* only successive—it does entail psychological atomism. We can leave development of this aside for now, but, as will be suggested immediately below (and see also Ch. 7, Sect. 4), such strictly construed succession would be impossible to unify into an experience of succession anyway.

self-ascription of them by a single consciousness will be. In any event for the sake of argument let us accept that all experience is successive. (Even if this is not true, even on some such weakened construal of it, it can be taken as a heuristic simplification that for accuracy would have to be transposed back to the fully general formulation, in terms that were not specifically temporal.)

The argument can then proceed as follows: The mere fact that our awareness of particulars is successive in this way gives us no grip on whether the items perceived are themselves successive existences. To make the successive nature of experience vivid one might imagine perceiving the world in effect through a blinking shutter. Confining ourselves for the moment to a single-modality shutter, we might place the blinking apparatus beyond the eyelids. Imagine, then, a strobe-light flashing in a bar. It flashes three times, say, so that I have the experience of seeing a bartender at t_1, at t_2, and at t_3. The perceptions are successive. But that tells me nothing regarding whether the perceptual content (as of a bartender) is of one and the same abiding bartender, or of a different one hired with every flash of the strobe. To get an answer to that question, no amount of attention to the content of those successive experiences would help. The perceptual content available is indifferent between the two options on offer. This is basically Hume's sceptical problem about establishing the independent existence of the external world.[77] The Kantian insight is that while the content of the serial experiences cannot strictly speaking tell me anything about whether there is an independent objective world that abides across those experiences, the very fact of one subject having successive experiences (regardless of their content) does suffice to establish, by way of presupposition, that there is such a world. This is what Hume missed, and what constitutes a refutation of problematic idealism or scepticism about the external world.[78]

The underlying insight can be brought out by imagining a situation in which indeed *nothing* remains as an abiding existent across the two perceptions. In that situation no room is left for experiences to be temporally ordered in experience, since no room is left in experience for relations of succession. Imagine that in that situation there is a self-conscious experience, say of a pain, or of seeing a bartender. Then, imagine further, there is another equally self-conscious experience: pain, or bartender. Since by hypothesis everything changes between the two, I could not experience this transition from the one to the other, or be in a position to judge that there had been two experiences: all monitoring devices have not merely been reset to zero, but have gone out of existence in the interim. The two experiences are thus strictly incommensurable. One or the other of them can be nothing for me. There could thus

---

[77] See *Treatise*, I. iv. 2 (1978: 187 ff.) in particular. (See Ch. 1 n. 126 above for further references.)   [78] See *Critique*, B274–5.

be no experience of succession if there was only bare succession. The experience of bare succession is not possible. For the experience of succession to be possible, there must be something that survives the demise of one episode, and which enables the advent of the second episode to be historically placed in relation to the first as indeed being second in the sequence. Now the question is, what is it that must survive?

Here we can turn back to the fact that the strobe-light actually constitutes a shutter to only one sensory channel, leaving the others intact. It might at first be thought that it is because it did not block out all experiential input in the interim between one flash of the strobe and the next that we remained able to plot the different visual experiences as successive to one another. A super-strobe, it might be thought, that cut out all experiential input would not just model, but would in fact effect, just the fragmentation of consciousness that we are considering. And this suggests that all that need survive from one experiential episode to the next, in order to preserve the unity of consciousness, is some intervening experiential input, for example, as in the case of the strobe, tactile and acoustic, primarily. In fact this is not the case, given the assumptions of succession and perceptual atomism that are at work. Interposing between the two visual experiences an interim tactile experience, or indeed an interim series of experiences, simply multiplies the problem. It would not even be right to say that it repeats the problem at more frequent intervals—at least not from the perspective of the experiencing mind. The content of each serial experience is self-contained, and so when it occurs would seem to be utterly insensitive to the occurrence of any preceding experience. For each of these, the question is how it is to be temporally placed in relation to the preceding experience. Merely increasing the population density of experiences (the description being from a sideways-on perspective) will not give rise to any experience of unity across experiences. So what survives between the demise of one experience and the advent of another, and serves to unite them, cannot be a further experience. Kant is perfectly clear about this (in a sentence that is as close as we get to a third edition of the *Critique*): 'But this permanent cannot be an intuition in me. For all grounds of determination of my existence which are to be met with in me are representations; and as representations themselves require a permanent distinct from them, in relation to which their change, and so my existence in the time wherein they change, may be determined.'[79] But appeal cannot be made simply to the abstractly conceived, bare temporal structure, since that is not in itself an object of experience. The appeal can only be to something that abides in the spatio-temporal structure, and exists across experiences, something that has a continuous history, in relation to which experiences can be ordered by the mind

---

[79] *Critique*, amendment to B275: see Bxl n. *a*.

as successive, some pertaining to earlier stages, some to later stages, of one and the same abiding world. That is in fact what we hold on to between the two flashes of the real-life strobe, and which affords us the possibility of placing both visual experiences, and all the intervening tactile and auditory experiences, in relation to one another. (In fact, this is why even without any of the intervening *other* sensory experiences, the mere absence of visual experiences between the two flashes would suffice—just in so far as we are in a position to describe that interim as *the world* having gone dark.) The series of experiences are thus united externally, by appeal to a constant independent backdrop, given the impossibility of any helpful appeal to anything internal to the series. And this is just to say that the unity of consciousness over time presupposes the unity of an objective world in our experience. We cannot therefore help ourselves to the former and still coherently doubt the latter; and any fragmentation of the latter is *ipso facto* a fragmentation of the former.[80]

We have so far seen two reconstructions conforming to the see-saw strategy designed to answer at the same time both Hume's question about the unity of consciousness and that about the existence of the external world. In fact, it is not only that there being a unified consciousness presupposes experience of an objective world; it works the other way round as well. There being experience of an objective world presupposes the unity of consciousness. As it is relatively easy to see why this is the case, and as it is also not relevant to the overall concern with subject-driven scepticism, we can here leave aside this strand of the argument.

4. TRANSCENDENTAL IDEALISM

Kant's strategy with the sceptic is to start from the premiss that even the most sceptical empiricist would have to accept: namely, that each of us has a unified consciousness over time. Hume accepted this, but on his model of the mind could not properly account for it. Kant shows how this is possible. It turns out, on the explanation given, that there is a relation of mutual presupposition between unity of consciousness and experience of a unified objective world, such that one cannot coherently assume knowledge of the subjective domain

---

[80] It is this last reflection that leads Kant on to the conclusion that there can be only one substance (in the transcendental rather than the transcendent sense) underlying all appearances, something itself necessarily unchanging, and in relation to which all change is plotted. The coherence of this proof of the permanence of substance need not, however, concern us here (see Ch. 7, Sect. 5, below). Similarly, we need not go into the next step, in the Second Analogy, with which Kant attempts to show that the empirical world must abide by causal laws. I have been concerned only to establish the more modest conclusion, namely the necessity of an external world for the unity of consciousness.

and still genuinely raise questions about our knowledge of the objective domain, as philosophers from Descartes to Hume thought possible. By way of refutation of the Cartesian epistemic strategy the Kantian shows that the very capacity for a unified mental stream of contents already settles the question of there being an objective world set apart from the subject in experience. By the time one has helped oneself to the former, it is too late genuinely to doubt the latter.

However, having noted this interdependence between the unity of consciousness and the unity of an objective world in experience, we are in a position to appreciate not only how this promises to solve the sceptical problems concerning the external world, but also how at the same time it has its price. This emerges particularly clearly on the first reconstruction of the Kantian argument, which does not attempt to take its distance from Kant's model of the mind. What Kant salvages is knowledge of empirical reality: the objective world as it is presented to us in our experience of it. But that empirical reality is in fact only the phenomenal world, the world as it (necessarily) appears to us. It is the way the world is delivered to us, subject to the forms of space and time, and the synthesizing operations in accordance with the Categories. That is as far as our knowledge can reach. It is not, and we cannot have, knowledge of the way the world is in itself.

This combination of positions—that we can know the empirical world which is not ultimately independent of human structuration, and cannot know the world as it is in itself—is what Kant calls *empirical realism* combined with *transcendental idealism*. The transcendental idealism combines a realist ontological claim—there is a way that the world is in itself—with an idealist epistemological claim—we cannot have knowledge of that world. The empirical realism conversely, and surprisingly, delivers the combination of a realist epistemic claim—there is a world that we can know—with an idealist ontological claim—that the world that we can know, although independent of the individual's empirical consciousness of it, is not ultimately real. Empirical realism is confined, then, to what is in fact mere appearance—transcendental appearance—relative to the world as it is in itself.[81]

That all of empirical reality is ultimately transcendental appearance casts an interesting light on Kant's answer to the sceptic. We can bring this out graphically by likening the sceptic to a sentry standing at the border between appearance and reality, asking all comers with what licence they think they can cross

---

[81] Transcendental appearance is distinguished from empirical appearance. Within the empirical world there are mere empirical appearances—for example, the colours of the rainbow—which are contrasted with the way empirical things really are: in this example, light refracting through droplets of water serving as tiny prisms. But the empirically real (the droplet of rain) is itself merely a *transcendental* appearance relative to the way the world is in itself. See A45–6/B62–3.

from the one to the other. With this picture in mind we can say that Kant's strategy is not to silence that sentry, or to answer him: instead Kant relocates both the border and the sentry.

The sceptic starts by asking how I can know that the world really is as I experience it to be. That is, it is a question of how a person can cross from their individual mental contents, subjective appearances, about which they cannot be wrong, to certainty about the world beyond their thoughts. This takes the appearance–reality distinction to be an empirical distinction: a distinction between how things seem subjectively to me and how they really are. The Kantian strategy alters this. The way the mind must work, to satisfy the presuppositions of there being unity of consciousness, means that that boundary between subjective appearance and reality is easily traversed: individual mental contents are linked to there being experience of an independent public world—but this simply expands the domain of appearance, so that it now includes not only the individual's subjective mental states, but also the transcendentally constituted empirical world in which they are located. All of that now falls within the domain of appearance (as transcendental appearance). And we cannot know anything beyond that domain.

The sceptic, who said all along that we could not know anything beyond appearances, that we could not know the world as it was, independently of the way it appeared to us, thus turns out to have been right. Kant has only transferred that sceptic (or, less metaphorically, has transferred the reference of his terms): from the *empirical* appearance–reality border to the *transcendental* one. But that makes all the difference. As long as the sceptic is talking of the impossibility of getting to know the world beyond empirical appearances, he is in fact raising the untenable prospect of the confinement of knowledge to our individual thoughts, our solipsistic mental contents, precluding knowledge even of such mundane items as tables and chairs. The Kantian strategy is to show how in fact, properly understood, the sceptic is pushed back to talking of the impossibility of getting to know anything beyond *transcendental* appearances. That is, the sceptic is allowed to carry on insisting that we cannot get beyond appearances, but by pushing back the boundary, Kant has expanded the domain of appearances. It now includes the entire empirical world. Consequently, whereas before the confinement to appearances (= subjective states of mind) was untenable, now the confinement to appearances is perfectly acceptable. In fact, it becomes a source of security.

This clarifies the way in which Kant's strategy with the sceptic ingeniously involves granting the sceptic's central claim and simply redrawing boundaries so as to render the claim valid but innocuous. In allowing that the sceptic is right, but about transcendental appearances rather than empirical appearances, Kant can consider that he has put the sceptic in his proper place. And so located, rather than posing a desperate problem that needs to be solved, the sceptic can now serve as a valuable sentry, warning us not to attempt to extend our knowledge beyond its proper limits.

But, for all this, it remains the case that we do not ever know the world *as it is in itself*, and live our lives confined to knowledge of empirical reality, which is ultimately a domain of transcendental appearance: the way the world appears to us, modified by our faculties. Notoriously, Kant does not see this shortfall of our epistemic reach as a problem, but as having restricted knowledge to make room for faith. His separation of domains enables him both to allow for the universality of causal laws, and at the same time to accommodate elements that are prima facie at odds with the deterministic world of science. At the level of empirical reality, of which we can have knowledge, the deterministic laws of science hold without exception, but they are limited to that phenomenal world. The world as it is in itself, not being governed by those deterministic laws, leaves room for God, free will, and the like: but we have no knowledge of them; they must remain for ever, and appropriately, objects of faith. I have already commented on the way in which this critical demarcation of a domain within which knowledge is unrestricted is expressive of the Enlightenment outlook.

However, regardless of the fact that for these reasons Kant regards this limitation of knowledge as a positive aspect of his system, it cannot be denied that his answer to the sceptic does seem to carry a price. Perhaps it is right that we have no need to secure knowledge of the way the world is in itself, and that we can live our lives comfortably in the confinement of knowledge to transcendental appearances. But the fact remains that (*a*) this is less than philosophers traditionally wanted as the answer to their epistemic quests; and (*b*) we have been given a fairly complex set of ideas concerning transcendental appearances (empirical reality) and transcendental reality. At the very least these are consequences of Kant's view that make it clear that alongside the positive anti-sceptical consequences of his account of the mind, all sorts of new and difficult questions have been ushered in by it.

Now some of these problems can seemingly be avoided by adhering only to the second reconstruction of the argument given above, which, basically following Strawson and Bennett, attempts to yield the anti-sceptical result without either Kant's transcendental idealism or his transcendental psychology. In fact, his transcendental idealism is a consequence of the transcendental psychology, and it can be argued that, properly shorn of the latter, the anti-sceptical conclusion is significantly weakened.[82] This latter perhaps needs explaining.

Kant, while not distinguishing clearly between the two reconstructions presented above, would in fact endorse them both. We might think of the relation between the two as being such that the first reconstruction affords us

---

[82] But see below, Ch. 8.

insight into—or at least a story about—the mechanism whereby the conclusions of the second are sustained. That is, the second shows only that there must be an objective world that is independent of our experiences, and the first shows how we are equipped to produce that world. Those who distinguish the two strands in this way might well be inclined to say that Kant would have been better off endorsing only the second reconstruction, thereby divesting himself of a lot of speculative philosophical psychology, and also avoiding some of the more disturbing ramifications, in particular the transcendental idealism, that are seemingly consequent upon those workings.[83] In particular, explicitly shorn of transcendental idealism, the argument might be put simply in the form of a *modus ponens* argument: The unity of consciousness requires that we have experience of an ontologically independent objective world. So, since we do have unity of consciousness, there must be such a world. Happily, for us, the world without which we could have no experience does exist. And so Humean scepticism is answered with a robust realism, rather than with some attenuated form of realism nested within a transcendental idealist framework that is thought to be, at best, far-fetched. That we might be the source of there being such a world, rather than it simply being real, is thought to be an unnecessary complication introduced by an insufficiently motivated account of the transcendental workings of the mind.

It is, however, not that clear that avoiding Kant's doctrine of transcendental idealism in this way results in an adequate response to the Humean.[84] It would seem that we are then left with a commitment to unqualified realism—what Kant calls transcendental realism—about the world of empirical objects around us. As Kant points out,[85] the danger with this is that it threatens to collapse into empirical idealism; i.e. into the inability to know anything other than our own mental states and internal representations. (The line between appearance and reality is now back where it was, too close to home.) The hope would be that the argument I have just outlined, along the lines of the second reconstruction, is precisely what enables us to bridge that chasm from mere representations to the way of a thoroughly realist world of tables and chairs. But for this to work satisfactorily, it would be necessary to do more than say that the possibility of our constructing the appearance of the world by virtue of transcendental workings of the mind is an unnecessary complication. It would have to be shown also that, with *or without* transcendental workings of the mind, there are no constructions of the mind that are capable of sustaining the experience as of an independent world, thereby getting in the way of the conclusion of the simple *modus ponens* argument.

---

[83] Again, see Strawson (1966) and Bennett (1966). [84] See e.g. Sacks (1989: 25–32).
[85] Fourth Paralogism, in particular A369–72.

And it is not clear how that could be shown. There are, after all, hallucinations, and within them there is no trouble about my self-consciously self-ascribing thoughts over time, and while that perhaps indeed requires the presentation of a domain that is independent of my representations, the brain, when hallucinating, is clearly capable of producing the requisite experience as of an independent object domain (albeit pretty much in the confinement of one sensory modality). And given that the mind has it within its resources so to construe an independent object domain, and without any appeal to transcendental workings of the mind, what is to assure us that the independent world is not generally construed by us in such a way, sufficient perhaps to sustain unity of consciousness, but in a way that—like hallucinations—is not assured of capturing the way of the actual empirical world of tables and chairs? Even if it is thought that it is in fact impossible to be completely immersed in a hallucinatory situation, there is nothing obvious to preclude there indeed being an external world with which we are in contact, sufficient to sustain unity of consciousness, but which we might be construing in a systematically distorting way.[86] Adducing further constraints, such as that our experience could not be as it is unless the external world abided by causal laws,[87] might seem to limit the scope left for such distortion. But, on the present realist reconstruction, the same problem arises again: that would help only if we could render secure that inference to the causal structure of reality, and that requires excluding the possibility that the causal structure is a mere representational imposition that has nothing to do with the way the empirical world is in itself.

What the Kantian sees is that there is another option, that since we cannot exclude the possibility of a representational imposition, we might do better if we can simply consolidate it. Given the impossibility of excluding the intrusion of such constructions, the Kantian converts them from worrying ineliminable possibilities to transcendental necessities about the workings of the mind. This is supposed to give a resilience to the appearances they sustain, such that they can themselves count as our empirical reality; we have the assurance that we will carry on experiencing the world in this way. It would seem, then, that the second reconstruction on its own might not in fact secure us the external world, and that even if it does, it cannot secure assurances of constancy in the way it holds together. That is what the appeal to the transcendental workings of the mind promised to do, and what might make it

---

[86] In recent years related questions have been discussed in terms of whether it is possible to be a brain in a vat (Putnam 1981). The scenario just outlined in the text is significantly more concessionary, however, in that it allows that the contact with the external world is not merely physical, but is epistemically rich enough to sustain unity of consciousness. (For discussion of the brain in a vat predicament, see A. W. Moore 1997; Forrai 1996; Forbes 1995; Wright 1994; Sacks 1989; Brueckner 1986.)

[87] As Kant does in the Second Analogy, A189–211/B232–56.

difficult to do without them. Of course, at best all this suffices only to bring out the inadequacy of subscribing to the second reconstruction on its own. It does not in any way count against an argument to the effect that nevertheless we have to make do with that, because the appeal to transcendental workings of the mind and transcendental idealism is simply incoherent or too untenable to take us any further than that.

However, for present purposes the debate over the adequacy of the second interpretation taken on its own, and the Strawsonian rejection of transcendental idealism, does not matter. There is a prior worry. Kant's entire anti-sceptical move rests on the need for the changing contents of experience to be combined into a unified consciousness. Now this need not be construed as proceeding from a form of psychological atomism. Indeed, the first reconstruction did not so construe it. But that argument seemed for various reasons to be unsatisfactory. The second and more promising reconstruction, however, does trade on a form of psychological atomism, as we have seen, and uses it as the central premiss from which to launch the argument. And this constitutes a possible weakness of the argument-strategy. While it is true that I cannot deny that I have a unified consciousness, it is not true that it cannot be denied that that unity is the result of an atomistic construction. The sceptic is thus offered a way of rejecting the entire argument at the first step. This is what I turn to next, in discussion of William James. In fact James takes issue not only with the atomism germane to the second reconstruction, but also with the distinction between faculties—such that contents of sensibility are wholly inarticulate until acts of judgement are applied to them from within the distinct faculty of the understanding—which is germane to both reconstructions. It should be clear that the two points of contention are related: in so far as one rejects Kant's conception of the involvement of two faculties in the generation of perception, the justification for his perceptual atomism identified above will be removed. Any remaining commitment to a form of psychological atomism may then be as much of an unmotivated—and easily displaced—assumption as it at first seemed to be.

3

James and Bergson: The Neglected Alternative

I TURN now to consider the Jamesian model of the mind. Interestingly, and at some cost, as the present reflections should bring out, James is not normally included in the story of modern epistemology that takes in Descartes, Locke, Hume, and Kant. This omission is all the more surprising given that James himself saw his work on the mind as a response to that story, taking up a position that rejected a common presupposition of both the empiricists and Kantians. That he clearly saw his philosophical psychology in this orientation is not to say that he saw clearly the significance it had for that orientation, as we will see. Again, I shall begin with an outline of James's conception of the mind, and the ways in which it differs from other views, in particular Hume's and Kant's; I shall then consider the wider philosophical ramifications of this view of the mind, and along with that the cost of standardly neglecting to consider the Jamesian response to Kant.

1. THE MIND-DUST THEORY

James sets himself in opposition to psychological atomism. In this he is self-consciously taking his distance from a presupposition seen as common to empiricism and to Kantianism. As innate ideas were to Locke, so atomism is to James; it is regarded as a presumed default position that has to be firmly ousted. He consequently launches an assault on atomism, or the 'mind-dust' view as he sometimes refers to it, before setting out his own preferred alternative. By 'psychological atomism' James means the theory according to which our mental world is constituted at root out of simple mental atoms, such as simple sensations, distinct from one another, such that each is a self-contained unit of whatever consciousness exists in it. All other more complex mental states are formed out of these discrete psychological atoms by way of compounding them—somehow—into larger molecular structures. Talk of atoms is not taken to imply extensionless points, and ruled unintelligible on those grounds: rather, such atoms are to be allowed whatever duration the simple experience requires, but not more than will accommodate a single indivisible experience. We might think of such atoms as the smallest packets of experience, out of which any larger unit of experience must be composed. (Such atomism accommodates the thought, endorsed both by common sense and by empiricists, that in the stock of psychological atoms there can be those that recur on different occasions, such as the simple experience of redness, of a certain sound, or of a pain.) James's rejection of such atomism is uncompromising. He considers atomism to be explanatorily deficient (strictly speaking unintelligible), introspectively inadequate, and theoretically pernicious. The full details of his case need not concern us here. For present purposes the interest is not in whether atomism is false and James's holism true, but only in the availability and viability of a significant alternative to atomism.

His initial and direct assault in the *Principles of Psychology* is set out in chapter VI, 'The Mind-Stuff Theory'.[1] He there argues that this atomism, for all its apparent explanatory appeal and theoretical simplicity, is in fact 'quite unintelligible'; an easily made, but obscure and theoretically confused assumption.[2] Some of the points made are worth rehearsing briefly. A central thought is that discrete units, whether material or mental, however intimately related they may be, cannot combine or integrate with one another to form a larger unity, just in so far as they individually remain discrete components set apart from one another.[3] At best the relations between them might constitute a larger structure that has unity for someone seeing it from an external perspective. When the entities involved are specifically mental, this is even more obvious:[4] a hundred discrete mental states, all atomistically conceived, as so many windowless monads, each contains an awareness of its own content, but none has access to that of any other. That is the atomist conception. Now imagine that they are so related to one another that a further experience somehow emerges— a consciousness of the hundred belonging together. However this emerged, it should be clear that it is not identical with, or a simple consequence of, there being a string of one hundred proximal but mutually impervious experiences. This is supposed to show that the series of atomistic experiences from which psychological atomism would have us start cannot possibly explain, or by itself result in, the unity of consciousness that holds across all those experiences.

James offers two examples that bring out in a particularly vivid way how the encapsulation of consciousness inherent in psychological atomism renders problematic the unity of consciousness across experiences. The first[5] involves taking a sentence of n words, writing each word on a separate piece of paper, then taking the n pieces of paper and distributing them in order and one apiece

---

[1] All page references to James are to the *Principles* (James 1981), unless stated otherwise.
[2] p. 148.   [3] pp. 160–4.   [4] p. 162.   [5] pp. 162–3.

among *n* people. Each person is asked to think hard about his or her word. It is clear that nowhere in this set-up is there any consciousness of the whole sentence, simply because all we have is a string of discrete conscious states, and this alone would not suffice to ensure the unity of consciousness across all of them, which is what we would need in order to have a consciousness of the whole sentence. And clearly it would not matter whether the *n* people were sitting around a room, or packed together in one cell, or indeed were so many homunculi or discrete conscious states within one brain. What matters is the encapsulation of consciousness in each, which is inherent to psychological atomism; as long as they remain psychological atoms, merely stringing them together, however tightly the atoms be compounded, will not suffice to render consciousness of the string of them. The second example, which brings this out even more clearly, is quoted from Brentano:

> Someone might say that although it is true that neither a blind man nor a deaf man by himself can compare sounds with colors, yet since one hears and the other sees they might do so both together.... But whether they are apart or close together makes no difference; not even if they permanently keep house together; no, not even if they were Siamese twins, or more than Siamese twins, and were inseparably grown together, would it make the assumption any more possible. Only when sound and color are represented in the same reality is it thinkable that they should be compared.[6]

James concludes from this that the atomist view taken on its own cannot intelligibly account for the unity of consciousness across experience, that we cannot '*explain the constitution* of higher mental states by viewing them as *identical with lower ones* summed together'.[7] Now this seems right, but it does not of itself show that there is no room for psychological atomism. It might be that there are good grounds for assuming atomism, and that some further work must then be done in order to account for the unity of consciousness. In particular, we might think of the Kantian grounds for a commitment to (what I referred to as) perceptual atomism. I will return to this question below. For now, the point is only to note that atomism itself has not so far been disproved. And James does not disprove it elsewhere in this chapter.

He does show that historically some of the motivation for adopting it was questionable, and that some of the phenomena in question could be explained without assuming atomism. Thus he argues that the fact that a physical phenomenon, such as a sound, is made up of many discrete events does not mean that the consciousness of the sound must itself be made up of mental atoms,

---

[6] pp. 162–3 n. 16. Quoted from Brentano's *Psychologie vom empirischen Standpunkte* (trans. James); Eng. trans. Brentano (1973: 159).

[7] p. 164 n. 17. The same note concludes: 'What Mr. Ward and I are troubled about is merely the silliness of the mind-stuffists and associationists continuing to say that the "series of states" *is* the "awareness of itself"; that if the states be posited severally, their collective consciousness is *eo ipso* given; and that we need no further explanation, or "evidence of fact".'

corresponding to those discrete events.[8] There is surely a sensitivity to all those teeming micro-events, without which consciousness of the sound would not arise. But that sensitivity might be registered 'in the nerve-world' rather than 'in the mind-world', as James puts it.[9] That is, the transformation of the micro-processes into a larger unity might be done at the level of mere brain tracts, below the threshold of consciousness, rather than in the mind, above the threshold of consciousness, as the atomists would have it. In this argument James seems to equate the 'mind-world' with that which is above the level of consciousness. This clearly makes his task easier, since it ignores the possibility of a form of atomism which holds that the unification might happen within the mind, i.e. to mental states, albeit not ones that are conscious. Atomism of this form might seem less obviously a non-starter, and could have richer explanatory power in comparison to James's alternative in which integration does not occur in the 'mind-world' at all.[10]

Later in the chapter[11] he does argue against a form of psychological atomism which is run at the level of the unconscious: our mental life is at ground level atomistic, although at a level that precedes the threshold of consciousness—by the time consciousness has arisen, these mental atoms have been combined. But James's arguments here are entirely constructed as replies to ten particular arguments for there being unconscious states of mind. Again, there is nothing to show that the position itself, as opposed to those specific proofs of it, is faulty. This is particularly relevant, given that his earlier arguments did not in fact tell clearly against this form of atomism.[12]

There are then weaknesses with James's argument against the explanatory appeal of atomism, and in any event pointing out explanatory inadequacies and the failure of some alleged proofs cannot establish conclusively that atomism is false. But for our purposes these shortcomings of argument and argument strategy do not matter. Since the concern here is not to reject atomism, but merely to establish that it is theoretically optional, it is enough if James has managed to loosen its grip. He further weakens that grip in the course of arguing that atomism is also introspectively inadequate.

---

[8] pp. 148–60.   [9] p. 157.

[10] In fact, in stating the benefits of his preferred view, James seems to think that it has been contrasted with this more reasonable form of atomism. Thus, 'On this supposition there *are* no unperceived units of mind-stuff preceding and composing the full consciousness' (p. 159). But in bringing out the inadequacy of the atomist explanation in the first place (pp. 157–8) he confines himself to the other more easily ridiculed form of it.   [11] pp. 165–77.

[12] It is incidentally interesting, from a strategic point of view, to note that James in rejecting atomism needs to preclude resort to the unconscious just as atomists like Locke and Hume needed to preclude it in their rejection of innate ideas and holism. (See above, Ch. 1, Sect. 2.1.) James writes in this connection that the distinction 'between the unconscious and the conscious being of the mental state... is the sovereign means for believing what one likes in psychology, and of turning what might become a science into a tumbling ground for whimsies' (p. 166).

2. JAMES'S HOLIST ALTERNATIVE

James is perhaps at his best when making the case for his model of the mind in terms of its greater introspective adequacy over the atomistic one. He argues that certain introspectible features of our mental life are easily overlooked, with the result that atomism gains currency. With due care and attention to phenomenological detail, the better fit of a non-atomistic conception of the mind would become obvious. The appeal of atomism is thus taken to trade on inattentiveness to the evidence, being a distorted description of our mental life as it is in fact presented introspectively. Part of the distortion results from certain basic errors that psychologists are prone to make,[13] in particular what James identifies as the Psychologist's Fallacy.

By the psychologist's fallacy[14] James means the mistake of confusing the psychologist's sideways-on perspective for that of the subject; confusing what the observer knows about the thought, the object it is about, and other related thoughts, for what is given just by *having* that thought. Elements readily get packed into the content of the experience, which are in fact not part of the experience, but part of what we know because of access to information related to but not contained within the experience in question.[15] A closely related mistake, to the point of being one particular instance of the psychologist's fallacy, is that of assuming 'that as the objects are, so the thoughts must be'.[16] In particular, as objects might come and go, might recur unchanged on different occasions, so it is considered that the thought of those objects too can come and go, can recur unchanged on different occasions. 'The thought of the object's recurrent identity is regarded as the identity of its recurrent thought' (ibid.). Although elsewhere essentially the same error is indeed included as a form of the psychologist's fallacy,[17] James initially (pp. 194–5) seems to introduce this sort of error as being distinct from that fallacy. It is at any rate clear

---

[13] See in particular 'The Sources of Error in Psychology' (pp. 193–6), in ch. VII, 'The Methods and Snares of Psychology'.   [14] See pp. 195–6, 268, 335, 911.

[15] 'We must be very careful therefore, in discussing a state of mind from the psychologist's point of view, to avoid foisting into its own ken matters that are only there for ours. We must avoid ... counting its outward, and so to speak physical, relations with other facts of the world, in among the objects of which we set it down as aware' (p. 196).   [16] p. 194.

[17] Thus on p. 268, presenting it as the psychologist's fallacy, he says that we 'have the inveterate habit, whenever we try introspectively to describe one of our thoughts, of dropping the thought as it is in itself and talking of something else. We describe the things that appear to the thought ... as if these and the original thought were the same.' It does not matter much how this sort of mistake is categorized, as long as it is recognized that James certainly means the psychologist's fallacy to be inclusive of more than just this, as is clear not only from his initial definition, but also from the use made of it elsewhere (e.g. p. 335).

why he thinks it important to set this form of error apart from others: although it does not entail, it readily leads to a pernicious atomism about the mental which, without that error, would not be sustained by any introspective grounds. James is very clear that in saying this he means 'to impeach the entire English psychology derived from Locke and Hume, and the entire German psychology derived from Herbart, so far as they both treat "ideas" as separate entities that come and go'.[18]

Let us then turn to see what view of the mind, avoiding these errors, is taken by James to be sanctioned on good introspective grounds. Starting from simple sensations, as if the simplest things are the first things from which to start psychological explanation, constitutes a theoretical step taken blindly at the outset by atomists, one which has no licence and which threatens to yield ineradicable problems. James withdraws from that theory-driven first move, and instead takes as his starting-point simply that thinking of some sort goes on, where 'thinking' is taken broadly (as in Descartes's *cogito*) to cover any sort of conscious experience whatsoever.[19] He considers that to be a theoretically neutral datum, from which explanation and analysis can proceed.[20] He then identifies five important characteristics of that process of thinking:[21]

1. Every thought tends to be part of a personal consciousness.
2. Within each personal consciousness thought is always changing.
3. Within each personal consciousness thought is sensibly continuous.
4. It always appears to deal with objects independent of itself.
5. It is interested in some parts of these objects to the exclusion of others, and . . . *chooses* from among them . . . all the while.

The discussion of these five features, which structures the rest of chapter ix ('The Stream of Thought'), covers the ground which concerns us here, taking us through an outline of James's alternative to atomism, and to the wider theoretical ramifications of this view.

That every thought is part of a personal consciousness is meant to highlight the fact that thoughts are not items such as exist in isolation in the world, items that might or might not be owned. On the atomist conception, there would be nothing to preclude this latter being the basic default situation. James is concerned to bring out that there is no basis for thinking that thoughts should be construed in such a way as to afford them that kind of isolation as the default, any departure from which requires explanation. In our experience thoughts cluster together in mutually exclusive larger wholes. No thoughts roam

---

[18] p. 195. [19] pp. 219–20.
[20] And, as he says, if (simple) 'sensations then prove to be amongst the elements of the thinking, we shall be no worse off as respects them than if we had taken them for granted at the start' (p. 219). [21] p. 220.

the world free of any such larger affiliation. In a crowded restaurant, say, there are many thoughts, but it would be a misguided theoretical move to consider starting our account of the mental by attending only to the totality of thoughts in a room. A salient fact is that all those thoughts divide neatly, with no remainder—at least as far as we can tell—between the number of people in the place. There are none that are left as stray orphan thoughts, wandering between the tables. Thoughts, or at least the only ones that are of concern to us, are owned. Moreover, while individual thoughts do not seem to be presented in insulation from other thoughts, at the level of the larger wholes to which those thoughts belong there is insulation, such that only I can have my thoughts, and only you can have yours (although, of course, we might communicate them to one another).[22]

How this characteristic of thought is to be accounted for remains to be explained; but that it is a characteristic of any thought in which we might be interested seems to be right. To that extent, the basic starting-point, 'the immediate datum in psychology',[23] is not merely that *thought exists*, or that *thinking goes on*, but rather that *I think*, or that *I have thoughts*. There is nothing about taking this as the starting-point that excludes atomism. It merely points out a constraint that atomist theory construction should not be allowed to ignore or undermine.[24] For our purposes here it is important to note that so far James's starting premiss, modified by this first characteristic of thought, essentially converges on Kant's starting premisses for the transcendental deduction and refutation of idealism: that there are thoughts, and that those thoughts are essentially indexed to thinkers. Given how basic these claims are (this, after all, is the strength of Kant's refutation of idealism), this is hardly surprising. It is worth mentioning, however, since I am going to go on to claim that it is James's departure from Kant's model of the mind, rather than any flaw in Kant's subsequent arguments based on that model, that undermines Kant's refutation of idealism. Evidently, we have not yet reached that point of departure.

The second characteristic of thought is that it is in constant change. The claim is not that experience is constantly changing such that no experience has any duration. It seems clear that there must be a minimal duration for the experience to register in consciousness, and James does not mean to dispute this.[25] The denial would anyway amount to a peculiar form of atomism,

---

[22] This points to the difference between James's psychological sense of *thought* and the sense of Frege's *Thoughts*, which are precisely not insulated within a personal consciousness, and in which sense two individuals can have the same thought (or Thought). [23] p. 221.

[24] Which is, of course, precisely what Hume came to appreciate in following through the consequences of his atomist account of the mind with regard to personal identity or the unity of consciousness. [25] p. 224.

a psychological pointillism, which would be precisely the sort of theoretical imposition James is eager to get away from. The claim that thought is in constant change could also mean only that there is a change in experienced content from one moment to the next, such as would be compatible with a repeating repertoire of experienced contents, of the sort that an atomist might think would be afforded by life on a merry-go-round: experiencing constantly changing contents *a, b, ..., f,* and then back round to *a* again ... But again that is in fact exactly what James wants to preclude. What he means is not just that thought is constantly changing so as to be different from what it was the moment before, but—more strongly—that what it was the moment before was unique, and can never recur again.[26] While the former is compatible with the constructivism and associationism of the empiricist 'theory of ideas', the latter is not. In effect this characteristic amounts to a swift rejection of the empiricist theory of ideas. Since we cannot have the same elementary experiences recurring, there is no room to appeal to principles of association to explain how the same simple ideas will come to be associated with one another, so that repetition of the one will call to mind the other; nor can we account for complex perceptions as recombinations of the same recurring simple ideas.

At first sight the assumption of recurring mental atoms, 'simple elements of consciousness that always remain the same' (p. 225), out of which all complex concrete states of mind can be composed, seems to be borne out by our experience. Sugar tasted gives rise to the same sensation of sweetness each time; hitting the same piano key with the same force seems to give rise to the same acoustic experience; the same blue sky looked at twice gives rise to the same visual experience, etc.[27] James, however, thinks that here we have a clear instance of introspective inadequacy. For all its easy appeal, in fact these descriptions fall foul of the psychologist's fallacy (on the broad conception of it outlined above).

What is got twice is the same OBJECT. We hear the same *note* over and over again; we see the same *quality* of green, or smell the same objective perfume, or experience the same *species* of pain. The realities, concrete and abstract, physical and ideal, whose permanent existence we believe in, seem to be constantly coming up again before our thought, and lead us, in our carelessness, to suppose that our 'ideas' of them are the same ideas. (p. 225)

In fact, once this error is avoided, and due introspective care is taken, we can see that there are reasons to doubt that we can ever have exactly the same experience twice. Changes in conditions external to us, as well as the 'colouring' offered by our internal states (moods, emotions, etc.), will mean that the

---

[26] '... the result on which I wish to lay stress is this, that *no state once gone can recur and be identical with what it was before*' (p. 224).   [27] p. 225.

same object will not be likely to be experienced in the same way on two different occasions.[28] Even if it did happen that the same object was experienced twice in identical external circumstances, there would always be grounds for doubting that it could be experienced twice in identical internal circumstances, and so for doubting that it could be experienced twice in the same way. Barring total amnesia, the second peal of the bell or sight of the blade of grass is experienced as different from the first precisely because it is second. The experience is coloured by the fact that it is a second experience, by the recollection of the first, however vague: it will have a familiarity to it that was lacking first time around. That familiarity will alter the experience. The experience of the first peal of thunder would not be identical to the experience of the second, even if the sound-waves are indistinguishable on the two occasions.

It might be contended in response that the basic experience is repeated, it is merely that familiarity gives rise to certain consequences, such as the experience of tedium, weariness, nostalgia, that were missing first time round—but that those experiences are additional to the basic experience that has been repeated. This would seem to salvage the recurring atoms of the empiricist theory of ideas. James's response to this, however, would surely be that it is again introspectively insensitive. The repetition of the same object alters not just the consequences of the immediate experience of that object, but the experience itself. The first taste of smoked mackerel, say, will not be the same as the taste that identically prepared fish will come to have for someone living entirely on a diet of smoked mackerel. It is not just that the same experience of taste comes to be regarded differently, with revulsion, say, but that the experience of the taste itself comes to be different.[29]

The idea is not only that every later experience of the same x stands to be modified by the awareness (however dim) of there having been other previous experiences of x. The experience of one and the same object stands to be modified by other experiences, or states of the experiencing organism. The sound of a bell announcing a break is not experienced as is the sound of the same bell announcing the end of the break. And again it would seem to be a blunt theoretical imposition that insisted that the experience of the sound was identical, phenomenologically invariant, and only the added different perceptions of its significance account for the difference in the two complex experiences. The experience of schoolchildren, at least if my own experience is anything to go by, is frequently as if two different bells are in use: one joyous and celebratory, the other a stern and piercing call of authority.

---

[28] p. 226.
[29] But do we not, nevertheless, judge that it is in all such cases the taste of mackerel? Yes, the response would be, but that does not require identity of some core experience, only resemblances across experiential states.

It would seem, then, that there is some support for the claim that we cannot have the same sensation, exactly the same, twice; there 'are facts which make us believe that our sensibility is altering all the time, so that the same object cannot easily give us the same sensation over again' (p. 226). This is all that James attempts to conclude from the introspective base. Strictly speaking, the conclusion is no stronger than that *'there is no proof that the same bodily sensation is ever got by us twice'* (p. 225). In fact the introspective evidence for the claim that thought is constantly changing is then supposed to be strengthened by the addition of 'another presumption, based on what must happen in the brain', establishing that it is not possible ever to descend twice into the same stream (p. 227). But the best that can be said for this further presumption is that the story told is not impossible; it is clearly speculative, and the argument weak.[30] Confining ourselves, then, to the yield of the introspective considerations, we rest with the weaker conclusion that there is at least room to doubt whether we can unproblematically help ourselves to the assumption of two experiences ever being identical.

James is clear about the significance of this assumption:

The proposition is more important theoretically than it at first seems. For it makes it already impossible for us to follow obediently in the footprints of either the Lockian or the Herbartian school, schools which have had almost unlimited influence in Germany and among ourselves. No doubt it is often convenient to formulate the mental facts in an atomistic sort of way, and to treat the higher states of consciousness as if they were all built out of unchanging simple ideas. It is convenient often to treat curves as if they were composed of small straight lines ... But in the one case as in the other we must never forget that we are talking symbolically, and that there is nothing in nature to answer to our words. *A permanently existing 'idea' or 'Vorstellung' which makes its appearance before the footlights of consciousness at periodic intervals, is as mythological an entity as the Jack of Spades.* (pp. 229–30)

So far, then, James's attention to introspective detail in the characterization of the workings of the mind suffices to put pressure on the viability of the

---

[30] The argument would, if successful, prove that 'no two "ideas" are ever exactly the same' (p. 229), and so would count as straightforward empirical evidence against the theory of ideas. Unfortunately, as the following typical passage makes clear, the argument is too tenuous to offer any such support:

Every sensation corresponds to some cerebral action. For an identical sensation to recur it would have to occur the second time in an unmodified brain. But as this, strictly speaking, is a physiological impossibility, so is an unmodified feeling an impossibility; for to every brain-modification, however small, must correspond a change of equal amount in the feeling which the brain subserves. (p. 227)

In fact what he has to say here about the brain (see pp. 228–9 and 229 n. 9) amounts only to a vivid biological analogue of his holism (along with a sketch of the brain's functioning that is suggestive of what came to be called connectionist or parallel distributed processing).

empiricist theory of ideas.[31] But it is worth noting that as yet the thesis of psychological atomism has not itself come under pressure. It might turn out that while experiences cannot be such as could recur, they are all registered atomistically. James is clear about this possibility. Thus he recognizes that the conclusion that thought is constantly changing 'would be true even if sensations came to us pure and single'.[32] And the discussion of this characteristic of thought ends with the implicit recognition that while Humean atomism, or at least the contention that thought is composed of independent and discrete parts, is an implication of the belief in recurring identical experiences, the argument against the latter is not *ipso facto* an argument against the former.

This possible combination of atomism with the impossibility of the same experiences recurring would clearly be enough to count against the empiricist theory of ideas, leaving traditional empiricists with atomist fragmentation, and no possible recourse to their only candidate mechanism—i.e. principles of association—for compounding units of experience into larger bundles. And as we have seen, this is James's primary target here.[33] But this envisaged outcome would not, for all that we have seen, be particularly troublesome to the Kantian's method of introducing unity into the plurality of experiences. As yet, then, we do not have any significant departure from, or repudiation of, the Kantian model of the mind.

The promised rejection of atomism comes in the course of setting out the third characteristic of thought, according to which within each personal consciousness thought is sensibly continuous. It is here too that the fundamental point of departure from the Kantian model is reached. James, in dealing with the third characteristic of thought, is addressing the question of how the stream of consciousness is unified. Kant too has a story to tell about how thought, or consciousness, is unified. In terms of this comparison the distinctive point of James's discussion resides in his claim that thought is *sensibly* continuous.

James clarifies in rough terms what is meant by saying that thought is continuous. By 'continuous' he means to identify 'that which is without breach, crack, or division'.[34] Such breaches clearly occur between different minds. The

---

[31] That James takes the conclusion to be much stronger than this by relying on his conception of the workings of the brain is clear from the following lines leading up to the passage just quoted in the main body of the text:

If so coarse a thing as a telephone-plate can be made to thrill for years and never reduplicate its inward condition, how much more must this be the case with the infinitely delicate brain?

I am sure that this concrete and total manner of regarding the mind's changes is the only true manner, difficult as it may be to carry it out in detail. If anything seems obscure about it, it will grow clearer as we advance. Meanwhile, if it be true, it is certainly also true that no two 'ideas' are ever exactly the same, which is the proposition we started out to prove. (p. 229)

[32] p. 227. [33] See p. 225. [34] p. 231.

question is, in what way can we conceive of them, as the atomist clearly does, as occurring within a single mind? James thinks that within a single mind we can conceive of such breaches only as gaps, interruptions, during which consciousness just goes on the blink, or alternatively as the result of changes in the content of the thought so radical that there is nothing to connect the earlier contents with those subsequent to the change.

Now the Kantian account of the possibility of both these kinds of discontinuity ultimately involves appeal to the representation of an abiding objective world. To accommodate a gap in consciousness there must be a representation of an objective world that persisted in existence throughout that gap, such that it is possible to make sense of there having been *a gap* in one and the same consciousness; a gap in a single process within the continuing history of an abiding world; a stretch of time during which the world did not contain any consciousness on my part. Without such an abiding world, rather than a gap in my consciousness, there would be just the world going out of existence and another (temporally unrelated one) coming into existence. That would obviously preclude any sense in which what happens after the gap is a continuation of my selfsame consciousness. Similarly, radical qualitative change is prevented from severing the unity of consciousness because in fact throughout such change there is some unity that is preserved. But, importantly for Kant, this is not the unity of sensible content. Throughout all change, there must be the representation of some abiding substance.[35] It is the representation of a permanent substance, abiding throughout all change, that ensures that, however radical the change in the content of sensations, in the stream of consciousness its unity will not be shattered, severed.

The Kantian preservation of the unity of consciousness, despite time-gaps in consciousness and changes in quality from one moment to the next, works by appeal to external unity; to features that are themselves external to the stream of *felt*, or *sensible* contents. James's view of the way in which the unity of thought is not disrupted by breaks in consciousness or by changes in quality from one moment to the next contrasts significantly with this. With regard to gaps in consciousness, if these gaps are unfelt, then no threat is posed to the unity of the stream of consciousness. But there are also gaps that are something for us, cases where we are aware that there has been a gap in consciousness, as when, for example, we wake from sleep and are aware that we have been unconscious. What, in these cases, makes it possible to unite the experiences before we fell asleep with those occurring after we wake up into one consciousness? How do we connect up post-sleep experiences with the right set of pre-sleep consciousness, rather than with someone else's? James, imagining Peter and Paul falling asleep in the same bed and then waking up together, reminds us

[35] See the First Analogy in particular.

that, however much Peter might know about Paul's last drowsy thoughts before he sank into sleep, this will be mere knowledge, and will not be suffused with the warmth and intimacy with which his recollection of his own last thoughts prior to sleep is suffused. And 'whatever past feelings appear with those qualities [of warmth and intimacy] must be admitted to receive the greeting of the present mental state, to be owned by it, and accepted as belonging together with it in a common self'.[36] The suffusion with warmth and intimacy establishes a unity, or 'community', among the person's mental states that cannot be severed by gaps in consciousness.

Now at this stage talk of 'warmth and intimacy' remains pretty unclear. Are these *criteria* by which we can tell which states belong together in cases of breaks in the flow, or are they themselves the binding force? Nothing James says here commits him to their being anything more than criteria, sure signs that the states thus suffused belong together. And, of course, if this suffusion with warmth and intimacy of different parts of the stream are mere criteria for identity, then this is perfectly compatible with a Kantian account of how this unity of consciousness is secured. It might be that the unity of consciousness makes essential appeal to an external object domain, but that the unity thus secured manifests a unique warmth and intimacy between its parts. The presence of this warmth and intimacy is then a sure identifying mark of states that are within one unified consciousness, without it itself being the unifying mechanism. But although, for all that is said here, the feelings of warmth and intimacy might be no more than criteria, James makes it clear from what he goes on to say that for him the unifying of consciousness is not brought about by anything external to the contents of the stream of thought.[37]

The case of abrupt qualitative changes brings this out quite clearly (pp. 233 ff.). James urges that in fact there is never absolute qualitative discontinuity in the content of experience. Again, there is a call for introspective rigour here. We all too readily tend to confuse the discontinuity that might obtain in the objects of experience—say, from a state of silence to a sudden explosion of noise, or from one bright colour-field to an equally bright but differently coloured one—for discontinuity in our experience of the objects. We do not introspect carefully enough to notice that in fact the discontinuity in the objects of experience is not paralleled by a matching discontinuity in our experience of them:

The confusion is between the thoughts themselves, taken as subjective facts, and the things of which they are aware.... The things are discrete and discontinuous; they do pass before us in a train or chain, making often explosive appearances and rending each other in twain. But their comings and goings and contrasts no more break the

---

[36] pp. 232–3.
[37] It is also clear from the later discussion of warmth and intimacy that he does not see them as playing a mere criterial role (see pp. 316–24).

flow of the thought that thinks them than they break the time and the space in which they lie.... The transition between the thought of one object and the thought of another is no more a break in the *thought* than a joint in a bamboo is a break in the wood. It is part of the *consciousness* as much as the joint is a part of the *bamboo*.... The thunder itself we believe to abolish and exclude the silence; but the *feeling* of the thunder is also a feeling of the silence as just gone; and it would be difficult to find in the actual concrete consciousness of man a feeling so limited to the present as not to have an inkling of anything that went before. (pp. 233–4)

While the silence is shattered by the thunder, and is no longer there once the thunder occurs, our consciousness is not equally discrete and discontinuous. In our consciousness the awareness of the thunder coexists with the awareness of the earlier silence, which will gradually fade as new contents register vividly on the basis of the fading clap of thunder. Our experience of an occurrence is thus always tinged with an awareness of what has just preceded it. Even if that earlier event is now no longer present, its 'vibrations' are still dying in our consciousness, and are thus still present alongside the consciousness of the new state.

Here we see very clearly that James, unlike Kant, is not explaining the unity of consciousness across abrupt qualitative changes of content by appeal to factors external to the series of sensible experiences, but is rather appealing to a feature internal to the stream of consciousness itself. Due introspective care reveals that in fact the contents of consciousness are not such as to change all that radically—even when there is radical change in the objects being experienced. In effect, introspection thereby reveals that there are no grounds for thinking of experiences as distinct and discrete existences in the first place, such as are in need of being held together by extraneous means. They are, internally, *sensibly* continuous to begin with. Thus James, famously, says:

Consciousness, then, does not appear to itself chopped up in bits. Such words as 'chain' or 'train' do not describe it fitly as it presents itself in the first instance. It is nothing jointed: it flows. A 'river' or a 'stream' are the metaphors by which it is most naturally described. *In talking of it hereafter, let us call it the stream of thought, of consciousness, or of subjective life.*[38]

James further develops the introspective case for thought being sensibly continuous from the outset, rather than being so many sensible atoms in need of unification, by distinguishing between 'substantive parts' and 'transitive parts' of the stream of thought. The substantive parts are those in which the contents of consciousness are changing slowly, there is a relatively stable configuration of states of which we are comfortably aware; the transitive parts are those in which the stream flows more quickly, there is rapid change, as we move from one substantive part to another.

[38] p. 233.

Now it is very difficult, introspectively, to see the transitive parts for what they really are. If they are but flights to a conclusion, stopping them to look at them before the conclusion is reached is really annihilating them. Whilst if we wait till the conclusion be reached, it so exceeds them in vigor and stability that it quite eclipses and swallows them up in its glare.... The rush of the thought is so headlong that it almost always brings us up at the conclusion before we can arrest it. Or if our purpose is nimble enough and we do arrest it, it ceases forthwith to be itself. As a snowflake caught in the warm hand is no longer a flake but a drop, so, instead of catching the feeling of relation moving to its term, we find we have caught some substantive thing, usually the last word we were pronouncing, statically taken, and with its function, tendency, and particular meaning in the sentence quite evaporated. The attempt at introspective analysis in these cases is in fact like seizing a spinning top to catch its motion, or trying to turn up the gas quickly enough to see how the darkness looks. (pp. 236–7)

The introspective difficulty involved in detecting the 'transitive parts' of thought can readily lead to false theories. Because these transitive parts are so difficult to hold fast and observe, there has been a tendency not to notice them, or indeed to deny them, emphasizing only the substantive parts of the stream. It is then that we might think that abrupt changes in the objects—as from silence to thunder—render an equally abrupt change in the mind, not paying sufficient attention to the fact that there is no 'break in the mind', since we register not only the substantive parts (silence, thunder) but also the transition of the mind from one state to the other.

James believes that ignoring these transitive states has led to two erroneous positions: empiricism and Kantianism (p. 237). He calls the first *Sensationalism*: viz. Humean atomism, whereby there is in the mind only a rapid succession of distinct states, which come to be united only by association. This can lead, as it led Hume, to the denial that there are strictly speaking any grounds for affirming the reality of relations between events out of the mind, as well as in it. The second mistaken view, based on the error of not recognizing that we are introspectively aware of transitional or relational states, is Kant's. James calls this *Intellectualism*:

The *Intellectualists*, on the other hand, unable to give up the reality of relations *extra mentem*, but equally unable to point to any distinct substantive feelings in which they were known, have made the same admission that the feelings do not exist. But they have drawn the opposite conclusion. The relations must be known, they say, in something that is no feeling, no mental modification continuous and consubstantial with the subjective tissue out of which sensations and other substantive states are made. They are known, these relations, by something that lies on an entirely different plane, by an *actus purus* of Thought, Intellect, or Reason, all written with capitals and considered to mean something unutterably superior to any fact of sensibility whatever.

But from our point of view both Intellectualists and Sensationalists are wrong. If there be such things as feelings at all, *then so surely as relations between objects exist in rerum natura, so surely, and more surely, do feelings exist to which these relations are known.*[39]

Again, we see clearly James's contention that it is not in Kant's way that the unity of consciousness is achieved: it is not by means of unifying factors external to the sensuous stream of contents. It is internally and inherently unified, at the base level of sensible content. Even the logical functions of judgement, which for Kant must be applied by a separate faculty, imposed on sensible content from without, are for James elements internal to the stream of consciousness as much as any other:

We ought to say a feeling of *and*, a feeling of *if*, a feeling of *but*, and a feeling of *by*, quite as readily as we say a feeling of *blue* or a feeling of *cold*. Yet we do not: so inveterate has our habit become of recognizing the existence of the substantive parts alone, that language almost refuses to lend itself to any other use. (p. 238)

In addition to transitive states James identifies further sensible aspects of the stream of consciousness that are so fleeting and intangible that they are not readily given individual names, and so tend to escape attention in careless theory construction about the nature of the stream of consciousness. Both empiricists and Kantians are taken to be guilty of this. He talks of feelings of 'tendency'[40] and of 'fringes'.[41] James is here perhaps at his introspective best; certainly at his most attentive. He gives various examples of what he means by feelings of tendency: the feeling of the tendency to pass from one thought to another, of the logical transition, 'always on the wing . . . and not to be glimpsed except in flight', from one step in an argument to its consequent step;[42] the felt tendency of the mind to anticipate in advance the completion of a sentence or a phrase, the direction in which it is going;[43] or the felt tendency to produce a name that for the moment eludes us, a casting about of the mind that is *felt* and that is already sensitive to the particular name that is as yet still absent (being on the tip of our tongue, we can tell immediately when the wrong name is proposed, proving that it is not merely a matter of a name being absent, a gap in consciousness, but that 'the gap of one word does not feel like the gap of another', the mind is already pulling in one direction rather than another).[44]

By 'fringes' he means to identify the way in which thoughts do not in fact impinge on us clean-cut, as information packets might in a computer. Each thought is suffused or fringed with a dim awareness, an echo of other thoughts. The case here is supposed to be biologically motivated—by certain considerations of what goes on in the brain[45]—as well as sustained by introspection. Rather than being discrete and sharply individuated parcels, any

---

[39] pp. 237–8. See also pp. 163 and 267–8, for example.   [40] pp. 240–6.
[41] pp. 248–50.   [42] p. 244.   [43] p. 245.   [44] p. 243.   [45] See p. 248.

thought or conscious state for James is tinged with an awareness of those states that have just begun to fade from consciousness, as well as with those that have just begun to increase in intensity. In his example, as I recite the alphabet and reach the letter 'e', the consciousness of that letter is fringed with an awareness of 'b, c, d' which are still echoing in my mind, each weaker than the next, just as on the other side, so to speak, the experience is fringed with the rising awareness of 'f, g, ...' each as yet stronger than the next.[46] This is just one way in which a thought might be tinged with a faint awareness of other mental relations and objects.

James is aware, specifically with regard to 'tendencies', that he might be accused of committing precisely the psychologist's fallacy he himself has identified. That is, the objection might be that he confuses his standpoint with that of the mental states under observation: the psychologist is aware of the tendency the subject has to move from one thought to another, and confuses that tendency for a constituent of the subject's own thought. From the inside, so to speak, those tendencies, so the objection goes, are not themselves sensible contents, only their end-results are.[47] Here James rests his case on description which he hopes captures in detail what should be introspectively familiar to us as our own undeniable sensible experiences.

Now what I contend for, and accumulate examples to show, is that 'tendencies' are not only descriptions from without, but that they are among the *objects* of the stream, which is thus aware of them from within, and must be described as in very large measure constituted of *feelings* of *tendency*, often so vague that we are unable to name them at all. . . . What must be admitted is that the definite images of traditional psychology form but the very smallest part of our minds as they actually live. The traditional psychology talks like one who should say a river consists of nothing but pailsful, spoonsful, quartpotsful, barrelsful, and other moulded forms of water. Even were the pails and the pots all actually standing in the stream, still between them the free water would continue to flow. It is just this free water of consciousness that psychologists resolutely overlook. Every definite image in the mind is steeped and dyed in the free water that flows around it. With it goes the sense of its relations, near and remote, the dying echo of whence it came to us, the dawning sense of whither it is to lead.[48]

The overall shape of the introspective case for psychological holism is this: when attention is carelessly concentrated solely on the substantive parts, as if there were only those parts, apparently disjointed and discrete, atomism is likely to seem right. But James believes that when due attention is given to the other more easily overlooked elements of consciousness, transitive elements, feelings of tendency, fringes, it will be acknowledged that the stream of consciousness is in fact already given as a sensible continuity and unity of thought, and that it is only by abstraction that the substantive parts can be

[46] Ibid., p. 248. See also pp. 269–73.   [47] p. 246.   [48] Ibid.

set up as so many discrete items still in need of unification.[49] The unifying characteristics of the stream are internal to it, 'a feeling like any other' (p. 247), rather than a principle externally applied to hold together the multiplicity of sensory contents.

3. PHILOSOPHICAL IMPLICATIONS

James is clear about what he takes to be the precise point of divergence between his view of the mind, as outlined above, and that of both the empiricists on the one hand and Kant on the other:

The ordinary associationist-psychology supposes, in contrast with this, that whenever an object of thought contains many elements, the thought itself must be made up of just as many ideas, one idea for each element, and all fused together in appearance, but really separate. The enemies of this psychology find . . . little trouble in showing that such a bundle of separate ideas would never form one thought at all, and they contend that an Ego must be added to the bundle to give it unity, and bring various ideas into relation with each other. . . . Now most believers in the ego make the same mistake as the associationists and sensationists whom they oppose. Both agree that the elements of the subjective stream are discrete and separate and constitute what Kant calls a 'manifold'. But while the associationists think that a 'manifold' can form a single knowledge, the egoists deny this, and say that the knowledge comes only when the manifold is subjected to the synthesizing activity of an ego. Both make an identical hypothesis; but the egoist, finding it won't express the facts, adds another hypothesis to correct it. Now I do not wish just yet to 'commit myself' about the existence or non-existence of the ego, but I do contend that we need not invoke it for this particular reason—namely, because the manifold of ideas has to be reduced to unity. *There is no manifold of coexisting ideas*; the notion of such a thing is a chimera. *Whatever things are thought in relation are thought from the outset in a unity, in a single pulse of subjectivity, a single psychosis, feeling, or state of mind.*[50]

Now, if what was said about Kant's perceptual atomism in Chapter 2 is right, then James's diagnosis here is not quite accurate. Atomism in Kant is then not the same thesis as the empiricists held; and it is not a premiss—we might say that it does not merely necessitate a judging ego, but is also necessitated by it. Kant's conception of the mind, which seems to be validated as the only means of coping with (perceptual) atomism, is in fact also a sufficient source of that atomism in the first place. But regardless of these differences, both the empiricists and Kant clearly do accept that in the first place the mind registers many separate ideas, something like a spray of experiential or perceptual

---

[49] p. 262.   [50] pp. 267–8. See also pp. 237–8 (quoted above).

atoms, which somehow then get united into a single consciousness. The way in which this uniting into a single consciousness comes about is where the empiricist and Kantian models of the mind diverge markedly. (I have addressed above some of the consequences of that divergence.) But, as distinct from these views, James does not accept the general starting-point common to both empiricists and Kantians, that there is at the outset a plurality of experiential atoms. For him there is rather a unified stream of consciousness at the outset, which can subsequently be analysed into constituent atoms—but these remain abstractions, symbolic parts, rather than genuine components from which experience starts and is composed.[51]

This divergence is important since James regards atomism not only as wrong, but also as theoretically pernicious.[52] There are several respects in which the explanatory inadequacy of atomism seems to be improved upon by Jamesian holism. I noted above that atomism ran into difficulty in explaining how there could ever emerge experiences of succession, or of spatial contiguity, for example.[53] It seems clear that with the rejection of psychological atomism the origin of these ideas is no longer problematic. But perhaps the most important defect of atomism is that it leads to the problem, or rather the pseudo-problem, of how the disparate psychological atoms can be united into a single consciousness. To James's mind this is something that empiricists simply could not explain, and that led Kantians to make further untenable hypotheses to accommodate the damage wrought by the initial false step. Given that this is the case, James sees his description of the stream of consciousness and rejection of atomism as a corrective that finally liberates us from the problem that confronts both empiricists and Kantians concerning the explanation of how the unity of consciousness is to be explained.

Unfortunately, one consequence of James's alternative account of the unity of consciousness, sidestepping the traditional problem involved, is that it thereby threatens to short-circuit the solution to another problem. Kant's model of the mind established the solution to the problem of the unity of consciousness as being at the same time a solution to the problem of our knowledge of the external world. The Jamesian alternative account of the mind seems to mean that a solution to the former is available which leaves the latter problem

---

[51] For an analogy that captures this conception vividly, see p. 268 n. 36:

> In a sense a soap-bubble has parts; it is a sum of juxtaposed spherical triangles. But these triangles are not separate realities; neither are the 'parts' of the thought separate realities. Touch the bubble and the triangles are no more. Dismiss the thought and out go its parts. You can no more make a new thought out of 'ideas' that have once served than you can make a new bubble out of old triangles.

[52] 'It is astonishing what havoc is wrought in psychology by admitting at the outset apparently innocent suppositions, that nevertheless contain a flaw' (p. 219).

[53] See Ch. 1, Sect. 2.3, above. See James (1981: 334–5) for a succinct articulation of some related observations.

unsolved. That is, if the Jamesian model of the mind is adopted, it would seem difficult to hold on to the refutation of scepticism about the external world that is sustained by Kant's model of the mind.

There are two preliminary ways of bringing this out. In James the unity of consciousness is secured at the level of sensible content, internally to the stream of thought, rather than being a conceptual operation applied to those contents. This means that the unity in question is no longer dependent on the unifying agency of any mechanism external to the manifold of sensible contents. In particular it is not dependent on acts of judgement applied to the stream of sensible contents by a separate faculty, in accordance with its a priori structures. Hence unity of consciousness does not entail the synthesis of the contents of sensibility to form an objective domain structured by and in accordance with those a priori rules. This is one way in which the hypothesis that the stream of consciousness is unified internally, rather than externally, means that we can no longer avail ourselves of the advantage of such external unification as it works in Kant.

But this is only one way of showing why James's account precludes the benefits of Kant's refutation of idealism. We have already seen that there might well be grounds for doubts about the rather elaborate transcendental psychology involved in this reconstruction of the Kantian argument, doubts that James clearly shares. Another way of bringing out the bearing of James's account on Kant's anti-sceptical argument addresses the second reconstruction of the argument seen above.[54] Here we leave out recourse to any external mechanism that has as a consequence the transcendental synthesis of an objective world, and address the contention that there being a representation of an objective external world is a *presupposition*, rather than a product, of the unity of consciousness. For Kant, given his perceptual atomism, the only thing that enables different atoms of experience to be united in one consciousness is the self-conscious judgement that they are all mine, but for that judgement to be possible, those experiences must be experienced as occurrences on the background of a unified objective world, one in which there is, moreover, sufficient order, e.g. causal order, to secure an ordered association of those experiential units. Again, then, unity of consciousness is dependent on factors external to the sensible stream of contents—viz. the unity of an external world. Were experiences atomistic, as in the case of the 'super-strobe' considered earlier, then appeal to an abiding external world might indeed be the only way of rendering experiences commensurable. But of course on James's view that model is wrong: two flashes of the strobe might be quite discrete occurrences, but the experience of them will in fact be sensibly continuous. And such internal grounds for the unity of the stream of consciousness, the fact that it is *sensibly* continuous, would

---

[54] Ch. 2, Sect. 3.3.

appear to render that unity independent of whatever else might obtain or not obtain in the world. (There is no need to appeal to some abiding world in order to be able to unify experiences: they are already unified.) And once the unity of consciousness is not dependent on external factors, such as the existence of an external world, those external factors can be doubted without undermining the unity of consciousness. Since it is only the latter that the sceptic could not countenance, now that it no longer follows from the former doubts, there is nothing to rule out such sceptical doubts.

Basically, on either of the two reconstructions, it would seem that the change in the model of the mind from Kant to James serves to unhook us at the outset from the entire train of thought involved in Kant's refutation of scepticism. Since the line of argument based on transcendental synthesis was manifestly resistible anyway, it is the impact on the second reconstruction that is of greater interest. In this argument atomism is undeniably central (in a way that it wasn't in the other). And it should be emphasized that, in terms of the impact on it, it does not particularly matter whether atomism is in fact wrong and James's alternative right; what matters here is only that while Kant's refutation turns on atomism, James's account of the mind offers a possible alternative to it. That would seem to be enough to release us from the compulsion of the Kantian train of thought.

There are accordingly at least two lines of objection that ought to be considered. According to the first, it can be questioned whether James himself has managed, for all his efforts, to offer a genuine alternative to atomism. According to the second, when it comes to reconstructing the Kantian argument, any assumption of atomism that Kant might make is merely a red herring, and is not essential to his anti-sceptical arguments. Both of these objections question the impact of the Jamesian model on the Kantian proof. I will consider each of them in turn.

Turning to the first, it might be thought that, for all the introspective detail, James cannot have succeeded in articulating an alternative to atomism. In the first place, it might be thought that since in Kant psychological atomism emerged as a conclusion of an argument, rather than as simply an adopted premiss, perhaps that same argument applies here. This might be further motivated by recognition of the fact that James attacks psychological atomism as a rashly adopted bit of theory, without considering comprehensively that it might rest on sound argument. In fact, however, the argument that James misses is not applicable to his position. Perceptual atomism seemed unavoidable on Kant's model of the mind, where there are two faculties—sensibility and the faculty of judgement (concepts).[55] James, as we have seen, precisely rejects that distinction. Of course, some care is needed in stating precisely what James is

---

[55] See pp. 76–8 above.

rejecting. Clearly he cannot deny that for an experience to be something for me it must be experienced as being of one sort rather than another, or—perhaps less question-beggingly—as having some distinguishing qualities. But he can arguably allow for this while denying that experiencing something as having a certain quality involves application of concepts by the understanding to otherwise blind sensible contents. Sensible contents, on the alternative view, are simply qualitatively self-intimating. We may still talk of 'conceptualization' here, as long as it is not thought to be the product of so many acts of judgement carried out by a separate faculty, one corresponding to every perceptual content. The latter would entail a commitment to perceptual atomism, as we have seen, but James's sensibly continuous self-intimating stream of experience stands to avoid that.[56] To that extent Kant's commitment to atomism does not extend to James's model. But obviously the inapplicability of that argument for atomism does not mean that no other applies. It is therefore worth turning more directly to the question of whether James has managed to avoid atomism. (This will also offer a way of following more closely what is involved in, and the viability of, rejecting the Kantian two-faculty model in favour of a model based on sensibility alone.)

Here I pick up on a question that was raised earlier.[57] At issue is the relation between the claim that experience is successive, and atomism. The shape of the objection is simple: that there is a general case to be made to the effect that thought is always successive, and that if thought is always successive, then we cannot escape endorsing psychological atomism.[58] Hence, the objection contends, however rich and nuanced James's descriptions might be, he cannot genuinely be offering an alternative to atomism. Moreover, it looks as though James in particular might be directly committed to accepting the premise of the argument, regardless of the general grounds for it. As we have seen, one of James's central contentions is that mental content is always changing. And if thought is always changing, then there is a sense in which it is always successive. The question is whether an objection along these lines works once the details have been filled in. It seems clear that it does not, but the reasons are perhaps worth spelling out.

Let us start with the general form of the argument, and address the final step first. It should be clear in what sense it is right that if our experiential contents are always successive, then they must be atomistically apprehended. The operative word here is 'always'. If experiential contents are *always* successive, then we can never have two simultaneously. But that means that we

---

[56] Whether they are to count as conceptualizations or not, the necessary discriminatory capacities in question here will play a significant role in the arguments in Ch. 7 below.

[57] p. 84 above.

[58] Which, of course, is not to say that the reverse is true, that atomism is committed to all thought being successive.

cannot have co-occurring experiences. There can then never be any complexity to what is apprehended at a time, which just is tantamount to an assertion of atomism. But the question is whether there is any reason to accept the first premiss of the argument, that experiential content *is* always successive *in this strict sense*.

Kant at times appears to have thought that there was. But it seems likely, as Kemp Smith claims, that he may have been led to think that all apprehensions of the manifold are successive in part by his emphasis (in the Analogies, at least) on temporal over spatial ordering of the manifold.[59] What does seem right—on Kant's model of the mind—is that experiences are discrete contents; but, as we have seen, that does not exclude discrete cotemporaneous perceptions, and so is not equivalent to a commitment to strict succession.[60] However, the claim that experience is always successive is perhaps true in one sense, which is given in the fact that I cannot turn my attention equally to two things simultaneously. It might be that I apprehend the table and the lamp on it at one and the same time, in one and the same experience, but the point seems valid that in so far as my apprehension of them is strictly simultaneous, I cannot be aware of my experience as being of two things—a desk and a lamp. Rather, I am taking in at once all the information comprising the desk + lamp experience, and to then become aware that what we have here comprises two things, a lamp and a desk, it does seem right to say that I must turn my attention, if only in thought, *first* to the one, *then* to the other. This brings out the sense in which we can perhaps claim that thought is successive, but it is clearly not the sense employed in the second step of the argument.

The equivocation can be brought out by distinguishing clearly between *apprehending* and *attending* to the content of experience. By the apprehension of content I mean registering it, such that it falls within the realm of that which we notice and can subsequently draw on. By attention is meant focusing selectively on something, foregrounding it. We capture the relation between the two by saying that *apprehended* content is available for us to *attend* to it or to part of it. What we attend to is then foregrounded; what we merely notice is rendered the background.[61] Now it is attention that is arguably always successive;[62] but it is only if the *apprehension* of sensory content is always successive—viz. in each and every instance—that succession amounts to atomism. Moreover, it is not easy to see how a move from one to the other could be made good. That attention is always successive, assuming for now that it indeed is, clearly does not imply that apprehension is always successive, and

---

[59] Kemp Smith (1962: 348).
[60] Kant nevertheless remains committed to perceptual atomism, precisely because cotemporaneous perceptions will be discrete on his account.
[61] For a treatment of attention, see James (1981, ch. XI: 'Attention').
[62] See e.g. James (1981: 386).

thereby lead to atomism. It is clearly possible in principle to conceive of attending specifically to only one item at a time, while allowing that that item is always possibly an element of a complex apprehended as a whole at a moment, in what James calls 'a single pulse of thought'.[63] The successiveness of attention does not preclude the item singled out from belonging to a complex that is not successively apprehended.[64] And there does not seem to be any direct argument from the successiveness of attention to atomism. So much, then, for the general form of the objection.

Regardless of the standing of the general argument, there is the question of whether James in particular has inadvertently committed himself to atomism, in virtue of his insistence that thought is always changing. In view of what has just been said, it should be clear that the sense in which this commits him to successiveness is not that which entails atomism. He clearly accepts that attention is, more or less strictly, successive, but that has been dealt with in the general argument and so is not relevant here. What is relevant is that he accepts also that across sensible intervals of time mental states are constantly changing, so that essentially what we have is never an abiding mental state, but rather always a succession of different sensible contents.[65] This is the sense in which thought is always successive for James, a succession of thought-contents each of which is what he calls a single pulse of thought, or experience. Now this might, as we will see immediately, give grounds for concern, but it should not do so on the grounds that it amounts to atomism. For the succession in question does not entail that apprehension is always successive (which, as we have seen, *would* amount to atomism). It would entail that, if each pulse of thought in the succession were simple. But it is, of course, clear that James means nothing of the sort. The perishing pulse of thought,[66] or single state of mind,[67] is not single in the sense of being a simple experience, but in the sense of being a single unified complex, precisely the kind of diverse but seamless and unarticulated complex that is apprehended *at once as a whole*, rather than successively.[68] So although James is committed to experience involving a succession of different thoughts or states of mind[69] in virtue of it constantly changing, just in so far as those constantly changing states themselves involve an apprehension of contents that is not successive, he is not committed to apprehension *always* being successive. So much, then, for

---

[63] e.g. pp. 383, 268. Of course the Kantian view as identified above precisely precludes this possibility, but since it does not entail strict succession anyway, that is of no relevance here.

[64] In fact, as I will point out later (Ch. 7, Sect. 4), there are reasons for thinking that successiveness of attention requires that apprehension not be always (i.e. strictly) successive.

[65] Where 'abiding' does not mean just having temporal duration, but extending beyond the minimum sensible interval. On this, see James (1981: 224 and *passim*).

[66] p. 350.   [67] p. 268.   [68] pp. 266–8, 383, and *passim*.

[69] James uses 'thought', in the sense familiar from Descartes, as synonymous with 'mental states at large' (see p. 186).

the first possible objection, to the effect that James cannot in fact be offering a genuine alternative to atomism.

Turning now to the second line of objection, the question is whether the availability of an alternative to atomism is of relevance to Kant's anti-sceptical results anyway. The thought is that to the extent that those conclusions are not premised on atomism in the first place, the possibility of unseating atomism will not threaten them. One way of bringing this out is to attempt to argue that even on the Jamesian alternative to atomism there is room for the Kantian see-saw strategy of the transcendental deduction to get a grip. It is here that a worry alluded to in the previous paragraph might be exploited. The fact that thought is constantly changing means that we have a constant succession of pulses of thought, each of which is qualitatively different from the other. Now, we have seen that given the nature of each 'pulse' this does not amount to atomism. But there might nevertheless be a problem as to how these different pulses of experience, particularly given that they are each unique, can come to be united into one consciousness. However richly textured each pulse is internally, and however 'closely packed' they are to one another, surely the mere fact that they are different pulses raises the question of how they are to form a larger unity, the unity of consciousness. What we are doing here, of course, is using against the Jamesian precisely the strategy he used against the atomist.[70] And the reason indeed is that it would seem that within the personal unity of consciousness such pulses, for all their inner complexity, function as just so many 'atoms' or units in need of combination. And to this extent it looks as though the Kantian argument concerning what is required for the uniting of such disparate (albeit complex) elements into one consciousness can get going here. It then follows that the Kantian link between the unity of consciousness and objectivity is perfectly compatible with the rejection of atomism.

Pursuing this objection in a bit more detail will serve to bring to the fore the grounds for regarding it as inappropriate. It might be thought that a response to the objection lies in the fact that the 'pulses' of thought that are to be united are after all not atomistic, but contain a heterogeneity. Consequently, one counter-objection would go, there are enough internal elements to serve as threads connecting the experiences internally, without any appeal to Kantian external means of unifying consciousness. The disparate elements of any such pulse of experience are such that while some alter between one pulse and the next, others will persist, providing sensible continuity across them, thereby weaving the pulses internally into a longer unity. The trouble with this is that, given James's holism, this talk of threads would already seem to be an unacceptable importation of atomism. The idea that every 'pulse' of experience is

---

[70] See James (1981: 160–4) and pp. 94–6 above.

made up of so many threads, each of which retains its identity independently of the others, is precisely the sort of atomism he is at pains to deny. His holistic explanation of why thought is always changing, such that the same experience cannot be had twice, relies on the fact that any change in the total mental state will alter the quality of any element within it. But this just means that there can be no such threads that persist unchanged and provide the sensible overlap between different pulses of thought. If there could be, there would precisely be the possibility of recurring experiential atoms that James denies. Given his holistic nesting, the mere fact that there are two different pulses of thought means that the elements of each—say, the persisting experience of seeing an unchanged blade of grass—will be different in each too. So, the response to the counter-objection has it, the pulses in question cannot be internally unified, and the field remains open to regard them functionally as just so many discrete units in need of Kantian unification.

However, by now the problem with this objection will, I take it, have reached the surface. Regarding such pulses of thought or consciousness as so many units in need of combination is just an extension of the problem of regarding each as composed of so many entwined threads. It is to redescribe the stream of thought atomistically; to ignore James's reasons for talking of *pulses*, rather than of units or stages. Of course, such description is possible, and does recreate the problem of how those discrete stages or 'atoms' come to be combined into some larger unity. But to James's mind that is like asking how so many potfuls combine to make a river, or how so many spherical triangles combine to make a soap bubble, and would be regarded as being 'as unfair as Zeno's treatment of the advocates of motion'.[71] For James the use of the term *pulses* is precisely supposed to indicate a taxonomy imposed on an already continuous organic process, such that pulses are recognitionally salient identifications but are not discrete items and do not have clear boundaries between them. To that extent, the question of how such pulses can then be combined looks like a confusion of recognitional priority for compositional priority. To that extent, the objection posed trades on a pseudo-problem that is just another instance of the theoretically pernicious consequences of an atomistic conception. Both descriptions, atomist and holist, are possible; but it is important not to beg any questions by inadvertently collapsing the two, which is what the objection does. It does not in fact, despite the initial moves, amount to consideration of the question whether the Kantian strategy can be run without atomism.

It might be best to address this question more directly, leaving to one side the particular development of the non-atomistic model in James, and the application of the Kantian strategy to it. The task can be brought out as follows. There

[71] The allusions are to pp. 246, 268 n. 36, and 237.

is an obvious sense in which a Kantian link between unity of consciousness and experience of a unified objective world can obtain without atomism. It might well be that, even without atomism, the transcendental workings of the mind would be operative, or that we would still resort—however unnecessary it may then be—to an abiding external world in the unification of our subjective contents. But this weak sense in which the link between subjectivity and objectivity can be maintained without atomism is not to the point here. The question is whether, without atomism, the argument for the *necessity* of that link would still work. What the Kantian would have us accept is that, given atomism, there is no other way of securing the unity of consciousness.[72] In other words, atomism is sufficient to drive the argument of the Transcendental Deduction. But there is no reason why the Kantian should insist that it is the only possible sufficient condition. With this in mind, the question behind the current objection becomes whether in setting aside atomism we are effectively unhooked from the force of Kant's argument, or are there considerations waiting in the wings, so to speak, that comprise other equally sufficient conditions for accepting the necessity of the Kantian derivation of objectivity? In that case, even without atomism the argument of the Transcendental Deduction and generally Kant's refutation of idealism would still run.

Now the general strategy expressed by this question is central to the larger concern here, and I will return to it later. For present purposes it is enough to consider the obvious moves that might be thought to render atomism inessential to Kant's case. If those moves do not work, we will have reason to accept, at least provisionally, that Kant's refutation of scepticism is indeed premised on perceptual atomism.[73]

The general shape of the Kantian argument is that the unity of consciousness presupposes self-consciousness, which in turn presupposes judgements about an objective world. Now I think we can accept that without atomism the first link does not obtain. Given atomism, it seems reasonable to think that the only way in which all those discrete experiences can be combined into a single consciousness, into what James calls a personal consciousness, is if they can be gone through and self-ascribed as being one and all mine.

---

[72] It should be clear from what we have seen above that James, for one, took this atomism to be Kant's starting-point. For a contemporary endorsement of this view of Kant, see Stern (1990, 1993). We have seen that although the form of atomism in question does not necessarily have the status of a premiss within Kant's system as a whole, it is indeed the starting-point of the Transcendental Deduction at least on one central construal of it. For the purposes of the present discussion we can ignore the former and concentrate solely on its role as a premiss in the Transcendental Deduction.

[73] In returning to the issue later (Ch. 7) the concern will be to show a way in which a recognizably Kantian position can in fact be sustained without taking atomism as a premiss. But the position defended will be quite far removed from Kant's, which is all we have before us here.

And that presupposes self-consciousness. But once we give up atomism, there is no manifold that has to be run through and held together by acts of self-ascription: it is already sensibly unified at the entry level, so to speak. Self-ascription and so self-consciousness, although possible, are not necessary for the unity of consciousness. So we might accept that the first step is indeed premised on atomism. But it hardly seems to matter that, without atomism, self-consciousness would not be presupposed by unity of consciousness, since it would anyway be undeniable that we are self-conscious, and do have the capacity to self-ascribe experiences. That is, it does not matter that, without atomism, the self-consciousness cannot be inferred from mere unity of consciousness, since the sceptic would allow both as premises. So the burden is shifted almost entirely onto the second presuppositional link, between self-consciousness and judgement of an objective world. If it can be shown that the argument for that particular link is not premised on atomism, that will suffice to establish that the Kantian case against the sceptic cannot be derailed simply by appeal to a Jamesian rejection of atomism.

James, for one, would consider that in fact without atomism there is no good argument for the second link. For Kant the move to self-consciousness is necessarily a move beyond the boundaries of sensibility; it involves a judgement about the contents of sensibility, which is construed as an intellectual operation of another faculty, the understanding, on the contents of the first. We have already seen why self-consciousness being understood on the model of judgement might entail the commitment to there being an objective world that is independent of our thought about it. So the question is whether this understanding of self-consciousness is forced upon us. And here it might be argued that to the extent that this conception is not combined with atomism, it is not.

Consider an occurrent simple experience of some sort. That it is occurrent is meant to get away from the question of whether it is atomistically individuated or not. For there to be self-consciousness of that experience, the Kantian would say there must be a judgement about the experienced content to the effect that it is mine, that I am having that experience. The Kantian construes that judgement as an intellectual act that takes that experienced, sensible content as its object. But the question is why we need to import any such separation of faculties. It would seem that this conception of self-conscious experience models itself on perceptual experience. The experience is thought of as an object, towards which the understanding is directed from outside it. But self-consciousness need not be understood as harpooning an experience and calling it mine. There would seem to be other available models of self-consciousness. It might be, for example, that self-consciousness is simply a certain characteristic of the experience itself, that the awareness that the experience is *mine* is not the result of judgement about the experience in question, but a matter of the content or character of that experience.[74] This is precisely the view that James takes.[75]

When we then pull back from the current experience to consider the entire range of a person's self-conscious experience, there is no obvious change for the non-atomist, there are no significant boundaries to be crossed, and the same two models can still apply. A person's entire mental life is just the single experience considered above, writ large. It is only if we adopt atomism (or a separation of faculties that forces such atomism) that we are compelled to say that even while within each individual experience there might be a choice between two models,[76] the internalist model that regards self-consciousness as an aspect of the sensible experience would at best be able to accommodate there being just so many distinct self-conscious experiences. In so far as the experiences are distinct, and self-consciousness is an aspect of the experience, there is no way of explaining how they could add up to a single self-consciousness that encompasses them all. That would now seem to require an operation that was distinct from the individual experiences, and so could range over them all. And it is difficult to see what would answer to those specifications other than the Kantian model of self-consciousness.

It would appear, then, that if we are not atomists, there is a choice between two models of self-consciousness. And as long as there is a choice, the fact that one of those models entails there being an objective world cannot count as a refutation of scepticism on that score. The only way to avoid that choice is to insist on atomism. But that is just to accept that, without atomism, the second link—between self-consciousness and experience of an objective world—may not obtain either.

However, there is a sense in which the alternative model of self-consciousness is not in fact as adequate as I have suggested it is when it comes, on the non-atomist conception, to accounting for the self-consciousness that a person has not just of a current state but of the wider span of their conscious experience. It is true that in so far as self-consciousness is a component of sensible experience, and sensible experience is sensibly continuous, self-consciousness will be sensibly continuous. And so the mere passage of experience will not result in so many distinct units of self-consciousness in need of further combination. But while the self-consciousness of a person can be explained in this way without appealing to acts of judgement, it is clear that it gives us only what might be called a present continuous self-consciousness. But a person

---

[74] For related discussion of these two models of self-awareness, see O'Brien (1995, 1996).

[75] See e.g. his discussion on pp. 314–24. On grounds of simplicity James prefers his model to the Kantian one (see pp. 341–50, in addition to the references in n. 39 above) which has to take on board a transcendental ego, which is not an empirical item—since as such it could not range over all other empirical items of experience—and also not a transcendent item.

[76] And, of course, there might not even be such a choice if it is a separation of faculties that forces the atomism.

does not merely have an ever present continuous self-consciousness. We also have the capacity to self-ascribe past experiences to ourselves. And that does seem to involve judgement.

Now some caution is needed here in identifying the precise point at which this requires judgement. It is open to us to claim, as James does,[77] that each thought, as it wanes, leaves its mark on the succeeding thought, so that every perishing thought contains within it the trace of preceding contents, and has access to all such contents which it has inherited (as part of the total brain state upon which it supervenes[78]). To the extent that something like this can be envisaged, it might not be right that judgements of self-ascription are required for my past experiences and their contents to be anything for me. But there is more than just an awareness of past experiences that goes on in the self-ascription of them. I also ascribe to myself that it was me, at such-and-such a point in time, who had that experience. That does involve more than an awareness of current contents, including current traces of my past experiences; it involves a judgement of how things were with me in the past. It is at this point, then, that it perhaps seems necessary to appeal to judgement if we are to give an adequate explanation of self-consciousness and the self-ascription it involves. The question is whether this point comes too late in the story to sustain the Kantian argument.

There are two reasons why it might be thought to come too late. First, the later the appeal to judgement comes, and the more specific the task for which it is required, the less effective it will be as an opening move in anti-sceptical argument. When it is insisted that such self-ascription requires appeal to an objective external world, the sceptic can simply accept the argument, and contend that it follows that since we have no right to the latter, we have no right to the former either. On the atomistic model that would have been an impossible conclusion, given that without such self-ascription there would be no unity of consciousness either,[79] and the sceptic cannot consistently deny that we do at least have unity of consciousness. But once it is granted, as it is on the non-atomist model, that we can have both unity of consciousness and basic self-consciousness over time without making any judgements of self-ascription, it is open to the sceptic to question our right to such judgements without absurdity. He can then contend with impunity that since the necessary conditions for making such judgements might not obtain, for all we know we have merely the illusion of making them.

Perhaps more significant is the second reason why this residual need to introduce judgement even on the non-atomist model comes too late. As we have seen, there are two routes from judgement to the existence of an objective

---

[77] See e.g. pp. 322–4, 350. [78] See e.g. p. 324.
[79] And Kant would have it that there was then no self-consciousness either.

world. The one, to the effect that judgement involves the categories and transcendental synthesis of objects in accordance with them, can be left aside for now as too dependent on insufficiently substantiated particularities of Kant's model of the mind. The other, which is relevant here, involves pointing out that self-conscious self-ascription of experiences involving past-tense judgements already commits us to an objective order. It commits us to there being an objective temporal sequence of events, to there being an appearance–reality distinction such that it makes sense to consider that there is a truth about what happened at a certain time in the past which might be different from how I now take things to have been. Now it seems to me that this simply does follow, and that anyone adhering to the non-atomist option would at least have to concede this much. But coming where it does, this concession is no longer enough to yield any interesting anti-sceptical conclusion.

On Kant's view, as we have seen, since time itself cannot be perceived, and the individual atomistic perceptions do not themselves sustain a representation of temporal structure, the representation of an objective temporal sequence requires that there be something that fills time, some abiding substance, in relation to which the multitude of discrete experiences can be plotted as forming a single history (temporal sequence), rather than there being as many unrelated worlds as there are moments of experience.[80] And, moreover, that unified world must be governed by laws that determine the order of events in it, since without that there would be no ordering of our own mental states.[81] But in the absence of the commitment to atomism there is no need to appeal to anything external to allow for our representation of a single temporal order. What 'fills' time, allowing our representation of a single temporal order, need be nothing other than the stream of thought. Moreover, since that stream is already internally ordered, there is no room for the inference to causal laws that hold true of an external world. In other words, the realm of objectivity that is entailed by our past-tense self-ascriptions need not extend any further than the contents of personal thought. And that again would seem to offer little by way of an answer to the sceptic about the external world.

It seems, then, that we can, if only tentatively, conclude that Kant's refutation of idealism will not work without the atomist premiss, and that consequently, in offering an alternative to atomism, James does unseat the Kantian answer to the sceptic.

That James himself indeed does not regard the unity of the stream of thought as linked to the unity of an independent objective world is made clear in his treatment of the fourth and fifth characteristics of thought.[82] It would seem

---

[80] See pp. 84–7 above, and Ch. 7, Sect. 5, below.
[81] On the way in which the argument for this conclusion can be construed so as to avoid the famous *non sequitur* objection, see pp. 281–2 below.   [82] pp. 262–73, 273–8.

that the only sense in which it may be true that the unity of the stream of thought *presupposes* objects would be that according to which 'the *Object* of your thought is really its entire content or deliverance, neither more nor less'.[83] On this conception, the object of my thought that the pen is on the table, properly speaking, is neither the pen, nor the table, but the entire content, which can be captured without loss only as *the-pen-is-on-the-table*. That is the proper specification of the substantive object of my thought. James considers it to be 'a vicious use of speech to take out a substantive kernel from its content and call that its object', or to 'add a substantive kernel not articulately included in its content, and to call that its object'.[84] The object of thought is 'all that the thought thinks, exactly as the thought thinks it, however complicated the matter, and however symbolic the manner of thinking may be. It is needless to say that memory can seldom accurately reproduce such an object, when once it has passed from before the mind.'[85] While it does not seem right to take James to be talking simply of an intentional object, it does seem that the conception is not meant to involve (or preclude) any commitment to objects in the weighty sense, as ontologically independent of the thought of them. It is rather as if we have here an object in the bracketed sense intended later by phenomenologists.[86]

And any move beyond there being objects in that sense to objects in the weighty sense, which on the Kantian view would be a precondition of experience, is regarded by James as an entirely contingent addendum. Thus, he holds that it is only relative sameness of content across different appearances that leads us to attribute independent existence to the objects of awareness. That two people have the same object of thought is what leads us to suppose that the object is external to and independent of the mental state of both of them; that a past thought and a present thought of mine have the same object leads me to extrude the object from both thoughts, and 'project it by a sort of triangulation into an independent position, from which it may *appear* to both'.[87] James is explicit that, without such experience of (relative) sameness, 'the question of reality being extra-mental or not is not likely to arise'.[88] And of course on his view there is nothing that necessitates that experience will exhibit any such sameness. It follows, then, that experience does not presuppose there being an independent external world. (In fact James assumes that children, prior to repeated judgements of sameness, will not have resort to

---

[83] James identifies this as the proper use of the term 'object' in psychology (p. 265).
[84] p. 265. [85] p. 266. [86] See e.g. Husserl (1997, §§8–9).
[87] p. 262. Here James's use of 'object of thought' can be taken in the more ordinary sense of the phrase, rather than in his technical sense. The explanation given of the origin of our belief in external objects is very reminiscent of Hume's account (*A Treatise of Human Nature*, I. iv. 2). (Hume, characteristically, concentrates on the case of intrapersonal rather than interpersonal triangulation.) [88] p. 262.

an independent world, and will experience the objects of their thoughts as being 'neither in nor out of thought'.[89]) Whereas for Kant an external reality is a presupposition of my now judging about thoughts I had earlier, rather than a 'triangulation' *from* such thoughts, on James's view, if there had been no experiences of sameness, there would have been no need to assume the existence of independent external objects, and no problem about sustaining a unified self-consciousness over time would have resulted. Nothing is presupposed by thought except objects in the proper psychological sense of the term, which remains ontologically uncommitted.

Not only does James not hold that the unity of the stream of consciousness is dependent on the existence of objects in the weighty sense, he allows that there is no one determinate answer to the question concerning which objects the independent world consists of. James offers an early and very clear statement of ontological relativity.[90] The object of thought, in the proper psychological sense, is indefinitely complex, and we inevitably ignore most of what we are confronted with, and single out for attention those elements that are made salient to us given our practical and aesthetic interests. Those elements are then elevated to the status of *things*. Things, as James puts it, are simply selected groups of sensible qualities which were made salient for us by our practical and aesthetic needs, 'and which we exalt to this exclusive status of independence and dignity.'[91] Different interests would mean different individuations of things.

> ... the world of each of us, howsoever different our several views of it may be, all lay embedded in the primordial chaos of sensations, which gave the mere *matter* to the thought of all of us indifferently. We may, if we like, by our reasonings unwind things back to that black and jointless continuity of space and moving clouds of swarming atoms which science calls the only real world. But all the while the world *we* feel and live in will be that which our ancestors and we, by slowly cumulative strokes of choice, have extricated out of this, like sculptors, by simply rejecting certain portions of the given stuff. Other sculptors, other statues from the same stone! Other minds, other worlds from the same monotonous and inexpressive chaos! My world is but one in a million alike embedded, alike real to those who may abstract them. How different must be the worlds in the consciousness of ant, cuttle-fish, or crab!
>
> But in my mind and your mind the rejected portions and the selected portions of the original world-stuff are to a great extent the same. The human race as a whole largely agrees as to what it shall notice and name, and what not.[92]

The statement of ontological relativity is not particularly well argued for in the text, but the commitment to it consolidates the sense in which James's

---

[89] p. 263.   [90] pp. 273 ff.   [91] p. 274.
[92] p. 277. The similarity between this elegant statement of ontological relativity and later developments of the idea in Quine and Goodman is of course not coincidental, although the line back to James is not always sufficiently well traced.

view of the mind is such that it places no a priori constraints on the construal of an object-world. James agrees that the objects we regard as independent existences are constructs, and so comprise what Kant would call a merely empirical reality. But Kant has it that there are a priori constraints determining both that and how the 'primordial chaos of sensations', the *matter* given to sensibility, will be transformed into a law-governed empirical reality. James emphasizes here that there is no one empirical reality we are constrained a priori to live in; it is rather a pragmatically determined matter, which might have been determined differently. The most that can be recognized as a priori is that where a conception of an independent external world has (contingently) come into play, for each of us there will be one 'great splitting of the whole universe', a dichotomy for the thinker between themselves (and their mental contents) and the rest of the universe, *whatever it might contain*.[93] But there will be little comfort in this for the sceptic.

James thus seems to develop his characterization of thought in a way that backs up the non-Kantian tolerance of a divorce, to which his view of the mind is anyway committed, between subjectivity and the existence and structure of the objective world. James himself does not attend to this consequence of his rejection of atomism. That he does not do so might seem surprising, given how attentive he is to assessing his alternative conception of the mind in comparison with the atomism of the empiricists and of Kant. The explanation for his lack of attention to these further ramifications is in part, doubtless, that these are epistemological ramifications, and James is not doing epistemology in the *Principles*, but philosophy of mind.[94] But the primary point is surely that the model of the mind developed by James has these epistemological ramifications only where it is embedded in a generally Cartesian framework of a fundamental split between subject and object. If the model of the mind as an organic and self-sufficient stream of consciousness is conjoined with a Cartesian distinction between subjective and objective domains as two poles that are taken as basic rather than as constructs, such that starting from the one we need to establish contact with the other, then the fact that the Kantian refutation of scepticism can no longer run is rendered pertinent. But James, even in epistemological mode, does not generally share this orientation.

The whole idea of an organic stream of consciousness seems to be bound up with the idea of that stream being unconditioned by any dependence on objects external to it. Yet at the same time there are numerous places where

---

[93] In discussing this (pp. 277–8) James is more concerned to bring out that it is also a priori that the line of division between the two halves of such a distinction is never drawn in the same way by two different people.

[94] Thus he talks in one place of himself as taking 'the *psychological* point of view, the relatively uncritical non-idealistic point of view of all natural science, beyond which this book cannot go' (p. 263).

James helps himself to appeal to the presence of external objects in explaining the unity of the stream of consciousness. For example, in the course of addressing a slightly different issue, he writes:

> Our own bodily position, attitude, condition, is one of the things of which *some* awareness, however inattentive, invariably accompanies the knowledge of whatever else we know. We think; and as we think we feel our bodily selves as the seat of the thinking. ... Whether the warmth and intimacy be anything more than the feeling of the same old body always there, is a matter for the next chapter to decide. (pp. 234–5)

Such appeals would seem to suggest a denial of any significant dualism, as an epistemological starting position, between subject and object.[95] The question of whether the combination of a non-Cartesian epistemological orientation with his particular views on the unity of thought makes good philosophical sense need not concern us here. While it perhaps remains unclear whether or not in the *Principles* James does still accept an alignment of the stream of consciousness with a Cartesian conception of consciousness, he had clearly moved away from this alignment by the time of his *Essays on Radical Empiricism*.[96] In any event, to the extent that the stream of consciousness is conjoined with the denial of any such basic distinction between the subjective and the objective, the subject-driven sceptical problem no longer arises, and with that as his epistemological orientation it would be clear why James would not be concerned with such scepticism,[97] and so would not regard the undoing

---

[95] A few years later we find James appealing much more boldly to the experience of physical phenomena as the basis of the knowledge we have of our own continued existence:

> Let the case be what it may in others, I am as confident as I am of anything that, in myself, the stream of thinking (which I recognize emphatically as a phenomenon) is only a careless name for what, when scrutinized, reveals itself to consist chiefly of the stream of my breathing. The 'I think' which Kant said must be able to accompany all my objects, is the 'I breathe' which actually does accompany them. There are other internal facts besides breathing (intracephalic muscular adjustments, etc., of which I have said a word in my larger *Psychology*), and these increase the assets of 'consciousness', so far as the latter is subject to immediate perception; but breath, which was ever the original 'spirit', breath moving outwards, between the glottis and the nostrils, is, I am persuaded, the essence out of which philosophers have constructed the entity known to them as consciousness. *That entity is fictitious, while thoughts in the concrete are fully real. But thoughts in the concrete are made of the same stuff as things are.* ('Does "Consciousness" Exist?' (1905), in James 1976: 19)

Clearly this thought might—but was not meant to—suggest a neo-Kantian interdependence between unity of consciousness and an abiding physical world. In fact it is rather evidence of James's pragmatism, which has here altogether eclipsed the salience of the epistemic polarity that is the Cartesian starting-point.

[96] See Myers (1986: 60–4). Myers claims that 'The exact status of James's concept of consciousness in the years before he introduced radical empiricism is difficult to determine' (p. 60). He goes on to outline why, apart from the lack of clarity in the early position of the *Principles*, even in his later radical empiricist stage, where his convictions against Cartesian dualism are clear, James seems committed to an ambivalent stand on the issue of whether or not the stream of thought is to be conceived as a genuine unity, occupying one side of a Cartesian dichotomy.

[97] Or indeed, given pragmatism, with any other.

of Kant's link between a unified subject and a unified object-world as being particularly troubling.

For present purposes what matters is precisely that if the stream of consciousness model of the mind *is* conjoined with the Cartesian epistemological assumption—an assumption which it might in any case be thought to sustain—the impact on the Kantian refutation of scepticism obtains.[98]

4. BERGSON

Having seen how James's rejection of atomism bears on the epistemological yield of the Kantian model of the mind, it is worth commenting briefly on the use Bergson makes of a conception of the mind that is essentially similar to James's.[99] Like James, Bergson distances himself both from the atomism of empiricists and from Kant. And it is difficult for anyone familiar with Bergson not to notice particular points at which James in the *Principles* seems to echo more than just the general opposition to atomism that they had in common. (In places, for example, James highlights the way in which language, far from being a vehicle for representing the truth, can serve to distort it.[100]) But unlike James's *Principles*, Bergson is primarily concerned to connect this conception of the mind with traditional epistemological questions. He ties the model of the mind to our capacity to know reality. A central idea is that psychological atomism distorts not only our understanding of the mind, but also our understanding of the world itself.

Unfortunately, this position is not substantiated by Bergson with detailed argument and, moreover, it is not clear that there is any room to replace the rich but broad brushstrokes with a more analytic attention to details (there

---

[98] While it is important to have identified the role played by that Cartesian assumption, the consequences of questioning it can, for the moment, be left aside. This is something that I will return to consider in Part II.

[99] The two were in increasingly close philosophical contact. At the time *The Principles of Psychology* was published, in 1890, Bergson was only 31, and not surprisingly there is only one mention of him in the book. Later contact was more significant. James wrote two essays on Bergson, 'The Philosophy of Bergson' (James 1909a) and 'Bradley or Bergson' (James 1910). Bergson in turn wrote on James, e.g. 'On the Pragmatism of William James' (Bergson 1992c, ch. 8). On the relations between James and Bergson, see R. B. Perry (1935, vol. ii, chs. 86–7). While the two were allies in their view of the mind, there is evidence that James took a polite distance from the more speculative moves that Bergson made on the basis of that view. See e.g. the final paragraph of 'The Experience of Activity' (1905; James 1976: 79–95).

[100] James (1981: 234). See also his comment on Zeno's treatment of motion (James 1981: 237), which is reminiscent of Bergson's subsequent treatment of those paradoxes (Bergson 1911b: 250 ff.). For an early statement, just prior to James's *Principles*, see also Bergson (1910: 112 ff.).

certainly isn't in terms of the theory itself).[101] This perhaps partly explains why, for all the initial excitement over Bergson, and for all the eloquence of the writing, he has subsequently been largely neglected. Nevertheless, as a flagged alternative, it is worth considering, if only for the light that it casts on other, better-worked-out epistemic strategies.

Bergson distinguishes between two kinds of knowledge, corresponding to two ways of knowing something:

> The first implies going all around it, the second entering into it. The first depends on the viewpoint chosen and the symbols employed, while the second is taken from no viewpoint and rests on no symbol. Of the first kind of knowledge we shall say that it stops at the *relative*; of the second that, wherever possible, it attains the *absolute*. (Bergson 1992a: 159)

In the second kind of knowledge we do not know the object in question from without, from an external point of view, sideways on. Rather we 'enter into it', and become identical with it. Although it is far from clear what this means, it is clear why this knowledge is taken to be absolute, rather than relative: there can be many different perspectives on one and the same object, but there is only one way of being identical with it. Moreover, this absolute knowledge is immediate, whereas knowledge from an external point of view will be mediated, will involve some representation of it, which presupposes a representational medium—a level of interpreted symbols, language. 'A representation taken from a certain point of view, a translation made with certain symbols still remain imperfect in comparison with the object whose picture has been taken or which the symbols seek to express' (1992a: 161). A form of knowledge that, by contrast, dispenses both with perspective and with representation closes off the source of a distinction between how things seem ('from here', or 'in these terms') and how they are. (On this view, it is a mistake to think of absolute knowledge of reality in terms of a thoroughly detached *absolute conception* of it, as if from a God's-eye viewpoint. The very phrase 'absolute conception' should be recognized as oxymoronic.)

The idea is that scientific knowledge is of the first sort, that which necessarily deals with concepts, representations, interpretations of symbols, and so is only relative. The second kind, which is what philosophers were traditionally after, can occur only when we have transcended all language, all conceptualization, all representation and translation, and reached direct identification with the object of our knowledge. 'Metaphysics is therefore the science which claims to dispense with symbols' (Bergson 1992a: 162). As such it yields

---

[101] For an interesting sympathetic comment on the way in which Bergson licenses silence rather than attempting to grapple with questions conceptually, see James (1909b, lecture vii, pp. 290–1).

absolute, non-perspectival metaphysical knowledge of reality. Here there is no distance left between representer and represented.

The two ways of knowing that sustain these two kinds of knowledge are identified as *analysis* and *intuition*. Analysis deals with symbols, so many sideways-on representational takes, in relation to which the object of knowledge becomes 'the piece of gold for which one can never make up the change'.[102] Intuition, which remains when we have transcended all such symbolic representation, and which enables us 'to enter into' the object, rather than skirting interminably around it, is unfortunately not defined in further non-metaphorical terms, except negatively, as that which does not involve conceptual representation or analysis.[103]

Now it is relatively straightforward to see how intuition might be a way of knowing the self, given that here the relation of identity between knower and known is trivially satisfied. Moreover, the application of the intuitive model in this case is viable even without making any special assumptions about the nature of the self, and in particular without rejecting psychological atomism. The now well-known problems about self-conscious self-identification can seem to indicate that the root of the problem lies in trying to provide a representational model of such identification. Sideways-on representations are such as will always leave a gap between the representational content, however rich, and the intended referent, the self.[104] The result is the elusiveness of the thinking subject, which always seems in danger of slipping out of the representational net. The problem can seem to result from trying to explain self-conscious self-identification on the wrong model: on the model of perception, using representations, rather than relying on the unmediated awareness of one's own actions. Such awareness simply *presents* us with the thinking subject *in the very act* of thinking or doing something, 'from within', and dispenses altogether with resort to sideways-on *representations* of it. To this extent it can seem to fall in with what Bergson regards as an intuitive grasp of the self.

But Bergson considers that intuition yields a much richer service to our knowledge of the self than just this. Intuition constitutes a form of epistemic access that delivers a radical alternative to the atomist construal of the self. Knowledge by analysis, using concepts, results in a study of the self 'in its passivity',[105] as an object to which a particular conceptual taxonomy is applied from a particular point of view. The result is the recognition of so many clearly individuated perceptions and mental events—the very taxonomy that constitutes the kind of atomism, generally speaking, that both Kant and the empiricists share. By contrast, unconceptualized from without, the unmediated simple

---

[102] 1992*a*: 161.
[103] See e.g. 1992*a*: 161–2. See also 'Philosophical Intuition' (Bergson 1992*b*).
[104] This is brought out particularly clearly, for example, in Perry (1993).
[105] 1992*a*: 163.

intuition of the self by itself[106] presents us with the continuous flow of consciousness which is ever changing and in which discrete states can be individuated only retrospectively, by a process of analysis. Intuition, then, circumvents representation and its consequent atomist model of the mind, to deliver precisely James's model of an organically unified stream of consciousness.

While James puts significant effort into a rich and detailed phenomenological description of that stream of consciousness by way of giving the lie to atomism, Bergson is more concerned with the direct contrast between two epistemic routes and their respective yields. When it comes to knowledge of the self we can make sense of there being two ways of coming to know it, from without and from within, corresponding to the methods of analysis and of intuition. And Bergson is clear that, of the two, intuition is the more basic, and delivers undistorted the reality underlying the various conceptualizations of thought. This follows immediately from his assertion that symbolic representations are always perspectival, such that alternatives to them are possible, whereas intuition transcends all perspective to deliver the object of knowledge as it is in itself. But he is concerned to make more of a case. The claim is that the psychological atomists take as proper parts of consciousness what are in fact only theoretical constructs. The clear-cut, distinct, and discrete perceptions are produced by analysis, they are the product of a certain conceptual taxonomy that is applied to the stream of consciousness—these products are in fact mere abstractions from the subjective stream of contents. As abstractions they are important, since without them the science of psychology would not be able to get off the ground.[107] But they remain theoretical constructs, abstractions from a given unity, and are only mistakenly regarded by atomists as proper parts out of which the unity of our stream of consciousness is constructed, or into which it could be disintegrated.[108]

Once this is allowed it is indeed clear that intuition and the model of thought to which it leads must be more basic. The unified stream of consciousness will allow for certain abstractions to be derived from it, by analysis, but there is no room for going the other way. The atomist taxonomy can carve up the underlying reality, resulting in what James described as merely 'pailsful, spoonsful, quartpotsful... and other moulded forms of water', but there is no way that, starting from those as our building-blocks, we might hope to do justice to the real flow of the river from which they are abstracted. Both traditional empiricists and Kant, then, are 'dupes of the same illusion', attempting to derive the continuity of our mental life from what are in fact themselves derivations from it.[109] In Bergson's own similar metaphors, the atomist's discrete states are merely the clear-cut crystals of some superficial

---

[106] 1992a: 169, 176. [107] 1992a: 170. [108] 1992a: 169–72. [109] 1992a: 172–5.

congelation or encrustment:[110] 'the sounding made on the sea floor brings up a fluid mass which the sun very quickly dries into solid and discontinuous grains of sand'.[111] These, for Bergson, remain of vital practical importance, but the point for now is that they can be regarded only as derivative from that underlying reality from which they are abstracted.

Bergson, then, like James, concludes that the self can have knowledge of itself as an enduring organic unity. There is no plurality of atoms that needs to be unified, and so no need for unifying acts of judgement or appeal to an independently existing object-world. It does not matter for present purposes that Bergson offers relatively little apart from storytelling and persuasive analogy by way of substantiating his case for the kind of intuitive knowledge that he takes to be available of the self as an organic whole. It is enough that he vividly portrays the alternative. To this extent Bergson, like James, seems to have provided the sceptic with the outline of a model of the mind the mere possibility of which derails any strictly Kantian argument from the unity of consciousness to the unity of an objective world. We are back with the possibility of having self-contained knowledge of our own minds, and of nothing else.

It should be noted that, apart from the rejection of atomism, Bergson's distinction between two kinds of knowledge suggests even more clearly than James did that, with atomism rejected, self-consciousness over time should not be thought of as involving the application of concepts, i.e. judgement, at all. The Kantian, of course, would object that this cannot be right, since, without concept application, there would be no way of experiencing something *as something*, as being an experience of one sort as opposed to another.[112] And to this extent we might think that Bergson's knowledge by pure intuition cannot be viable. However, as we have seen, this criticism results from being too firmly in the grip of the two-faculty model Bergson and James are opposing. They resist the idea that experiencing something as *red* rather than *round*, for example, necessarily involves conceptual operations of the understanding. There is no reason to think that conceptualization forces a distinct faculty of judgement and, consequently, perceptual atomism. And the minimal conceptualization in question—if indeed conceptualization it is—does not *on its own* seem to be such as would sustain a refutation of solipsism, particularly given the doubts about the Metaphysical Deduction of the Categories. There is no reason to think that such minimally construed conceptualization would imply a fixed set of world-constituting categories with which we will all be forced to comply.

---

[110] 1992a: 163.

[111] This is quoted slightly out of context, since Bergson is not talking here solely about the stream of consciousness (1992a: 193).   [112] See pp. 77ff. above.

The prospect of methodological solipsism, and scepticism about the external world, is one that Bergson himself raises:

> But if metaphysics is to proceed by intuition, if intuition has as its object the mobility of duration, and if duration is psychological in essence, are we not going to shut the philosopher up in exclusive self-contemplation? Will not philosophy consist simply in watching oneself live, 'as a dozing shepherd watches the running water'?[113]

Now we have seen that James was basically removed from the Cartesian epistemological orientation, and was satisfied to resort to pragmatism in response to questions of what has existence that transcends the stream of consciousness. Bergson differs in this latter respect from James, in that he is specifically concerned to establish absolute metaphysical knowledge of reality, although as the following, which is said in response to the question of the dozing shepherd, indicates, it would equally be a distortion to saddle him with a Cartesian epistemic agenda:

> To speak in this fashion would be to return to the error I have not ceased to emphasize from the very beginning of this study. It would be to fail to recognize the particular nature of duration and at the same time the essentially active character of metaphysical intuition. It would be to fail to see that only the method of which we are speaking allows one to pass beyond idealism as well as realism . . .[114]

In Bergson's view, intuition, the grasp of something from within, coinciding thereby with what it is in itself, and so producing absolute knowledge of it rather than perspectival representations from without, is available not only for the self, but for reality as a whole. To this extent, the reliance on intuition, far from creating an epistemic predicament, is thought to be the fundamental resolution of one: intuition is what enables us to have absolute knowledge of reality as it is in itself.

Getting a clearer view of what is involved here is not straightforward. Whereas we could with reasonable ease conceive of the grasp of ourselves from within, since we simply are identical with ourselves, it is more difficult to follow Bergson in thinking that the same kind of knowledge is available for objects other than ourselves. One might think that here we have to resort to a metaphorical understanding of intuition—that is, understanding *as if* from within (or, to put it differently, *identifying* with the object even though not *identical* with it). And indeed Bergson does talk of intuition as 'the *sympathy* by which one is transported into the interior of an object in order to coincide with what there is unique and consequently inexpressible in it'.[115] This would clearly be a significant weakening of the alternative epistemic route he has in mind, since identifying sympathetically with something so as to see it as if from within

---

[113] 1992*a*: 184.   [114] Ibid.   [115] 1992*a*: 161; his italics.

itself remains a perspectival representation for all that it attempts to downplay its perspectival coloration. It might, therefore, be more charitable to consider that in such passages Bergson is, from his point of view, speaking with the vulgar. He seems here to accept an alignment of first-person intuition with the Cartesian dualist conception of the subject (over here) that then needs to extend that intuition to the rest of reality (over there). Covering the gap is what forces resort to 'sympathetic identification with', instead of straightforward 'identity with'.

Bergson's considered view is clearly that that Cartesian dichotomy, which also seems responsible for facing us with the choice between idealism and realism, is itself only a particular representation (a static encrustation) that should not be taken as metaphysically basic, and one that his own method tries to get behind. He advocates a conception of the underlying reality as a single process of what he calls pure duration, which is said to be an undifferentiated process of change, or mobility, containing no divisions and which as such is resistant to law and measurement.[116] We can again leave aside for now that it is not at all clear what this amounts to. (Note that Bergson would be the first to admit that in so far as it has no determinate structure, we cannot have an adequate articulation of it in representation. That is precisely what he contends anyway.) The point for now is that if *this* is what is known by intuition, then there is no room left to think, as there is on the Cartesian conception, that strictly speaking what is thereby grasped from the inside is only one part of reality. Intuition no longer presents itself as a way of delving deep into *myself*, as if that could be hived off from the rest of reality as one particular locus with which I am identical. There are no such fundamental boundaries. Hence what is grasped in the process of intuition, what is entered into, far from being merely myself, can be nothing short of reality itself. It is in this way, then, that intuition, in the absence of a Cartesian construal of what is intuited, is thought to deliver not the threat of solipsism, indeed, but absolute knowledge of reality as it is in itself. And since the reality in question is devoid of any Cartesian dichotomy, it is clear that the position in question would be neither idealist nor realist: what is known cannot be classified either as purely mental, or as material.[117]

---

[116] 1992*b*: 124.

[117] It should be noted that there is some tension between this position and Bergson's contention (particularly in *Creative Evolution*; Bergson 1911a) that there is a distinction between the spiritual (the living) and mere inorganic matter. Even within *Creative Evolution*, however, Bergson still affirms that the whole is of the same nature as the self, such that in knowing the latter fully one also comes to know the world itself. One obvious way of resolving the tension is to hold that this taxonomy is not meant to be regarded as metaphysically basic, and is operative only when the world is already conceptualized as a domain of study by one of the sciences. (On this, see Lacey 1989: 171–2 and *passim*.) But the viability of this need not detain us here, where the concern is not with the consistency of all parts of Bergson's thought.

So far by way of a charitable description of Bergson's basic metaphysical picture. Although not strictly necessary for present purposes, it is worth pausing to note two further points. Both concern the relation between ordinary and metaphysical knowledge.

The ordinary conception of the world as consisting of discrete things, external to one another, each with its own spatio-temporal locus, such that the thinker—located in one corner of the vast expanse—can know from the inside only one such locus: that conception, in Bergson's view, results from a pulverization[118] of the underlying reality by our own sensibility and understanding.[119] The Kantian resonance here is important. The measurable spatio-temporal world comprising discrete objects is not taken as ontologically basic, as Cartesian extension, but as a construction implemented by our faculties. This leaves room to address what goes on beneath the level of that construction. And it is this 'space' that Bergson utilizes. It means that rather than choosing between the two conceptions, he can set them up as at different levels. There is the level of empirical realism, on which Kant and Bergson might well have agreed in essence: it is a world as we construct it, in conformity with our representational capacities, and as such it does not deliver the world as it is in itself. But whereas Kant conjoins empirical realism with transcendental idealism—which involves a claim that we cannot get beyond empirical reality to know the world as it is in itself—Bergson by contrast conjoins a form of empirical realism with what Kant would regard as transcendental realism—the claim that we can in addition have absolute knowledge of reality as it is in itself. Bergsonian intuition can get behind empirical appearances constructed by our representational faculties.

The explanation for this difference between Kant and Bergson is not that Bergson introduces the notion of purely intuitive knowledge—after all, Kant too allows that the alternative mode of knowledge, which would give us access to the world as it is in itself, is a mode of intuition. The difference resides rather in the fact that Bergson thinks we can *employ* such intuition, whereas Kant considers 'intellectual intuition' to be available only to God, or to any being with different faculties, whose experience is not bound up with sensible contents.[120] The reason for this difference is that, for Kant, the intuitive knowledge in question would require, as Bergson puts it, 'transport[ing] ourselves outside the domain of the senses and of consciousness'.[121] That

---

[118] The metaphor of reducing some living whole to so much dust, grains of sand, dry crystals, is one that Bergson, like James, uses repeatedly; in the present context, see Bergson (1992b: 126).

[119] 1992b: 124–8.

[120] See Kant, *Critique*, B307–9, B71–2, B145–6. See also, in connection with what follows, B314–15. There is no reason to think that Bergson's notion of philosophical intuition is the same as Kant's notion of intellectual intuition, but it does not seem worth pursuing the details. Even if they had the same notion in mind, Kant would not have thought we could employ it.

[121] 1992b: 127–8.

James and Bergson

transcendence (impossible for us) would be required because, within that domain, in so far as intuition is subject to the conditions of human experience, it is always a partly passive epistemic encounter with discrete particulars, which are either internal to the mind or external to it. By contrast, once we have in play Bergson's notion of reality in itself as 'pure duration', as 'indivisible mobility', then there is no such restriction on sensible intuition. We then supposedly have scope within the domain of the senses for 'an indivisible apprehension'[122] with no distance to be covered between knower and known, no encounter with particulars, and no distinction between an intuition of our merely internal contents and intuition of external reality as it is in itself. In this way Bergson thinks that it is only because Kant operated with only one notion of time and change—the dust to which our consciousness has reduced the mobile reality[123]—and did not recognize the availability of this other notion, that he was not able to see how intuition *in us* could deliver absolute knowledge of reality. 'A vision of this kind, where reality appears as continuous and indivisible, is on the road which leads to philosophical intuition.'[124]

Bergson's general strategy here, of reaching behind empirical appearances to absolute knowledge of reality, is, of course, familiar from rationalist philosophy. The similarity is of interest, given that Bergson uses the strategy to offer a clear subversion of rationalism. Rationalist philosophers (from Plato, through Descartes, to Leibniz) typically assume that by relying on innate ideas we can get beyond the merely phenomenal world of the senses. It is, of course, that extension of knowledge that Kant was concerned to deny. Now Bergson too holds that the mind can have access to the reality behind the veil of empirical appearance—only in his view not by way of relying on innate ideas that take leave of the senses to approach a timeless reality, but by precisely rejecting reliance on concepts and ideas altogether, clearing the way for a non-intellectual grasp of the contents given to consciousness in all their immediacy and transience.[125]

---

[122] 1992*a*: 161.   [123] 1992*b*: 128.

[124] 1992*b*: 127. The idea is that intuition delivers knowledge of reality as pure duration, and that in fact it is only in so far as reality is that way that we could have knowledge of it by means of intuition at all. There is no vicious circularity here. The problem is rather that it remains quite unclear what pure duration is, and whether intuition delivers anything of the sort.

[125] This anti-rationalist inversion comes to the fore in a particularly poignant way in various comments that effect implicit inversions of Plato's Analogy of the Cave. Thus Bergson says that through concepts (= ideas, representations) all one can *ever* grasp are mere shadows of reality (1992*a*: 167), that what is got by the scientific viewpoint on the world is nothing more than the play of shadows on the wall (1992*a*: 173); and whereas for Plato emergence from the cave into the clear sunlight offers the paradigm of veridical conceptual grasp, Bergson talks of the fluid mass of reality 'which the sun very quickly dries into solid and discontinuous grains of sand', thereby abstracting fixed, distinct, and immobile concepts from, and so serving only to distort, the intuition of duration (1992*a*: 193).

Now while Bergson does hold that absolute or metaphysical knowledge can be had only by intuition, and that reality can only be falsified by conceptual representation, it would be wrong to think that he—any more than Leibniz—thought that knowledge by means of empirical representations is without value. It remains pragmatically necessary. Without it science, and generally our practical needs and interests in the world, would not be served. Philosophical knowledge, by intuition, is absolute but essentially inarticulate and devoid of practical use; scientific knowledge, by conceptual representation, is therefore all the more important in our coping with the world. The mistake is only to think of it as absolute, or even as disinterested knowledge. Here Bergson anticipates the irreverent attitude towards science that became more widespread in the second half of the 20th century. Scientific explanation, far from being an impartial view from nowhere, is inherently interest-relative and perspectival. It is our interests and particular needs that determine those features of reality that are salient for us, those that we give dominance to and select for in our representational taxonomies. And it is that world, so cut up by our interest-relative taxonomies, that science proceeds to investigate. In that sense, at least, science is indexed to our interests, investigates the world relative to those interests, and so is assured its pragmatic value. The mistake, then, is not in relying on science, but in relying on it to produce knowledge of the world as it is. Being based on representations, which are essentially always only perspectival abstractions, it could not hope to do that.

It is helpful here to contrast Bergson with Kant again. For Kant, too, scientific explanation, which is essentially all that immanent metaphysics accommodates, i.e. the investigation of empirical reality, is perspectival rather than absolute. It is after all indexed to a particular set of representational capacities (namely, ours) which result in a perspectival construal of the world, and it is only to that construction of reality that science answers. But saying that scientific knowledge is perspectival rather than absolute is not yet to say that it is interest-relative in Bergson's sense. It might be interest-relative, but only in the sense of being relative to human interests as such. In so far as Kant takes the representational faculties in play to be transcendentally determined, there is one fixed construal of the world, such that, however perspectival it might be, it is a perspective that all humans of necessity share. It is that which imparts to empirical reality, and to the scientific investigation of it, intersubjective universality. Bergson, however, does not accept any such fixed essential representational faculties. In the absence of transcendental constraints, there is room for different interest routes through the world, sustaining different representational taxonomies, and so different scientific explanations. This brings out more clearly the difference between the empirical realism both Kant and Bergson take our representational capacities to sustain. For Kant there is only one such empirical reality, transcendentally determined; for Bergson there can be many empirical realities, determined by contingent interest-relative representational taxonomies.[126]

It is in this connection that we can understand Bergson's repeated diagnosis of the problem of diametrically opposed philosophical systems and schools of thought. These result from different interests giving salience to different conceptual abstractions from the world, with the result that when these different representational takes are put together, the world reconstituted by each of these systems of thought is different. Each construct expresses different interests and points of engagement. The mistake is in not noticing this, and proceeding as if the conflict is one that needs to be adjudicated, and one that can be, as if any of these might turn out to embody the truth about the world as it is in itself. More specifically the mistake comes in that they are all inappropriately employing a representational method of knowledge, which is inherently interest-relative and should only ever serve for pragmatic purposes. The corrective is to see aright the value, and the proper limits, of representational knowledge, and so come to understand that securing absolute knowledge of reality, of the sort that philosophers are after, requires a different form of knowledge rather than the futile misappropriation of the scientific model.[127]

In view of this we can understand why Bergson claims that in the absence of his proposed alternative, knowledge by intuition, we are in fact denied anything that can count as philosophical knowledge. All we are then left with is pragmatic knowledge of the sort that science can provide.[128] The latter, which Bergson considers insufficient in relation to his agenda, is all that James wants by way of securing our knowledge of the world. This brings out clearly the difference between James's pragmatist orientation and Bergson's more traditional epistemic aims.

Returning now to the main thread of the discussion: However appealing Bergson's strategy might be, it is unlikely that we will take on the full Bergsonian metaphysic. In part because it is not clear that it is coherent, in part because it does not seem constructive. The incoherence threatens in the fact that for intuition to deliver absolute knowledge of reality (and not just of the self), the duration intuited must, as we have seen, be such as is prior to any significant subject–object dualism; but if that is so, then it is not clear that we are left with anyone to do the intuiting, or with any conception of

---

[126] This aspect of Bergson, reminiscent of James, has clear affinities with the later Wittgenstein's emphasis on the way in which ontological taxonomy is bound up with our involvement in contingent practices, such that ontological prominence is afforded to those features which our practices render more salient. Different practices, different construals of reality.

[127] In relation to the points made in this paragraph, see e.g. Bergson (1992a: 168, 178, 189 (iv), 198–9).

[128] Thus, 'Either there is no philosophy possible and all knowledge of things is a practical knowledge turned to the profit to be gained from them, or philosophizing consists in placing oneself within the object itself by an effort of intuition' (Bergson 1992a: 178).

there being someone (the subject) who has any epistemic ground to cover.[129] And intuition of reality had better not collapse into simple self-identity of reality with itself. Questions of coherence aside, the intuitive knowledge of reality is in principle such as cannot result in representations. It remains inarticulate, mystical, and so seems beyond intersubjective agreement or indeed any detectable convergence. An absolute grasp of reality which is such as cannot allow for a distinction between what seems right and what is right is not likely to offer much satisfaction to the epistemically critical, however much they might welcome the deflationary effect on the pretensions of science.

Bergson is not, it seems, insensitive to this point. Thus he several times insists that his concern is to point out that only intuition delivers genuine knowledge of reality in a way that reliance on conceptual knowledge cannot, but that that is not to say that knowledge by intuition cannot subsequently avail itself of conceptual activity. This is so both because science employs concepts, and metaphysical knowledge cannot be divorced from the sciences, and also—which is the relevant point here—because while intuition is needed for the original grasp of reality, what is grasped then gets unpacked, articulated, using concepts in the employment of knowledge by analysis.[130] But it seems clear that no appeal to concepts, to knowledge by analysis, can answer the worry about the radical inarticulacy of intuitive 'insight'. By Bergson's own insistence, to the extent that what is intuited is brought to the surface, is analysed, it is already after all falsified.[131]

So what if, as is overwhelmingly likely, we do not accept the full Bergsonian metaphysic as outlined? It seems clear that we might well withdraw from the more extravagant claims regarding intuition affording exhaustive knowledge of reality as it is in itself. We might, however, still allow some plausibility to the contention that we can each know ourselves from within, with non-representational immediacy. It is in application to the self and the unity of consciousness that Bergson's notions of intuition and duration are at their most plausible, and in relation to which his criticism of the atomism of empiricists and rationalists seems to have some force.[132] Moreover, to the extent that it is only in this use that we take on the appeal to immediate, non-representational knowledge, the problem that such knowledge remains inarticulate is no longer

---

[129] Bergson clearly says that 'There is at least one reality which we all seize from within, by intuition and not by simple analysis. It is our own person in its flowing through time, the self which endures' (1992a: 162). But it is not clear how that is compatible with the assumption that what is grasped in intuition bears no demarcation between the self and the rest of reality.

[130] See Bergson (1992a: 199). For the previous point, see 1992a: 168.

[131] It is interesting to compare here the use at 1992a: 199 of the metaphor of intuition as a way of plumbing the seabed with that made of the same metaphor at 1992a: 193.

[132] See e.g. (1992a: 162–76). The debt to James's description of the stream of consciousness is particularly salient here, both in content and in terminology. For reasons indicated above, Bergson does not always distinguish clearly between intuition and duration applied to self-knowledge, and to knowledge of reality *tout court*.

relevant. The inarticulacy no longer matters because Bergsonian 'intuition' of our own duration is no longer needed to serve any descriptive role: it suffices to establish the unity of consciousness over time, and knowledge of it, however inarticulately. Should we wish for a description of it, we can appeal to conceptual representation, forewarned of the distortion that results—in particular, aware that any resulting fragmentation is only at the level of representations, and should not be confused for ground-level fragmentation of consciousness that is in need of unification from without.

To this extent, as in the case of James, we are again left with a model of the mind the unity of which, and knowledge of the unity of which, does not require the sort of reliance on an external world that sustains the Kantian refutation of idealism. From both James and Bergson we come away with the possibility of that alternative model of the mind, as an internally unified organic whole, regardless of whether we share their particular reasons for disengagement from the Cartesian epistemic structure (pragmatist reasons in James, metaphysical ones in Bergson). But with that model of the mind introduced into the traditional epistemic structure, the Kantian linkage between the unity of subjectivity and the unity of an objective world no longer obtains.

The discussion so far has taken something of the form of a selective historical survey. We have seen how different philosophical models of the mind have wider ramifications, in particular concerning the possibility and nature of our knowledge of an independent world. We should accept, then, that models of the mind should be assessed not only in terms of their internal adequacy, but also in terms of their wider philosophical ramifications, their fit within a comprehensive theory. We have so far not found a model that, when so assessed, is not seen to carry an epistemic cost. And the question arises whether an adequate comprehensive philosophical theory should commence from a model of the mind at all.

That is, a presupposition of the discussion so far was that there is a well-defined self-contained subject, set over against the rest of the world, such that knowledge involves crossing an epistemic divide between the two. With that assumption in place, it makes sense to think that securing epistemic success involves first finding the optimal model of the subject (with the result that the former is a further test for the latter). But the question is whether the assumption of a gulf, which philosophers from Descartes to Kant sought to bridge, between the subject at home with its own thoughts and the rest of the world was not simply an unfortunate theoretical move to begin with—a rash bit of epistemology, and an unthinking assumption about the mind, which mutually sustained one another despite there being no good theoretical reason for either. We have noted, and so far resisted, the pressure under which this traditional epistemic structure comes from both James and Bergson, for very different reasons, as early as the turn of the century. In recent years this structure, and in particular the associated conception of the Cartesian individual, has been widely attacked from both directions—epistemology and philosophy of mind. It will be appropriate, then, at this point, to leave aside the traditional assumption underlying the discussion so far, and consider how things look when we do not take the Cartesian agenda as our starting-point.

II

World-Driven Scepticism

WORLD-OTHER SCEPTICISM

4

From the Egological Subject to the Domestication of Reason

MUCH of philosophy in the past sixty years has been directed at, or has at least resulted in, questioning the traditional assumption of an epistemologically significant breach between subject and object. This raises the issue of the epistemic impact of this move. It might have been thought that in the absence of that assumption, with the subject regarded as perfectly at home in the world, epistemology would no longer be faced with sceptical worries, which might well have been the point of rejecting the traditional assumption. The three chapters comprising this part of the book make a case for thinking that no such simple deliverance ensues.

It would be a mistake to think that rejecting the traditional assumption simply and incisively releases us from the related epistemological agenda. The orientation that brings about the blurring of that Cartesian dichotomy has been intimately bound up with other commitments, such as the withdrawal from metaphysics. And the combination of naturalism and the dissolution of the Cartesian chasm do not add up to an end to our epistemic troubles. As we will see, the new orientation ushers in its own acute problems: in particular regarding the scope and legitimacy of fundamental normative structures. In both cases, despite coming from different directions, the result is a strikingly similar threat to objectivity.[1] It seems that we escape the clutches of one form of sceptical worry (subject-driven) only by falling into those of another (world-driven)—and in the latter case, in fact, indifference to the problems may be far less easy.[2]

---

[1] As we will see later (Part III), this is because of the common conception of objectivity underlying both.

[2] I note that this shift, after the demise of the traditional epistemological agenda, from subject-driven to world-driven scepticism has recently been put succinctly by Taylor (1999: 158–9), albeit not in just these terms. His suggested response to this problem is, however, unsatisfactory for reasons that will emerge below (see Ch. 8 n. 52).

1. THE EGOLOGICAL CONCEPTION OF THE SUBJECT

We begin by noting how the new orientation stands in relation to what I will refer to as the egological conception of the subject (or self). The egological conception regards the subject as one whose core normative structures are autonomous—independent of contextual features—and so attributes rational autonomy to the subject. An egological conception, as I shall be using the term, is meant to be distinct, at least in definition, from what is referred to as Cartesian individualism. Unlike Cartesian individualism, which is specifically a semantic thesis to the effect that the individual's meanings do not presuppose for their individuation the existence of any thing in the external world other than that individual, the egological conception is concerned rather with the nature of the subject that employs semantics. (The relation between Cartesian individualism and the egological conception will emerge in due course.)

There is little room to doubt that philosophers working on the traditional assumption by and large endorsed this notion of an egological subject. This is not to say that their ready endorsement of it was not problematic. The main considerations that militate against that conception apply even in that context. Nevertheless, the demise of the traditional assumption was bound to leave the conception of an egological subject more exposed to scrutiny than it had been as part of the traditional package. And in the context of thoroughgoing naturalism that scrutiny is of increased significance. As we will see, without the withdrawal from metaphysics to naturalism, the demise of the egological subject would not be of such consequence; but equally, without the demise of the egological subject, naturalism would not carry that significance. The issue, to put it briefly, concerns the status of reason and normative structure generally. On at least one conception of reason, that according to which it is the core normative furnishing of the autonomous individual, any attack on the egological subject threatens to constitute an attack on the objectivity of reason. It is to this that I turn in the present chapter.

The threat to the egological subject, and thereby to the conception of reason traditionally associated with it, is an appropriate starting place in part because it has arisen independently in recent years across disparate philosophical traditions, in different ways, and to different effects. To this extent it bears witness to the general scope that we might expect of world-driven scepticism in what follows. But the threat to the egological conception of the subject is particularly relevant in the case of the analytic tradition, and as such deserves separate emphasis: it arises squarely from recent developments central to that tradition, and yet threatens to undermine one of the key assumptions of the tradition. It seems to me not only descriptively true, but also unsurprising—

given the general realist and logicist orientation of the early analytic tradition —that this egological view of the subject served as the default within analytic philosophy.

The egological conception is conducive to a realist or objectivist view. This is so in two senses. First, such a view of the self is conducive to a sharp dichotomy between the self and everything other than it, which is then set apart as an independent object domain. I will not make much of this in what follows, but it is worth noting that this is not to say that the egological conception *entails* the traditional assumption, although it does underscore a natural affinity between them. That affinity would suffice to explain their common co-occurrence in the history of philosophy. Secondly, and this is the primary concern here, such a view of the self is conducive to the expectation of convergence on what counts as rational thought, what counts as a good reason, or as an end worth pursuing. The link between an egological self and there being objective rules for the direction of the mind is obviously not one of entailment (pluralist individualism is a possibility). Nor is it the case that not adhering to such an egological conception of the self would imply the absence of any such convergence (as we will see with reference to Hegel below). The link is simply that to accept this conception is to render the subject independent of environmental features, such that the individual can be stripped of all contextual coloration to reveal what it essentially is: and where that is possible, there is room for the hope that, so stripped, all normal human minds would be seen to be functioning identically, to be running the same programs, so to speak.

Now it will readily be recognized that such a self is at the heart of Enlightenment philosophy. And it is of particular relevance that the Kantian Copernican Revolution relies heavily on just this assumption of an egological subject. On the Kantian view, at the level of the fundamental faculties of the mind, any individuals, just in so far as they are human and are functioning properly, will function in the same way. This conception could be preserved as a more or less unattended default within the analytic tradition, in part precisely because that tradition was not deeply involved in questioning the basis of Kant's transcendental idealism, or much concerned (in part because of this lack of involvement) with a reflexive turn to the nature of the self. Even when that tradition did turn to the problems with Cartesian individualism, the issue of the egological subject was not so salient as to lead to general recognition of the impact of those developments upon it.[3]

---

[3] It is, of course, precisely in so far as it retained the default assignment of the egological self that the analytic tradition can, in this respect, look naïve or undeveloped from the perspective of other traditions that did not shy away from discussion of the subject in the same way. This is perhaps particularly so from the perspective of that tradition in German philosophy concerned with the critique of reason, for which the question of the appropriate philosophical conception of the subject was, since Kant, consistently at the centre of philosophical concern. The fact that between these two traditions there is today room to detect convergence on matters relating to the topic of the subject is therefore all the more interesting.

2. THE REJECTION OF THE EGOLOGICAL CONCEPTION OF THE SUBJECT

Beyond the confines of the analytic tradition there has been a lively and sustained interest in, and criticism of, this egological conception of the subject.[4] This concern has, however, been particularly central in recent German philosophy—in part, no doubt, because of an abiding interest in transcendental idealism, and in the status of Kant's critique of reason. It is not necessary to go into the details of this long history here.[5] The attack on the Cartesian–Kantian conception of the self came in various forms, two of which have been helpfully identified recently by Wellmer and Honneth.[6] The attack could be directed at the kind of psychological transparency that that conception readily assumed the mind's workings to have, and which formed the basis for a central notion of moral autonomy. An attack on this conception came from the direction of thinkers from Nietzsche to Freud, who identified forces at work within the individual which were essentially unconscious and beyond the control of the subject. This line of approach is of less concern in the present context, given that what is at issue is the egological conception of the subject's cognitive capacities, whether these are transparent to the subject itself or not. The interest here is not in the critique of the subject based on internal psychological considerations, but in the philosophical assumption that the explanation of the subject's basic normative structures can proceed in essentially individualistic or egological terms; or, to put it in terms that already anticipate a converging development within the analytic tradition, the assumption that the unit of explanation is the individual taken on its own.[7] (The latter is, more or less, the second line of attack that Wellmer and Honneth identify.)

The result of this critique of the traditional egological conception of the subject has been a perceived need to reject that conception. There is—across much of what is called 'continental' philosophy—a widespread admission that the traditional egological model of the subject is now defunct. Thus Honneth, for example, can talk of the conclusion being *'largely accepted* in philosophy today' that the classical notion of subjectivity is destroyed.[8] These 'self-evident' conclusions,[9] the result of the 'century-long' reflexive attention to the subject, are not at all *self-evident* within, and are in marked contrast to, dominant working assumptions made within the analytic tradition, in which the egological subject survived more or less intact by escaping critical attention.

---

[4] The critique of the Enlightenment subject in recent continental philosophy perhaps owes most to Foucault. See, in particular, Foucault (1970, 1972).

[5] For a partisan introduction to this history of the theory of the subject, see Henrich (1992).

[6] See Wellmer (1991); Honneth (1995a: 261–3).   [7] Burge (1982: 116–18).

[8] Honneth (1995a: 262); my italics.   [9] Ibid.

The Egological Subject

In consequence, from the point of view of the analytic tradition, some of the questions into which other philosophy has been led after 'the fall of the subject' have seemed rather alien. As indicated, we will shortly see that in fact the agenda facing the analytic tradition today is not that different. But it will be helpful first to say a bit more about the course that the critique of the egological self has taken.

Perhaps the most prominent alternative to the traditional egological model of the self derives from Hegel, and can be thought of as dialogical or sociological. The self emerges, as does the reflexive consciousness of its identity, only within a social context of intersubjective recognition; the encounter and interaction with others structures the identity of the subject and guides self-consciousness of it. This Hegelian dialogical model runs counter to the Enlightenment ideals for which the egological model was so well suited. After all, on the Enlightenment view, it is the naked individual, stripped of all features and standards that depend on sociocultural context, who can stand back and assess the order of things, and can do so as any other free-thinking agent would. On the dialogical model there *is* no such naked, core individual such as could step back from all sociocultural structuring as a free thinker. That conception turns out, ironically, to have been an unnoticed fictional construct at the heart of the Enlightenment project; stripping away all cultural and historical layers does not reveal any naked kernel of the subject, or at best reveals only a brute animal subjectivity that does not have the content with which to engage in any substantive thought or judgement.[10] But while this much is true, it is not the case that this Hegelian model also counts against the objectivity of reason and convergence of rational conduct that was encouraged by the egological model. The reason for this is that the objective structure of thought, on at least one reading of Hegel, has simply been displaced: there is still a blueprint that imposes constraints on rational thinking, a program for the direction of the mind, only now, rather than being individualistic and context-independent, it is rooted in the socio-historical space across which individuals range. It is because of this that while the individual cannot abstract himself from socio-historical context and still lay claim to being a rationally guided thinker, nevertheless, *qua* embedded subject, the individual is indeed subject to the very same constraints on rational thought that apply to all others in that context. Moreover, since for Hegel (again on at least one reading of him) the logic that drives intersubjective recognition also drives the transition between historical states, there is no ultimately contingent historicity, such that the convergence between what count as rational thinkers is always only internal to one socio-historical context or another, leaving others in other contexts to their own devices. To the extent that all are subject to the same

---

[10] I will return to this distinction shortly.

unchanging blueprint (that unchanging structure that governs all change), across contexts individuals can expect to converge at the end of the day: either in discussion by recognizing the socio-historical context each is at, and what is appropriate at that stage; or in fact by having reached, finally, the same socio-historical stage of development.

So the Hegelian rejection of the egological conception of the subject for a dialogical or intersubjective model does not count against the kind of objectivity in reason and rational thought that egological accounts could sustain. It does, however, appear to involve some pretty heavy metaphysical machinery —at least as heavy as the baggage carried by the traditional egological view— with some significant anti-Enlightenment consequences. Put crassly, whereas on the egological model the individual is fully empowered to structure society, on this Hegelian model society (in some form) is fully empowered to structure the individual.

Both positions came to be widely rejected in contemporary non-analytic philosophy. This reaction was in part motivated on purely philosophical grounds. Such metaphysical hypotheses, be they in the egological or the Hegelian sociological mould, no longer seemed sustainable. The rejection of what are essentially uncritical dogmas, and the philosophical systems constructed upon them, betokens a shift from a metaphysical to a post-metaphysical orientation. Such rejection of metaphysics is, of course, not new, dating back at least to Kant. It is simply more pervasive and rigorous: pointing out, for example, that Kant himself, for all his rejection of metaphysics, still held on to what was basically a dogmatically accepted metaphysical model of a given egological self as the fixed basis of his purportedly universal critique of reason.[11] The pervasiveness of this contemporary rejection of metaphysical models that transcend the empirical has to do with the fact that the reaction against metaphysics was in part also political.

The Hegelian appeal to a fixed metaphysical system that is not up for revision, and which structures the individual and dictates which socio-historical moves are possible, and to which the individual must be true, is, as we have seen, a clear reversal of the Enlightenment priority of the free-thinking individual over society. The politically conservative nature of any such Hegelian appeal to metaphysical systems that govern social progress and the possibilities of individual human action is clear, and perhaps particularly in Germany in this century the dangers of it are all the more palpable. But the egological model does not escape the charge of being politically conservative. The appeal to a fixed subject, which is not up for revision and to which one must be true, can be seen to serve as a politically and intellectually conservative measure, imposing limits on human freedom. Reason, logic, fundamental taxonomies,

---

[11] This criticism of Kant is not new, and dates back to Kant's near-contemporaries.

possibly values, all then get set up as structural features from which we cannot depart without deviating from the normal, which now means—from our true nature. Such a self can be seen as a fiction, the endorsement of which is a fake philosophical, but real psychological and political, imposition on the human freedom to revise and modify the world without any a priori limitations. Seen in this light, the Enlightenment individual paradigmatically conceived of on the egological model is not more free, but is simply the internalization of the authority to which adherence and subservience are required. By being brought within the subject, the authority of those structures is set up as inalienable. Moreover, the imposition involved might be thought to be all the more pernicious for not being as obvious in the case of the egological model as it is in the Hegelian dialogical or sociological model.

It is, then, in part in consequence of this too that there has been a move—and here again contemporary Critical Theorists fall in with a much wider trend—to take some distance from any residual metaphysical impositions.[12] On the one hand, there has been a rejection of anything like the Kantian egological subject, the transcendental structure of the mind that is the source of synthetic a priori judgements. On the other hand, there has equally been a move away from the Hegelian *metaphysical* system of intersubjective constitution. Instead, philosophers like Habermas, Honneth, and Wellmer have turned to a (maximally) metaphysically purged form of Hegel's dialogical model of the subject. This naturalized Hegelian account has led to a renewed interest in the American pragmatists, and in particular in George Herbert Mead. The idea is that the dialogical model, the account of subjectivity in terms of intersubjective recognition, allows for the right understanding of the intimate connections and interdependencies that obtain between individuals, and between the individual and his or her society, in a way that the simple egological model, with its stark opposition between the isolated thinking subject and the juxtaposed objective world, does not. But, at the same time, by avoiding the Hegelian metaphysical system, it avoids the subjugation of human freedom to an imposed metaphysical order. The promise is that we will have an adequate understanding of the nature of the subject and its place within a normative structure, without restricting the scope of possible variation by the imposition of a Hegelian grid (from without) or an Enlightenment one (from within).

The details of this dialogical account of subjectivity need not concern us at this point. It is perhaps worth noting that the obvious problem—which we might think of as the bootstrapping problem—has not gone undiscussed in the literature.[13] How can intersubjective recognition ground the identity

---

[12] Within the German context, see e.g. Habermas (1992), Honneth (1995b), and Wellmer (1991).
[13] See Dews (1995) for a helpful entry-point to the discussion.

and self-consciousness of the subject? After all, it would seem that in order to have such intersubjective recognition, there must already be an active subject, minimally aware of itself in order to recognize as relevant those other items in the world that are like it in central respects (intersubjective recognition is to be set up between subjects, not between a subject and his object-world), but that seems to require as a presupposition of the process precisely what is supposed to be the product of that process. There are, not surprisingly, reasonable responses to this problem. (I say that this is not surprising, on the assumption that there is a palpable sense that the question might gain its force from our being gripped too tightly by the very picture to which an alternative is being offered: hence Habermas's talk of a paradigm shift.) There is no need to go into them here. We can in fact avoid the problem by upholding a distinction between a rudimentary subject, comprising only a brute responsive capacity, which precedes intersubjective construction, and the substantive subject that results from it. It could then be claimed that while the substantial self is a social construct all the way down, a result of processes of intersubjective recognition and structuration, the rudimentary subject is not constructed, and so can be unproblematically presupposed by the intersubjective account, thus avoiding the threatened vicious circle. (Something like this seems to be accepted by Mead in his distinction between 'me' and 'I';[14] and Habermas too has come to acknowledge that there must be some rudimentary relation-to-self.[15]) In any event, the relevant point here can be made even on this more moderate rejection of the egological model. Any insistence on extending the intersubjective account all the way will only strengthen the case.

The relevant point is that, with the rejection of the Enlightenment egological conception of the (substantial) subject and the avoidance of any Hegelian metaphysical interpretation of the dialogical alternative conception, we seem to be left with a self whose nature and normative constraints are entirely context-dependent, where the context itself—given a consistently post-metaphysical orientation—lacks any non-contingent normative structure. There is now no normative structure, whether within or without the subject, that transcends local intersubjective set-ups. The horizons of normativity are exhaustively set by contingent socio-historical processes. In particular there is no rational subject that outstrips and can neutrally evaluate all local norm-sustaining practices. To assume that there is some such subject is in fact to impose normative canons on all localities on the unsustainable pretence that those canons of rationality themselves have something more than a local legitimacy. It is on this sort of view that the Enlightenment emerges as a form of cultural imperialism.

---

[14] See Mead (1934: 173 ff.); cf. discussion in Honneth (1995a: 266–7) and Habermas (1987: ii. 40–2, 58–60, 97 ff.).

[15] See Habermas (1992: 27 n. 18); see also discussion in Dews (1995).

The Egological Subject

Habermas of course stands out as a notable exception here. He does not intend normative structure to be rendered local and contingent by the naturalized intersubjective model he advocates. While withdrawing from metaphysical commitments, whether Hegelian structures or the Enlightenment egological subject, he hopes to sustain an Enlightenment conception of universal rationality. The assumption of the universality of rationality is one that is common to Habermas and the analytic tradition. But, as we will see below, it is far from clear how it can in fact be maintained in the absence of metaphysical underpinnings, in particular of the Enlightenment egological conception of the subject. Habermas's appeal to the presuppositions of an ideal speech situation, if genuinely shorn of metaphysical underpinnings, would seem to leave open the cultural indexing of the conception of that ideal situation, and so too of its normative presuppositions.

The pluralism, this indexing of *all* normative structures to local contexts, that results from the naturalized intersubjective model of the subject, can be captured by talking in terms of rigid normative structure. On the Enlightenment egological conception of the self, normative structures of rationality, say, could be taken as rigid, i.e. as being the same across all possible local contexts. On the alternative under consideration, normative structures lose that rigidity. Normative structures become fragile, nested within a local context, and, as we might put it, they do not travel well. We are left with the intersubjectivity *and* the contingency of all normative structure.

Now many of those who endorse the naturalized intersubjective model of the subject may well be inclined to welcome these consequences as being suitably non-conservative. After all, there is now no imposition of normative order on the individual, either from within or from without, that cannot in due course (whether of space or of time) be overturned. But there is reason to think that this liberal optimism, along with Habermas's, is misplaced. This is something to which I will return shortly. For the moment we can leave the story here.

3. FURTHER PRESSURE ON THE EGOLOGICAL CONCEPTION

We can leave the story there, in order to point out that in fact, within the analytic tradition too, there have been developments—not the same ones as in the context I have been canvassing—that suffice to put pressure on the received egological model, leading to the same consequences just outlined. Interestingly, these moves go beyond rejecting the egological self as a matter of switching paradigms, in the sense of loosening the grip of the old paradigm merely by way of developing alternatives to it. Rather, what we find here are certain developments that seem to constitute firm arguments against there being any scope for an egological core. And, as we will see, these arguments count against the egological model not only in so far as it involves objectionable metaphysical postulation, but even on a naturalized construal of it. But, ironically, and importantly, within the analytic tradition these pressures have not been clearly perceived to bear on the egological model, and that model is still the dominant default. Recognition of those pressures has, by and large, tended to serve simply as an exit ticket for the bearer from that tradition.

That the pressures in question were not perceived is, in some cases, simply because they were such as *could* be held at arm's length. The rejection of the egological model of the self, with all the Enlightenment trappings, has certainly not been confined to literature unfamiliar to those working within the analytic tradition. Rorty, for example, has been rejecting that model, in favour of intersubjectivity and radical contingency of all normative structure, including rationality, for the past twenty years or so. And there were certainly those who saw him as posing a challenge to the dominant conception within the analytic tradition. But there were also those who simply took their distance, assuming that Rorty had gone over to some other way of doing philosophy, which need not concern the analytic tradition and its way of going on. A more interesting example, perhaps, is the debate within the 'communitarian' literature, also over roughly the past twenty years. That literature has specifically argued for the rejection of the egological conception that delivered the Enlightenment self.[16] It has done so while adhering to the canons of argumentative clarity typical of the analytic tradition, and has not been particularly dependent for its theoretical base on similar moves in contemporary literature outside the analytic tradition.[17] The debate takes place squarely within political philosophy as it is standardly carried out within the analytic tradition. This makes it all the more significant that the challenge to the dominant egological model of the subject has not been taken up more widely within the analytic tradition. What we find, in effect, is that in analytical circles philosophical discussion of the nature of the subject, and the implications for rationality, objectivity, and epistemology, remain largely contained within social and political philosophy. The result of this confinement is to protect the dominant conceptions at work within the rest of analytical philosophy from criticism of the egological model. Any contemporary student within the analytic tradition must surely be puzzled by the way in which discussions of rationality, epistemology, the nature of the self, are basically pursued in two parallel streams: one within the mainstream of the analytic tradition, the other within analytical political philosophy. (By

---

[16] Taylor (1989); Walzer (1983); MacIntyre (1981).

[17] While Taylor has been attentive to that literature, and was deeply influenced by Hegel, his understanding of Hegel is fairly analytical, and there is no sense of his having rejected analytical philosophy in favour of some other approach.

contrast, within contemporary German philosophy, for example, there has not been this schism: conceptions of the subject at work within political philosophy have been taken up and discussed in a wider context.)[18]

Now these are all tangential pressures on the received and still-dominant egological conception of the subject, which could therefore be kept at arm's length. But there are also pressures on that conception which, although not yet widely acknowledged as such, cannot be kept at arm's length. (That they can't might contribute to an explanation—largely non-philosophical—of why the pressure they exert on the egological subject has been slow to be noticed.) These are pressures that arise from within developments that are so central to the analytic tradition that they are ultimately inescapable.

One source of pressure on the analytic tradition's implicit conception of the subject emerged with Wittgenstein's comments about meaning in the *Philosophical Investigations*.[19] Plato's Theory of Forms in principle freed the individual from being essentially indexed to, grounded in, any one socio-historical context. The individual, by having independent access to language and ideas, was in principle cut loose from social context, in much the same way, structurally, that centuries later natural rights were a reaction to, and an emancipation of the individual from, a system of defining social (feudal) roles and entitlements. In both, the human being was assured standing as a significant individual, with normative structures, quite apart from any grounding in social context. Wittgenstein, in rejecting the received individualist picture, is in effect threatening that independence of the individual from society. On the Wittgensteinian view, throwing off social constraints and still remaining a language-user would in fact—despite the mythical conception taken up by the Enlightenment—be impossible.

Now, the impact of the Wittgensteinian considerations on the conception of the egological subject has not been lost on those concerned with this issue outside the analytic tradition.[20] Within the analytic tradition it has not been

---

[18] There is an interesting diagnostic point here that ought to be brought out. In part because analytical political philosophy has, via the encounter with communitarianism, addressed the wider questions of the nature of the subject, it has become a point of interest to philosophers working outside the analytic tradition. This would be a natural bridge between the two traditions, were it not for the irony that while not being ignored outside the analytic tradition, this work is being held at arm's length within the rest of the analytic tradition (e.g. philosophy of mind).

[19] I have argued elsewhere (Sacks 1990), on different grounds, that there is a sense in which the analytic tradition can be regarded as bookended between the early and the later Wittgenstein. In both cases the idea is that there has been a delayed recognition, in the analytic tradition, of the relevant impact on it of Wittgenstein's later work.

[20] See e.g. Wellmer (1991, esp. 64–71), McCarthy (1992: 252), or Habermas (1987: ii. 16–22). Indeed it is largely this strand of Wittgenstein's later thought that explains why he has been so readily taken up as central to traditions other than the analytical, thereby constituting another natural bridge between traditions.

so readily recognized. This is all the more noteworthy given that the problem has not been left as something internal to Wittgenstein's thought and of interest only to those who might refer to themselves as Wittgensteinians. Thanks to Kripke (1982) the problem that seems to lead to the conclusion that language-use essentially requires appeal to an intersubjective structure, so that the individual can engage in conceptual thought only in so far as he or she is socially embedded, has been shown to be a problem seemingly of general validity, that does not trade on any uniquely Wittgensteinian presuppositions which might not be generally shared. Moreover, Kripke's generalization of the problem in this way meant that it was exported effectively from any possible confinement to the attention of those within the Wittgensteinian camp, and was put centrally on the agenda of those working generally in philosophy of mind and philosophy of language. Given Kripke's forceful generalization of the impetus towards the intersubjective paradigm, and the wide exposure that his treatment has had, it comes to seem peculiar that the pressure thus put on the egological conception of the subject could pass relatively unnoticed in the analytic tradition.

Part of the explanation for this might be simply that the issue of the egological subject is indeed implicit in, rather than an item on the agenda of, the analytic tradition. But it might also be thought that the appeal to intersubjectivity is required only for the working of semantic and linguistic rules, and that this leaves in place the notion of an underlying rational individual, whose very capacity for rational processing and reason explains the capacity for, and so has priority over, any effective social interaction or intersubjective recognition.[21] But this thought, which would serve to salvage the egological conception, does not in fact survive the full impact of Kripke's treatment (or of Wittgenstein's). If Kripke is right, then all rule-following, on pain of paradox, requires the constraints of a social context. But clearly, being rational just is abiding by certain very fundamental rules. So we cannot hold on to the idea of the naked individual—taken privately—as already being a rational thinker.

It might be thought that the individual taken on his own already has a *propensity* to engage in rational thought, even though this can be actualized only upon socialization, and that this explains why individuals of the same species equipped with the same propensities end up converging on canons of rationality subsequent to socialization.[22] And in this sense we could then

---

[21] It might also be thought that the most basic preferences, values, and patterns of perceptual salience remain egological, and that it is only the articulation of them that requires resort to intersubjective processes. In fact it can be argued that even these cannot be coherently attributed to the egological subject. This extension of the case is more thoroughly Wittgensteinian, and is not brought out quite so strongly in Kripke's treatment. For present purposes we should perhaps leave aside this further strand of the case against the egological conception.

[22] Something of this sort seems to be held by McDowell (1994), to which I will return below.

still hold on to there being an underlying egological core. But this would in fact be to miss the full force of the intersubjective impetus both Kripke and Wittgenstein identify. It might be right to say that the individual brings with him a certain propensity to behave in certain ways. But whether that propensity counts as a propensity to be rational, or indeed to follow any system of rules, will depend entirely on what—in part dependent on the propensities to behave that others have—comes to count as rational subsequent to socialization. Once socialized, we can say of a given person by way of retrospective judgement that before socialization he had the propensity to be rational. But *without* socialization that propensity that the individual might have to behave in certain ways cannot count as a propensity to be *rational*, since there is as yet nothing that counts as being rational, or as being any other kind of normative (rule-governed) structure. Talk of the naked individual already having a prototypical normative structure is simply confused about the extent of the connection between normative and social structure. Fully understood, the insights about rule-following leave no room to talk of *any* normative structure at the level below the social.

Propensities to behave are, *as such*, no more propensities to be rational than they are to be irrational. Norms of rationality, and hence the rational subject, are established only at the level of, and so are indexed to, the conventions and practices of the community. And it would seem that they may then in principle be different in different social or sociobiological set-ups (which does not mean, of course, that in any of these set-ups what counts as rationality is a matter of choice). The propensities of what we might regard as an aberrant individual would count as underpinning rationality in a community of sufficiently like-minded others. All of this can be seen to lead from the heart of the analytic tradition to the emphasis on intersubjectivity and the fundamental contingency of our core normative commitments, which is just what we have seen to result generally from the displacement of the egological subject in favour of a naturalized (or post-metaphysical) intersubjective paradigm.[23]

This pressure on the traditional egological conception of the subject is not confined to this development within analytical philosophy. Equally, if not more

---

[23] There may be room here for a middle position, one which insists on the *publicity* of normative structure, but stops short of regarding such norms as *socially* or intersubjectively determined. On such an individualist view rules cannot be private, but that is not to say that they are determined by—and indexed to—conventions and practices of communities or sociobiological set-ups. They would be indexed only to what *could be* (whether or not they actually are) the conventions and practices of some community. I thank Adrian Moore for raising this point. Obviously, this possibility just on its own would not yet suffice to yield convergence across individuals (or communities) rather than the space of normative possibilities varying from one publicly established set of rules to another. More to the point, however, it is not clear that this middle position does in fact survive the full impact of the rule-following considerations; and in any event, as we will see next, there are other pressures that apply directly to this position just insofar as it is still a form of individualism.

significantly, that conception comes under pressure from the debate about semantic externalism. It is not important for present purposes whether or not externalism is right. All that really matters is the recognition of what is at stake in the debate about whether or not it is right.

We can confine attention here to two early moves in the debate which are still central. Putnam (1975) first introduced the case for externalism, arguing that in the case of certain terms, particularly natural-kind terms, or those that have an indexical element, what goes on in the head underdetermines meaning, so that it is not possible to think of the subject as having command of his language and thought independently of the contribution of the world. Moreover, the external contribution is not just of the object-world, but also of other speakers, in the form of experts to whom the relatively uninitiated will defer in the use of certain terms. All this already threatens the isolation and self-sufficiency of the Cartesian subject supposedly at home alone with its thoughts. But the case is restricted: it applies only to certain thoughts—those with a *de re* element—and even then there remains a well-defined mental content, narrow content, which the subject taken in isolation can retain (it is just that that narrow content is not sufficient to determine meaning). There is a fixed internal content that remains the same in any two individuals that are in identical physical and behavioural states. One way of putting this is to say that there is still a notion of narrow content that supervenes on the individual person's physiological states. While this might not be enough to secure meaning, it is enough to secure an individualist conception of mental content.

Now this is precisely what does not survive the extension of the externalist case argued by Burge, McDowell, and others.[24] On this view it is not only the structure of *de re* attitudes that introduces the appeal to social and physical factors beyond the individual. As long as that was all, we could carry on thinking in terms of a two-component model of propositional content: narrow belief-content, which is individualistic, and a second component, the *res*, which in varying might vary the propositional content without varying the narrow content that is applied to it. But, on Burge's view, even expressions occurring obliquely in content clauses identifying the contents of psychological states, and which are purported to specify *narrow* content, essentially require appeal beyond the individual. In effect this means that externalism applies all the way in: there is no longer any preserved domain of narrow content over which the subject is an authority. Psychological states and mental content do not supervene on physiological states of the individual. This means that the subject, taken on his own—without appeal being made to the social or physical context in which he is embedded—cannot authoritatively detect changes

---

[24] See Burge (1979, 1982, 1986); McDowell (1986).

in his or her belief-contents, and so cannot be said strictly speaking to know what his or her beliefs are.

These consequences are, of course, not unnoticed in the literature on externalism.[25] Davidson (1994), for example, was concerned with them early on—in a way that he says externalists by and large had not been[26]—and attempted to resolve the seeming conflict between externalism of the sort advocated by Burge and others and the strong Cartesian intuition that we can know, with first-person authority, what we are thinking.[27] In a subsequent paper, partly responding to Davidson, Burge (1994) is explicitly concerned to show how externalism regarding individuation of thoughts is compatible with allowing that the subject has direct, immediate knowledge of his or her own thoughts. Burge identifies a sense in which I can be said to know what I believe: whatever the content of p is, once it is non-individualistically fixed for the first-order belief, it is available for use in a reflexive second-order judgement—if I have a belief that p, I can also state that I know what it is that I believe, namely: p. However, this technical sense in which I can know what I believe has nothing to do with being able to explicate authoritatively what one believes. Burge concedes this readily:

> One clearly does not have first-person authority about whether one of one's thoughts is to be explicated or individuated in such and such a way. Nor is there any apparent reason to assume that, in general, one must be able to explicate one's thoughts correctly in order to know that one is thinking them . . . One should not assimilate 'knowing what one's thoughts are' in the sense of basic self-knowledge to 'knowing what one's thoughts are' in the sense of being able to explicate them correctly—being able to delineate their constitutive relations to other thoughts.[28]

Thus the sense in which Burge establishes the compatibility between externalism and knowing what one's beliefs are serves only to emphasize the extent to which the sense relevant to the egological conception of the subject has indeed been undermined. If externalism is right, I may have (and know that I have) a belief that p, but that does not mean that I am in a position to identify or explicate comprehendingly the content of my belief, or to track whether and what changes there have been in its content. This leads back to the relevant sense in which it remains the case that, given externalism, I cannot strictly speaking claim to know what my beliefs are.

---

[25] For recent discussion, see e.g. Boghossian (1997, also 1989), Wright et al. (1998).
[26] Davidson (1994: 50, originally published in 1987).
[27] Davidson's own diagnosis of where the externalists go wrong, and his suggested way back to first-person authority, seem not to do justice to the force of the case from externalism to denial of individual authority; in particular, that it does not necessarily rely on the myth that thoughts require mysterious mental objects (1994: 63–4).
[28] Burge (1994: 78).

And to the extent that the individual does not know what his or her thoughts are, whether they have changed, or consequently how they might stand in relation to other thoughts that that individual or some other has, it seems pretty clear that he or she cannot count as engaging in autonomous rational deliberation. Thus, for example, the application of formal concepts such as *modus ponens* requires the capacity for the reidentification of thought-contents across premises. But given that a thinker is not authoritative about the semantic contents of his thoughts, he will fail to be authoritative about such reidentification. And not being authoritative about such identification precludes being autonomous in adherence to rationality.[29]

It might be thought that, regardless of the identity of the particular thought-contents processed (which may be conceded to be externalistically determined), there are nevertheless formal structures of thought-processing which any individual will abide by. But it is not clear why externalism should respect the distinction between material concepts and formal rules. There is good reason to consider that the individuation of inferential patterns between thoughts is as much a matter of concept application as is the individuation of the thoughts processed:[30] both reduce to the application of rules. And the case for externalism may consequently apply to the one as much as to the other. Cases of the kind that establish externalism regarding concepts governing the use of terms like 'arthritis' (or for that matter 'gold') can equally be constructed for concepts governing the use of terms like *modus ponens*. Similarly, there is no reason why the rule-following considerations adduced earlier should not apply to formal and material concepts alike. And if it is said in response that by 'formal structures of thought-processing' nothing other than a biological mechanism is meant, then we are back with the problem of how normativity can arise individualistically from that alone, for all the reasons that the rule-following considerations bring out.

Now it is true that semantic externalism is not universally accepted—although for some time now there has been a clear sense that internalists are fighting with their backs to the wall.[31] But, taken together, the two developments—semantic externalism and the rule-following considerations—are significant enough to pose a severe challenge to the received egological model and any associated default ideals. What emerges is a view according to which the individual subject, considered in isolation from social and physical context, cannot properly know what his beliefs or desires are, is no authority on their

---

[29] Some externalists have indeed endorsed this consequence; see Millikan (1993: 280 ff.).
[30] See e.g. Peacocke (1992).
[31] Even Fodor, while still insisting that a Language of Thought is necessary, and that without individualism there is no explanation of the causal efficacy of propositional contents, has been forced to make significant concessions to externalism: concessions such as that although there is narrow content, we cannot say what it is (Fodor 1987, ch. 2); Fodor (1995) goes still further.

content or relation to other thoughts, cannot tell whether or not they have changed, cannot use language or more generally follow rules, and (in consequence of all this) cannot engage in rational deliberation, or indeed be said to be rational in any sense. Far from being an independent agent that applied itself to the social fabric, the subject would seem instead to be a construct in the wider social and physical context. We have here, in other words, a striking push towards a non-egological view of the subject of just the sort that we saw arising in non-analytic philosophy as a reaction against the egological conception.

Something of this shift was clearly stated by Burge himself in his early work on the subject.[32] He recognized that it is a consequence of his externalism that traditional psychology is mistaken in taking the individual subject as the unit of explanation; instead, he holds, the unit of psychological explanation should be the wider social context, with the individual being approached only indirectly, via that context. Burge (1979) explicitly mentions Hegel, as the philosopher whose conception of the individual in relation to society perhaps posed the right non-individualist model. In the present context, this should precisely begin to echo the parallel move towards a naturalized Hegelian view in contemporary non-analytic German philosophy.

Nevertheless, within analytical philosophy the debate has not really developed on the basis of a clear identification that what is at issue is the egological conception of the subject; the threat to the egological conception of the subject has not been placed squarely at the focal point of the discussion. Rather the concern has been focused on the tension between externalism and first-person authority, with little attention given to the consequences that revised conceptions of self-knowledge will have on the conception of the subject. Perhaps because of the dominant concern in this tradition with linguistic meaning rather than with the subject, the case against Cartesian individualism has been taken as a semantic thesis that can somehow be taken on board alongside the default assumption of the egological subject. But it is not only that the pressure on the egological conception of the subject has not been directly appreciated; the conception that has come under pressure, and is only illegitimately retained, in fact serves to sustain a central assumption of the analytic tradition itself. This remains to be seen more fully.

It is worth first saying more about how within the analytic tradition the demise of Cartesian individualism was not seen as a threat at all, at least not to anything essential to the analytic tradition. For one thing, the move towards semantic externalism was a move away from the importance of interiority, and is broadly supportive of the latent behaviourism that has proved attractive to philosophy of mind in the analytic tradition. Secondly, there is a sense

---

[32] Burge (1979: 73–4; 1982: 116–18).

that semantic externalism shows Cartesian scepticism—what I referred to as subject-driven scepticism—to be simply incoherent. It turns out that, understood aright, there is no way that the individual could be as he is, and yet not be embedded in a social and physical context—so raising the question is not a genuine philosophical (as opposed to psychological) possibility.[33] This might be thought of as a de-transcendentalized Kantianism. Thirdly, in so far as externalism is right, meaning and value are not things that are confined to the individual, leaving him or her in confrontation with an alien and possibly unresponsive external reality. If externalism pertaining to meaning can be extended to value and reason, then the individual, his or her society, and the external world are together a unitary domain within which meaning, value, and reason obtain. There is then no room for worry about the applicability of our values or reasons to the external world—all are elements internal to the domain of meaning. This latter move is, of course, that attempted recently by John McDowell, and can be seen to be a natural extension of his earlier externalism about meaning.[34] McDowell, who defends a form of what he calls 'naturalized platonism', in fact explicitly connects this move with a (naturalized) Hegelianism. He ends with an appeal (however loose) to Gadamer. Here the two lines I have traced, which have so far been kept apart, come together.

4. CONSEQUENCES OF DE-CENTRING THE SUBJECT

We have seen that in both a non-analytic context, and in the analytic tradition, there has been pressure towards convergence on a naturalized Hegelianism, and that in both—albeit for different reasons—there has been some enthusiasm over this reorientation. It is now time to say why it is that in both cases this enthusiasm seems to be misplaced. This will also bring out the reasons for thinking that in the analytic tradition the reorientation with regard to the egological subject threatens one of the central assumptions of the tradition.

The move that I have been considering, away from an egological conception of the subject, towards a naturalized Hegelianism, can all too easily be taken to have a liberating nature. There is no longer any non-empirical imposition on the individual: either from without (reason at large) or from within. This liberation from the imposition of all authority may be seen to invite radical pluralism, an absence of any distinctive human essence which

---

[33] See Burge (1982: 116–17).
[34] McDowell (1994). Some have seen tension between McDowell's earlier endorsement of semantic externalism and his appeal to the space of reasons expanding to include the natural world; see Wright (1996).

could not be overcome. These consequences might readily be regarded as an affirmation of freedom and liberalism. It is this optimism that seems to be misplaced, for reasons that are familiar from the discussion of communitarianism. If the self, or at least the substantial self, is an intersubjective construct all the way down, the individual cannot transcend his or her socio-historical setting. There remains no trace of the Enlightenment self that can step out of any community in which it is embedded, taking its critical capacities with it, to make an independent judgement about that community. The norms of critical judgement would themselves have been left behind. There are, to exploit Taylor's metaphor, only inherited horizons of significance,[35] indexed to contexts from which they were inherited. Now if this is the situation, then, far from being liberal, the picture threatens to be strikingly conservative. With reason itself a product of a particular tradition, there is ultimately only the authority of tradition. We have the inversion of the Enlightenment order: rather than tradition being subservient to reason, reason is subservient to tradition. This can be captured by saying, simply, that there are then only traditional societies.

Moreover, it cannot be claimed simply that reason, although essentially a social construct indexed for its validity to tradition, is nevertheless not indexed to a *particular* tradition, but is germane to anything that can count as a tradition. Let us take it that we have a convincing argument to that effect. The worry would be that any such argument would have to assume the very thing that it was supposed to establish: namely, that the argumentation was not good only for one particular tradition. It would seem, then, that on this view reason might set itself up as universalized; but that could never be anything more than universalization as it is carried out *from here*, where that picks out a particular community. To assume otherwise would seemingly be to accept that there is, after all, a non-empirical structure of reason which imposes itself—be it from without or from within. Strictly confined to a naturalized intersubjective model, though, we are left with the voice of reason—and hence the voice of the would-be independent critic—tamed, parochialized. There is nothing that can be said to those traditions that might regard fundamental faith, rather than reason, as the way to establish basic tenets of society and the good life (with reason and rational debate being a mere pragmatic ordering device).[36] In particular, there is nothing that could be said when, within that society, those who do stand out as rational critics are regarded as pathological deviants. Thus, with only inherited horizons of significance, the enquiring individual has become

---

[35] Taylor (1989, esp. chs. 1–2).

[36] That kind of society might be combated from without, but there is no room to expect reasoned, rational adjudication between reason- and faith-based societies. The very phrase has itself now become an obfuscation: *rational adjudication* would be nothing more than cultural imposition by one society on another.

answerable to society after all, rather than society being answerable to the enquiring individual. The liberation from fake metaphysical structures might be appropriate, then, but the post-metaphysical fallout should not be thought to deliver any simple liberation. We seem to end up with the unchallenged authority of tradition, with subservience of the individual to the contingent order that wholly defines him or her.

The attempt by Habermas to safeguard rationality as a universally binding normative structure similarly seems unable to distinguish itself from communitarian parochialism. There are two primary lines of criticism. One, already indicated above, has to do with the fact that the very conception of *open discourse* already assumes a normative judgement. This would appear to render the entire project circular. We cannot comfortably use a particular normative judgement as the basis for establishing the universality of all normative judgement. The underlying normative judgement might be nothing more than a local commitment, which will come to be rejected elsewhere. The resulting universality is then indexed to the context in which that local commitment is made; it is merely universalization from a given locus. Other loci, other universalizations. In particular, anyone not accepting the value of equal respect and participation in discourse, or who draws different boundaries delimiting the set of those who count as equals, might end up with a different normative universalization. Secondly, even where the underlying norm is adhered to, it results in the intersubjective constitution of reason and rationality only given a certain pattern of reaction of the interacting individuals. But those patterns of reaction are, in a post-metaphysical orientation, contingent on the individual animal make-up. With a different participating animal, the constitution of intersubjective normative patterns might produce different results, or indeed might fail to produce results at all. Either way, then, it would seem that the intersubjective paradigm could ground only locally valid universalizations of norms of discourse. What counts as an ideal speech community, what its presuppositions are, will always, it seems, be relative to conceptions of one historical community or another.

Now the same considerations that reveal this conservative predicament into which the naturalized intersubjective paradigm seems to lead, also reveal the problem to which the demise of the egological subject leads within the analytic tradition. Perhaps the egological subject, while being the default, is not itself a central tenet of the analytic tradition, so that there is no immediate reason why the demise of this conception of the subject should be of concern. But there is at least one conception that seems fundamental to the analytic tradition, at least in its classical robust form.[37] This is the conception

---

[37] It is of course conceivable (indeed likely) that something preserving the style and methods of the analytic tradition will survive, under this name, even after the formative central conception has been displaced.

of reason and rationality as having validity that is not merely historically or culturally grounded. This is in fact an extension of the anti-psychologistic approach of this tradition.[38] Canons of rationality and reason should not be the product of any one tradition; which, of course, is not to deny that perhaps rationality and reason are such that they are always at work only within a tradition. That is, perhaps—trivially—one cannot think outside any tradition, but that is not to say that one's thought-structures and -contents are entirely a product of, and valid only within the horizons set by, a given tradition. The analytic tradition can readily accept the former, but seems to sit uncomfortably with the latter. Yet it is precisely the latter that threatens after the demise of the egological subject, which is brought about from within the analytic tradition by various forms of externalism.

In so far as the individual taken on his or her own cannot be said to follow rules at all, and all normative structure essentially first arises at the intersubjective level, canons of rationality and reason would again seem to be normative structures grounded in the mode of social organization. And given naturalism about the possibilities of social organization, that would seem to suggest further that rationality and reason inherited the contingency of the social structures that grounded them, such that different social structures might bring with them, and impose on their constituent individuals, different normative structures. Rationality and reason then become fragile, entirely internal to a tradition, localized to one way of going on, in just the sense that undermines their presupposed universality.

Furthermore, given that rationality and reason are themselves only one local form of normative constraint, given that what the subject finds practically and theoretically significant might itself vary from one local setting to another, the conception of reality as a context-independent given, the true structure of which can be impartially mapped, also comes into question. With all theoretical and practical patterns of salience being essentially local, there is little hope that the same features of reality, and the same subsequent theoretical explanations of them, will be picked out across different local contexts. Reality seems then to emerge as internal to a local context; as we might say, it is merely an *empirical reality*, but unlike the Kantian conception it is indexed now not to the fixed structure of the mind, but to local normative structures and patterns of significance. The fragility of such structures will generally encourage a lack of objectivity about our construals of an external world.[39] To this extent, even the refutation of scepticism about the external world is weakened to something like a form of empirical realism without the transcendental guarantees of constancy in the construal of those empirical

---

[38] For clear statements of the anti-psychologistic orientation of the analytic tradition, see e.g. Hylton (1990). [39] See e.g. Pettit (1993, p. xi) and also McDowell (1994: 93).

objects. This is something to which I will return in more detail in the next chapter.

It is important to remain clear about what is, and what is not, being claimed to constitute a departure from a central assumption of the analytic tradition here. The way in which the construal of reality is indexed to, and so varies with, local practices and patterns of salience is reminiscent of William James's early statement of ontological relativity[40] and, of course, of Quine.[41] And while there are reasons for thinking that with Quine the analytic tradition has run its course,[42] the mere thesis of ontological relativity clearly does not betoken any break with analytic philosophy. The point is only that this breakdown of realism is seen here as a result specifically of the rejection of universal objectivity about *reason and rationality*. That canons of rational thought—like logic—are *not* locally or historically indexed is recognizable as a central orientating assumption of the analytic tradition; one that was, it would appear, sustained by the default egological conception of the subject.

Here it is appropriate to consider the move that McDowell has recently attempted.[43] He accepts that a human being cannot single-handedly come to possess the normative structures in question. He sees canons of rationality as essentially linked to a culture, a tradition, an educational process, as those structures within which alone the human being is inducted into the space of reasons. Our question then arises, how can any such view avoid that space of reasons into which the individual is socialized, being locally indexed, such that alternatives are available in other traditions with their different acculturation processes? One answer would be to think that there is a necessary structure of the social world, such that different societies constitute nothing other than different stages in the development of one and the same social order. However, that Platonic-cum-Hegelian metaphysical view is not the one that McDowell takes—any more than anyone else in the analytic tradition today.[44] McDowell's view is rather that what rules out such indexing of rationality and reason to a culture, such that alternatives to them are possible in other cultures, is that those normative canons are not in fact constituted by the culture in which they are embedded. Traditions and cultures do not constitute rationality and the space of reasons; they simply function as the enabling conditions for the development of what is in fact second nature to the human animal. Given that acculturation serves to bring out what is already latent in

---

[40] See James (1981: 273–8) and above, pp. 126–7.   [41] See e.g. Quine (1969*b*).

[42] See Romanos (1984), Sacks (1990), and, for quite different reasons, Hacker (1996*b*: 189 ff.).

[43] This move is also relevant to Habermas's attempt, indicated above, to sustain the universality of reason in a post-metaphysical setting.

[44] Here the importance of the naturalism of the contemporary analytic tradition comes to the fore.

this animal, and simply could not *develop* on its own, in isolation, it follows that there will be that latent structure common to all human cultures.

But this way of establishing the objectivity of reason and rationality in the face of the rejection of egological models of such normative structures seems to be a case of McDowell wanting both to reject the cake and to eat it. After all, we are here once again attributing to the human being, *qua* individual animal, a well-defined determinate normative structure, but one which becomes explicit only in some cultural context or another. This appears to commit McDowell to holding both that the space of reasons gets going only within the intersubjective structure, and that the individual is already constrained by it prior to any socialization. Quite apart from the internal tensions within McDowell—who would now appear both to deny that normativity is individualistic and to assert that it is[45]—this would be to revert to the very position that has been seen to come under pressure from within the analytic tradition.

Now it could be said that McDowell is not committed to anything as strong as that the individual human animal, pre-socialized, is already the bearer of a *normative structure*. That would perhaps introduce into his position the tension just alluded to. But possibly all he needs to say is that it is a biological fact about normal humans, as they happen to be, that upon socialization a second nature will develop such that, however different the social contexts and educational practices within which the process of maturation takes place might be, there will always be a common rational core. All normal humans will then have the latent compulsion to a core rationality, in the way that all normal human beings have, say, two kidneys. Now some such appeal to hypothetical biological structure might be our best bet. But, barring metaphysical appeals to an underlying form, whether Platonic or Aristotelian, any such biological facts—even if they could in principle sustain some such core rationality—are themselves merely contingent (not all humans have two kidneys), and there would be no objective sense in which any deviations or changes in them could be said to be deviations from the *correct* form, except relative to some socially endorsed norm. There are two distinct problems here. Regarding the latter, the idea was for biological form to underpin the social nesting of normativity, not the other way around. Secondly, apart from that, any core rationality underpinned by such biological facts is a merely contingent feature that cannot be said to inhere rigidly in human second nature. McDowell seems to be conflating his naturalized Platonism, which is all he can justify, with Aristotle's immanent Platonism, which is what he wants,

---

[45] The *denial* explains our being able to have knowledge of the world; the *assertion* explains why rationality and the space of reasons are not fragile nestings within one tradition or another.

but which brings in individualist metaphysical assumptions that he cannot defend. Confined to the former, the space of reasons, which encompasses the individual and his or her world, cannot be universalized as the space applicable to any and all acculturated human beings.[46]

We have seen one manifestation of the general problem referred to at the outset as world-driven scepticism: that across traditions the disintegration of the egological model, in favour of naturalistically conceived intersubjective models, forces recognition of the challenge facing our Enlightenment trust in rationality and reason.[47] The problem does not turn primarily on the fate of the egological conception, but on the general absence of scope for metaphysical groundings. It is, however, made more acute, and hence more salient, by the demise of the egological model. It is made more acute because as long as the egological conception survived, the threat to rationality and reason was, in the absence of metaphysical underpinnings, at least as resilient as biological structure. With the demise of that conception, we stand to lose even that source of resilience.

It would seem that without a metaphysical conception of the social or biological sphere, reason and rationality can inherit their stability only from resources internal to the social and biological set-ups to which they are indexed. Given their domestication, what resilience such normative structures have will then be entirely determined by the extent to which the scope for variance across such domestic contexts is restricted. The question, then, is just how restricted such variance is.

---

[46] It could be universalized as the space of reasons applicable to any and all acculturated human beings, *as human beings were at a certain historical–biological location*, but that is precisely to see rationality as historically indexed, and does not sustain the kind of rigid normative structure or rationality that is germane to the analytic tradition.

[47] Specifically, with regard to the analytic tradition, we have seen the sense in which the demise of the egological subject should perhaps not be seen as just another twist in the continuous development of that tradition, but rather as a threat to one of its central and formative assumptions. That threat seems to come not only from those who set out to challenge the tradition, but even—unwittingly—from some of those who would be among its staunchest defenders.

5

The Scope of Objectivity

THE significance of the apparent demise of the egological subject can be estimated properly only when seen in the larger setting, since it constitutes only one source of pressure on our ideal of the universality of reason. Moves against the egological subject in principle leave open other routes by which the objectivity of reason and rationality might be established.[1] If the subject is essentially indexed to, because structured by, the social and material fabric of the world in which it is located, its normative structures stand to inherit whatever stability or instability that environment has to offer. At issue, then, is whether external nesting can make good the loss consequent upon the demise of the egological subject. The question before us thus shifts to the objectivity that can be sustained, not about reason narrowly, or the individual's normative structures, but about the experienced object-world within which reasoning subjects and other objects are located. This is the concern of the present chapter.

The obvious way of securing objectivity was once thought to be metaphysical realism regarding some domain—whether that domain be the natural world, Aristotelian or Platonic Forms, the logical form of the world (or, for that matter, God). But the problems with such ontological appeals need no rehearsing, and I will continue to take it for granted that in proceeding to assess the available scope of objectivity, the discussion should take its initial bearings from the well-motivated and almost universally shared withdrawal from such metaphysics. This withdrawal can make something like the Kantian Copernican Revolution seem attractive, as offering an alternative and metaphysically minimalist way of securing a form of objectivity that is more than merely contingent. But any appeal to transcendental idealism, whatever other problems it might have, must seem insufficiently motivated as long as there is room to consider that we can withdraw altogether from all metaphysical grounding, and that naturalism provides all the resources we need in order to secure the required grip on objectivity. In the previous chapter I have in fact already briefly raised some specific reasons for doubting whether this is so. But the appeal

---

[1] The linkage between the universality of reason and an egological conception is indeed a fairly late historical development. For a reminder of this, see Taylor (1989: 155 ff.).

1. UNADORNED NATURALISM

The naturalist's naïve realism is, of course, in principle open to the standard sceptical worries, of a traditional epistemological sort, to the effect that if the world is assumed to be real and utterly mind-independent, we cannot be sure that it is as we in fact experience it to be. But a naturalist equipped with a robust sense of realism and the good sense to have avoided neurotic quests for certainty, such as may have been fuelled by adherence to the traditional assumption, is unlikely to find such worries motivating.

There is, however, a further worry, not entirely unrelated, which seems more significant. Consider the question, how is it that we *can* (granting that we undeniably *do*) have knowledge of objects? That is, in virtue of what are we in a position to make sense of experience—to have experience presented to us—as being experience *of objects*?[2] It clearly will not do to respond to this by saying no more than that there are objects, including physical objects, with which we causally interact. Although true, that does not answer the question. There are all sorts of things that interact causally with objects which do not thereby have experience at all, let alone experience that presents itself as experience of objects. More needs to be said about the details of the causal interaction: about how whatever experiential input there is (sensory or other) comes to be processed as experience of *objects*. The problem here is not that the naturalist can have no account to give. The account will presumably be a thoroughly naturalist one, ultimately concerning the neurophysiological workings of the brain, possibly in conjunction with functional and social levels of explanation. The problem lies elsewhere. (And here we approach, in one form, one of the weaknesses of the appeal to naturalism that will emerge more clearly in what follows.)

Let's assume that we have a completely naturalist story of how the brain comes to deliver up experience as of objects (and let's also assume for the moment, merely for simplicity, that there is no social overlay to the story). By a completely naturalist account I mean that there is no hidden or background appeal to some non-empirical story. Given that we are dealing with a naturalistic account of the workings of the brain, and that the facts in question can then be regarded only as contingent, there is obviously nothing to

---

[2] By 'objects' here I do not mean only full-blown ontologically independent objects constituting ourselves and the external world, but any item that can be regarded as distinct from the subject, and from other such items, such that the subject can be intentionally related to it.

secure the account from that contingency; it will undergo whatever changes and modifications correspond to those that might befall the brain structures it describes. The question then is what precludes such a change in the workings of the brain as would render experience as no longer being *as of objects*. We cannot now conceive in positive terms of what experience would be like in that case, but that is hardly surprising, and might have something to do with the fact that our brains have not in fact undergone the change envisaged. But if there were to be such a change, there would be no reason—and possibly no conceptual capacity—to think in terms of there being objects in the world.

It would not do to claim in response simply that while there might be such a change, we could not survive it, given that we live in a world of objects, and that this means that the fact that a creature has survived is sufficient to guarantee that its experience will be objectual. That will not do because it is not obviously true that survival requires objectual representations of the world. There are enough examples of forms of life that survive perfectly well and yet to whom it seems inappropriate to attribute objectual representations of any sort. And given that we could survive such a change, it looks as though our claim to be living in a world of objects, simply on the basis of our being biologically so constituted as to experience and theorize in those terms, can be counted as no more than an extrapolation from the way we are wired. Given different wiring, we would extrapolate from it differently. It seems, then, that on the naturalist story about how we come to have experience as of objects, the assertion that there are objects in the world has to be defended against the threat of empirical idealism.[3] The assertion is indexed to beings with our biological make-up, which might, simply, change.

There are of course various ways of handling this prima-facie pressure on naturalism, two of which are obvious. First, it may be said that the claim that there are objects is taken as premised, and is not based in any way on the fact that we now have experience as of a world of objects (as such, the claim would be independent of factors which might be relative to our constitution). Secondly, it might be argued that there could in fact not be a form of experience, rightly so called, that did not involve objectual representations. The point here, however, is simply to note that both of these obvious responses would involve extending beyond the naturalist's brief: the former by making a metaphysical realist claim (i.e. one which transcended all possible empirical evidence), the latter by endorsing a form of transcendental necessity. One might be inclined to say that the plain assumption of there being an objectual world need not extend beyond the naturalist's brief to any *metaphysical*

---

[3] Here the naturalist, although for not exactly the reasons Kant had in mind in saying the same of the realist, seems to be forced later to play the part of an empirical idealist. See *Critique*, A367–80.

claim, but can rather be presented simply as an inference from the available evidence (such as it is) to the best explanation. But it would then have to be granted that what counts as the best explanation would depend not only on evidence which may be relative to our own constitution, but also on explanatory routes which may equally be indexed to the way we happen to be. As such it would not provide an escape from the idealist pressure identified.

It should also be noted that the instability of the naturalist yield identified here cannot be classified simply as fallibilism. The problem is not that despite our best efforts we might be getting the world wrong, such that present errors might be corrected at a later date. That kind of fallibilism requires appeal to reality as in principle outstripping but fixed across enquirers and enquiries, of the sort that a metaphysical realism or transcendental idealism might provide. Fallibilism involves a fixed framework, such that open-ended enquiry can gradually approach it: whereas the pressure identified here in the case of an unadorned naturalism is precisely on there being a framework that is assured of such fixity. (Metaphorically, the worry identified is not whether a goal will be scored successfully, but whether the goalposts will remain in place.)

2. THE NATURALIZED COPERNICAN TURN

The threat of an unacceptable form of idealism that is inherent in unadorned naturalism thus perhaps helps to explain why it is appropriate that naturalism rarely *remains* unadorned. And in the context of a withdrawal from metaphysics, it is at this point that some form of Copernican turn to a form of transcendental idealism can seem attractive.[4] That our brains are such as to deliver experience as of objects is then no longer a source for concern that we might not be getting right the way of the world as it is in itself—unlike the metaphysical realist, we are no longer directing knowledge at anything beyond how the world necessarily appears to us. But more importantly, that the world so appears to us—e.g. as being necessarily objectual—is now no longer, as it was on the unadorned naturalist account, conditional upon any contingency of our biological make-up, such that were it different, our experience might not be so structured. The structure of experience is rendered resilient. Basically, that experience is objectual and (whatever other fundamental characteristics it might have) is not *determined* by the biological facts, it is simply implemented by them. There is now another, transcendental,

---

[4] Of course, in Kant transcendental idealism is bound up with appeal to precisely the sort of egological subject that we have seen come under pressure in the preceding chapter. That is one, sufficient reason for talking here cautiously only of *some form* of Copernican turn to a form of transcendental idealism.

explanation of why our experience is essentially of objects. And in so far as what does determine that structure are non-empirical constraints, the related inconceivability of experience being any other way does now stand to be a guide to impossibility, whereas on the purely naturalist account it was not.[5]

Such is the thinking behind the Kantian form of transcendental idealism, according to which there are non-empirical constraints on anything that can count as experience, which render the structure of experience resilient in the face of merely contingent changes (which is just to say that there are certain synthetic a priori truths)—and it is only of the world as presented in that form of experience that we can have knowledge. This way of bolstering naturalism (or what Kant would call empirical realism) has clear advantages. But it will be noted that although it clearly embodies a withdrawal from traditional metaphysics, it would be wrong to think that the non-empirical constraints in question are upheld in Kant in a way that avoids making any metaphysical claims. Indeed, it is not clear that without such metaphysical underpinnings we can make sense of there being non-empirical constraints (or, consequently, of transcendental idealism being coherent). This is something that I will return to later. For now, however, the more important point to note is that even if we allow such minimal metaphysical appeal to be made, it does not follow that Kant is right in thinking that just because non-empirical constraints render experience resilient in the face of empirical contingencies, it follows that it is rendered resilient.

After all, there is the possibility that non-empirical constraints themselves might change. This is not to deny them the status of non-empirical constraints, since the change in them need not be thought to be brought about by mere empirical fluctuations (in the face of which they and the implemented structure of experience might indeed be resilient). This of course recalls a central Hegelian view. Such non-empirical structures as there are might either be thought to fluctuate in a quite uncontrolled way, without this impugning their status as non-empirical constraints for as long as they are operative, or—should this be thought too weak—as part of the unfolding of some non-empirical order (which perhaps need not entail any untenable regress of meta-levels of non-empirical constraints.) In any event, to the extent that non-empirical constraints can be modified, it is wrong to think that there is one unchanging structure of experience, resiliently fixed by non-empirical constraints, and which Kant can regard as the set horizons within which any naturalist account of the empirical world will be nested.

Now if the singularity of the mind-imposed order comes into question when we are considering metaphysically grounded structures, this weakness can be expected to be all the more pronounced when it comes to a post-Kantian move

---

[5] These are themes that I will have opportunity to return to later; see primarily Ch. 6.

to mind-imposed structures that are merely empirical. By the latter move I have in mind specifically a kind of naturalized Copernican Revolution, a product of the withdrawal from metaphysics that can be found across various philosophical developments in the nineteenth and twentieth centuries. In social and political philosophy a form of naturalized Hegelianism has been fairly mainstream since Marx, and is evident through the work of thinkers like Weber, Durkheim, Mauss, and up to Adorno, Horkheimer, Marcuse, and Foucault. In all we find the awareness that central structures that we read off the world around us are not merely descriptions of a natural order that is there to be mapped, but of an order that in fact reflects the effects of the most fundamental institutions and forces of our social epoch. Although these are entirely empirical constraints, they function in one important respect as naturalized counterparts to transcendental structures: they are imposed, so to speak, behind the back, or beneath the surface, of our critical attention, such that we can then readily read them off the world as given to us, which in a sense they are, rather than as made by us, which in another sense they are too. This epistemic duality is precisely characteristic of transcendental idealism. And where there is this duality, there is also, consequently, the scope for critical understanding with which to unmask the way in which what initially might be taken as brutely given can be revealed to have been our own construct. This identifies one sense in which the critical turn of Kant's Copernican Revolution can be seen to be carried through right up to Critical Theory. The basic structure of the Copernican turn, whether transcendental or naturalized, creates the space for critical understanding, such that not to unmask the given empirical structures, to leave them to be taken at face value, as a simple impinging reality, is to allow them to retain a fictional force that does not survive critical reflection.

Now when it comes to social and political reality, this form of understanding of it is clearly not surprising, since the structures that are being dealt with here are so obviously and intimately tied up with human actions and interests anyway, that it makes sense to consider that even some of what we would take to be externally imposed can in fact be revealed to be the inherited sediment of just such entrenched actions and practices. And it is also in these cases easy to see why the Copernican turn takes the form of a naturalized Hegelianism, rather than naturalized Kantianism. Aside from the obvious relevance of intersubjectivity to social structure, those social structures that are experienced as presuppositional need not be such as cannot change over time. Given that the fundamental structures we inherit are shaped by the accumulation of preceding practices, it makes sense to think that as our practices might gradually shift, so too might those fundamental structures that future generations inherit from us. Barring determinism, there is no reason why the sediment of convention should not gradually shift as subsequent conventions do. (Indeed, a critical theorist might contend that they had better alter, if we are not to be so completely bound down by the weight of the past as to preclude all significant free movement.) Here the Wittgensteinian metaphor of the changing riverbed, always a relatively solid framework in comparison to the waters that flow over it, but nevertheless constantly shifting because of that flow, is particularly apt.[6] In fact Wittgenstein is talking there not about social reality, but about logic—which takes us on to the next step.

The naturalized Copernican turn, and the same dualistic structure that is characteristic of it, has been taken further, and applied quite generally, i.e. beyond the confines of social reality narrowly conceived. One way in which this has been done is as an extension of the treatments of sociopolitical reality, thereby blurring the distinction between that reality and the rest. Thus, for example, it has been argued that some of what are standardly regarded as medical conditions, and thought to be best described using the irreducible taxonomy of the relevant natural science, are in fact merely our own concealed sociopolitical constructs.[7] These cases may be well made, but clearly the further into the natural world such extensions of the sociopolitical order are pushed, the more shallowly programmatic—and plainly immodest—they are bound to appear.[8] But the implementation of a naturalized Copernican turn has also been brought about by quite general theoretical moves, which do not pertain specifically to sociopolitical philosophy, and so amount to more than simple expansive appropriation by the sociopolitical domain.

The general theoretical impetus towards a naturalized Copernican turn was prevalent in analytic philosophy in the second half of the twentieth century. This can be traced back largely to the influence of Carnap's naturalized Kantianism.[9] And in so far as the naturalized as opposed to transcendental version of this Copernican turn is all the more likely to allow for changes in the imposed structures, what we have here—far from bolstering naturalism in the way that transcendental idealism promised to do—is in fact the uncovering of a further source of concern regarding unadorned naturalism. The key

---

[6] Wittgenstein, *On Certainty* (1969; §97).

[7] See e.g. Foucault on madness (Foucault 1967, 1973; also 1988). (On even logic and basic categories (space and time) deriving from social organization, see Durkheim 1976; Durkheim and Mauss 1963. On the category of the person, see Mauss 1985.)

[8] The accusation of immodesty, as well as that of succumbing to a fear of reality or of loss of control over it, is bound to plague transcendental idealism, given that whereas the unrestrained realist hopes only to be able to know the world (and allows for fallibilism at that), the transcendental idealist claims to have made that world in his own image. The more programmatic and unsustained by solid theoretical considerations such transcendental idealism is, the more pertinent those worries will be.

[9] Carnap's importance within the analytic tradition should not be allowed to obscure the fact that at roughly the same time Mead was working on what he regarded as naturalized Hegelianism, and that Dewey and Mead (and their brand of pragmatism) were important formative influences on the course of the analytic tradition in the United States. Carnap's reception in that country ought not to be viewed in abstraction from that background.

figure for bringing out this pressure away from the singularity of imposed structure, towards relativism, is perhaps Quine.

Quine's reasons for advocating the holistic view that the unit of meaning is not the individual sentence but the whole of language are well rehearsed: There is no pre-given articulation of the world such as to select some sentences as true descriptions of corresponding bits of the world regardless of what else is going on in the language. Reality, as that which is independent of any conceptual scheme or theoretical construction, is a constraint only on language taken as a whole. How that reality is cut up into objects is not a matter of its own self-intimating individuation, but of how it is articulated by our linguistic construal of it. In effect this means that Quine can, however unwillingly, be held to something like a Kantian empirical realism—according to which the reality we know is not independent of the order we impose on it—alongside a counterpart to Kant's transcendental idealist claim to the effect that the world as it is in itself is not something that we can know. Except that here the source of the articulation of empirical reality is not the imposition of the transcendental structure of the mind, but of the empirical structure of some linguistic framework or other.

This may be thought of as linguistic idealism—in so far as what exists is made relative to language. What matters for our purpose here, however, is only that, like Carnap, Quine's naturalized Kantianism can be seen as conforming to the essential structure of transcendental idealism in these two central respects. First, he seems in effect to accept that there is a way that the world in itself is, independently of any conceptual structure that we impose on it, such that it imposes a constraint on theory construction but is not what we have knowledge of.[10] Secondly, regarding the latter epistemological claim, he implicitly accepts what I identified above as the essential epistemic duality of transcendental idealism: that of which we do have knowledge is presented in one way to the naïve understanding, namely as the way of the world in itself, but critically understood is unmasked as in fact comprising individuations that are merely internal to our conceptual scheme, the results of the way we ourselves have carved up the world.[11]

And with the carving up done not by means of any fixed structure of the mind, but by language naturalistically conceived, there is clearly no reason why there cannot be alternative languages, driven by different theoretical and practical concerns, which cut reality up into objects in different ways. The ontological commitments of one theory might be quite different from those of another; each will have its own posited ontology, and there is nothing more to determining the furniture of the world than choosing one or other of the

---

[10] For more on the grounds for this claim, and the charge that Quine still conforms to a form of transcendental idealism, see Sacks (1989: 32–7).

[11] These two strands of transcendental idealism, although both retained here, can in fact come apart, as we will see in Ch. 8.

available construals. As Quine famously insists, to call something a posit is not to patronize it,[12] since that is all we can hope to come by: it is merely to recognize empirical reality for what it is. But there is no longer any purported fixed set of posits that we are all bound a priori to recognize.

It is important to note that these conclusions, and in particular the thesis of ontological relativity, do not trade on Quine's behaviourism, from which we might of course readily take our distance. This is so both because the behaviourism is not in fact needed for the radical indeterminacy of translation beginning at home,[13] and because anyway radical indeterminacy of translation beginning at home is not needed to sustain ontological relativity. In fact these conclusions would seem rather to be the simple fall-out of reflections about the workings of language, combined with a withdrawal from metaphysics. And by the latter I mean, of course, not merely the withdrawal from a metaphysical conception of language—i.e. the rejection of what Quine calls the museum myth of meaning, which is unworkable regardless of any behaviourist premisses Quine himself might have for his doubts—but also the withdrawal from external questions, in Carnap's sense. Questions such as what *really* exists, independently of all conceptual frameworks, cannot now be answered,[14] and so we are left with only the mechanisms internal to the linguistic frameworks available for determining the ontology of the world. And given that such frameworks are not transcendentally determined, there is no reason why there cannot be starkly competing ontologies, none of which has any privileged claim, any claim to metaphysical truth, over the others. Different theories, different posits, without there being any a priori reason for thinking there will be any significant overlap between them.

Here, then, we have quite general theoretical grounds—i.e. not specifically targeted on the sociopolitical domain—for a move to a naturalized Copernican Revolution, with all the consequent relativist pressure on naturalism. Whereas the introduction of transcendental idealism promised to bolster naturalism, the possibility of a pervasive naturalized form of the same Copernican turn seems only to worsen the instability of unadorned naturalism.

3. ON THE IDEA OF A CONCEPTUAL SCHEME

There would therefore be good reasons for resisting naturalized Kantianism. Given the grounds on which this latter turn is premised, there would seem to be two general and not incompatible strategies for doing this. Both would

---

[12] See Quine (1960: 22).

[13] On this, see Kripke (1982: 40–54, 14–15, 55–7). See also discussion in Sacks (1990: 185–6).

[14] Quine regards the attempt to answer such questions, as even the attempt to explicate the notion of existence involved, as a forlorn cause: see e.g. Quine (1953b: 15–19) ('On What There Is'), or Quine (1969a: 96–7) ('Existence and Quantification').

involve denying, albeit in different ways, that we can only ever address internal questions. The one, while it need not deny that there are questions internal to given conceptual frameworks, would simply deny that we need be strictly confined to such internal questions, such that there is no theoretical scope for settling the relativist stand-off between them. This would be to resort to full-blooded metaphysical realism (or perhaps merely to transcendental idealism) in the hope of externally validating one set of internal answers over whatever rival frameworks there might be. But since this really seems like a desperate capitulation to the problems facing naturalism, the other strategy is likely to be more attractive. This too tries to argue that there are good reasons for denying that we are confined to only ever raising internal questions, but not because we can get beyond those questions to answer some external ones as well, but rather because there is something incoherent—or at least unmotivated and resistible—about the idea of such confinement to questions internal to a framework in the first place. The idea of such confinement, on this view, is the result of a particular conception of language, and of the linguistic framework, which we would do well to question.

The central conception here that has come under scrutiny, largely thanks to Davidson, is that of the scheme–content dualism, according to which language is regarded as involving a conceptual scheme set apart from some neutral uninterpreted content—whether this latter is thought of as reality or raw sensory experience—such that the former can be said to organize or be made to fit the latter.[15] Now it is certainly right that this distinction seems to be employed freely by Quine (and others), and is conveniently used to underpin his conception of radically divergent ontological individuations. And it is important to consider both whether that use is legitimate, and what the consequences would be of rejecting it. In response to the first of these questions, Davidson considers that the use of the scheme–content distinction is illegitimate on the grounds that it is incoherent.[16] In response to the second, he assumes that without that distinction the threat of relativism in question does not arise.[17] But Davidson might be thought to be a little too quick in both answers. Let us briefly consider each of these questions in turn.

Regarding the first question, about the legitimacy of the Quinean use of the scheme–content distinction, there is no need for present purposes to go into much detail of Davidson's well-known attack on the intelligibility of the distinction. But it is nevertheless worth noting some of the salient points of that treatment in passing.[18] Davidson's main case for the unintelligibility of

---

[15] Davidson (1984a: 191).   [16] 1984a: 189.   [17] 1984a: 198.

[18] These points will be concerned solely with Davidson's argument in his seminal paper 'On the Very Idea of a Conceptual Scheme' (1984a). This is standardly regarded as the *locus classicus* of the appraisal of the scheme–content distinction. The argument is also widely assumed to be self-standing, and for that reason it is worth examining it on its own, and independently of the rest of the Davidsonian programme.

the distinction in 'On the Very Idea of a Conceptual Scheme' appears to turn on first selecting which metaphors to introduce in informally unpacking the distinction (pp. 191–2), and then showing that those metaphors cannot be rendered coherent (pp. 192–5). But trade in metaphor is always tricky, and it is not clear either that the metaphors are guilty as accused, or at least that there are not other metaphors that might have been chosen, or indeed non-metaphorical ways of putting the relevant point.

Davidson makes the distinction depend crucially on the notions of *organizing* or *fitting* some neutral content, conceived of either as *reality* or as *experience*. The problem with a conceptual scheme as that which *organizes reality*, or for that matter *experience*, is taken to be that one cannot make sense of organizing a single object.

> We cannot attach a clear meaning to the notion of organizing a single object (the world, nature, etc.) unless that object is understood to contain or consist in other objects. Someone who sets out to organize a closet arranges the things in it. If you are told not to organize the shoes and shirts, but the closet itself, you would be bewildered. (p. 192)

So for the metaphor to work, it must be that the reality, or experience, which gets organized is taken to consist of a plurality, of events or objects. But for that individuation must occur, and Davidson considers that that will require individuation according to familiar principles, so that we will still be talking about languages that are essentially like ours; and, I take it more importantly, about contents that are essentially ours, rather than being anything external to our conceptual scheme, such that different schemes might organize it differently.

There are at least two problems here. First, it should be noted how hard Davidson is working the image of *organizing*. It seems clear that while one perhaps cannot make sense of organizing a single object, one can *break down* or *divide up* a single object.[19] So if the metaphor of organizing reality or nature will not suffice to render a neutral reality such that we can make sense of different schemes organizing it differently, all we need to do is alter the metaphor and talk of that single reality being divided or cut up, parcelled out, in different ways. Indeed, when first introducing the metaphor of a conceptual scheme as *organizing* something, Davidson regards it as shorthand for a group that also contains '*systematize*', and '*divide up*'.[20]

The second problem here is that it is anyway not clear that the image of *organizing something* is itself problematic in the way Davidson assumes.

---

[19] Thus Quine says famously that we persist in breaking reality down somehow into a multiplicity of objects ('Speaking of Objects'; 1969d: 1), without falling into any of the manifest silliness that Davidson associates with talk of organizing reality.

[20] 1984: 191.

Obviously one cannot organize a single object, but it is not clear why it follows that the plurality required should be individuated according to our familiar principles (thereby belying the possibility of that reality being neutral and uninterpreted such that there could in principle be conceptual organization of it that was radically different from our own). Davidson says that 'whatever plurality we take experience to consist in—events like losing a button or stubbing a toe, having a sensation of warmth or hearing an oboe—we will have to individuate according to familiar principles'.[21] But it is a mistake to think that the plurality in question is that which *we take experience (or the world) to consist in*. Of course the latter plurality is individuated according to our familiar principles. And of course that would have to be the sort of plurality in question if the organization was a deliberate act of an individual empirical agent, like the act of someone organizing his closet, in which one must first pick out the elements of the plurality before organizing them. But the *organizing* here is specifically not supposed to be an empirical sorting of objects internal to the scheme by an agent embedded within it, but rather is a presupposition of such activity. And once it is allowed that the *organizing* in question is not of items internal to that individuated reality, but is rather what sustains those individuations in the first place, we can recognize that the plurality must be conceived of as one that precedes our empirical individuations. Since a single object—reality or experience—cannot be organized, we can simply regard the reality or experience that gets organized in this way as comprising a state of flux, a chaotic *tohu vavohu*, a swarming Kantian manifold of intuition. It would be the contents (or elements) of that flux that get ordered in one way or another by a conceptual scheme, resulting in the familiar objects or events we take experience to consist in, and which can then be organized in the homely sense. It is the latter *domestic* organization that requires individuation of the organized plurality according to familiar principles that belie alternative conceptual schemes. That is the sense of *organization* that Davidson bases his argument on. But it is the former sense of organization, a process which goes on behind our cognitive backs, that is relevant. And that seems to require only that there be a given plurality for the conceptual scheme to go to work on—not that we be able to individuate and refer to the elements of that plurality prior to organizing it—and so would seem to leave room for different conceptual schemes organizing the given unindividuated chaos in different ways.

The matter might not be as straightforward as this suggests. In particular it might be thought that just in conceiving of the reality in question as containing a plurality, we are already applying our principles of individuation, and so are not genuinely conceiving of some altogether neutral and uninterpreted

---

[21] 1984: 192.

content that could be cut up in a radically different way by some conceptual scheme other than ours. It is in fact already being individuated in accordance with our individuating principles, and could not be conceived of were this not the case. Essentially, this counts against the picture of a neutral domain external to all perspectival individuations, by denying the ground on which we would have to stand to produce such a non-perspectival map. This is the kind of difficulty Kant faces in trying to say anything positive about his conception of the thing in itself. For present purposes we need not evaluate the strength of such an argument.[22] It should be noted only that it is distinct from Davidson's. Davidson's argument turns specifically on the idea that organizing a plurality would require that our principles of individuation apply to it. This other argument is general, and turns on the mere *conception*—as opposed to *organization*—of something external to all conceptual schemes. Indeed, the claim that our principles of individuation are involved just in so far as we conceive of the content purportedly external to our own conceptual scheme, is valid, if it is valid at all, whether that content to which conceptual schemes apply is conceived of as a plurality, or as a single object.

The problems detected above, if they hold, would be sufficient to impugn the case in Davidson (1984*a*) against the intelligibility of the scheme–content distinction. It is only to the extent that these arguments are upheld that the discussion of the second image, that of a conceptual scheme as something that *fits* reality or experience, becomes the focus of attention. Here too there are problems. Davidson proceeds as follows. He notes that 'It is sentences that predict . . . sentences that cope or deal with things, that fit our sensory promptings, that can be compared or confronted with the evidence' (p. 193). The implicit assumption of uniqueness here (i.e. not just that sentences can be said to fit x, but that wherever something is said to fit x it must be a sentence; or, what comes to the same thing, that the only *fit* in question is that of a sentence) is clearly wrong. A round peg fits a round hole, but it is not a sentence. So the conclusion that the fit in question means that we can equate conceptual schemes to whole sentences or theories (since sentences may include whole theories) is invalid. But this is the crucial move—from that point on it is relatively plain sailing: in saying that sentences or theories *fit* the facts, we mean simply that they are true to the facts. But 'the notion . . . of being true to the facts, adds nothing intelligible to the simple concept of being true' (pp. 193–4). 'Our attempt to characterize languages or conceptual schemes in terms of the notion of fitting some entity has come down, then, to the simple thought that something is an acceptable conceptual scheme or theory if it is true' (p. 194). That in effect does away with the structure according to which there is a single domain, whether of things or of facts, which different

---

[22] For an argument along these lines, see Sacks (1989, ch. 7).

schemes, with their points of view on it, must fit. All we are left with, by way of accommodating the idea of radically different conceptual schemes, is the notion of one theory being true but untranslatable. And, given appeal to Tarski, it follows that we could not then have a test for a conceptual scheme that was radically different from ours (since that would mean that it was true but untranslatable, which is precisely the separation Tarski's Convention T will not allow). Of course, one might here reject the reliance on Tarski, and say that testing for radically different conceptual schemes might be impossible but that that is not to say that there being such alternatives is unintelligible. But leaving such moves aside, let us go back to the crucial move: the move from the assumptions that conceptual schemes are said to fit *x*, and that if something fits *x* then it is a sentence, to the conclusion that conceptual schemes are (groups of) sentences.

This argument works, obviously, only if the sense of 'fit' in the two premisses is the same. But it seems clear that it need not be. The fit of conceptual schemes might be no more than a matter of the conceptual scheme coping with, accommodating, whatever external constraints are imposed on it, be it by experience or by reality. The conceptual scheme might be said to fit the external constraints upon it if there is no mismatch between the two such that the one cannot be applied to the other. But the match in question, such that it enables the conceptual scheme to cope with the constraints without remainder, is certainly supposed to underdetermine the conceptual scheme, so that there could be many incompatible schemes that all matched or fitted the same external constraints equally well. Such *fit*, then, cannot simply be equated with *truth*.[23] Indeed, it seems right to say that conceptual schemes are not the sort of things that can be said to be true anyway. They are ways of doing something, not descriptions of what has been done. Sentences or groups of sentences (theories) are true. If we are to countenance conceptual schemes, then it is right to say that sentences presuppose conceptual schemes, and their truth is relative to them. But being presupposed by the bearers of truth is not the same as to be a bearer of truth. It would be inappropriate, therefore, to say that the fit in question is that of truth. It is rather the fit of a tool to a task. The way to bring this out is to notice that the two images, of *fitting* and of *organizing* (or *cutting up*), are in fact rarely meant to be kept distinct by those who talk of conceptual schemes. The connecting idea is that a conceptual scheme *fits* the external constraints on it if it can cope with the task of doing something to it: namely, *organizing* it. Now, effective applicability is not the same as truth, although the metaphor of *fit* can cover both. Once this is recognized, it should be clear that it does not follow that just because

---

[23] I notice that this criticism, and something of the one that follows, is made in Hacker (1996*a*: 297).

conceptual schemes are said to fit experience, this must mean that they fit as sentences do—which would indeed boil down to saying that they are true to the facts or to experience, where the latter drop away as redundant.

There are other problems with this leg of Davidson's argument. We need not, however, settle the matter of the adequacy of Davidson's case for the unintelligibility of the scheme–content distinction; or indeed the question of whether any other case for that unintelligibility can be made out.[24] For present purposes it is more important to note that the question of the *legitimacy* of employing this distinction should not be so readily run together with the question of its *coherence*. Davidson seems to suggest that it is an unacceptable dogma *for being unintelligible*.[25] Now, of course, being unintelligible would be one good reason for being unacceptable. But in an important respect the question of the coherence of the scheme–content dualism is beside the point when it comes to the question of assessing the legitimacy of its employment in the context of empiricism. Whether or not it is coherent, a strict empiricism, or for that matter naturalism, cannot simply help itself to it. The scheme–content distinction is clearly a piece of philosophical artifice. It is a philosophical picture which, for all its possible merits, cannot claim to have a structural role such as precludes its being displaced. In terms internal to the picture the distinction might be foundational, but there is no reason—and in particular none that the naturalist can give—for thinking that the picture and its structural presuppositions are compulsory or privileged over others. Just as naturalized Kantianism is led to the possibility of a variety of competing conceptual schemes, none of which could claim absolute priority over the others, so consistent adherence to that naturalist stance should in turn lead to the recognition that the structuring distinction of that naturalized Kantianism is itself only another conceptual device to which there are alternatives, and over which it cannot claim any absolute priority. Questions of coherence aside, this seems to be enough to impugn the legitimacy of the Quinean use of the scheme–content distinction as if it were a universal presupposition, an a priori structural feature, of any form of linguistic experience.

Now it might be thought that here the threat of relativism reveals itself to be self-stultifying. That is, that the consistent pursuit of the naturalist line has led to the recognition that the scheme–content distinction, even if it is coherent, is itself not immune to displacement, and so the naturalized Kantian position stands to collapse, and with it the exacerbated relativist pressure it seemed to impose on naturalism.

Here we reach the second of the two questions raised above, namely what the consequences would be of rejecting the scheme–content distinction. The suggestion seems to be that rejecting that distinction would put paid to the

---

[24] As I think it can; see Sacks (1989). [25] 1984a: 189.

kind of relativism sustained by Quine's naturalized Kantianism. Davidson, we have said, agrees with this. Thus he concludes: 'Given the dogma of a dualism of scheme and reality, we get conceptual relativity, and truth relative to a scheme. Without the dogma, this kind of relativity goes by the board.'[26] Of course, trivially, to the extent that we no longer talk about conceptual schemes, there will no longer be room to talk of truth being relative to such schemes. But the question is whether this really counts against conceptual relativism and ontological relativity, rather than just against one particularly vivid way of articulating it. It is here that Davidson can again appear a bit too quick: 'In giving up the dualism of scheme and world, we do not give up the world, but re-establish unmediated touch with the familiar objects whose antics make our sentences and opinions true or false.'[27] The idea would seem to be that having extricated ourselves from the grip of the scheme–content distinction, we can return simply to the natural scientist's preferred model of a pre-articulated reality the way of which is self-intimating rather than imposed. This would still be susceptible to the basic instability of naturalism identified at the outset,[28] but would at least avoid the additional relativist pressure brought to bear by the naturalized Kantian view.

It is worth bringing out why this might be too quick. At issue here is how much falls away with the scheme–content distinction; how big a step the rejection of that distinction licenses us to take. There are at least two possible sources of concern here. The one is that while the scheme–content distinction might dispose of naturalized Kantianism, there might be other sources of pressure on naturalism, such that the mere disposal of the former does not suffice to leave an unadorned naturalism in place. This is perhaps too vague a possibility to be a real source of concern, rather than simply requiring open-minded circumspection. More significantly though, there is the question of whether the scheme–content distinction does get to the heart of naturalized Kantianism sufficiently for the rejection of the one to count as a rejection of the other. While Quine clearly avails himself of the distinction, arguably it might be little more than a convenient prop, or at least may be so reconstructed, such that even without it the central insights that sustain the pressure exerted on naturalism by a naturalized Kantianism would obtain. To that extent, the position would survive the demise of that distinction. The mistake would then, once again, be that of concentrating attention on an image or metaphor that was wrongly taken to be weight-bearing rather than a mere prop. What is needed, consequently, is to establish that the rejected feature is indeed as essential to relativism as it is taken to be. The point could be either that the

---

[26] 1984a: 198.

[27] Ibid. In fact, Davidson's strategy is not altogether clear, and, as we will see, this criticism cannot be levelled without qualification.   [28] See Sect. 1 above.

scheme–content distinction is not needed for there to be resort to conceptual schemes, or that such resort is not necessary for the relativist pressure of naturalized Kantianism anyway. Without ruling out both, the conclusion that with the rejection of the scheme–content distinction we simply reestablish unmediated touch with a self-intimating way of the world must seem premature.

It should be noted here that in fact Davidson's discussion is not simply restricted to this line of argument. He does take the scheme–content distinction to be central to conceptual and ontological relativism, and then argue directly against the intelligibility of the former. But he runs that line of argument alongside another which allows that in principle conceptual relativism, and hence the idea of conceptual schemes, might not hinge on the scheme–content distinction. He sets out (p. 185) to examine the idea of a conceptual scheme and of different conceptual schemes in terms of translatability of languages, and distinguishes two parts to his discussion: one dealing with total failure of translation (pp. 185–95), the other with partial failure (pp. 195–7). These two parts in effect implement different strategies, for good reason. To the extent that we are making sense of *total* failure of translation, we cannot appeal to accessibility from one scheme (= a set of languages, according to Davidson) to another, so attention has to be turned to the conception that would make such a tourist-free plurality possible, i.e. to the intelligibility of the scheme–content distinction. When it comes to partial failure of translation, attention can turn directly to consideration of the kind of access that there is between languages, to see whether such failure of translation as there can be sustains a case for conceptual relativism.[29] For the moment it is this second part of the argument that is of interest here, since such conceptual relativism stands to be established without resort to the scheme–content distinction. The argument against it thus provides, in principle, a possible response to relativist pressure that does not concentrate directly on what might be no more than a convenient but inessential metaphor in which relativism is commonly cloaked.

The brief argument appears to be that identifiable cases of translation failure, cases of disagreement, rest on significant assumptions of agreement; charity is not an option, Davidson reminds us, but a precondition of identifiable and meaningful disagreement.[30] But in the face of that it is always open to us to accommodate such disagreement as there is either as a difference of concepts (operating with a different taxonomy, they mean something different

---

[29] It should be clear that this leg of the argument cannot stand without the previous one: if partial failure of translation does not sustain the possibility of conceptual relativism (and conceptual schemes), the weight would shift entirely to the question of whether total failure of translation might. This explains why Davidson regards the scheme–content distinction as central to his argument.   [30] 1984a: 196–7.

by their words) or equally as a difference in beliefs about the world (operating with the same scheme, they disagree on which of our shared concepts best describes the facts in question). Nothing can force the one construal of the difference in question over the other. This direct argument against conceptual relativism seems, however, problematic for a number of reasons. Without a verificationist premiss, the fact that we might take a given case of disagreement to be a matter either of conceptual relativism or of disagreement of belief would seem to indicate two ways of interpreting the available evidence, with the aim of establishing the truth of what is going on with those with whom we differ. That is, the disputants are either concepts apart, or merely beliefs apart, but whichever it is would seem to be a matter of fact. And so the mere fact that we can interpret the evidence so as not to count as conceptual difference cannot count as establishing that there can be no such difference. With a verificationist premiss, which would itself be objection enough, things are hardly any better. If in cases of disagreement there are two ways of interpreting the linguistic behaviour of the others, and there are by hypothesis no evidence-transcending facts, then there is nothing more to deciding how things are with others than what we on our most charitable interpretations dictate. But if charity can work in different ways, as it surely can, there is no reason why all parties to a dispute with a given linguistic group would decide on the same charitable interpretation of what conversants from that group were up to. And that again opens up the threat of Quinean relativism.

In general, the primary weakness of an appeal to charity to establish the impossibility of significant conceptual or linguistic relativism results from the construal of the link between conceptual relativism, the interpretability condition, and verifiability. *Pace* Davidson, it is not meaningful disagreement, but rather *the possibility of identifying or detecting* the meaningful disagreement, that requires agreement in basic conceptual structure. The two—meaningful disagreement, and the possibility of detecting it—can clearly come apart, in a way that leaves room for significant conceptual relativism even after Davidson's appeal to charity has been given its due. This needs some explaining, to bring out exactly where the two come apart (and where they don't). It should, after all, be agreed that it would not make sense to say that there are two languages that use conceptual apparatuses so different that there is no room to say that there is meaningful disagreement between them. It is also arguable, and can be granted, that there could not *be* meaningful disagreement that could not in principle be detected. Furthermore, to be detectable, there must be some matrix in relation to which the conceptual apparatus of the disputants can be calibrated. So far, the link between the possibility of conceptual variance and detectability holds. But this is to say no more than that there must be some language, translation into which renders a detectable disagreement: how matters stand from within some other languages, or objectively—as if from no framework at all—is not at issue here. In particular, this is not to say that the difference need be detectable by the parties to the disagreement. *They* might not have the conceptual resources to recognize one another as cognitive at all. Anything that we *can* identify as a different language won't be all *that* different; but that is not to say that there cannot be languages so different from ours that *we*, given our resources, *cannot* identify them as such. Davidson asserts the former, without seeming to recognize that the link between conceptual relativism and the interpretability condition is not so tight as to require interpretability *by us* (the speakers of one of the languages in question). We can bring the point out in terms of the intransitivity of translation.[31] Given that translation can be only partial, either because part of the language cannot be translated, or because the full meaning of any concept of the language cannot be translated, translation must be an intransitive relation. It follows that there could be meaningful disagreement between L_1 and L_n which could not be detected from within either L_1 or L_n.

Returning now to the main thread of our discussion, let us, despite the above, simply accept the direct argument against the possibility of significant conceptual relativism based on partial failures of translatability. Talk of conceptual schemes would then rest pretty squarely on the scheme–content distinction. Let us also accept the argument to the effect that that distinction is unintelligible. The question is where this leaves us with regard to the relativist pressure on naturalism. As we have seen, Davidson here takes it to lead straight back to the reassurance of contact with the ordinary empirical objects of the natural world. It would seem, however, that even given the success of the arguments in question, there is no such easy return to a (relatively) comfortable naturalism. The reason for this is that the scheme–content distinction is after all not a necessary condition of the relativist pressure on naturalism. Even without talk of conceptual schemes, it does not follow that we are left with a self-intimating individuation of reality.

4. RELATIVIST PRESSURE WITHOUT CONCEPTUAL SCHEMES

As long as there is still room for the epistemic duality identified above as one of the characteristics of the naturalized Copernican turn, there will in principle be room for relativist pressure on naturalism. The duality is between the order of things uncritically regarded as the self-intimating way of the world which

---

[31] Davidson raises and disposes of the issue rather quickly earlier in the paper (p. 186), before moving on to consider partial translatability. On this, see also n. 43 below.

is given to us, and critically recognized to be the way that the world is constructed by us.[32] What sustains that duality is a structuring of experience that is ultimately our doing, in one way or another, but to which we are not normally attentive, and perhaps cannot be fully attentive. And as long as that is in place, there would seem to be room for the projected order of things, which is presented uncritically as brute fact in the way that the naturalist takes it to be, to change along with the structure to which critical attention reveals it to be indexed. In this way the scope for relativist pressure on naturalism is inherent to the epistemic duality of a naturalized Copernican turn.

This epistemic duality can, of course, be tidily presented in terms of conceptual schemes, by recourse to the scheme–content distinction, as it is by Quine. But that is really little more than a matter of presentational convenience, and the operative duality can be maintained without that distinction. There are perhaps historical reasons why the separability of the two was obscured. Initially this probably had to do with the fact that the understanding of that duality was embedded within the context of a Cartesian conception of the mind, which is clearly at work in Kant, in which context the structure of objectivity imposed by us is unthinkingly taken to be the result of an intra-individual scheme. The linguistic construal of that scheme, also already partially present in Kant, was further reinforced by the linguistic turn in this century. The result is that the epistemic duality in question has, from the outset of modern philosophy, been couched in terms that run it along with the distinction between content and conceptual or linguistic scheme.

Nevertheless, it need not be. The epistemic duality can be maintained in virtue of certain common practices and established routines, by virtue of certain entrenched conventions and related power relations. These result in some individuative structures being rendered more salient than others, with the consequence that certain ontological individuations are given more significance than other possible taxonomies. The more entrenched these practices and power relations are, the less aware we will be that the taxonomies in question are our—social-based, rather than individual-based—impositions. The weight of authority, primarily the authority of entrenched custom itself, but also specifically of experts generated by that custom, sustains the sense of those domains of knowledge introduced by custom, being domains to which we are simply introduced. That is, the ontological individuations and fields of knowledge in question will seem to be domains that are given to us, imposed upon us, the result of our discovery of them, when they in fact stand to be revealed to critical reflection as rooted in practices and structures that we ourselves have imposed: a fictional force allowing what is in fact invention to be passed off uncritically as discovery. Of course, none of this is incompatible

---

[32] See p. 174 above.

with talk of conceptual schemes, and it is not meant to be. Should conceptual schemes be found coherent and attractive, they can be pinned onto these accounts, as a gloss on what is going on in them. But the point here is that there is no need for any such theoretical imposition of conceptual schemes. Custom, practices, power structures, salient routes of interest, would all seem to be such as might necessarily be regarded as involving some conceptual components, but it is clearly an extra theoretical move to think that those should be hived off from other factors that are not strictly conceptual, or narrowly linguistic, to form conceptual schemes, such that they alone explain the construals in question.[33] Factors such as brute behavioural patterns, intuitive preferences, sentiments, and structures predicated on being *unmediated by concepts* might all seem to play an important role in sustaining such construals.[34] The philosophers germane to this line of thought—such as Foucault or Wittgenstein—serve in this way to sustain relativist pressure on naturalism without particular reliance on the scheme–content distinction. In this they constitute an interesting alternative to those who, like Quine and Davidson, appear to take ontological relativity as hinging on that distinction.

It would seem, then, that the scheme–content distinction is just one structuring metaphor in which the operative epistemic duality may be cloaked. It is not essential to it. Not being clear about this, about how much actually stands to fall away with the rejection of the scheme–content distinction, can result in inappropriately targeting that distinction for attention. That is, doing away with the scheme–content distinction might be interesting in itself, but it does not stand to eliminate relativism and re-establish naïve realism in the way that Davidson, for one, assumed. Even having disposed of that distinction, it remains the case that the identification of those 'familiar objects whose antics make our sentences and opinions true or false' might not be anything other than internal to an order that is familiar because it is our own imposition, and is such as might change.

It should be noted that this means that the Davidsonian identification of the scheme–content distinction as just another dogma (regardless of whether it is coherent), far from eliminating relativist pressure on naturalism, in fact

---

[33] Although of course conceptual schemes might themselves be determined by those construals. On this, see remarks in Wittgenstein, *On Certainty* (1969, §§(61–)65).

[34] The narrowness of the scheme–content distinction, such that it is indeed a merely optional theoretical construct, can be brought out further by noting that it is not just the 'scheme side' of the distinction that is artificially hived off from the forces that actually sustain the detected world-order. The 'content side' too is frequently construed artificially as comprising not reality but rather raw sensations or experience, something like a veil of impressions—and, of course, the notion that there must be some such purely non-conceptual intermediary content on which our schemes go to work is yet another ubiquitous but optional piece of philosophical machinery. The relevant epistemic duality no more needs to hive off that aetiolated sense of content than it needs to work with an aetiolated conception of an ordering scheme. Both the ordering forces and what gets ordered can be nothing other than the structures of the empirical world.

stands to extend Quinean relativism significantly. As long as relativism seemed to be predicated on conceptual schemes, displacing the latter—either as unintelligible or merely as an uncritically endorsed dogma that should not play any essential role in a thoroughgoing naturalism—seemed to collapse that relativist threat. But once it is recognized that that relativist pressure is not predicated on the scheme–content distinction, Davidson's rejection of that distinction threatens only to exacerbate further the relativist pressure, in so far as we do not even have a stable given structure that will be common to all forms of experience. Rather than any fixed Quinean scheme–content framework, with the reassurance that ontological relativism will occur within conceptual schemes, we find relativism now being applied to that framework itself. Talk of conceptual schemes is at best an optional dogma, which retains its grip only in so far as we are locked into a particular picture, and which—as we have just seen—we might come to discard.

Wittgenstein's orientation is of particular relevance at this stage of the discussion, given the historical roots of the scheme–content distinction. Both the Cartesian conception of mind, and the conception of language as a well-defined and self-contained structure set apart from the rest of the world, were targets of his later philosophy. It is largely in consequence of this that he would no longer be tempted to buy into conceptual schemes as anything more than a bad picture that once held us in its grip. To that extent the fact that his later thought at the same time still leaves room for the epistemic duality characteristic of the naturalized Copernican turn, and for the relativist pressure on naturalism, offers a particularly clear exemplification of the superfluity of the scheme–content distinction: neither the epistemic duality in question, nor the relativist pressure on naturalism, are predicated upon it.

What objects we identify, what structures we take to be basic, is determined by our form of life, by the practices and routines in which we are enmeshed.[35] But this is not a connection that is readily noticed in the course of our engagement with those practices etc.[36] And this is in itself sufficient to introduce the epistemic duality in question. It is reasonable to construe the later Wittgenstein as holding that we read off the world as a discovery the structure that our practices have in fact themselves introduced. This duality applies not only to social and political structures, say, leaving an underlying physical reality which is itself genuinely of a self-intimating nature. Thus Wittgenstein

---

[35] Wittgenstein's talk of 'language games' in such contexts should not be taken narrowly to be reducible to conceptual schemes.

[36] And perhaps it could not be rendered transparent without undermining or at least altering our engagement with the practices and routines that make up that form of life. This is a sense in which reflection perhaps stands to undermine knowledge. We will return to this source of tension below.

considers there to be a straightforward and symmetrical stand-off between the case of those who consult a physicist as their authority, and those whose equivalent authority is an oracle.[37] This indicates acceptance that even at the level of physics there is no escape from the epistemic duality of the naturalized Copernican turn; that what is identified as the basic ontological substratum is nothing more than the projected presuppositions of our practices and salient routes of interest. If that were not the case, there would not be a stand-off in this case. The stand-off results only to the extent that it is accepted that with such different practices, and with the reinforcement of such divergent figures of authority, there will be only correspondingly different ontological taxonomies in operation, and corresponding differences in what counts as knowledge of the world. And what goes for physics goes for any other domain. There is in fact no room left for non-dogmatic resort to a privileged domain the way of which is genuinely self-intimating. Any such assertion would stand to be revealed as in principle just the sedimentation involved in a particular established orientation, such that the establishment of alternative authoritative practices would invite alternative identifications of privileged domains, themselves then taken to be of a self-intimating nature. Indeed even logic, which might be regarded as foundational, can be taken as fixed only relative to a given form of life, a given set of practices.

Relativism results directly from this pervasive duality, simply from the fact that where the central practices are changed, so too will the structures made salient by them; and in a naturalized form of the Copernican turn, there is nothing to preclude or restrict such changes. Even logic might therefore change, should it be the case that the form of life in which it is presuppositionally nested changes sufficiently. Here we come to the full intended force of the comment from *On Certainty* alluded to earlier:[38]

> 97. The mythology may change back into a state of flux, the river-bed of thoughts may shift. But I distinguish between the movement of the waters on the river-bed and the shift of the bed itself; though there is not a sharp division of the one from the other.
> 98. But if someone were to say 'So logic too is an empirical science' he would be wrong. Yet this is right: the same proposition may get treated at one time as something to test by experience, at another as a rule of testing.[39]

Logic is clearly not an empirical science; the truths of logic cannot be established as are empirical truths, since there can be no method of establishing them that does not employ them. But to say that they are presuppositional

---

[37] Wittgenstein, *On Certainty* (1969, §§609(–612)).   [38] p. 175 above.
[39] See also Wittgenstein (1969, §§318–21).

is in itself not to say that they cannot change. In principle the presuppositions of our practices could change, as the practices to which they are presuppositional themselves change, such that certain new rules come to occupy the privileged presuppositional role.

Now we ought to be clear here about the kind of relativism that is at issue. There is no need, for present purposes, to assert that there can be relativism so radical that there is nothing in common between the forms of experience in question. It is perhaps still unclear whether such radical relativism is coherent. This should not be because of doubts about talk of conceptual schemes: as we have seen, both because it is not clear that such talk is as problematic as it has come to be regarded, and—primarily—because relativism does not require talk of conceptual schemes in the first place. Rather, there might be other reasons for holding that talk of a form of experience radically different from our own does not makes sense; that relativism can always amount only to local and perfectly accessible variations.[40]

In particular, it is sometimes argued that we cannot coherently conceive of radical relativism, say, of a form of experience quite different from our own, since we are then involved in trying to say both that something is a form of experience, and that it is unlike anything that we take experience to be. We cannot have it both ways: if it is unlike anything we take experience to be, what sense does it make to say that we are conceiving of a different form *of experience*? Of course it must be granted that *that* doesn't make sense. But to conceive of there being a different form of experience is not the same as to conceive of that different form of experience. This in fact seems to accord with the insight Wittgenstein is concerned to promote when he identifies practices so different from our own that they seem very strange, but which nevertheless always still have enough in common to be recognizable to us as language forms of such-and-such a type.[41] The limitations of our current recognitional capacities should not be taken to imply that the seemingly fixed riverbed is indeed such as cannot change.[42] Given the intransitivity of familiarity, those whose behaviour patterns are strange but still recognizable to us_{now} as forms of x, might encounter behavioural patterns strange and yet still recognizable to them as forms of x, where the latter would be so strange to us_{now} as to be unrecognizable to us_{now} as a form of x. Being unrecognizable to us_{now} is then not the same as being unrecognizable as a form of x, and is not to say that we cannot conceive of there being some such form of x. It means only that identifiable shifts in the riverbed will be small steps in a very gradual process. But that is no constraint on very far-reaching gradual processes, or indeed

---

[40] On this question, see B. Williams (1981a, b). I owe much to both papers.
[41] See B. Williams (1981b: 160). [42] See *On Certainty* (1969, §99).

on uncharted shifts such that we cannot say more than that things might not always everywhere be like *this*.[43]

However, as indicated, the coherence of the attempt to state radical relativism in the above sense is not really of any importance in the present context. What matters here is that, even if radical ('untranslatable') relativism is strictly speaking inconceivable, it remains the case that such change as there can be would seem to be *unconstrained*. The relativist pressure on naturalism seems to be such that the potential for change in our construal of the world is unstructured, unrestricted, by anything other than current contingent forces. There is nothing, not even logic, that is such that in principle it could not change; all construals seem only relatively stable, subject to brute shifts to the way human practice—as well as changeable forces of nature—have shaped them (these two are obviously not independent of one another, a fact that we will have opportunity to come back to later[44]). Even if such relativism falls short of radical relativism, it does constitute a significant source of pressure on the conception of a fixed objective world as the target of our epistemic endeavours.

On such a view the possibility of transcendental arguments, i.e. of arguments yielding anything like universal presuppositions of experience, comes under pressure along with any other attempt to secure a univocal construal of universal truths about an objective world. All such attempts might take us

---

[43] Of course, if we_{now} could not recognize an alien behavioural pattern as a form of x, then neither could we recognize something in the intermediary group(s) as a *recognition* that that thing is a form of x. (I thank Adrian Moore for raising this point.) But we could recognize them as making *a claim* to recognition of it as a form of x. We could not go beyond that to verify or substantiate the claim, but we could distinguish, in the usual variety of ways, between genuinely meant (serious) recognitional claims and mere pretence. We might, of course, consider or suspect the claimants to be genuine but deluded—but that is just what we should expect the intersubjective dynamics to be when it comes to intransitivity of familiarity. It does not count against the coherence of such intransitivity. (And with further experience of consistency on the intermediary's part we might become more inclined to trust that their claims are in fact genuinely recognitional, although we_{now} still could not establish that they were. In the long run this unsatisfactory situation would perhaps facilitate an unseating of the way we_{now} are. I will return later to the way in which such synchronic variation can effect diachronic change.)

This incidentally also bears on Davidson's rapid dismissal of the intransitivity of (direct) translation (Davidson 1984a: 186). What goes for recognition-claims in general also goes for translation-claims in particular. Of course we could not recognize what the intermediary was doing as a *translation* of x, but there would be the usual ways of establishing that they were at least genuinely meant translation-claims. We might wonder whether the intermediary's claims to be translating something that to us is mere babble (if even that) were not perhaps evidence of mere delusion on his part. Again, that is just what the intransitivity in question would look like at the points of disruption. But writing off these cases, as Davidson does, by saying that perhaps *we* were mistranslating the *intermediary* to begin with, and that his seeming translation-claims were in fact nothing of the sort, would seem to be uncharitably inattentive to the kind of fine grain indicated above that would be readily available in these cases.

[44] See Ch. 6, Sects. 2–3, Ch. 8, Sects. 2–3, below.

to the identification of necessary presuppositions, which might even seem inescapable to us, but they will remain necessary conditions only relative to one orientation, one set of practices, to which alternatives exist, with alternative arguments for alternative conclusions. The more established the practice, and consequently the sources of authority within it—whether these be texts, rituals, or roles (shamans or physicists)—the more power and influence the orientation will exert, and the more difficult it will be to recognize that the convictions and conclusions of arguments that are indexed to those practices do not have the universal validity which they present themselves to those under their influence as having. The influence in question, although in part exerted by the figures of authority, should not be thought of as based primarily on deliberate manipulation by those figures of authority; it is most effective when it is a manipulation *of them*, as much as of those subject to them, by the orientation in practice to which they are all *uncritically* subject.[45]

Here we come to the significance of the fictional force that is at work wherever we have the implementation of the epistemic duality in question. Unaware of the way in which our practices and interests shape our conception of the objective order, behind our cognitive backs, we read that order off the world merely as something discovered, quite independent of us. Of course, that order is independent of us in a sense—namely, independent of our conscious decisions and choices. But it is only to the extent that it is taken at face value as presented, as simply given to us, ontologically independent of any structuration introduced by us, that it is so readily taken as having universal validity.[46] And it can be taken as such only as long as we refrain from critical reflection that would unmask the way in which what is presented as an impinging reality is not all that it is cooked up to be.

5. CONCLUSION

It is time now to take stock of the strategic significance of this source of relativist pressure. I started by pointing out the inherent instability of naturalism, viz. the instability of contingent brute natural forces in sustaining our conception of the objective world. This pressure towards relativism is then

---

[45] Whereas Wittgenstein identifies this only in an abstract and schematic way, we find Foucault attempting to expose in some detail the mechanisms that explain how the sedimentation of a seemingly universal order comes about in relation to a practice (or set of practices). On this, see e.g. the discussion of power and knowledge in Foucault, in Detel (1996).

[46] The point holds even if the discovered order, taken as ontologically independent of any structuration by the subject, happens to concern the structure of the mind itself. Indeed it is only as such that Kant claims for the mind the kind of universal structures required for the stability of his transcendental idealism. For more on this, see Ch. 6 below.

significantly exacerbated by the incorporation into a thoroughly naturalistic framework of the epistemic duality inherent in the Copernican turn. The result is the threat of there being no fixed limit on the empirical variation possible in the construal of an objective domain, on the possible fluctuations at the level of the practices and routines that yield our ontological individuations (which are themselves subject to the blind intervention of those natural forces). And, as consideration of both Wittgenstein and Foucault helps to see clearly, the relativist pressure results directly from taking on board the epistemic duality of a naturalized Copernican turn, and is not predicated on any other philosophical devices such as the scheme–content distinction with which that duality may be burdened. This is significant because the simple epistemic duality in question cannot readily be rejected on grounds of incoherence or unintelligibility, since it can be clearly seen at work in ordinary mundane cases ranging from paranoid delusions to scientific paradigms. And yet where that duality has come into play, we are essentially confined to asking internal questions; questions internal not to a conceptual scheme, but to a practice or form of life.

One way of avoiding this relativist pressure would be to grant the duality in question, but deny the generality of its application. But the denial of its application to certain central cases—e.g. logic, mathematics, or physics—must be more than a sudden and revealing entrenchment within a practice, a point of blind acquiescence, a refusal to engage in critical understanding of it. That would still readily be construed as a play within the epistemic duality, simply refusing critical insight, rather than constituting an effective exclusion of that duality from the cases in question. An appeal to a metaphysical order, such that in these privileged cases the epistemic duality is excluded because we simply are confronted here with the self-intimating way of the world as it is in itself, might suggest itself. But again, within a thoroughgoing naturalism there is no room for such an appeal.[47]

It might help here to refer back to what was said earlier, to the effect that there would seem to be two ways of resisting the relativist threat posed by a naturalized Kantianism.[48] One was to give up on the withdrawal from metaphysics, and so in this way deny confinement to internal questions. The other strategy was to deny the intelligibility of the central conception that underpins the naturalized Kantian position, and so in that way deny the intelligibility of thinking that we are confined to internal questions. Given that the former resort to metaphysics seemed like a desperate response to the

---

[47] Thus Wittgenstein in *Philosophical Investigations* (1952: II. xii, p. 230ᵉ): 'if anyone believes that certain concepts are absolutely the correct ones, and that having different ones would mean not realizing something that we realize—then let him imagine certain very general facts of nature to be different from what we are used to, and the formation of concepts different from the usual ones will become intelligible to him'. [48] See pp. 177–8 above.

threat facing naturalism, the latter seemed like the only alternative. But we have now seen that, rightly identified, the central conception that underpins the naturalized Copernican turn is so mundane that it cannot be rejected as unintelligible in the way that the scheme–content distinction, as a piece of philosophical artifice, could be. It is in this way, then, that, with the identification of the epistemic duality in question, we can come to appreciate the extent and resilience of the exacerbated relativist pressure purportedly exerted by a form of naturalized Kantianism.

Significantly, the relativist pressure on naturalism that has emerged here bears on the conclusion of the previous chapter. We saw there that the notion of a timelessly fixed egological subject was one that we could no longer avail ourselves of. Rather, we seemed to be forced to accept the view of the subject and its normative structures as structured by the wider context in which it is located—both biological and social. That meant that subjects stand to inherit whatever instability, and only as much stability as, the context to which they are indexed might have. Something of this is implicitly accepted by Charles Taylor. Rejecting the idea of the self as ahistorical, completely independent of socialization, of its place in a culture, a history—what we have called the egological self—Taylor regards the individual subject as essentially social: 'one cannot be a self on one's own'.[49] He regards the embeddedness of the self in a culture, its existence only within, and dependent upon, 'webs of interlocution', as an essential, inescapable condition—a 'transcendental condition'—of the individual having projects, purposes, normative structures. We can free ourselves from one such context, from one web of interlocution, only by resort to another. There is no getting away, however, from the dependence and essential indexing of the individual subject to some such webs of interlocution that set its horizons of significance.[50] Given the relativist pressure that has now been seen to apply to these wider contexts, such that normative structures, even at the deepest level, stand to be nothing more than local colouring, the subjects indexed to those contexts are similarly not afforded any universal normative structures that can be known to apply across contexts.[51] In this way we seem to be driven to the conclusion that the instability of naturalist construals of the objective world consolidates the normative instability that emerged as a clear threat after the demise of the egological subject. Just as we can no longer help ourselves to the egological subject as a source of universal-

---

[49] Taylor (1989: 36).

[50] Taylor (1989: 38–9). The Wittgensteinian connections are explicitly brought out, e.g. pp. 34, 38.

[51] Given that Taylor objects to the 'monolithic relativism' to which Foucault is committed, it is of interest to attend to the relativist commitment germane to his own position. There are certainly differences, but it is not at all clear that Taylor's response to Foucault's relativism (see Taylor 1985b: 180–3) is sufficient to free his position from essentially the same consequence. (See also Ch. 8 n. 52 below.)

ity or objectivity, so equally the way of the world at large cannot constitute a source of stable universality for normative structures of individuals embedded in it.

However, the assumption that the relativist pressure on the construal of an objective world is ultimately not constrained by anything other than the current contingencies, which has so far not been questioned, needs to be addressed more carefully. We saw earlier the strategic use of transcendental idealism against scepticism: the seemingly ineliminable possibility that we might be distorting the world in representing it is dignified and tamed by insisting that we do indeed distort it, but do so necessarily and necessarily in the same way.[52] We are constrained *non-empirically* to have certain well-founded illusions. In principle the same kind of strategy could be used to tame the relativist pressure sustained by the epistemic duality of a naturalized Copernican turn, by showing that it was not the case that the scope for change in construals of the world was unrestricted. I said above that it is only to the extent that the objective order detected in the world is taken uncritically as it is presented, i.e. as an ontologically independent order given to us, discovered by us, that it is *so readily* taken as having universal validity. But it would not be right to say that it is only as long as it is taken at face value as presented that it can be credited with universal validity. That order detected in the world could in principle be regarded as having universal validity precisely because it was recognized that it was imposed by us *but in accordance with structures that were universally valid, i.e. to which there could be no alternatives.* This would deliver a genuinely stable conception of the objective or universal order: one that, while still indexed to our practices in ways that commonly escaped critical attention, nevertheless survived critical reflection on that fact.

A mere return to Kantian transcendental idealism, however, would not constitute an advance.[53] It consequently becomes relevant here to consider that a form of transcendental idealism has been identified in Wittgenstein's later work. The question, then, is what this form of transcendental idealism amounts to, and how it might differ from the Kantian position. This is the issue that will be addressed in the next chapter, in the course of which the conceptual terrain relevant to the relativism of this chapter will emerge more clearly. The question is whether *all* presuppositions of our contingent practices might change as the practices themselves change, or are some more resilient than that?

---

[52] See above, pp. 92, 172–3.
[53] To appreciate why, it is sufficient for the moment to refer back to the point made at n. 46 above.

6

Transcendental Constraints and Transcendental Features

THE epistemic duality inherent to the Copernican turn has been identified, as well as the pressure it stands to exert on the conception of objectivity in the context of a fully naturalistic account. One way of taming that duality is by bolstering naturalism with transcendental idealism. Embedded in the framework of transcendental idealism, the epistemic duality still leaves a gap between the assumed and the real source of the objective order detected in the world, but it does not—at least in theory—still leave room for significant alternative construals of objectivity. But this form of transcendental idealism, even if it did stand to restrict relativism, would be unlikely to be accepted today given the prevailing naturalist (or pragmatist) orientation, in the context of which Kant's transcendental idealism seems excessively metaphysical. This is so despite the fact that Kant's transcendental idealism was conceived as, and constituted, a well-motivated withdrawal from traditional metaphysics. It is at this point that it becomes relevant to consider the form of transcendental idealism that has been identified in the later Wittgenstein, whose orientation is still more clearly post-metaphysical. In virtue of this it might stand to bolster naturalism against relativism without the excesses that make the Kantian version unacceptable. The aim of this chapter, then, is to contrast these two purported forms of transcendental idealism: Kantian and Wittgensteinian. Clarifying the distance between them leads to a distinction between *transcendental constraints* and *transcendental features*. In terms of that distinction some of the problems facing the naturalist, or what might more generally be referred to as a post-metaphysical orientation, can be brought into sharper relief.[1]

---

[1] It should be understood from this that the discussion will not primarily be concerned with the interpretation of either Kant or Wittgenstein. The concern is rather to engage in what might be thought of as philosophical geography—becoming clear on the nature of certain positions that constitute significant philosophical landmarks. These positions would be deserving of this attention even if it turned out that strictly speaking they did not fit thinkers who have, perhaps too conveniently, been saddled with them here and elsewhere in the literature.

1. KANT, WITTGENSTEIN, AND TRANSCENDENTAL IDEALISM

By transcendental idealism Kant seems to mean the thesis that *(a) we cannot know the world except as it is subject to the a priori structures imposed by the mind;*[2] *and (b) this world which we can know—empirical reality—cannot be the world as it is in itself.*[3] The second part of this thesis has been much discussed in the Kantian literature. It would seem, at first, at least possible that structures imposed by the human mind happen not to alter in any way the world as it is structured in itself.[4] The contours of the world as it is in itself might match those we necessarily impose on it—the way in which, say, one might project the image of a chessboard onto a backdrop that is in fact an isomorphic chessboard, or a bread-slicing machine might be applied to a ready-sliced loaf of bread. Kant's grounds for denying this possibility have not been clear. The denial seems at odds, in any case, with the claim that we cannot know anything about the world as it is in itself.[5] One way of sustaining this part of the Kantian claim is to argue that the structures imposed are essentially *perspectival*, such that in the world as it is in itself, devoid of all perspectives onto it, those structures could not possibly obtain.[6] Leaving this aside, my interest here is rather to concentrate on the first and primary claim involved in Kant's transcendental idealism. Until we are clear about this, there is little possibility of discussing the appropriate interpretation of the second claim, in so far as it is largely consequent upon the interpretation of the first.

That the interpretation of the second claim depends on the interpretation of the first should be clear from a Strawsonian approach to the first claim. The first claim can be taken to mean either that the possibility of the world being experienced depends on its being *presented in conformity* with certain structures of our minds, or that it depends on its being *shaped* by those structures. The latter, in contrast to the former, readily invites (although does not imply) claims to ontological dependence: the notion of a world that could not exist without the structures of the mind, since those structures *produce* it. This motivates the thought that the world in itself cannot be the world as we experience it to be, whereas the former more Strawsonian interpretation

---

[2] Kant would take this to mean specifically the human mind, but we can overlook this restriction in the present context.
[3] See in particular *Critique*, A28/B44, A36/B52–3, A369, A507/B535.
[4] The sense of the term 'impose' here perhaps differs slightly from its usual meaning: for any x and y, x will be said to *impose* on y just to the extent that where x is successfully applied to y, y will subsequently have the form of x, *whatever form y had previously*.
[5] As is frequently pointed out by commentators (e.g. Walker 1978: 130).
[6] Allison (1983: 111–14) suggests a response along these lines.

does not: there is here no claim that the mind *makes* the world, *constructs* it, such that that world could not exist just as it is without the mind. It says only that for us to have experience, the empirical world of which we have experience must be a certain way. We do undeniably have experience; hence the empirical world we experience must be that way. This might sound like a way of establishing straightforward realism. Arguably, however, it can be seen still to constitute a form of attenuated transcendental idealism. It is still acknowledged that our identification of the essential features of the world is not dictated to us by the world, but by the structure of any experience that *can be made intelligible to us*. And as the essential truths about the world are thus read off from constraints of the mind, it is only of the structure of the world *qua dictated by the mind* that we can have knowledge. As for the world in itself, although it remains possible that it is as it is presented in our experience, that it is (or is not) remains something we cannot know. (A world could be presented in conformity with certain structures, even if they were not true of the way it is in itself.) While this renders a *minimal* reading of Kant's transcendental idealism, it is still recognizable as a form of transcendental idealism.[7] And precisely because it is weak, it is worth examining. Any problems that arise within it are likely to be problems for transcendental idealism in its other, bolder, formulations as well.

The central claim that I want to discuss, then, is that any necessary features of the world of which we can have knowledge are essentially those imposed— not necessarily in any ontogenetic sense—by the experiencing mind. Another way of putting it is to say that the structure of the mind *determines* the nature of any world in our experience of it. Leaving behind further elaboration of transcendental idealism in Kant, we can perhaps fruitfully set our discussion of the minimal thesis just identified in the context of the later Wittgenstein.

Wittgenstein has been read, by Bernard Williams and others, as retaining a form of transcendental idealism in the move from the earlier to the later work.[8] Williams identifies three ideas as central to the idealism (solipsism) of the early Wittgenstein: (1) The limits of my language are the limits of my world; (2) those limits cannot be staked out from both sides, but are revealed rather by the fact that certain things simply do not make sense; and (3) the subject to which certain uses of the first-person pronoun relate is not an item *in* the world (i.e. is not an empirical subject).[9] Williams contends that these ideas are carried over in modified form to the later work, rather than abandoned; and it is because of this that the later work, like the earlier, comprises a form of transcendental idealism. Thus Williams writes:

---

[7] On Kantian transcendental idealism as involving an idealist epistemological claim, alongside a realist ontological claim, see also Sacks (1989: 28 ff.).   [8] See B. Williams (1981*b*).
[9] 1981*b*: 146.

my chief aim will be to suggest that the move from 'I' to 'we' was not unequivocally accompanied by an abandonment of the concerns of transcendental idealism. To some extent, the three ideas I mentioned are not so much left behind, as themselves take part in the shift from 'I' to 'we': *the shift from 'I' to 'we' takes place within the transcendental ideas themselves.* From the *Tractatus* combination ... of empirical realism and transcendental solipsism, the move does not consist just in the loss of the second element. Rather, the move is to something which itself contains an important element of idealism. (1981*b*: 147)

Jonathan Lear too recognizes an idealist position in the *Philosophical Investigations*.[10] Both Lear and Williams recognize that the idealism in question is transcendental, rather than empirical. The question is, what does this transcendental idealism amount to? It would appear, from the foregoing, that the shift from first person singular to first person plural would result in a form of idealism according to which the limits of our language—where language is not taken narrowly to mean a formally defined structure that is semantically interpreted—are the limits of our world; these limits cannot be charted from both sides; and the 'we' in question does not pick out one empirical group nested in its environment such that it and its limits can be seen sideways on. The first-person plural is rather taken globally, as widely as possible, to include any local 'we' amongst which anthropologists might travel.

The question here is what sense we can give to the notion of 'limits', when it is said that the limits of our language are the limits of our world. It might initially seem that this form of first-person-plural idealism conforms by and large to the weak version of transcendental idealism that we have gleaned from Kant. Above I articulated this weaker version of transcendental idealism by dropping the denial that the world as we experience it to be might be the world as it is in itself, whilst maintaining the claim that there can be knowledge (or experience) only of worlds that are presented in conformity with the a priori structures of anything that can count as a mind.[11] I will refer to this weaker form of transcendental idealism as T_1:

(T_1) There are transcendental constraints imposed by the mind on what can count as an object in experience, such that we can know (experience) objects only in conformity with these constraints.

The claim that the limits of our language are the limits of our world can seem to imply something like T_1. The way we are minded, to use Lear's phrase, constrains the recognitional routes available to us in encountering the world around us; the classificatory taxonomy we can detect in the world is dependent on the language games available to us within our form of life.

---

[10] See, in particular, Lear (1982, 1984).
[11] It should be understood that the concept of *mind* in play here need not be taken to involve Cartesian individualism.

Before going on to bring out that T_1 is nevertheless not quite the idealist position attributable to the later Wittgenstein, it is worth reiterating how weak the claim made by T_1 is. There is no transcendental psychology here whereby the empirical object is the result of synthesis by the transcendental subject. It is in eliminating this that T_1 takes its distance from a fully Kantian version of transcendental idealism. T_1 does not involve any claim of *ontological* dependence between world and mind. It might well be, according to T_1, that the world in our experience is in itself just as it is experienced to be. All that is claimed is that to be an objective world in our experience, it must accommodate certain constraints which are imposed by the structure of the mind. This is not to say, of course, that the claim made by T_1 is incompatible with there being some ontological dependence, such that the experienced world (Kant's empirical reality) could not exist just as it is independently of a transcendentally structuring mind. But, as we have seen, even without that additional claim, there is still room for a recognizably transcendental idealist position: the structure of the mind dictates, non-empirically, the fundamental structure that an objective world in our experience will display. Consequently, our representation and knowledge of fundamental characteristics of the world is always only of structures imposed by our minds, and we can say nothing about whether or not the world itself shares these fundamental characteristics.[12]

Now although the explicit definition of T_1 leaves it weak enough to remain neutral on the metaphysical question of the way the world is in itself (whether it is or isn't as we experience it to be), I want to argue that this neutrality cannot readily be extended to the question of whether there is such a world. T_1 would appear to presuppose a metaphysical realist claim after all: or, more precisely, would appear to presuppose the *ontological realist* component of metaphysical realism.[13] To bring this out, consider that if there are constraints imposed by the mind on what can count as possible objects of experience, if there is something about the way we are minded that dictates that certain moves are intelligible and others are not, then there must surely be some answer to the question of the source that secures those constraints. It seems that we cannot simply remain silent on the source of these constraints: that would render

---

[12] If Kant were to substitute agnosticism for the denial made in (*b*) above, then he would be in conformity with the weak form of transcendental idealism outlined here. But, as indicated, the interpretational question of which position should be taken to be Kant's canonical one need not concern us here.

[13] I take metaphysical realism strictly speaking to consist of two components: ontological realism and epistemological realism. Very roughly, by *ontological realism* I mean the claim that there is a way the world is in itself, and by *epistemological realism* I mean the claim that we can know the way of that world. For related discussion, see Sacks (1989, §§1.4, 2.1). In what follows I will, for simplicity, use the phrase 'metaphysical realism' as shorthand for what should strictly speaking be referred to as the ontological realist component of metaphysical realism. In doing so I will be obscuring the other component, epistemological realism. In the present context this will not be of any consequence.

unjustified their status as constraints. Now in so far as those constraints are transcendental, their source too would seemingly have to be non-empirical. And this would appear to leave only two options open in answering the question. We can attempt to ground them transcendentally, but obviously grounding transcendental constraints by appeal to further transcendental constraints only defers the question back a stage. Alternatively, we can take a fixed metaphysical bedrock as the non-empirical source of those constraints. Of course, as we saw in the previous chapter, it is not clear whether appeal to a metaphysical reality could ultimately constitute a satisfactory explanation. But—and this is the point here—it is hard to see how else such constraints could be grounded. We thus are pushed to ask what grounds these constraints, and on pain of regress to take a fixed metaphysical reality as constituting those grounds. If that reality were not fixed, or at least if any change in it were not in accordance with a non-contingently fixed order, there would be no transcendental constraints, since any such purported constraints would be susceptible to change that was merely contingent; and constraints that can be undone by merely contingent factors would not count as transcendental constraints.[14] In this way, I suggest, this form of transcendental idealism is in fact predicated on a form of metaphysical realism as the only available explanation of transcendental constraints, however inadequate it might be suspected to be. It should, of course, be clear that the fixed reality here need not be something that is independent of the mind; it could include, or be nothing other than, the fixed structure of the mind: but we would still be saying that there is something that exists quite independently of any merely contingent structuring, and which determines the limits of our empirical experience.[15]

Now this idea, that transcendental idealism rests on a form of metaphysical realism, is difficult to resist as long as we take transcendental idealism to be defined as in T_1. Transcendental idealism as defined in T_1 appears to presuppose such realism in virtue of being committed to transcendental constraints imposed by the mind, and therefore being committed to whatever grounds them. This metaphysical commitment will, of course, not necessarily be regarded as problematic. Within a Kantian framework, the conclusion that transcendental

---

[14] The precise sense in which this is true will emerge shortly.

[15] Thus, for example, we find Kant saying: 'This peculiarity of our understanding, that it can produce *a priori* unity of apperception solely by means of the categories, and only by such and so many, is as little capable of further explanation as why we have just these and no other functions of judgement, or why space and time are the only forms of our possible intuition' (*Critique*, B145–6). What is admitted here to be a brutely given, inexplicable fact must be given a metaphysical realist construal. That is, being brutely factual should not be conflated with being contingent. If it were, then the construal of empirical reality could no longer be regarded as necessary and universal, and hence as sustaining strictly a priori knowledge. Any change in the contingent base would threaten to undo what are presented as transcendental constraints on possible experience.

idealism presupposes an ontological commitment to there being a thing in itself may not be a worry, given that Kant's transcendental idealism—in part for the same reasons—makes just that commitment. However, much work has been done to make us at least question the nature of such metaphysical realism and doubt its explanatory value; and to the extent that we withdraw from a commitment to such grounding in metaphysically real structures, and thus identify ourselves with a post-metaphysical orientation, the conclusion that transcendental idealism presupposes a form of that realism will count against it. There would, however, be no reason, at least as far as these doubts go, to withdraw from a form of transcendental idealism if it did not threaten to entail any such metaphysical realist commitment. It is here that the discussion of the idealism implicit in the position of the later Wittgenstein seems promising.

The commitment to a fixed, transcendent reality, which we are taking as a presupposition of T_1, is one that Wittgenstein rejects. Any such commitment is precisely the result of being in the grip of one picture, one language game from which—by a healthy diet of alternatives—Wittgenstein intends to liberate us.[16] If there is anything to be learned from the *Philosophical Investigations*, it is that the more we explore the various discourses possible, the more we will realize that what we took to be a fixed, immutable, universal reality resulted only from a fixed picture that held us in its grip. Of course, this insight also prevents Wittgenstein from advocating any other philosophical position, or even setting out systematically the grounds for this withdrawal (since that would only be to fall in with a further picture). But the claim made is that the insights that sustain this lesson show that some sort of transcendental idealism must be right.

Given this, and Wittgenstein's explicit statements to the effect that there is no fixed hard rock of the riverbed,[17] and that any such identification is essentially indexed to a practice,[18] it would clearly be inappropriate to suggest that the commitment to transcendental idealism that philosophers like Williams and Lear detect in the later work in fact rests on the assumption of just such a transcendent (immutable) reality. Yet we have seen that that would be the suggestion if the transcendental idealism in question were T_1. Hence, if we are to take Wittgenstein to be a transcendental idealist, it must be of quite a different sort.

Wittgenstein's transcendental idealism, on this reading, can be roughly characterized as follows: any individuations of objects and events is essentially relative to, and dependent on, language games, contexts of human practice and interests, such that different practices and interests (language games) will result in different perceptions of salient features, which will in turn determine

---

[16] Wittgenstein, *Philosophical Investigations* (1952, §§402, 114–15).
[17] Wittgenstein, *On Certainty* (1969, §§96–7).   [18] Ibid. (1969, §103).

different ontologies, different ways of taxonomizing a world. What we identify—and, more relevant here, what we *can make sense of identifying*—in the world is a consequence of 'the way we are minded'.[19] The 'we' here, as both Lear and Williams point out, is not meant to pick out one empirical group amongst others. Taken in that way, any dependence on mindedness would, if it counts as a form of idealism at all, amount only to a form of *empirical* idealism. 'We' is meant to be taken globally, to encompass any form of life that can—either directly or indirectly—enter into communication with us (taken narrowly). Wittgenstein considers contrasts between local communities—e.g. us (taken narrowly) and some remote tribe, such as might consult an oracle rather than a physicist to find out what there is good reason to believe[20]—but the aim seems to be to explore the limits of the empirical variety that 'we' in the global sense can accommodate. By looking at the full variety spanned by the global community, we get a sense of what *our*—global—limits are. The remote tribe is on the horizon, the limit, where comprehension fades. The exotic contexts of such language games draw attention to the limits of comprehension, thereby enabling recognition of the fundamental ways in which we are minded. By seeing where the horizon darkens, we are in fact coming to grips with the transcendental limits of the way we—in the global sense—are minded.[21]

Yet all this remains radically internalist. The limits to what moves and individuations are possible are not imposed by any transcendent reality or metaphysical order, by any thing in itself, by any fixed structure (whether of mind, or of world—the difference hardly matters). Thus, for example, we find Lear saying:

One task of philosophy is to explore this twilight that constitutes the outer bounds of our mindedness. Further, one need not, with Kant or the early Wittgenstein, assume that one is investigating a forever fixed, ahistorical framework of thought.[22]

Or, still more clearly, in a later paper:

In contemporary discussion, the phrase 'transcendental investigation' is often used to describe an inquiry into the necessary structure of the mind, of the world, or of both.... But I am suggesting an alternative.... Wittgenstein's later philosophy can then be seen as a transcendental inquiry even though it displays *no interest in necessary structures*.[23]

---

[19] Lear (1982: 385; 1984: 229; 1986: 275).
[20] Wittgenstein, *On Certainty* (1969, §609). [21] See Lear (1982: 389).
[22] Lear (1982: 390). It should be noted that this in fact must also exclude a (stereotypical) Hegelian reading of a historical framework of thought, since any necessity to the unfolding of that framework over time would then be in accordance with a blueprint which itself was fixed, and eternal.
[23] Lear (1986: 270); my italics. Lear does not bring out how weak such transcendental investigations stand to be, where no appeal is made to necessary structures. Part of the concern here is to bring out the importance of being clear about this weakness: for this we need the distinction between transcendental constraints and transcendental features introduced below.

The transcendental limitations do not derive from any fixed, independent structure that imposes upon us, but from what moves (language games) are now available to us. What *we* are engaged in doing fixes the limits of what it makes sense to do. The limits of coherence and our ontological individuations are not determined by something given from the outside, so to speak; they are determined by no more than the language games, the practices, in which we are enmeshed.[24]

This certainly seems to hold out the promise of a position which might be regarded as a form of transcendental idealism that does not presuppose any metaphysical realist commitment. We might offer a definition of transcendental idealism along these lines:

> (T_2) Anything that is a possible object of experience is ultimately an expression of our activity—where that is taken to include human concerns, interests, actions, beliefs.

In effect, T_2 is attributed to the later Wittgenstein by both Williams and Lear. Thus we find Williams saying:

> The fact that in this way everything can be expressed only via human interests and concerns, things which are expressions of mind, and which themselves cannot ultimately be explained in any further terms: that provides grounds, I suggest, for calling such a view a kind of *idealism* . . .[25]

And Lear, having said that the later Wittgenstein is not exploring (with Kant or the early Wittgenstein) a fixed framework of thought, goes on to explain why, none the less, this does not—in his view—open the door to a philosophically significant form of relativism. (I will return to the issue of relativism below.) He then characterizes the resulting position as transcendental idealist, and this in a way that takes its distance from T_1 in much the same way that T_2 does:

> To accept the claim . . . [that only because we are minded as we are do we see the world the way we do], but deny that it delimits one possibility among others, is to accept a Wittgensteinian form of transcendental idealism. This transcendental idealism is Wittgensteinian, as opposed to Kantian, because it does not depend on a scheme/content distinction, nor does it depend on the existence of a noumenal world.[26]

It is important to note that this alternative definition of transcendental idealism (T_2), although constructed here in relation to Wittgenstein, is not

---

[24] It would be a mistake to think that such a view can be dismissed simply by citing as counter-examples so-called natural objects such as mountains or rocks. On this view it will simply be denied that our distinction between the natural and the artefactual amounts to a distinction between those objects that are merely discovered and those which are expressions or products of human activity and practice. [25] B. Williams (1981*b*: 153).
[26] Lear (1982: 392).

merely an *ad hoc* stipulation tailor-made to accommodate his views. It has a wider currency. A very similar definition is, for example, offered by Rolf-Peter Horstmann in addressing Kant's transcendental idealism. He writes:

Kant's contemporaries—philosophers like Jacobi, Maimon, Reinhold, Fichte, and Schelling—were very much convinced of the attractiveness of what they took to be the major claim of transcendental idealism: *That there is nothing in the world which is not ultimately an expression of some mental or spiritual activity.*[27]

This similarity between the gloss on transcendental idealism implicit in the later Wittgenstein, and that which concerns post-Kantian German Idealists, is perhaps not coincidental. Both, after all, share the rejection of certain theses central to Kant, such as the commitment to a thing in itself, which are just the respects in which T_2 is weaker than T_1. T_1 is committed to there being transcendental constraints that impose the empirical order, and such constraints seem to presuppose fixed grounds of those constraints, and so an element of metaphysical realism. T_2 no longer asserts that there are such constraints, and so is more attractive to those who would reject any commitment to a form of metaphysical realism (at the limit, to a thing in itself).

Having identified T_2, we might want to give some preliminary consideration to the question of whether T_2 is in fact still a form of idealism at all. It can be argued, and has been argued by Bolton,[28] that the mere fact that all possible objects of experience are essentially expressed in terms of 'human interests and concerns . . . which themselves cannot ultimately be explained in any further terms',[29] contrary to Williams's claim, does not constitute idealism. Human interests and concerns, Bolton argues, are not specifically bound up only with mental states such as beliefs and desires: Wittgenstein argues that human interests and concerns cannot be merely a matter of what goes on inside the head or indeed inside any other peculiarly mental domain, that such interests and concerns are bound up with the world in which, and on which, we act. So, to say that everything is ultimately an expression of human interests and concerns is not to assert that something specifically *mental* is fundamental: what is fundamental is a life form which has various elements, some mental, some material or physical, that is, an integration of what were traditionally categorized as the mental and the physical. It is then not so much that everything is ultimately 'an expression of mind', as Williams puts it (1981*b*: 153), but rather that everything is an expression of the integration of mind and objectual world, which individual categories should no longer be taken as basic. At this point, as Bolton puts it, we have gone beyond either realism or idealism: 'the concept of life bridges the old dichotomies between idealism and materialism'.[30]

---

[27] See Horstmann (1989: 169); my italics. [28] Bolton (1982: 276 ff.).
[29] B. Williams (1981*b*: 153). [30] Bolton (1982: 275–6).

In response to this objection Lear has claimed that it trades on too narrow a definition of idealism.[31] Bolton sees idealism as involving a commitment to a transcendent reality upon which all appearance in the empirical world is dependent, and which is specifically mental or immaterial.[32] Clearly in this sense Wittgenstein's later philosophy is not idealistic, both because he rejects the idea of a fixed transcendent reality, and because he rejects the Cartesian conception of the mental. But Lear, citing the passage from Williams quoted earlier, defends the claim that there is a sense of idealism in which the later Wittgenstein's position can be seen as idealistic:

Bolton says that in Wittgenstein's lifeforms, 'what is taken as fundamental is . . . human action, and this being so there is no reason [here] for calling this philosophy a kind of idealism' (272 [sic: 277]). But if it is human *action*, not behaviour, that is fundamental, and action is the expression of beliefs, desires, interests, concerns, then there is reason for calling this philosophy a kind of idealism . . .[33]

Lear can be taken to be pointing precisely to a form of idealism along the lines of T_2: the mere fact that everything is bound up with human activity, i.e. is an expression of human interests, beliefs, etc., provides grounds for calling this a form of idealism. And Bolton's point that human activity is not specifically *mental* is held to be of less importance than the fact that nothing can be held to be altogether independent of human activity, altogether non-mental, which is what the realist held. It is not dependence on the specifically mental, but the essential involvement of human experience, that constitutes a case against realism, and so—it is said—in favour of idealism. While this is persuasive, it can seem like an insistence on playing the game in terms of old dichotomies which, as Bolton's remarks suggest, are bridged once we realize that the human life-world, which is taken as fundamental, is an integral whole in which form of experience and an independent physical or material domain can be distinguished only as abstractions. (Bolton does not put it quite like this, but a reformulation along these lines is clearly well within the spirit of his paper.)

Whether everything being bound up with human activity should count as a weak form of idealism (T_2), or as a position which has moved beyond anything that is usefully still called idealism, would seem to be a moot question. Let us, however, allow for now that T_2 does express a form of idealism, and that on certain readings of Wittgenstein such idealism can be attributed to him. As a form of idealism it clearly seems not to be a form simply of empirical idealism, but of *transcendental* idealism. The limitations of our

---

[31] Lear (1984: 239 n. 49).
[32] See Bolton (1982: 273 and *passim*). Bolton here and throughout, as Lear notes, seems to conflate 'transcendental' and 'transcendent'. [33] Lear (1984: 239 n. 49).

mindedness do not have a source transcendent to the empirical world, but neither can they be identified as a part of the empirical world. One way in which this can be brought out is by reiterating that no particular group or practice that we can identify can be taken by us as the determinants of these limits. Were we to take any empirical group as the referent of the first-person-plural pronoun used in T_2, the thesis would be rendered false. Given this, T_2 seems to indicate limitations—the way we are minded—which apply to everything we can experience without themselves being empirical items in the world. It is this liminal status as presuppositions of the empirical which are not themselves located as empirical facts in the world that allows us to take these limitations as transcendental characteristics of experience. These transcendental elements with which experience is bound up might be thought to 'condition' or 'determine' everything we come to experience. Thus, to quote more of the paragraph in which Williams characterizes the transcendental idealism of the later Wittgenstein:

> *our* language, in this sense in which its being as it is has no empirical explanation, shows us everything as it appears to our interests, our concerns, our activities, though in the only sense in which we could meaningfully say that they determined everything, that statement would be false. The fact that in this way everything can be expressed only via human interests and concerns, things which are expressions of mind, and which themselves cannot ultimately be explained in any further terms: that provides grounds, I suggest, for calling such a view a kind of *idealism* . . .[34]

Now although Williams shows appropriate caution here in distinguishing what can be said from what can only be shown, it can appear that at the same time he is running together two distinct claims about what it is that can only be shown and not said. The passage talks in the first sentence of interests etc. *determining* everything, and in the second of everything being *expressible* only via those interests etc. And prima facie the *determining* here could be taken so that the first claim was stronger than the second, in just the way that T_1 is stronger than T_2. But that would be to attribute to the later Wittgenstein a form of idealism he would clearly reject. While it might be right that the move from the *Tractatus* does not involve the simple abandonment of transcendental idealism, it is important to bear in mind that the shift from one form of idealism to another does involve the abandonment of any notion of a fixed, eternal structure (the *logical form* of the *Tractatus*). So any talk of transcendental elements *determining* our experience had better not be such as to make implicit appeal to some such structure in the way that the talk of constraints in T_1 apparently does.

To put it differently, the first-person-plural counterpart to Tractarian solipsism asserts that the limits of our language are the limits of our world.

[34] B. Williams (1981*b*: 153).

It is this talk of the limits of language that at the outset seemed to invite the introduction of T_1—that our world, the world as we can know it, is dependent upon, or *constrained by*, our language or our capacities. And this seems to involve saying more than merely that it is an *expression* of, or is *enmeshed* with, those linguistic or mental features.

Some care must therefore be taken if this talk of transcendental elements *determining* everything (or serving as 'conditions'[35]) is going to be rendered compatible with the weaker form of idealism attributable to the later Wittgenstein (T_2), rather than illicitly reintroducing the earlier, Kantian,[36] form of idealism (T_1). To see how, in what sense, T_2 still allows talk of transcendental elements that determine everything, more needs to be said about the difference between the two candidate forms of transcendental idealism, T_1 and T_2.

2. A DISTINCTION BETWEEN TRANSCENDENTAL CONSTRAINTS AND TRANSCENDENTAL FEATURES

I have argued that presupposed by the stronger version (T_1) is some fixed reality that imposes constraints on the empirical forms of experience (or language games) that are possible. Kantian transcendental idealism can be construed as being of this sort. The weaker candidate form (T_2) avoids this metaphysical realist underpinning of T_1—there is no reliance on a fixed, atemporal reality that imposes limitations on the forms of life that are possible. Rather, the claim is that the grounds for rejecting some such metaphysical realist underpinnings themselves constitute a form of transcendental idealism. We come to appreciate that all ontological determinations are bound up with our interests and practices, which determine what we might think of as salient recognitional patterns. It is these patterns that lead us to identify 'substantive kernels' in our experience as real.[37]

But so far perhaps this seems merely to amount to ontological relativity: different patterns of prominence result in different ontological commitments. While such ontological relativity is today immediately associated with Quine, and possibly Wittgenstein, it is, as was noted earlier, already very clearly stated in William James:

But what are these things? Nothing, as we shall abundantly see, but special groups of sensible qualities, which happen practically or aesthetically to interest us, to which

---

[35] B. Williams (1981b: 152).

[36] It should be noted that what makes this position Kantian has nothing to do with Kant's transcendental psychology as such—only with the appeal to *some* fixed order, be it that of psychological or of logical form.

[37] The quoted phrase is from William James (1981: 265).

we therefore give substantive names, and which we exalt to this exclusive status of independence and dignity. But in itself, apart from my interest, a particular dust-wreath on a windy day is just as much of an individual thing, and just as much or as little deserves an individual name, as my own body does.[38]

Unlike Wittgenstein, both James (at least in the *Principles*) and Quine still seem to presuppose some form of the scheme–content distinction.[39] In this respect Quine and James remain Kantian.[40] They still accept or at least leave room for a distinction between *our* ontological individuations, and the way things (reality or content) are in themselves, independently of those interest-relative individuations. While acceptance of this distinction is not itself a sufficient condition of endorsing T_1 (as we will see when we return to James below), it does seem to be a necessary condition of it. Wittgenstein in effect rejects the scheme–content distinction as itself just one more picture, made salient within one more language game. Freed from the grip of that picture, there is no room to assume a domain—with a structure of its own—that lies beyond, and is protected from, the vagaries of our imposed individuations. It follows that it is individuation *of the world itself*, and not merely *our construals of it*, that is bound up with our own interests and practices, with our form of life.

Now clearly if *all* ontological individuation is an expression of our language games, then there is no room for an independent ontological individuation that imposes constraints on the empirical variety of language games available to us. How, then, on this view that is being attributed to Wittgenstein, *is* the possible variety of language games determined? We know now how it is not determined—viz. by the structure of reality. But we also assume that it must be determined *somehow*. There would after all seem to *be* limitations on the variety of language games we (taken globally) can encompass. There seem to be points beyond which we can no longer make sense of certain behavioural patterns as possible moves within a form of life. This is just the sort of insight the later Wittgenstein is concerned to bring out. But he avoids any appeal to a fixed transcendent structure as that which determines the limits in question.

The suggestion is rather that we explore the full variety of language games available to this global community, and that it is this variety of available language games that determines those elements to which alternatives cannot be considered. Those elements, such as *modus ponens*,[41] or the truths of arithmetic,[42] then have transcendental status. They are still essentially bound

---

[38] James (1981: 274). See also p. 277, quoted above, p. 126, for a particularly clear statement of ontological relativity.

[39] In James's case the organizing scheme is not narrowly *conceptual*, but is rather our interests and salient practices, as in Wittgenstein; but unlike Wittgenstein, James does leave room for a pure content to which those organizing factors are applied.

[40] Although both are, of course, quite radical in the departure they take from Kant's transcendental psychology.   [41] See Lear (1984: 238).

[42] See Lear (1982: 389).

up with human practices, with our recognized patterns of salience—but we cannot begin to make sense of a practice (language game) which displaces them. Attempting to do so we find that rather than stretching ourselves by imagining a different way of going on, we simply begin to lose our grip. This is what Williams has in mind when he writes:

> the business of considering [alternatives] is part of finding our way around inside our own view, feeling our way out to the points at which we begin to lose our hold on it (or it, its hold on us), and things begin to be hopelessly strange to us. The imagined alternatives are not alternatives *to* us; they are alternatives *for* us, markers of how far we might go and still remain, within our world—a world leaving which would not mean that we saw something different, but just that we ceased to see. (B. Williams 1981*b*: 160)

It is important to appreciate that what is being said is not merely that by considering a variety of language games available to us, we come to recognize those elements to which there are no alternatives. That would be compatible with the claim that while that is a way of *discovering* elements of our worldview that are not merely empirical, what *explains* their transcendental status is the way in which some transcendent reality dictates the structure of any empirical form of experience, thereby rendering these elements invariant across all language games. The claim is, rather, that in the absence of the possibility of any such external source of transcendental necessities, it is the empirical order that itself determines—rather than merely reveals—what appear to be transcendental limitations: which moves are possible within our form of life, and which are not.

Now this may seem flatly to count against this being a form of idealism that allowed transcendental elements to determine experience, contrary to Williams's apparent contention that this is what is shown (even though it cannot strictly speaking be said) to obtain.[43] Such determining as there is seems to go in the opposite direction—from the empirical to the transcendental. But it would be inappropriate to conclude that Williams has simply run together the two forms of idealism identified. On the form of idealism attributed to the later Wittgenstein—according to which it is not that the language games possible are determined by the fixed way we are minded—it would indeed seem that there is no room to speak of constraints that transcendentally determine what possibilities there are for us (taken globally). Nevertheless, this does not rule out the possibility of there being framework limitations that have some restrictive force.[44] To clarify matters the contrast between the

---

[43] See p. 209 above.

[44] We can talk of framework limitations without being committed to there being anything like raw material which is prior to, and structured by, those limitations. In this way talk of framework limitations does not imply a reintroduction of a scheme–content distinction.

two positions in question needs to be further elucidated, and to this end it will help to introduce a distinction between transcendental constraints and transcendental features.

Roughly, a *transcendental constraint* indicates a dependence of empirical possibilities on a non-empirical structure, say, the structure of anything that can count as a mind. Such constraints will determine non-empirical limits of possible forms of experience. This gives us the direction of determination that runs from a certain transcendental structure, say of the mind, to the range of empirical forms of experience that can be actualized. A merely *transcendental feature*, on the other hand, is significantly weaker. Transcendental features indicate the limitations implicitly determined by a range of available practices: a range comprising all those practices to which further alternatives cannot be made intelligible to those engaged in them. Now if the range of such practices was fixed, they would yield transcendental features that were absolute. But in the context of a naturalist orientation, that is precisely what cannot be had. Human practices, concerns, interests, etc. will then stand to vary with empirical contingencies. There is still room for transcendental features, but in so far as it is the entrenched empirical order that fixes what structures are transcendental, the features in question will only ever be relative. We can say, then, that transcendental features indicate the limitations on what, at a time, can be envisaged as possible by us (construed as widely as possible), and to which alternatives cannot be made intelligible as long as those features retain their transcendental status. But given that such features are rendered transcendental only by the empirical variety of language games currently available, it follows that while transcendental features indicate limitations on what can be envisaged, those limitations, just in so far as they are determined by no more than empirical facts, can themselves change over time, and moreover can change in a way that is not subject to any constraints whatsoever. To put it metaphorically, such transcendental features are no more than a shadow of necessity cast by whatever practices are current. Consequently, those transcendental features of what we can currently envisage are not constraints on what is possible. When it comes to such transcendental features, inconceivability is no guide to impossibility.

Now this distinction between transcendental constraints and transcendental features underpins the distinction between T_1 and T_2. It would seem that whereas T_1 can appeal to transcendental constraints, T_2 can appeal only to transcendental features. Where there is no (possibly implicit) appeal to any transcendent source, it looks as though there is no scope for a dependence of the variety of empirical possibilities on transcendental constraints; certain transcendental features can emerge from reflection on the practices in which we are engaged, but these features are dependent on those practices, rather than the other way round. We then have to concede that at best transcendental features might create in us the illusion that we are subject to transcendental constraints.

We can now, before moving on to the more general significance of this distinction between transcendental features and transcendental constraints, finally explain the sense in which it might still be said, within T_2, that everything is *determined*, or *conditioned*, by transcendental elements.

It seems clear that when it comes to the later Wittgenstein, there is no room to identify transcendental elements other than transcendental features. At the moment we cannot imagine alternatives to certain transcendental features (and consequently perhaps cannot properly articulate those features)—but that is no more than a consequence of the way our mindset is fixed by currently salient practices, which might change. It will *look* to us at any given point as though there are no alternatives to certain features, but that does not mean that there *are* no alternatives to them. We might change in such ways that certain transcendental features lose that status, and others come into existence. Such is the instability of practice-driven manufacturing of transcendental items.

The fact that in this way transcendental features are contingent, and might shift in response to contingent factors, raises a question of whether they can be said to be genuinely transcendental. However, we can take them to be transcendental for the same reason that we allowed that T_2 could be thought of as a version of *transcendental* idealism: where they obtain, they are presuppositional features relative to the world we can experience and describe, such that they cannot be established to obtain in the manner of empirical facts. In this way, it seems that their contingency, resulting from possible changes in practices, need not undermine the transcendental status of these features. However, their contingency does affect the status of these features—however transcendental they are—as *constraints*. Transcendental features, expressing limits of what we can currently envisage, might serve as constraints on what projects we undertake, what we can recognize as a viable option, etc. But the contingency of these transcendental features means that their force as constraints is in no way privileged over that of ordinary empirical constraints. This is because it is a contingent matter whether they are sustained, rather than a shift in our practices sustaining alternatives to them, whether or not we can now make those alternatives intelligible.

Whereas merely transcendental features thus constitute at best ordinary empirical constraints, we rightly call those transcendental elements that constitute non-empirical constraints on the possibilities of experience 'transcendental constraints'. The difference between transcendental features and transcendental constraints, then, is not that the former cannot serve as constraints at all, but that, unlike the latter, they are at most empirical constraints. (In fact, since it is empirical practices that determine transcendental features, saying that transcendental features are empirical constraints on empirical practices is just an elliptical way of saying that sometimes current practices can act as empirical constraints on other practices in ways that we cannot clearly articulate.)

Having identified the sense in which transcendental features might be seen as constraints, we can understand how the later Wittgenstein can be taken to introduce a form of idealism according to which transcendental elements *determine* everything, without this involving an inappropriate retreat from T_2 to T_1. While not appealing to anything more than (what we are calling) transcendental features, Williams can consistently regard Wittgenstein as committed to the view, albeit strictly unsayable, that our interests, concerns, etc., taken as transcendental elements, *determine* everything—as long as the distinction is made between transcendental determination or constraint and transcendental features serving as merely empirical determinations or constraints. It is only in the latter sense that talk of transcendental elements *determining* everything can be rendered compatible with the weaker form of idealism that is attributable to the later Wittgenstein.[45]

3. THE SIGNIFICANCE OF THE DISTINCTION

The distinction between the kinds of constraint operative in the two forms of idealism outlined is of some importance. Not being clear about it can result in the assumption that we can withdraw from the residual metaphysical commitments of Kantian transcendental idealism, and still hold on to there being transcendental constraints that are sufficient to establish universal and objective limits to empirical relativism. Some such position is essential, no doubt. But what we have seen so far is that we cannot simply help ourselves to it.

We can bring this out as follows: A gradual withdrawal from metaphysics reaches a limit in Kant's rejection of transcendental realism for transcendental idealism. But Kant still maintains a residual appeal to a metaphysical order. This withdrawal from metaphysics, from a commitment to a transcendent order, can, however, continue beyond its residual Kantian stage, as in the move from the early to the later Wittgenstein. And what we have seen here is that, with that move, there is apparently no room left for transcendental constraints. Whatever transcendental features are operative cannot count as transcendental constraints; that would require that they be governed by an order that is not up for merely contingent alteration, which is precisely what we can no longer help ourselves to. It is in fact because this is not readily appreciated that it is so tempting to think that what we have in T_2 is a form of transcendental idealism, with all the certainties but none of the unwanted baggage of T_1.

---

[45] This also seems to be the sense in which Lear can say that Wittgenstein offers a transcendental investigation in the absence of necessary structures—see n. 23 above.

At this juncture it might again seem that there is not much point in claiming a position which leaves room only for transcendental features (which serve at most as contingent constraints) rather than transcendental constraints, to be a form of transcendental idealism, rather than of radical *pragmatism*. If there are no transcendental constraints, then there are obviously no fixed non-empirical conditions governing human change. There are, then, just the variety of practices from which at any given time we can read off transcendental features, but those features will not be unchanging (or such as change only in accordance with a non-empirical blueprint). This is just the radical pragmatism that thinkers like Rorty attribute to the later Wittgenstein. It is arguable that the distinction between transcendental constraints and transcendental features precisely differentiates between transcendental idealism and pragmatism, rather than between two forms of transcendental idealism. Certainly it seems right that what makes William James a pragmatist rather than a transcendental idealist is precisely that for him, although there is a way the world is in itself, there is no related imposition of a non-empirical order on our experience; there are no transcendental constraints, the only constraints are internal, empirical, and contingent.[46] Whether or not we ultimately want to strip the position of the later Wittgenstein of its title as a form of transcendental idealism is not something we need to settle here. It should be noted, however, that there is prima facie no reason not to consider Wittgenstein's purported transcendental idealism to be a form of pragmatism—as long as it is recognized as a form which gives a particular presuppositional status to certain ultimately contingent structures. What really matters is that we seem to be forced to recognize two quite distinct positions: one which allows transcendental constraints, by still appealing to a metaphysical order, and one which prescinds from metaphysical commitment, and affords us no more than transcendental features. And the choice between the two is not a happy one.

If we opt for there being transcendental constraints, that would hold out the possibility of standards of evaluation that are not merely contingent and cultural. But such constraints seem to require appeal, however minimal, to some sort of unexplained and possibly inexplicable transcendent grounds.

If, on the other hand, we confine ourselves to the recognition only of transcendental features, we can avoid all metaphysical 'dogma'. But we are then left with the possibility of ultimately unrestrained empirical relativism sanctioned by T_2.[47] All standards of evaluation are then ultimately indexed to a given set of practices, to the tradition in which we participate. It might be

---

[46] This aspect of James's pragmatism is brought out nicely by Bergson, in his paper 'On the Pragmatism of William James', in Bergson (1992c).

[47] It is helpful to bear in mind that—as we saw in the previous chapter—there is no need here to insist on the viability of radical relativism. The worry arises merely from empirical relativism, once the full scope for it is admitted.

thought that we could aim here for universalizability by again construing 'we' as widely as possible—globally—and hoping for canons of evaluation that would be agreed to by all concerned. But in the absence of transcendental constraints, in effect the global 'we' seems to be left devoid of any resilient normative unity. Radical contingency just does mean that there are no limits to how far 'we' may come to extend, however inconceivable such extensions may be to *us here and now*. Without some transcendental constraints governing possible variety, there is no apparent reason for trusting that there will be any significant common ground between all different localities. Transcendental *features* might arise, but they too are ultimately local: they indicate local limitations on conceivability which do not translate into limitations on possibility.[48]

It is important to recognize that *this* is the position that seems to be implicit in the later Wittgenstein. The grounds for concern over this view being *de facto* accepted should be clear. Moreover, if the authority for all our fundamental commitments, which in non-reflective mode seems to transcend the merely empirical, is upon reflection said to be merely the shadow cast by our entrenched practices, the point of adhering to those commitments might come into question. Thus our fundamental commitments might have the status of fictions, which function successfully only when our critical eye is turned away from them.

We thus seem to have, on the one hand, a position that makes highly problematic metaphysical claims, and, on the other, one which threatens to offer little more than ultimately uncritical participation in local practices. Clearly what is called for is some middle ground; some way of showing how, without mysterious metaphysical underpinnings, we can nevertheless have what transcendental constraints promise, rather than mere features masquerading as such constraints.[49]

It is, of course, not at all clear how this combination of genuinely resilient universality and metaphysical abstinence can be secured. And it is just this difficulty that is obscured by the failure to distinguish clearly between transcendental constraints and transcendental features. Without that distinction in place, it was possible to see the move to the later Wittgenstein as a move to a post-metaphysical orientation that still retains the operative force of transcendental idealism. Once the distinction between transcendental constraints and transcendental features is made, we can come to recognize that, barring

---

[48] A particularly central question, of course, and one to which I will return (in Ch. 8), concerns what transcendental arguments can be taken to establish: transcendental constraints or transcendental features? Kant clearly took them to establish the former. But to the extent that transcendental arguments are merely locally indexed, i.e. are merely relative to a socio-historical context, they will be sufficient to establish only transcendental features.

[49] Also, whereas the two obvious alternatives that pose the problem are inadequate in part because neither sits comfortably with critical reflection, the middle position would have to avoid this sort of instability.

further work, what the later Wittgenstein retains of the transcendental ideas (namely, transcendental features) is seemingly sufficient only to constitute a position which may be considered as unacceptable as the metaphysical option to which it is opposed.

Of course, not everyone would feel the pull of this difficulty. Wittgenstein, for one, seemed prepared to accept that there is room only for what I have described as the radical contingency of involvement in one set of language games or another, and would surely have accepted with equanimity that where we would look for transcendental constraints, there are no more than transcendental features. Consistently with this, he inclined towards giving up philosophy in a kind of Pyrrhonist acquiescence. But it is important to emphasize that this withdrawal from philosophy does not leave everything as it was. The conception of reason, and of normative validity in general, that we come away with after giving up the philosophical study is not at all the conception with which we entered that study. While some will accept this Wittgensteinian post-metaphysical position, others, like Habermas, Putnam, or Rawls—to name only three—have been concerned that a post-metaphysical framework be shown to be compatible with universal and objective constraints.[50] For those who share that concern, the problem focused here in terms of the distinction between transcendental constraints and transcendental features will remain pertinent.

---

[50] Although Putnam has tried to accommodate a degree of normative convergence within his 'internal realist' position, it is not clear that he is sufficiently attentive to the difficulties involved. On this, see Sacks (1992).

III

Conceptions of Objectivity

7

A Compulsion to Objectivity in Experience

THE first two parts of this book set the agenda for this final part. In this chapter I will take a look at some arguments designed to pick up on the insights of the philosophers canvassed in Part I, while allowing them to stand uncluttered by doubtful characteristics of one model of the mind or another. The essentially Strawsonian attempt will be to uphold the interdependence between subjectivity and objectivity, but without reliance on any transcendental psychology. This is intended to get round the various problems seen earlier, in particular the fact that the availability of a Jamesian alternative to the Kantian model of the mind threatens to derail the train of the Transcendental Deduction at the outset. These arguments, however, have the character of transcendental arguments, and the upshot of Part II has precisely been to cast doubt on the credentials of any such arguments. The possibility of such arguments will accordingly be taken up again in Chapter 8, where I will provide grounds for thinking that the arguments in the present chapter may not succumb to the relativist pressure on objectivity identified in Part II, and in fact provide a way of resisting it.

In Part I we saw the difficulties that ensue for various philosophical models of the mind; in particular, we saw that the issue of psychological atomism proved problematic. In the context of traditional empiricism the theoretical commitment to atomism, itself seemingly conducive to the rejection of innate ideas, gave rise to problems internal to the account of the mind, as well as to external world scepticism. At the same time, the rejection of atomism, either in the context of James's radical empiricism, or in the context of a like rejection of empiricism (Bergson), does not fare much better in dealing with traditional epistemological questions. And in the context of the Kantian framework, psychological atomism seemed to figure as a commitment that could well be rejected, as indeed it was by James (along with many other features of Kant's transcendental psychology, in particular the division of labour between transcendental faculties of sensibility and of judgement). Yet without that commitment the more viable reconstruction of the argument of the Transcendental Deduction does not run.¹

We might expect to get further, particularly with a Kantian argument, if instead of introducing psychological atomism as a consequence of an optional model of the mind (or indeed simply as a premiss) we can reveal it to be an unavoidable conclusion of an argument that starts quite a bit further back. To this effect we would do better to expunge all concern with the theoretical construals of the right model of the mind, and in particular for the question of whether the mind first registers contents holistically or atomistically. Instead we might take our start from the simple question, what must the most minimalistically conceived experience be like for it to count as an experience at all? The intention is not to proceed from this to an adequate model of the mind, but rather to accommodate the valid insights of Part I without entangling them unnecessarily with contentions about transcendental, or indeed empirical, psychology along the way at all.

1. MINIMAL CONCEPTIONS OF EXPERIENCE

The sense in which the question from which we take our start involves taking a step back from the Kantian starting-point can be brought out as follows. Kant is interested in the interdependence between the experience of objectivity and the unity of consciousness. Without unity of consciousness, he tells us, my experience would be nothing for me; it would be fragmented into so many unowned experiences. 'These perceptions would not then belong to any experience, consequently would be ... merely a blind play of representations, less even than a dream.'² His starting-point, then, is that we must, in fact on pain of inconsistency, accept that the individual person does have such unity of consciousness, the question then being about the preconditions of that unity obtaining. But while it is perhaps right that we cannot coherently question our unity of consciousness, it might be of interest to ask what would in fact remain subsequent to the disintegration of that unity. Kant's interest is in the fact that to the person, once he has lost his unity of consciousness, these experiences ('representations') are nothing. The concern here

---

¹ As we have seen, the argument of the Transcendental Deduction might arguably still run without Kant's atomism, on the version that accepts not only that all experience is fundamentally conceptual, but also that the Metaphysical Deduction of the Categories, and the doctrine of synthesis, are right at least in principle, if not in detail (see above, Ch. 3, Sect. 2). But the latter are not likely to be accepted.

It should be pointed out that the more viable version of the argument (Ch. 3, Sect. 3, above) was seen to have weaknesses in the absence of the safeguards promised by the psychological mechanisms described on the other reconstruction (pp. 91–3 above). The argument as developed here should not similarly require such safeguards (see Ch. 8, Sect. 3, below).

² *Critique*, A112.

is, nevertheless, to take that step back, not to rest at the level of personal unity of consciousness, and to ask what each of these fragments—the individual experiences that might supposedly survive the disintegration into a 'blind play of representations', but which can equally be unified into a single personal consciousness—must be like for them to count as so many experiences at all.

It seems clear that the mere disintegration of personal unity of consciousness itself leaves it underdetermined whether we should say of the resulting disunity of items only that there is no one owner for all of them, or more strongly that, for any one of them, there is no owner. All Kant needs for his purposes is the former, weaker construal, namely that with the loss of personal unity of consciousness the various experiences are no longer held together in one consciousness; he need not deny that there is consciousness of each individually. Even if individually each of the items in question still belongs to a discrete single consciousness, the loss of single ownership of them all renders what was the single owner's experience even less than a dream. At the same time, there is nothing as yet to stop Kant endorsing the stronger thesis as well.

If, however, we want to consider the fall-out of the disintegration of personal unity of consciousness to be *experiences*, then it seems clear that this weaker thesis is no longer optional.[3] If the resulting elements are not even individually owned, in the minimal sense of there being, for each one, a subject that is conscious of it, it is difficult to see how they could, following the disintegration of personal unity of consciousness, still survive *as experiences* cut loose in the world. For something to count as an experience there must be something that it is like.[4] The question then is, what are the conditions under which there

---

[3] For his purposes, Kant does not need to consider the disparate items to be experiences. He refers to them as representations or intuitions, and although it is not very clear what his view on this question is (cf. e.g. *Critique*, A111–12 and A122 or B131–5) it seems open to him to say that in themselves, devoid of the unity of consciousness of the person, they would not count as *experiences* at all. Nothing fundamental to his argument-strategy depends on his saying otherwise. Nevertheless, that would be a counter-intuitive view, which there is no reason to adopt here.

[4] This familiar line of thought is well expressed by Nagel (1974). For opposition, see e.g. Carruthers (1992a, ch. 8). The case of blindsight (Weiskrantz 1986), now standardly appealed to and which Carruthers uses too, does not show that there are non-conscious *experiences*, and hence experiences the having of which is not *like* anything. It can—more convincingly, I think—be regarded as evidence of information-carrying brain states which are not themselves experiences. Carruthers, although not endorsing it, allows for such a construal himself (1992a: 173). This is not to deny that, given a suitable functional role, such non-conscious states may count as *perceptions*; and that we might come to be conscious that we have them.

It should generally be acknowledged that not every cognitive or mental state has a typical feel in the way that experiential states do. Thus the belief that nationalism is a necessary evil, for example, may not have associated with it something that it is typically like to have it. But again it seems right that for the belief to count as an *experience*—rather than as a non-experiential cognitive state—it must be associated with some qualitative state. If it isn't, then I may be conscious that I have it, but what I am conscious of having is not itself an experience. In short, by holding fast to the claim that experiences are such that there is something that it is like to have them, we also retain the recognition that not all cognitive or mental states are experiences. And it is with the necessary conditions of having experiences that the main text is concerned.

can be something that a given experience is like? It would seem that we have no way of making sense of this requirement except by saying that it must involve *consciousness of content*. Moreover, it can count as an experience only to the extent that the content is present to a *single* consciousness. An individual experience must, then, involve within its parameters a unity of consciousness.

Here we have a minimal constraint on the nature of anything that is to count as an individual experience, considered in isolation from whether or not it is bound up with some larger unity of consciousness that constitutes an individual person. We can take it as our starting-point, then, that any experience, to count as an experience, must involve a distinction between two components: the subjective component (that for which there is something that it is like), and the content component (the something that it is like). We might also attempt to capture this in terms of a distinction between a recognitional component and the content recognized, although talk of recognition is tied to conceptualization in a way that will require some caution.[5]

Now this latter distinction is familiar from Strawson,[6] and the contrast with his treatment of it is illuminating in the present context. He says, in the context of discussing the dependence of unity of consciousness on experience being of a unified objective world, that

> There can be no experience at all which does not involve the recognition of particular items *as* being of such and such a general kind. It seems that it must be possible, even in the most fleeting and purely subjective of impressions, to distinguish a component of recognition, or judgement, which is not simply identical with, or wholly absorbed by, the particular item which is recognized, which forms the topic of judgement. (Strawson 1966: 100)

The notion of recognition said here to be inherent to every experience seems to be close enough to the one I have articulated, with the caveat only that we should not so readily conflate this recognition, and the conceptual content it involves, with an act of judgement—at least not as that would be understood by the Kantian, namely as the operation of a non-sensuous faculty of rules.

Strawson goes on to identify simple individual experiences (such as a momentary tickling sensation) 'of which the objects (accusatives) have no existence independently of the awareness of them'.[7] The question at issue for Strawson is whether we can have unified consciousness that consists entirely of this sort of experience, and thus is not of objects in the weighty sense, thereby refuting the Kantian claim that unified experience is necessarily of objects in that sense. Strawson seems to consider that the reason that we cannot is that such experiences would not leave room for the distinction between the recognitional component and the content recognized. There would be nothing here to save the recognitional component from absorption into the

---

[5] See below, pp. 232–3.   [6] Strawson (1966: 100 ff.).   [7] 1966: 100–1.

recognized content, and so nothing left to save the character of the experience as an *experience*.⁸

The idea is that, in so far as these experiences involve experience of objects that cannot be conceived of as having an existence independent of the particular experience of them, the distinction between recognitional component and content recognized is endangered. Now in fact it is not at all clear what the connection is supposed to be between an experience leaving room for conceiving of its object as existing independently of the experience of it, and its leaving room for conceiving of it in terms of a distinction between the content and the recognition of it. It is not clear why the denial of the former precludes the latter. But we can leave this aside for now. (It is in fact also not clear that the example given, of a momentary tickling sensation, is one in which the object—the tickle—cannot be conceived of as having existence independent of, or at least distinct from, the experience of it,⁹ but no doubt there are other such momentary experiences—e.g. a pang of conscience, a flurry of anxiety—of which this is true.)

For Strawson, what saves the recognitional component from collapse into the content, in such cases, and so what saves them as experiences, is that they are part of a larger personal unity of consciousness such that they can be recognized by that person (their 'owner') as one of their experiences. And that recognition, the self-consciousness that these are all my experiences, can be shown to involve a distinction between a subjective order of appearances and an independent objective order, thereby showing why there cannot be only pure 'sense-datum experiences'. Some experiences must be such as 'contain the basis' to sustain the distinction between a subjective order of experiences and an objective order of which the former are experiences:

Granted that these distinctions are implicit in the conceptual character of some experiences ... we are free to allow that there are *also* experiences which lack this conceptual character altogether, i.e. the objects (accusatives) of which are not such as must be conceived of as existing independently of the experience of them. What is excluded is that experiences should be entirely of the latter class.¹⁰

---

⁸ Ibid.   ⁹ See pp. 52–3 above.
¹⁰ Strawson (1966: 101). It is as well to remember here that the distinction between a subjective and an objective order should not be said to be implicit in one kind of experience rather than another, as if it were entirely grounded in those different (non-purely-'sense-datum') experiences, for all the reasons familiar from discussions of empiricism (see above, p. 40). The strength of the Kantian position is that that distinction emerges as a transcendental condition of individual experiences being arranged in certain ways, rather than as sustained by the content of some experiences as opposed to others. It is true that there cannot, for Kant, be a purely sense-datum form of experience, and also true that such experiences entail that there be other experiences that are as of an objective order that is independent of the experience of it; but it would not be right to construe the latter as *sustaining* that distinction solely in virtue of their content.

There are several moves that are unclear in this discussion. We can reconstruct it partially by noting that there seem to be two senses of recognition in play. The first, which is the sense we are interested in here, is the recognition internal to an experience of the content of that experience. It is in this sense that recognition is necessary to avoid the collapse of an experience into a mere event (albeit possibly a cognitive one). The second is the recognition fundamental to self-consciousness: the recognition of an experience or item as being one of mine. Strawson seems to argue that in the face of a threat to the former in the cases of certain experiences, what saves their status as experiences is the possibility of recognition in the second sense. The way in which this might work seems clear enough. In recognizing the experience in question as one of mine, I must recognize it as something, as being of one sort rather than another, and that is precisely to recognize its content. The gap between recognition and content is maintained not within the confines of the individual experience itself, but by the application to it of recognitional resources external to it. In this way, even in the absence of resources internal to the experience, the distinction between recognition and content that makes it into an experience is saved.

It is not clear, however, either that this line of argument is necessary, or that its consequences are acceptable. The reason it might not be necessary is this: It seems legitimate to argue that by taking up their place in the nexus of the larger unity of consciousness of the individual person, with all the recognitional capacities required for self-conscious self-ascription of the individual experience, 'experiences' could in principle be accommodated which did not within their own narrowly conceived parameters contain the required distinction between recognition and content. But it is not clear that we should accept that there are any such experiences. If the experience of a tickling sensation, to stick with Strawson's example, really does not internally leave room for recognition of content, then it is not clear why *it* is to count as an experience at all, rather than being a mere datum for another experience, viz. that involving the self-ascription of the (possibly perceptual) datum, the recognition of it as one of mine (the second sense of 'recognition'). That would suffice only to sustain the experience of self-ascription, which is not the same as the self-ascription of an experience. To talk of there being self-ascription of an experience, rather than the self-ascription of a datum, what is self-ascribed must be something that in itself feels a certain way. And that involves the distinction between recognition and content being operative within the experience. If it is not, then that distinction can come into play only once the putative experience is self-ascribed; which means that as a merely possible item of self-ascription, i.e. before it is actually self-ascribed, it does not yet have the structure required to count as an experience. If this is so, then there are no experiences of the sort that do not contain in themselves the distinction between recognitional component and content, and so there is no need for the argument designed to accommodate such experiences.

The above considerations lead on to the second point mentioned, namely that it is not clear that the consequences of that argument are acceptable. It would seem to follow from this argument that the experiences in question are such that they can be had only by creatures that, like ourselves, are capable of self-conscious ascription of them. Without that capacity they would not count as experiences at all. It is one thing to allow that if we have self-consciousness and the possibility of recognition in the second sense, then we could accommodate such experiences as may not themselves exhibit a component of recognition (recognition in the first sense). It is another to argue, as Strawson does, that the possibility of self-conscious self-ascription is not only a sufficient but also a necessary condition of recognition in the first sense.[11] This yields the counter-intuitive result that creatures that do not have self-consciousness cannot experience pain or tickles (while they might be able to have all sorts of other experiences that do allow for the distinction between a recognitional component and content). That mice, say, do not have self-consciousness seems plausible; that it follows that they cannot experience a tickling sensation or pain seems highly implausible.[12] Yet this is a consequence of the argument under discussion. It may turn out that this consequence is unavoidable. But that it is so counter-intuitive clearly constitutes one reason for taking note of the fact that the argument that has yielded it is not forced on us, and for exploring alternatives to it.

The alternative to be pursued here takes as its starting-point that the distinction between a recognitional component and content recognized, which Strawson too acknowledges as necessary for something to count as an experience, is inherent in every experience, even the most simple, taken on its own. The latter part of the claim, the reasons for which were outlined above, is the primary point of departure from Strawson. The strategic results of this difference are

---

[11] He seems in fact to suggest that the possibility of self-conscious self-ascription is a necessary condition not only of saving the recognitional component of the kinds of momentary experiences that do not internally sustain the distinction necessary for them to count as experiences, but of there being a recognitional component in any experience whatsoever. Thus: 'The way out is to acknowledge that the recognitional component, necessary to experience, can be present in experience only because of the *possibility* of referring different experiences to one identical subject of them all. Recognition implies the *potential* acknowledgement of the experience into which recognition necessarily enters as being one's own, as sharing with others this relation to the identical self' (Strawson 1966: 101). While the first sentence is ambiguous ('can' can be taken in the sense of *might*), the second and the rest of the text seem to make it clear that the claim is general to all cases of recognition, not only to special circumstances.

[12] Implausible as it is, it has been defended by Carruthers, who generally sees consciousness as presupposing self-consciousness, and so is also prepared to draw the conclusion that like these mice, so too human infants, prior to the development of self-consciousness, cannot experience pain. See Carruthers (1992a, b); see also Rosenthal (1991).

significant. Strawson's conception of these most rudimentary experiences means that the recognitional component for such experiences comes from outside them, such that considering them as experiences immediately involves their integration into the mental life of a person. One consequence of this is that having these experiences is immediately, and counter-intuitively, bound up with self-consciousness and the capacity to self-consciously self-ascribe those experiences. Another consequence is that it falls in too readily with a form of psychological atomism, according to which such experiences are nested within a series of other experiences, all bound together only by the possibility of being self-ascribed by one and the same owner. As a reconstruction of Kant, this is probably right, as we have seen.[13] But it results from at least partial acceptance of Kant's transcendental psychology and as such Strawson in particular ought to be wary of it, given his explicit effort to expunge from his reconstruction of Kant all elements of transcendental psychology. More to the point, since psychological atomism is a view to which alternatives are conceivable, it does not constitute a stable foundation on which to rest the argument of the Transcendental Deduction and the refutation of idealism.[14] If, on the other hand, we allow that such simple experiences, considered in isolation, already contain the minimal structure necessary for them to count as experiences, then we can avoid both of these consequences. We can then proceed to explore further the structure of the simplest experience taken on its own, without being compelled immediately and possibly heavy-handedly either to link it with self-consciousness, or to endorse psychological atomism. In both of these respects, the investigation here can be seen to take its start from a point that is more rudimentary than, and so constitutes a step back from, the Kantian starting-point.[15]

2. DOMAINS OF PRESENTATION

Taking our start, then, from consideration of the individual experience, of which we know that it at least leaves room in the identified sense for the necessary structure of recognition, the question is, what more can be said about its

---

[13] See the discussion of Kant above, especially Ch. 2, Section 3.3.

[14] As we saw in discussing the bearing of James's psychological model on Kant; Ch. 3, Sect. 3 above.

[15] In fact the claim that even the simplest experiences contain within themselves the structure of recognition is merely convenient for present purposes, and is not strictly necessary. Were it argued successfully that in fact there are items that count as experiences in the context of the whole person, but which could not do so if taken in isolation from that larger nesting, then we would simply have to start instead from consideration of the simplest individual experience that taken on its own *does* allow for the recognitional structure.

structure, considered strictly on its own, prior to adding it to a unified series of other such experiences (which would take us back to Kantian terrain, asking about the experience of the individual person, rather than about the individual experience)? We have seen that the content component of such an experience must be presented to a *single* consciousness for it to count as a single experience. But nothing so far has been said about this presentation requiring conceptual activity; for all that we have seen it requires no more than immediate acquaintance, as in direct and inarticulate demonstrative contact with the presented content. The point at which conceptualization emerges has yet to be identified. In terms of terminology, then: to avoid the possibly premature assumption of conceptual activity that the term 'recognition' carries with it, at least as Strawson construed it, it might be helpful if the individual experience as a whole is thought of as neutrally as possible as a *domain of presentation*, and the content component within it is then identified with equal neutrality merely as the *presented domain*.

Given the intention to start from the simple experience, we should not assume that it is temporally extended. We are talking for now about a momentary unity of consciousness.[16] Even so there seem to be two possibilities that need to be addressed separately in considering the necessary internal structure of any such domain of presentation. The domain in question might be either *homogeneous* or *heterogeneous*. Heterogeneity of the domain of presentation means no more than that there is room to distinguish (different) properties that pertain to the presented domain. Homogeneity of the domain of presentation is then defined as there being no room for more than one property pertaining to the presented domain.[17]

Let us start with the simpler notion, of a homogeneous domain of presentation. It is not clear that such a domain is in fact fully intelligible. Certainly, some care is needed in considering just how restricted such a domain of presentation would be.

It should be clear that the presented domain in such cases cannot comprise a foreground–background distinction. That would clearly involve there being at least two properties in the presented domain, sufficient to distinguish between the foreground property, and that of the background to it. There being

---

[16] A momentary experience should be conceived of as the briefest temporal span that can be psychologically significant, or the minimum sensible interval. On this, see James (1981: 573 ff.), and for more recent discussion and references, Hoerl (1998: 158–9). Hoerl also offers a valuable discussion of why the fact that a single act of apprehension is temporally extended does not in itself suffice to equip the subject of the act with the grasp of temporal concepts.

[17] Talking here of there being no more than one property, rather than of there being no room to distinguish more than one property, is important, since the latter would suggest that there is the possibility of distinguishing at least one property, and, as we will see shortly, it is not clear that that is possible within a homogeneous domain of presentation. This provides grounds for doubting the intelligibility of such domains.

such a distinction within the presented domain is then incompatible with its being a homogeneous domain of presentation. It is important also to see that there is no room to think of such a domain simply as comprising a uniform background empty of any foreground features, some homogeneously extended field. On the most immediate construal, such a field would be spatially extended—and as such it could not be homogeneous in the sense defined. Even if all the locations in the field have one and the same property, say, a colour, it will be true that there is more than one property applied within the presented domain. For to say that all the different spatial locations are, say, brown, is to say that we can rightly apply not only the property of being brown, but also the spatial properties which suffice to pick out one colour point from another. In the visual field there is room to construct a grid, such that although all points on it might be brown, there is room to say of one point that it has the property of being brown and of being A3, and of another that it has the property of being brown and of being B4. And that, of course, immediately intimates the other relational properties that pertain uniquely to location A3, or B4. This will be the case just in so far as any such uniform extended field must involve some spatial structure, where that means a plurality of locations systematically linked into a single matrix by different relational properties true of each location.

This, however, might seem not to be a general point, but merely one pertaining to the kind of visual field with which the notion of a uniform background is so readily conflated. It might be thought that a homogeneous domain of presentation can be construed as a mere uniform background without relying on the visual (or tactile) modality which introduces the experience of a differentiated spatial structure. The idea might be to rely on something that has only a quasi-spatial structure, of the sort that Strawson's sound-world comprises.[18] The master sound serves to establish a space analogue, in that other sounds are located relative to that sound. The relevant point is not that hearing the master sound does not entail hearing all those other sounds as well; seeing brown uniformly did not entail seeing any other colours either. The point is rather that in hearing just the master sound on its own, there would be no way of identifying various 'places' at all of which the same sound could be heard, which is what could happen—substituting visual content for sound—in the case of the colour field. In the case of the visual field we have a way of identifying a spatial location which is independent of the specific colour of that location (although not independent of its having any colour at all). Because of this it is possible in the case of the visual field to pick out various locations, and then realize that they all have exactly the same colour property; or to pick out different locations within the same

---

[18] Strawson (1959, ch. 2).

expanse of colour, however small it might be. In the case of the sound field, there is no such independent access to various locations.

Of course, this is not to say that there cannot be different locations in the confinement of an acoustic domain. It is just that they are fixed by their differing relations to the specific property of the master sound, so that it is not possible to determine the location as being different while the sound 'at that location' is identical. (Assuming otherwise immediately implies that the term 'location' is not being used as strictly internal to a sound field.[19]) It is the relations of other possible sounds to that master sound that enable us to construct out of them a quasi-spatial structure, a plurality of locations systematically linked into a single matrix by the different acoustic relational properties that hold true of each location. But once we have constructed a background space in that way, it is even more clear than in the case of the colour field that the various locations in it have different properties, such that *it* is no longer a candidate for a homogeneous domain of presentation. At the same time, and by the same token, it becomes clear that the master sound, taken on its own, cannot be considered to constitute a background on which other properties can make an appearance.

At this point we can begin to appreciate how rudimentary such a structure of experience must be. We are pushed towards the conclusion that the presented domain in a homogeneous domain of presentation not only cannot instantiate a background–foreground structure, but cannot constitute a mere empty background either. The question is, what is left of the notion of a homogeneous domain of presentation once we steer clear of either of these two dead ends?

We might start from the experience of the single master sound, precisely because taken on its own it did not suffice to constitute a background field, and see whether taken in that isolation from other sounds it could constitute anything that would count as a homogeneous domain of presentation. We are to conceive of an individual experience which consists entirely of 'hearing' a certain sound.[20] This will exclude even the possibility of 'hearing' the sound as something that could be other than it is, sharper or flatter, say; or as something that could be accompanied by some such other sound but in fact is not. For that to be possible there would again have to be an acoustic quasi-spatial matrix within which those possible sounds could be plotted as possibilities alongside and in relation to the actual sound, and that is just the kind of background structure that cannot be accommodated within a strictly

---

[19] This is not quite accurate, since we can allow for differences of volume and timbre, rather than merely of pitch. But for present purposes we can confine attention to the case of acoustic homogeneity, where we assume that there are not such additional variations.

[20] The use of scare quotes is meant to indicate that the word 'hearing' here should not be taken to entail the existence of ears or of a processing brain. It is meant to capture only the subjective experience of an acoustic event.

homogeneous domain of presentation. In the absence of the sound matrix on the background of which to make sense of such sortals the sound experienced will not have the scope to be experienced as being one tone rather than another. (It should be noted further that this same consideration equally excludes the contrast of the sound experienced with the absence of all sound, a silence within which the sound is occurring.[21] Again, that would not count as a homogeneous domain of presentation since it would be operating with a background of acoustic space, some parts of which had the property of being acoustically void, unoccupied, in contrast to at least one part of it which had the property of being occupied.)

We can readily see how this rudimentary structure of the domain of experience puts pressure on the notion of the content of the experience. The experienced content in such a presentational domain, being isolated from alternatives to it, cannot be determined by way of a contrast with something else, either actual or possible. But where that kind of contrast between properties cannot be drawn, there is no room to distinguish between things being of one kind rather than another. And that is just to say that there is no room to experience the content as being of a kind. Essentially, such experience seems to preclude even the weakest appeal to a conceptual component by means of which the experienced content is subsumed under a sortal. Sortal concepts require contrasting one kind with what it is not, and cannot get going where that contrast is not available.

Now it might be thought that experience is necessarily conceptual in this sense, since for any property to be experienced just is for it to register subjectively in one way rather than another, *as being of one kind rather than another*. It might therefore be argued that where there is no room within the domain of presentation for the experience of at least two properties, there is no room to talk of experiencing any properties, in the sense of there being something that it is intrinsically like to have that experience.[22] And that would simply be to say that a homogeneous domain of presentation cannot, taken on its own, count as an experience (such a domain would not leave room for the essential distinction between subjective component and content). If this is the view taken, then we would have to start from heterogeneous domains of presentation, and the assumption that all experience must be minimally conceptual; and the possible difference noted above,[23] between identifying the characteristic fundamental to any experience merely as there being a subjective component that registers content, as opposed to requiring that there be a

---

[21] The idea here is not of the silence before and after the sound occurs, since we are considering momentary experiences, but of a silence as the domain within which sounds occur.

[22] To give a different construal of the underlying view, we might say that it rests on the assumption that all experienceable properties are relative. Relativity requires plurality. Homogeneous domains of presentation taken in isolation preclude plurality. Which is why on this view there cannot be experience of a homogeneous domain of presentation.   [23] See p. 224.

recognitional element involved, would come to nothing. There could be no apprehension without recognition, however minimal.

We might, however, wish to allow for its not being the case that all experience must be 'experience as'. It might be that there is room for something to count as an experience, such that the content experienced is exhaustively specified as a single instantiation of only one property, even though taken on its own that content cannot be experienced *as* an instance of that property (or of any other). On this view the recognitional component would have to be external to the experience—as Strawson has it—but that would not mean that it cannot still count as an experience considered on its own. Here an internal recognitional component is not taken as necessary for something to count as an experience. A more slender conception of experience comes into play: a domain of presentation strictly requires only that there be room for subjective *apprehension* (rather than *recognition*) of the content presented. While we have left room for this conception, and so for a homogeneous domain of presentation, it is worth noting just how rudimentary the content of such experience is, taken strictly on its own. What we are left with is the brute experience of content: there will be an experience, without any internal recognition of its being *as it is* rather than some other way. Although this seems to leave scope for there actually being a difference in subjective feel between different homogeneous experiences—a pain being different in feel from a colour sensation—the identity of the experience would be unavailable within the domain of presentation. This, given the extrusion of all conceptual content by the constraints of homogeneity, is the rudimentary notion of content that can be allowed to obtain within a homogeneous domain of presentation. It might in fact be argued that the role of conceptual content is more pervasive, so that in its absence there is no room to allow even for there being, within the domain of presentation, any actual (albeit undetectable) difference in subjective feel between different experiences. There might be only an altogether inarticulate raw feel, a mere something that it is like to have presented content rather than not (overlooking the residual conceptualization seemingly necessary even for that), but no scope to make sense of there being a difference between different contents.

Either way, it looks as though even if a homogeneous domain of presentation is possible, the only experience that can be of much interest to us must be minimally conceptual, and as such must involve a heterogeneous domain of presentation.[24] But before turning to the latter, it is worth noticing some further features of the homogeneous domain as we have identified it.

---

[24] Again, it should not be thought that the recognitional component involved in conceptual experience immediately requires resort to a capacity for self-conscious judgement, as Strawson—following Kant—seems in places to assume. As we have seen, there is room for a weak construal of the conceptual recognition involved, such that it might not even be a matter of the content of a cognitive judgement.

What we are considering is the experience of an object domain which itself has no parts, no extension in any modality; an item of experience without any background to it, and which cannot itself constitute a background. Now it is worth noting, first, that on this construal of the domain of presentation, the material provided within the presented domain is too rudimentary to sustain any internal explanation of the dissolution of the unity of consciousness involved in the experience. There is not sufficient scope to explain how the unity of consciousness might disintegrate. In the case of a *heterogeneous* domain of presentation the complexity of the presented domain enables us to distinguish elements, the experience of which can come apart, such that unity of consciousness is lost. This can be the case even where the experience is considered momentary. The momentary experience might consist, say, of something red, and something hard. We can conceive of the unity of consciousness having been lost simply in virtue of there being no common owner of the experience of hardness, and of redness. This is precisely what the paucity of material in the homogeneous domain of presentation precludes. Here the unity of consciousness cannot come apart, simply because there are no parts to it. But that, of course, is not to say that it cannot terminate.

Here we should note, secondly, that the dissolution of the unity of consciousness that can occur in the heterogeneous domain of presentation need not involve any change in the properties of the original domain of presentation.[25] The basic 'object domain' remains; it is merely the experience of it that alters. In the case of the homogeneous domain of presentation, by contrast, there is no room for the unity of consciousness to lapse leaving a previously presented domain unchanged. As long as the presented domain is unchanged, the unity of consciousness cannot be threatened. And the termination of the unity of consciousness is also the end of the presented domain; there is no room to consider that consciousness might fade while the content persists unchanged, since any such extension would count against the homogeneity of the domain of presentation.

The homogeneous domain of presentation thus involves a kind of internal 'immortality'—there are no resources internal to the domain of presentation sufficient to explain the dissolution to the subjective component—that goes well with the conception of a form of experience that would see its world in its simple, and exhaustive, unity. It is the shift from the homogeneous to the heterogeneous domain of presentation that marks the point at which we first encounter the possibility of an explanation internal to the experience of the

---

[25] The domain of presentation is determined precisely as that domain within which there is unity of consciousness. So after the loss of the unity of consciousness the original domain of presentation is no longer there. It cannot therefore be that the unity of consciousness is lost without the domain of presentation altering its properties: rather, the properties of that domain of presentation, although now distributed across two or more distinct domains of presentation, have not changed. The only change is in the parcelling, not in the content that is there to be parcelled out.

dissolution of the unity of consciousness; and also—not coincidentally—the point at which we first encounter, in rudimentary form, experience and object domain being set apart such that there is scope for the object domain to be conceived as in principle existing independently of the experience of it. That which is experienced as red and hard need not change, and yet the unity of consciousness that enables experience of it could disintegrate.

Let us now leave behind the homogeneous domain of presentation, and take our start from this heterogeneous domain of presentation. Saying that the heterogeneous domain of presentation provides the materials out of which the distinction between a subject (unity of consciousness) and an object domain that is independent of consciousness of it can be drawn is, of course, not to say that such a domain of presentation itself instantiates the distinction. We are, after all, drawing the distinction starting from no more than the meagre notion of a momentary experience exhibiting two or more properties. It would seem that for the distinction between subject and independent object-world to be manifest entirely from within the domain of presentation, that domain would have to present materials considerably richer than those considered so far. We need more than just the momentary heterogeneous domain of presentation.

There would, again, seem to be two ways of proceeding from this point to enrich the conception of the form of experience. The one would be to enrich the external description, adding the momentary heterogeneous experience to other such experiences, whether homogeneous or heterogeneous, and so assuming a plurality of such experiences bundled together under the ownership of a single unified consciousness. This would again lead us to Kant's starting-point in the Transcendental Deduction, asking about the conditions for such discrete experiences being ordered under a single consciousness of them all. The other possibility, which is the one being pursued here, is to uncover more of the internal description of the domain of presentation. This, again, is in effect to start a transcendental argument at an earlier step than Kant does, from an even more rudimentary and hence less debatable premiss. Starting from the single heterogeneous domain of presentation, as externally specified, we can show that in fact the internal structure it exhibits must be richer than we have so far appreciated. The guiding idea here is that there might be a contrast between what the presumed structure is, as seen from the outside, or sideways on, and what the structure is as presumed from within.[26] The sideways-on description might be of a structure significantly less complex than the structure presupposed from within.[27]

[26] On the relevant difference between the two perspectives, see Cassam (1989: 79 ff.).

[27] This is basically the insight that lies at the heart of the Kantian explanation of how some of the traditional philosophical problems can be avoided: those problems arise because the complexity between subject and object of experience is taken to characterize the external rather than the merely internally presupposed structure. (That is what it is to say that the subject and object are taken to be *transcendentally* real, rather than merely *empirically* real and transcendentally ideal.) For related discussion, see Ch. 9 below.

3. TIME

The notion of a momentary experience, whether homogeneous or not, is something that has been simply assumed in the discussion so far. But obviously characterizing it as momentary requires that there be a temporal span in which the experience itself occupies one place, which is thought of loosely as something like a geometrical point on a continuous line.[28] To us, who are not confined to the internal structure of that momentary experience, it is recognizable as being preceded and followed by a time span, of which it does not encompass more than the briefest period, and in relation to which it can be recognized to be momentary. The characterization of it as momentary is thus external to the experience; it is the way it seems from sideways on. What has not been addressed so far, regarding the temporal dimension, is how what is thus externally characterized as a momentary (homogeneous or heterogeneous) experience seems 'from the inside'.

I have identified two exclusive and exhaustive kinds of presentational domains, homogeneous and heterogeneous, and it might seem at first that both could be such as to leave no room for a temporal dimension to the experience they sustain (where that obviously does not mean that they are experienced as being momentary—i.e. as they are externally seen to be—but that they are strictly atemporal).

It is relatively straightforward to appreciate that a homogeneous domain of presentation not only *can* exclude, but indeed of necessity excludes, the experience of any temporal dimension. If the domain of presentation is presented as temporally structured, it would involve not just the experience of P but the experience of P-at-t_1 and P-at-t_2, etc. Now in so far as these are not experienced *as* different, there would be only the homogeneous presentation of P, *tout court*, with no way of setting different moments of the experience alongside one another, temporally or otherwise. So in so far as P-at-t_1 and P-at-t_2 are not experienced as different, there is no experience of temporal extension; yet in so far as they are, the domain is no longer homogeneous but requires the subject to experience P *as* temporally indexed. Thus temporal structure of the domain of presentation, like the spatial or quasi-spatial structure discussed above, precludes its homogeneity.

It should be noted here that the argument from temporality to heterogeneity of the domain of presentation does not rest on any assumption of time itself

---

[28] Again, in talking of the experience being momentary, the idea involved is not that it really is extensionless, a mathematical point, but that it is psychologically indivisible. (See above, n. 16).

being an experienced property.²⁹ The thought is not that in addition to the property P there is a temporal property t (or a spatial property s) which is experienced, such that the domain of presentation involves both P and t (or s), thereby relinquishing homogeneous status. This is just as well, since that assumption—while it would do for present purposes—is as untenable as Kant took it to be.³⁰ The thought here is rather that in order for there to be a temporal structure within the domain of presentation, there must be a distinction between whatever is experienced at t_1 and then at t_2, if only of the sort that at t_2 the experience is *P-again*, i.e. there is not only the experience of P but also some incremental value, added baggage in the form of familiarity, or even of the awareness of having had that experience before. It is in virtue of that difference, rather than anything to do with an experience of a pure 'temporal component', that the operative difference between the content of P-at-t_1 and of P-at-t_2 will be provided.

We have seen that if the domain of presentation is to remain homogeneous, it must be non-temporal; or, conversely, that to the extent that the domain of presentation is temporally structured, it must be heterogeneous. But that is not to say that the heterogeneous domain of presentation could not also accommodate a strictly non-temporal experience. It is perhaps less immediately obvious that a heterogeneous domain of presentation is *necessarily* temporal. Given how extensive the category of the heterogeneous domain of presentation is, it might seem likely that while the more complex of them can sustain temporally structured presentation of content, at least the simplest— say, the simple experience of a single foreground property on a homogeneous background—can be non-temporal in just the way that a homogeneous domain of presentation is. In fact this is not so.

An argument to this effect might be set out along the following lines. Starting now from a domain which is heterogeneous, we must ensure that the conditions are satisfied for the presentation of different properties. Clearly, for there to be experience as of different properties within the domain of presentation, there must be some experienced contrast between the properties. If this condition is not met, then however many properties are identified from sideways on, no distinction will be made internally between different properties: the domain of presentation will be internally homogeneous. But experienced contrast presupposes commensurability, which in turn presupposes relative

---

[29] Nor should it be thought that the previous reflections concerning space—to which I will return—rested on an assumption that space itself is an experienced property, additional to its occupants. The fact that the arguments regarding space and time run along parallel lines (as in Kant's expositions of the status of space and time as the a priori forms of intuition, in the Transcendental Aesthetic) is not without reason. They are two forms serving essentially similar commensurability functions.

[30] See e.g. *Critique*, B225 ff. This denial that bare time can be perceived has a long pedigree prior to Kant—most notably, perhaps, Aristotle (*Physics*, IV. 10–14, esp. 219ª22–5).

individuation, individuating the properties so that they can be placed in relation to one another. So for a contrast between properties to be registered, it must be possible to experience there being a property at one point distinct from another at another point.

What we mean by 'point' here requires immediate clarification. Of course, if 'point' is taken to mean temporal point, so that the different properties must be located at different temporal points, it follows immediately that the heterogeneous domain of presentation must be temporally structured. But that would obviously be too quick, since there is no reason to think that it is location at a *temporal* point that is required. Property differentiation requires location, but the locations can be points in, and across, any of the different modalities of experience. We could, for example, imagine a case of the two properties in question being located at different spatial points, or perhaps the one at a visual spatial point, the other at some point on an acoustic or olfactory scale. While cross-modal orientation of this sort might make it difficult to compare the properties for likeness, it is certainly enough to allow the required contrast to be drawn within the experience between two distinct properties.

But it nevertheless remains the case that for the contrast between two properties to be drawn, it must be possible to attend distinctly to each point. And that can only mean that it must be possible to attend first to the one, then to the other. And this already presupposes the availability of temporal relations. It is not that there must necessarily be a temporal sequence to the occurrence of the two properties. They might well be coexisting. It is not even that there must be a temporal sequence to the initial apprehension of them. But there must, internal to the experience, be the resources to attend to the properties in temporal sequence. Without assuming at least the possibility of temporal succession in attention there would be no room to make sense of their being experienced as two distinct properties. Without that possible separation, the experience would simply be as of one comprehensive property, rather than of two. Hence, to the extent that the domain of presentation is to remain heterogeneous, it must involve recourse to relations of temporal succession.

A more explicit statement on the way in which temporality is being introduced here might be helpful. I have said that the separation in experience whereby we can distinguish different properties—can in principle attend first to one property and then to another—presupposes temporal relations. This should not be taken to mean the introduction of temporality as though that were some extra ingredient, some further ontological commitment.[31] Rather, the separation between properties in attention itself constitutes a temporal structure. Nothing more is needed. The experience of different properties, by

---

[31] This point is distinct from the one made a few paragraphs back, to the effect that time is not itself an experienced property.

itself, brings temporal relations into existence, as the background structure involved in the differentiation of one property from another. This also explains the transcendental status of time. It is essentially *presupposed* by any differentiation of properties. Consequently, it cannot itself be differentiated as having certain properties. Time itself has no independent properties, and any attempt to attribute such properties to it must essentially result in contradiction. Which is why, as Kant put it, bare time cannot be perceived, but only things in time.[32]

We can then conclude, so far, that not only must a homogeneous domain of presentation be non-temporal; but also, any non-temporal domain of presentation must be homogeneous. But we have seen how rudimentary such a domain of presentation must be. It is therefore significant that it follows that a heterogeneous domain of presentation, however simple it may be (and even if externally it would be characterized as momentary), necessarily involves temporal structure.

Now it follows also that a heterogeneous domain of presentation, even if externally characterized as a single momentary experience—say, to take a simple case, of a red patch on a green background—will internally give grounds for being regarded as comprising a synthesis of different contents, each content separable from the others, ultimately in a way that its own parts are not separable from one another, corresponding to the different simple properties individuated (red, green, colour, extension . . .). But to say that there are such different contents, constituting separable moments of the experience, is just to say that it consists, internally, of discrete units of experience. And to the extent that that is taken to constitute a form of Kant's perceptual atomism, which is the starting-point of his Transcendental Deduction (on the strongest construal of it), and yet does so without reliance on his transcendental psychology, we might then simply allow Kant's argument to pick up from there.

But there is reason to resist that option. It would not be appropriate, since these different contents are here such as constitute only *separable* moments of experience, not *separate* moments. From within the heterogeneous domain of presentation they might seem separate, and in need of unification, but in fact they are already unified as so many moments within a single domain of presentation. And pursuing the internal structure of the simple heterogeneous domain of presentation—bearing in mind just how impoverished anything more simple would be—we can in fact go further. It might be helpful to have a general and schematic overview, before turning to spell out the details.

---

[32] The above argument for the transcendental status of time is Kantian, and is analogous to the thought that Allison (1983: 82–6) identifies in the first Metaphysical Exposition of the a priori nature of space. (It is unfortunate that while this charitable interpretation seems to fit the spirit of the text of the *Critique*, there is only scant evidence of it in the parallel section, the first Metaphysical Exposition of the concept of time. See A30/B46.)

It is only in so far as the various properties in the domain of presentation are experienced by one and the same consciousness, that there can be any experienced contrast between the properties; and we have seen that, without that experienced contrast, there would be no room to talk of there being experience as of different properties within the presented domain. If the experience of each property were a unity of consciousness unto itself, the heterogeneous domain of presentation would have disintegrated into so many homogeneous domains of presentation. The question then is, under what conditions can we preserve the unity of consciousness within the heterogeneous domain of presentation?

And the response is in essence as Kantian as is the question.[33] The unity of the subjective component presupposes unity of the objective element of the presentational domain. For the different experiences to belong to a single consciousness, there must be some way of relating them to one another. For that to be possible there must be a background matrix, or grid, onto which those experiences can all be plotted. If that grid itself changes, there are two possibilities. Either that change falls outside the experiential capacity of the unity of consciousness in question; or else, if that change from one grid to another can itself be experienced by the unity of consciousness in question, it must be possible for that consciousness to relate the two 'grid-phases' to one another. And that again means being able to plot them onto some yet more basic grid or matrix that underlies them. If that further matrix changes, then again, either it turns out not to have been the most fundamental matrix within which all change occurs, and some other such matrix is presupposed; or else, if there is no further common matrix, then with the change in it, the unity of consciousness comes to an end as well (for there is now no longer any way of relating the experiences prior to the change to those subsequent to it). Either way, then, there is no room to experience a change in the fundamental matrix onto which all change is mapped. The unity of consciousness requires a single unified and unchanging matrix onto which all change can be plotted. And that is just the unity of the objective world.

What is of interest is how this results from consideration of nothing more than the conditions for there being a simple heterogeneous domain of presentation. Shatter the unity of the 'objective' matrix within that domain of presentation, and the unity of consciousness is correspondingly shattered; persistently shatter the unity of consciousness, and there is ultimately no room for the recognition of differentiation between properties; and, without such differentiation, there is no experience of a heterogeneous domain of presentation.

We can now fill in some details.

---

[33] See in particular Kant's treatment of substance in the First Analogy, *Critique*, A182–9/B224–32.

4. SPACE

We have seen that the heterogeneous domain of presentation must internally have recourse to temporal structure. We can now turn to see that it must also have a spatial structure.

Let us start from consideration of the heterogeneous domain of presentation considered at a moment. Although we can conceive of a domain of presentation that is heterogeneous at a moment, we have not yet seen an argument to the effect that any heterogeneous domain of presentation must be heterogeneous at any moment. This remains to be shown.[34] For the time being, then, we start with only the conditional that *if* a domain of presentation is heterogeneous at a moment, then it must be spatial, if only in the most generic sense.[35]

The truth of this conditional follows more or less directly from the claim that space in the generic sense can be defined in terms of time, as that which is required for there to be awareness of a difference between coexisting moments of experience.[36] I will refer to this awareness of simultaneous experiential properties being different as an awareness of difference in simultaneity. The

---

[34] See pp. 251 ff. below.

[35] The phrase 'generic space' is meant to apply to any framework that consists of loci the properties of which are entirely structural (that is, they have no inherent sensory properties), such that any of those loci can be related formally to any other, and the whole of which is not necessarily extended in time. It is generic in that it is not necessarily physical space, and clearly need not be specifically Euclidean, or indeed strictly mathematical. There is, however, no reason to construe generic space as a lesser candidate for objectivity than physical space.

For present purposes there is no need to distinguish this generic spatial structure from what is sometimes referred to as a quasi-spatial structure. On the notion of quasi-spatial structure see e.g. Evans (1985a: 252). See also Strawson (1959: 74–81).

[36] It is interesting to note that it cannot work the other way; that time cannot be defined in terms of space, as difference without coexistence, for example. Coexistence is itself a temporal notion. This gives a sense in which time can be regarded as conceptually more basic.

This perhaps brings out the interesting truth implicit in the Kantian effort to accord to time a wider scope than to space. Kant holds that space is the form of outer appearances only, while time is the form of both inner and outer appearances. There is an important asymmetry between the two, but its importance is perhaps not best brought out in this way. In part this is because while it is true that inner appearances are *presented* in time but not in space, their being inner nevertheless presupposes space. This is because space is required for the conception of there being *inner* experiences as distinct from outer items. Indeed, this is a point Kant himself, at least on Allison's charitable reconstruction, seems to appreciate in his first proof of space being an a priori representation (in the 'Metaphysical Exposition of the Concept of Space'): 'For in order that certain sensations be referred to something outside me ... the representation of space must be presupposed' (*Critique*, A23/B38). If we follow Allison (1983: 83) and take 'outside me' to mean logically distinct from me, then space is equally presupposed in order to make sense of saying that something is *not* 'outside me' in this sense, i.e. that it is inner. So while inner appearances are not presented in space, they would not be possible without space. But what does seem right, beyond the phenomenological point regarding the mode of presentation of different contents, is that the temporal structure of experience is conceptually prior to the spatial structure, and has wider scope, in so far as space can be defined in terms of time, but not vice versa.

claim is that for an awareness of difference to be maintained between simultaneously experienced properties, there must be a specifiable difference of locus between the two properties.[37] Without that, there could be no encompassing within a single consciousness of the two as different, since there would be no one matrix on which they could be plotted, and by means of which they could be related to, and so distinguished from, one another. But the difference of location need not, so far at least, be a difference specifically of geometrical structure.

This latter might not be clear immediately, if by chance we choose to concentrate on the visual modality. Two simultaneous red patches, say, can be experienced as different from one another only in so far as they are in different *places*. Without that difference in location of the two, given that they are simultaneous and are not in different consciousnesses, there would be scope only for the experience of one red patch (if that). The requirement has nothing specifically to do with the experiences being qualitatively identical (with respect to their non-relational properties). A red patch and a green patch equally require different locations *if* they are to be encompassed within a single consciousness.[38] But the requirement here of a location in ordinary space is simply a peculiarity of the fact that the contents of the visual modality are made in space, i.e. that that modality presents its contents in physical, or at least ordinary, geometrical space. The matter is different if, say, we take an example from the acoustic modality.

For two simultaneous sounds to be registered as different in one consciousness it must be possible to relate them to, and so distinguish them from, one another, and that means putting them in their respective places, but the places need only be places in an acoustic field (or on an acoustic scale). It is interesting to point out that in this case there is no room for two (or more) qualitatively identical simultaneous sounds to be experienced as such—namely, as the same *sound* coming simultaneously from different places.[39] This is precisely because the places on the acoustic scale are differentiated only by their tonal properties and relations to one another, and with that as our only matrix onto which to plot experiences, two tonally identical sounds would be forced to share the same place, and would be experienced as one and the same. This brings out clearly the general point, the necessity of spatial location, in the most generic sense, for recognition of difference in simultaneity. It is true that as soon as we widen the resources to include not only the 'space' within the acoustic modality, but physical space, there is no problem in experiencing qualitatively identical

---

[37] It is important that we are speaking here of an *awareness of* difference in simultaneity. Mere difference in simultaneity, even difference between simultaneously experienced properties, does not in itself require a *specifiable* difference of locus. There might be a bare qualitative difference, or indeed a bare numerical difference. But that can only work if the two experiences are in different unities of consciousness. What is right is that in order to allow for difference in simultaneity, either we must give up on unity of consciousness, or we must maintain that there is a specifiable difference of location for the two experiences. What forces the second disjunct is talk specifically of *an awareness* of difference in simultaneity.

[38] On this, see pp. 49–51 above. [39] On this, see pp. 230–1 above.

simultaneous sounds as such—one might come from the left, say, the other from the right. But of course there is no necessity for a heterogeneous domain of presentation to leave room for simultaneous experience of qualitatively identical contents as distinct, and so this extension to ordinary physical space is not necessary.

This identifies the sense in which the experience of difference in simultaneity requires a generic spatial structure, *and no more than that*. It is important, however, to be clear that if a sensory modality is taken to serve as the spatial structure in question, this does not mean that the spatial structure in question itself has sensory content. Rather, the loci of that structure can be occupied by sensory content. This is important because the generic conception of space should retain that quality of physical space, that it is a background onto which the perceivable can be plotted, but is not itself perceivable (for reasons that will become clear immediately).

Now this is in fact the case when we concentrate, as we have so far, on differentiating properties within a single modality. In a heterogeneous domain of presentation confined to a single modality, that modality will serve as a single background matrix onto which the experienced contents can be plotted, but there is no sense in which it itself will be a bearer of sensory content, and so an object of perception. That would require some background onto which it itself could be plotted, which is precisely what, by hypothesis, we do not have here: if we did, then *that* background would be the generic space in question, the non-sensory structure in relation to which this one sensory modality could be distinguished. Another way of putting this is to say that in a single-modality heterogeneous domain of presentation, that sensory modality, say an acoustic modality, would enable the distinction between different sounds, because of the differences between them—their differing addresses on the acoustic matrix—but it would not enable the experience of them all *as being sounds*. That common denominator cannot be experienced as sensible content in the confinement of that modality, since it has no unique locus within it—at best it takes the whole matrix as its address—and so cannot be distinguished as a separate content from all others in relation to that matrix. For that experience to be possible, there would have to be some way of experiencing the distinction between what is a sound and what is not a sound, and that is not something that can be accommodated within the acoustic modality.[40] It requires the addition of

---

[40] It might be thought that it can: that all we need are gaps of silence, the absence between sounds, and that there is a place for them on the acoustic scale. If there is, however, then this shows only that the experience of them counts against the possibility of there being experience of them in the confinement of a single-modality domain of presentation. For the silences would not be possible objects of experience in such a context, since bare space (or time) is not itself an object of experience, and there would be nothing else available to 'fill' the silence, such that there could be experience of it as a silent stretch. If this is not meant to be just a peculiarity of the acoustic modality, but a general point about any sensory matrix needing to contain 'gaps'—empty loci that must be experienced as such—then it follows that a single-modality heterogeneous domain of presentation is impossible, either at a time, or over time.

another sensory modality. And that is just what we do not have, by hypothesis, in the cases considered so far. It follows, then, that in the case of the single-modality heterogeneous domain of presentation, if it is possible at all, the operative modality will itself necessarily function as a generic spatial structure, i.e. one which is not itself experienced as having sensible content of its own.[41]

The question now is what happens when the heterogeneous domain of presentation, considered at a moment, is not taken to be confined to single-modality contents, as it has been so far. It might be thought that here there is no longer any need for a spatial structure. In fact, although the argument is not quite as direct, it is as difficult to resist and has perhaps a clearer yield.

If at one and the same time we have the experience of a certain sound, say, and of a certain taste, then the difference of modalities maintains the required difference in simultaneity. Nevertheless, the required awareness of difference in simultaneity, even if directly it presupposes only a distinction between modalities, does indirectly still presuppose a generic spatial structure. This can be brought out in two steps: (*a*) If there is awareness of simultaneous experiences in different modalities, there must be some common matrix onto which those modalities can be plotted. (*b*) That common matrix must itself not be a further sensory modality, since if it were, then it too would have to be plotted relative to other sensory modalities onto some further matrix. The final matrix in the chain, then, must be a structure onto which sensory modalities can be plotted, but which is not itself subject to the form of a sensory modality; which is just to say that it is a structure of the sort that cannot be experienced as inherently having sensory content, as itself impinging on any sensory mechanism, although things *in it* do. This matrix would be generic space, as we have defined it: the things in it would be the contents that fill space.

Steps (*a*) and (*b*) both require clarification. I begin with (*a*). Why is it that there must be some common matrix onto which the different sensory modalities can be plotted? The answer to this, again, is thoroughly Kantian in spirit. Assume that the different modalities are entirely separate from one another in this sense: there is no way that the experience of a sensory content in the one modality can be placed in any relation to the experience of a sensory content in the other modality.[42] The contents of *each* modality are then internally related, but there can be no relation from a content in one modality to a content in another. Such incommensurability simply precludes a unified consciousness across the two experiences. For wherever there was a

---

[41] This is not to say, of course, that the single modality might not continue to function in that way if the domain of presentation is no longer considered merely at a moment; it is just that it is then no longer obviously necessary in order to keep the different contents apart.

[42] This must be assumed to be so even if both modalities are thought to pertain to the causal powers of a single brain.

unified consciousness of contents across modalities, there would have to be some way, however loose, of relating one content to another; a way that is available to consciousness.[43] It would seem that where the modalities are entirely incommensurable, there could not be any unity of consciousness ranging over the contents of each.

But even if this is so, is it right then to say further that for the different sensory modalities to be brought into some sort of relation, they must be plotted onto some common matrix? That is, is it right that unplotted in this way, they must remain incommensurable? The answer to this must, I think, be positive. Being commensurable, however minimally, just is occupying positions that can be located within the same system or framework. It might be suggested that that encompassing system, the whole within which those experienced modalities take up a position, might be nothing other than the single unified consciousness of them. But it turns out that to be encompassed within a single consciousness just is for them to be plotted onto a common background matrix. We can bring this out in detail.

We are concerned now with awareness of difference in simultaneity that is secured not within a single-modality domain of presentation (which was seen immediately to introduce a generic spatial structure) but across sensory modalities. To take an example, at one and the same time there might be an experience of, say, a shrill sound (acoustic modality) and of sweetness (taste modality).[44] What is it that makes it an experience of two properties, rather than of just one? It is simply not helpful to say that they are qualitatively different. The question at hand is, in virtue of what can they be experienced as different properties? That there is a sideways-on perspective from which the properties can be recognized as different is not sufficient to ensure that they will be so discriminated in the experience of them. (Here it is helpful to think of the varying discriminatory powers across the animal kingdom.)

---

[43] Most commonly, of course, we might have the experience of having one *here*, and the other *there*. It should be noted, perhaps, that it is not an option here to say that they might simply be related as temporally successive, thus short-circuiting any argument for the necessity of an appeal to space, since we are for the moment considering specifically what is required to maintain a domain of presentation that is heterogeneous at a moment.

[44] Here I have taken as examples sensory experiences that are not obviously spatial themselves, as are the tactile or—more obviously—visual sensory inputs. I have also tried at the same time to take experiences that are not essentially extended in time (beyond the minimum required for sensibility), given the focus in the discussion on heterogeneity at a moment. (In fact, what is required is only simultaneity in the sense of occupying one and the same temporal stretch, rather than being confined to one and the same instant or minimal temporal stretch.) Interestingly, there is some tension between these two constraints: a play-off between temporal and spatial extension of the sensory experiences. The visual and tactile seem to give rise to experiences that are closer to being instantaneous, but the contents of which are spatially extended. The contents of the auditory experience are not spatially extended, but are more obviously temporally extended.

To get a handle on what is involved here, let us symbolize different modalities by means of capital letters ($A, B, ...$) and loci within them by means of the respective lower cases ($a, a', a''; b, b', b''; ...$). Now supposing experience to be actually extended over time, it seems that we can distinguish between two qualities, a and b, because the experience of them has at times come apart, such that there has been experience of a on its own, or in conjunction with some other member of the B family, say b', just as there has been experience of b either on its own, or in conjunction with a', say. But, of course, the same can be secured at a time. And it would seem right that where there is experience of there being two qualities, a and b, what makes it the case that the experience is as of two distinct qualities, rather than just of one undifferentiated experience, is just that content a is experienced as possible on its own, or at any rate as possible without b. The experience of a shrill sound, in my example, is such that it might be just as it is without the accompaniment of the sweet taste.[45] So far, this would seem only to count against the claim that the experience of difference in simultaneity presupposes a spatial matrix. That a spatial matrix is nevertheless presupposed can be brought out by attending in turn to the two different ways in which it can be said of experience a that it is possible without b.

It is not *always* the case that the possibility of experiencing a without b can be construed as the possibility of experiencing a on its own. This is not always possible because there might in some cases be a type–type dependence across modalities. Let us address this kind of case first, since here the argument is more straightforward. To take an example, if a = tactile experience of a rough surface, and b = visual experience of a blue expanse, it is not necessarily true that there could be an experience of a on its own, although it is true that there might have been a without b. At least where all the sensory modalities are up and running, in so far as there is experience of a rough surface, there will also be an experience of its having *some colour* as well—there is a type–type dependence between the two.[46] But the token–token pairing in such cases might have been different. It might, say, have been a *green* rather than a blue rough surface. Now it seems clear that in such cases the experience of

---

[45] Where there is no further room for such separation, we could not make sense of there still being experience as of two qualities, rather than of one. This accords with the empiricist view of what a simple impression is, namely one which leaves room for no further separation within its content. (See Hume, *Treatise*, I. i. 1; 1978: 2.)

[46] There could certainly be an experience of a on its own here if not all the modalities were working; precluding visual input there might be an experience of roughness on its own. This would not, however, generalize to the statement that two contents are distinct only if the one could be experienced on its own in the face of the shutdown of all but one modality, given (i) that precisely because of the type–type dependence it is not clear that such shutdowns are always conceivable, e.g. olfactory and taste sensations, and (ii) that the distinct qualities need not be in distinct modalities.

difference in simultaneity across modalities requires that within each modality the property in question be assigned a place amongst other possible places within that modality; and also that it be possible to discriminate, for any given collection of properties, which share the same perceptual matrix (= modality), and which lie outside it, in another matrix. This will be so in any case in which the distinctness of the two contents, such that a can be had without b, is thought to be maintained not because a could be experienced on its own, but because it could be experienced as conjoined with some b' which is exclusive of b. It would not do, for example, to think that a shrill sound (= a) and a sweet taste (= b) were shown to be distinct simply because of the possibility of an experience combining a shrill sound (= a) with experience of a pink colour patch. The latter does not show that a can occur without b. For that, the new quality must exclude b, in a way that being pink, for example, does not exclude being sweet. Selecting the appropriate alternative thus requires the ability to tell, for any given content, with which other contents it is clustered together as comprising different loci on a single matrix, which are thereby rendered in principle mutually exclusive of one another. And since this holds for any content, this is just to require that there be some way of plotting different matrices in relation to one another; from which it is a small step to the conclusion that there must be a background matrix.

So far so good. But now we must return to the other, and more obvious, way in which one content may be held distinct from another: it may be thought to be distinct not because it can be combined with some other content which effectively displaces its previous cohort, but because it is in no need of any such partner. What keeps a distinct from b may be simply that a can be had without b, *on its own*. There may be no type–type dependence between a given A and some B. To this extent, clearly, it may seem that the argument just given would no longer be relevant; that there is no longer the requirement that it be possible to identify different matrices, groups of loci, within each of which one locus effectively excludes all others, in a way that typically does not hold between loci of different matrices. But this is not the case. In fact the difference between the two ways in which it might be possible to have a without b—either conjoined with some b' which excludes b, or simply all on its own—is not as significant as it might at first seem.

It is important not to take the notion of the experience of a all on its own, at least as that is involved in the awareness that a might be had without b, too simplistically. Consider what would be the case if the experience of content (= ab) were in fact to be compared strictly only to the experience of a taken simply on its own. The contrast between the two experiences so conceived could not suffice for the conception of its being possible for content a to be had without b, of a being distinct from b. There would be no room here to distinguish the second experience as involving one component of the first experience, only taken on its own: nothing in virtue of which a on its own could be individuated in the same way as it is when a component of content ab. For that to be possible it would have to be the case that a was experienced along with a dummy place-marker that secured the appropriate demarcation of content, such that it then made sense to say that where previously a was combined with content b, now the place of content b is empty. Say, where before there was a sweet taste along with a loud noise, now there is just that sweet taste, accompanied by silence. Without that, there would in effect simply be two different experiences, one of which could be described from sideways on as heterogeneous, but both of which from within would have been equally simple (although obviously different). So if the possibility of having a on its own is to sustain the possibility of recognizing the distinctness of content a from b, that one can be had without the other, then having a on its own must be construed as the experience of that content in the company of the relevant neighbouring dummies, the place-markers that give meaning to its being all on its own rather than in the company of some other contents.

But that construal of the possibility of having a all on its own in effect collapses the relevant difference between the two ways in which it seemed that we could make sense of a without b. The various dummies, the sensory blanks, which serve to sustain the individuation of content a, and so to make sense of its being *that* content that is had all on its own, all do so by playing an exclusionary role within other matrices. They are, in effect, the empty locus, the zeroth, in each of the neighbouring modalities.[47] The possibility of having a on its own thus in fact comes down to having a along with b' rather than with b. This is so at least to the extent—which is all that matters for present purposes—that the possibility of having a on its own is to serve in the explanation of an awareness that a is distinct from b (and so that content ab exhibits cross-modal heterogeneity at a time).

It would appear, then, that for any cross-modal heterogeneous experience, i.e. whether or not we take it to exhibit type–type dependence between its contents, the distinctness of content a from b—without which it would not be experienced as heterogeneous—can be sustained only by appeal to the various combinatorial possibilities across modalities, and to the exclusionary relationships within modalities (since the former are dictated by the latter). And we have already indicated that that appeal requires being able to plot the different modalities in relation to one another. We can now set the matter out more concisely: distinguishing properties requires the possibility of analytically separating them; that analytical separation presupposes (apart from

---

[47] This further supports the possibility raised earlier, that each sensory modality will include an empty place amongst its loci: see n. 40 above.

temporal relations) awareness of combinatorial possibilities and more specifically impossibilities; that, given the relations between properties that exclude some combinations and not others, involves plotting the properties in question onto their respective matrices; which in turn requires distinguishing matrices from one another, each as having its own address, just as properties within a matrix were distinguished from one another in relation to that matrix. And this is just to say that there must be a further background matrix, one presupposed—but possibly also exhaustively constituted—by the fact that each of these matrices has its own locus, distinct from and yet commensurable with that of other matrices. That is, for each property to be allocated not merely the appropriate place in a matrix, but the appropriate matrix, in a form of experience that includes different sensory matrices, there must be a single unified background matrix that encompasses all the various sensory matrices, allowing references to each as distinct in relation to the others. We can conclude, then, that cross-modal heterogeneity at a moment requires that there be some common background matrix onto which those modalities are mapped in relation to one another.

So much, then, by way of establishing the first point above.[48] It remains to establish the second, viz. that the background matrix in question must still be non-sensory. The basic point here was easy to see: if that further matrix were sensory, then it too would have to be plotted onto some yet further background matrix, ultimately coming to rest on a background matrix that does not constitute a sensory modality. (There is no real threat here of an infinite regress: what precludes it is the simple fact that experience is not infinitely rich in sensory modalities.[49]) But as it stands, so baldly stated, the point has an air of empty formality about it, and it will perhaps be helpful to dispel that impression by setting out the point in more detail.

It seems undeniable that the background matrix in terms of which the various modalities (themselves constituting matrices) are plotted in relation to each other, must be distinct from those modalities. For if it were identical to any one of them, then the one modality with which it was identical could not be plotted onto it; it would, so to speak, simply 'dissolve' in the process—or rather, could not have been distinguished from it in the first place. And it seems equally clear that if it is distinct from those modalities and yet is experienced as a sensory matrix, then it cannot serve as the required background

---

[48] See p. 244.

[49] It is perhaps interesting to point out here that were there to be such an infinitely rich form of experience, such as would perhaps have to be attributed to God, it would follow—given what is argued below, Sect. 5—that for such a form of experience the notion of categorial existence will not be necessary. That is, the transcendental argument developed here would not apply to a form of experience of that sort. This is suggestive of the sense in which the existence of an invariant objective world can be seen as a parochial necessity. On this, see Ch. 8, Sect. 3, and Ch. 9.

matrix. If it were an additional sensory matrix, there would have to be individuation of it as one sensory matrix amongst others. It would have to be such that the properties pertaining to that matrix were suitably bound together, as having a common denominator that kept them distinct from those pertaining to a range of other sensory matrices. Now if the latter consisted of the very matrices whose commensurability is being accommodated, this would mean the additional matrix taking its place alongside those other matrices, rather than itself being the background against which sensory matrices are plotted in relation to one another. Alternatively, the background matrix might be such that its quality as a sensory matrix is not thought to be brought out by any distinction between its sensory content and that of the various modalities that are plotted onto it, but by way of contrast with several *further* sensory modalities, so that at that further level there is the same scope to plot out relative differences as at the first level. But then either those further modalities are accessible to the subject in question, in which case the problem is simply repeated at that further level (and indeed the distinction between levels collapses), or they are not. And if they are not, then for the subject in question the background matrix—in so far as it cannot have sensory content that can be distinguished as being of a kind either in relation to the sensory modalities that are plotted onto it, or in relation to still further modalities—cannot itself function as a sensory modality. It follows that the ultimate background matrix onto which all sensory modalities are plotted, to the extent that it functions as that background, cannot itself be experienced as having a distinctive sensory content. To be a background of the required sort, it must be neutral.

The point here is essentially the same as was seen above when it was noted that experience strictly confined to just one sensory modality, while it could be such as would allow for placing different experiences at different loci in a unified matrix, could not be such as to allow for the individuation of that matrix as itself being of a certain qualitative kind.[50] For that would require a contrast between that kind and some other, which is precisely what there is no room for here, just to the extent that we have indeed reached the background matrix.

It follows, then, that difference in simultaneity, considered across modalities as much as within the confines of a single modality, presupposes a neutral unified background. Which is just to say that it presupposes a unified spatial structure, such as can be filled with, but does not itself *qua* empty structure have any inherent sensory content. So much then by way of establishing the conditional set out at the beginning of this section, namely that if a domain of presentation is heterogeneous at a moment, then it must be spatial.

[50] See pp. 243–4 above.

It is perhaps worth noting briefly the sense in which this background spatial structure must be comprehensive. Any sensory modality whose loci are distinguishable by one and the same subject must be such that they can be plotted onto this background common matrix. In so far as there is some rogue modality ($= R$) the loci of which cannot be plotted in relation to other sensory modalities (A, B, C, etc.), there is no way that the same subject that experiences contents of the latter could also experience contents of the rogue modality. That would require an awareness that there is some content, say ar, which, as we have seen, counts as an experience of a and of r only where there is room to conceive of content a, say, as having been conjoined not with r but with r' (or at least minimally with r^0), which appeals precisely to the combinatorial possibilities that are excluded by the incommensurability of R with all other modalities. The incommensurability between R and other modalities thus entails a schism between the subject that experiences the contents of the former, and that which experiences contents of the latter. And this is just to say that the rogue modality cannot be included within the same unity of consciousness as the contents of the other modalities. This brings out the way in which we have here, at this rudimentary stage, and without any reliance on transcendental psychology, the Kantian conclusion that the unity of consciousness entails a unified framework onto which the various sensory properties, via their respective modalities, are all plotted. I will pursue this further below.

What we have seen so far is only the conditional that any rudimentary domain of presentation, just in so far as it is considered heterogeneous at a moment, will presuppose appeal to what is essentially a spatial structure. This is, of course, not sufficient to allow us to conclude without further ado that any heterogeneous domain of presentation will involve this sort of spatial structure. For it would seem possible to consider a domain of presentation which is heterogeneous, but not heterogeneous at a moment. That is, prima facie, it would appear possible for there to be a domain of presentation in which at any given moment there is only one property being experienced, such that that property is not contrasted in any way with other properties experienced at that moment. (Considered merely as it is at a moment, this would be a homogeneous domain of presentation.) What nevertheless makes the domain of presentation heterogeneous is simply that it is not confined to the moment; that the property experienced at a moment is contrasted with other properties had later and earlier.

To the extent that this is feasible it would seem that not every heterogeneous domain of presentation presupposes heterogeneity at a moment; and so, since we have so far argued only that heterogeneity at a moment implies spatial structure, there might remain room for a heterogeneous domain of presentation that does not involve a spatial structure.

In fact, however, it is not difficult to show that every heterogeneous domain of presentation does after all presuppose heterogeneity at a moment. We know that every heterogeneous domain of presentation must internally allow for the experience of temporal succession.[51] The experience of temporal duration clearly requires that there be some experience of change. But the question is what sort of change this must be. If the change is in the experienced quality, such that one content is replaced by another that is qualitatively different from it, the way to the desired conclusion would be clear of obstacles. But the prior question at hand here is whether the experienced change might be merely that of bare temporal passage. If that is the case, then the content (what fills time) need not change from one experience to the next for there to be an experience of, say, 'sweetness, still' or 'still the same sound'. And in such a case the matrix required to plot the two properties alongside one another would seemingly be no more than the temporal matrix itself—and so we would have heterogeneity over time without any need for heterogeneity at a time, and so without spatial structure.

Now there are various possible lines of response to this. One might, for example, be inclined to argue that even the mere judgement 'same still' requires the ability to identify that one experience is qualitatively identical to the preceding one; and that judgements of qualitative sameness, no less than judgements of difference, require utilization of a background matrix onto the space of which qualities can be mapped, sufficiently to tell that the same position is being occupied on two separate occasions. Although I think it valid, I will not attempt to rest anything on this argument here.[52]

A more rewarding line of response is available, one which grants the argument but again simply rejects the premiss that bare temporal succession is itself a possible object of experience.[53] I start with the case of a persisting simple experience. If at any given moment there is exactly one experienced quality, then that moment considered on its own counts as a homogeneous domain of presentation, which, as we have seen, leaves no room for an experience of the persistence of one and the same consciousness over time. As long as there is just a sequence of moments each comprising *that one quality*, there is no possible experience of temporal duration. For there to be experience of temporal duration there must be some perceived difference between a-at-t_1 and a-at-t_2. That is just to say that at the very least there must be some property

---

[51] Whether because it is heterogeneous at a moment—or because it isn't.
[52] But see Sect. 5 below.
[53] This line of argument resembles the earlier argument (pp. 236–7 above) to the effect that homogeneity precludes temporality: but whereas that left it open that temporality might entail no more than heterogeneity over time, the present argument concludes that it is specifically heterogeneity at a moment that is required.

pertaining to the one experience that is missing in the other. And since by hypothesis bare temporal properties cannot by themselves be objects of experience, the changing property in question cannot be merely temporal. Yet any *non*-temporal property changing, alongside the sequence of identical and simple contents, would immediately entail heterogeneity of content at a moment—the one moment involving $a + b$ (whatever b might be), the other involving $a + \textit{not-b}$.

Moreover, this line of argument is clearly not confined only to those cases where temporal heterogeneity is based on what appear to be qualitatively identical contents, but can readily be generalized to any experience of temporal duration, however different the contents at different temporal moments might be. For there to be experience of temporal duration—i.e. a domain of temporally extended presentation, and not just a temporally extended domain of presentation—at least two conditions must be satisfied: (*a*) there must be something within the domain of presentation that changes, and (*b*) there must be something within the domain of presentation that remains constant throughout the change. If nothing changes between *content*-at-t_1 and *content*-at-t_2, then there is internally no difference between the two experiences, and so no distinction between them. (This, within the bounds of the domain of presentation, is just the identity of indiscernibles.) We then do not have a heterogeneous domain of presentation after all, but are back with a homogeneous domain of presentation, which, as we have seen, leaves no room for temporal extension. So much by way of establishing the necessity of the first condition.

But if the change is so radical that nothing remains constant between the two moments, then there remains nothing to bind the two moments together as moments of one and the same temporally extended domains of presentation. If nothing remains constant across the two, then there is no structure enabling the two to be plotted in relation to one another within a unified domain of presentation. In effect, the complete incommensurability of the two means that there is nothing in virtue of which they constitute a single domain of presentation. They are then rent apart, each moment being a homogeneous domain of presentation that leaves no room for temporal structure. What from the outside we might characterize as two distinct homogeneous domains of presentation, following one another in temporal succession, would from the inside be as insulated from one another as Leibnizian monads. If we are to avoid this, there must be some content that remains invariant across changes, which is what the second condition sets out. Without both an invariant element, and some change, we could not have the grounds both to distinguish two or more moments of experience, and yet to leave them combined within a single domain of presentation.

This means that for a given domain of presentation to be temporally structured, it cannot be that any given moment in it might contain only one experienced property. There must at any given moment be at least two experienced properties: one by the elimination and replacement of which change can be implemented, the other by means of which change can be experienced, contained within the domain of presentation. But where there are two distinct properties at a time, we have a domain of presentation that is heterogeneous at a moment.

This constitutes an important link in the argument. We have already seen how heterogeneity at a moment involves spatial structure. We have now established that any temporally structured domain of presentation must be heterogeneous at a moment. So temporally structured domains of presentation must also be spatially structured. And since heterogeneity of a domain of presentation can only mean either heterogeneity at a moment or heterogeneity over time, it follows generally that *any* domain of presentation, just in so far as it is heterogeneous, presupposes a spatial structure. (Indeed, since even the most rudimentary heterogeneous domain of presentation must accommodate temporal structure, we can also draw the general conclusion that any domain of presentation, just in so far as it is heterogeneous, presupposes a spatio-temporal structure.)

5. AN ABIDING SUBSTRATUM

We can pursue further the line of argument developed so far.

The general conclusion established thus far regarding spatial structure can be only that any heterogeneous domain of presentation will involve spatial structure *at a moment* (difference in simultaneity). This would seem to leave open the possibility that while any given moment within a domain of presentation will involve some such spatial grid, enabling us to plot the various coexisting properties onto it, there might not be the same spatial grid for all such moments (and that at the limit there could be a different spatial structure for every such moment). But it does not take much effort to appreciate that the argument seen so far extends readily to strengthen this conclusion, to show that it will not do to have the spatial structure confined to a moment —that it must in fact be one and the same spatial grid that abides across different moments of the domain of presentation.

To distinguish two or more temporal moments of experience, and yet leave them unified within a single domain of presentation, we required both a change in experienced content, and an element of content that remains the same across the change. But experiencing that change, that one content is replaced by another that is qualitatively different from it, and equally the fact that something remains unchanged across the change, requires that there be an abiding background matrix, unchanged throughout the temporal extension in question, in relation to which the properties experienced in different moments of experience can be recognized as different or the same. Otherwise the contents of the two heterogeneous moments would each be plotted onto their respective spatial grids, enabling distinction between the properties at a moment; but there would be no point of comparison across the two moments. The two moments would have been rendered incommensurable. A unified heterogeneous domain of presentation thus presupposes not just that at any given moment there is a background spatial matrix onto which differences between properties can be plotted, but also that the same spatial matrix be operative across different moments. For different moments of experience to be unified into a single domain of presentation, there must be a unified spatial grid that remains invariant across them.

It is important to be clear that this point, that there must be a single spatio-temporal matrix that remains invariant across different moments of one and the same domain of presentation, is not the same as the previous point, that for experience of temporal duration there must be some experience that remains constant across a change. Both are necessary; and the former is a presupposition of the latter. But it seems clear that while experience of temporal duration requires that there be some experienced quality that remains constant while some other experienced content changes, there need not be one experienced quality that remains invariant across all experienced change. Thus the experience of something square and green might be followed by the experience of something square and red; then the experience of something square and red might be followed by the experience of something rectangular and red. In contrast, it is being pointed out that across different moments of one and the same domain of presentation there is just one invariant underlying spatio-temporal grid onto which all these properties are mapped, and so placed in relatively determinate relations to one another. This being so is simply a requirement for the commensurability of all those moments, without which they could not be contained within a single domain of presentation.[54]

This conclusion might, of course, be questioned. It might seem that the above confuses sufficient and necessary conditions. There being just one invariant underlying grid across all moments of experience is certainly a sufficient

---

[54] Note that this requirement holds even if we take a Jamesian view of the unity of the stream of consciousness.

condition of the commensurability of all those moments—but is it also a necessary condition? Could we not envisage the underlying matrix being sufficiently stable for it to be possible to plot simultaneous and successive moments of experience in relation to it, but still gradually shifting over time, so that it was not one and the same, invariant, throughout the domain of presentation? The thought is, in other words, that this background matrix might be analogous to the shifting sands of the riverbed, rather than to the logical space of the *Tractatus*. In fact this is not possible.[55]

Such a shift could not be anything to the experiencing subject, and strictly speaking we cannot even conceive of it. Within the domain of presentation all change is plotted in relation to that background matrix, so there simply isn't the material available within the domain of presentation to make sense of the possibility of that basic matrix itself changing; there is not the logical space for such a change. Making sense of a spatio-temporal matrix undergoing a change requires foregrounding it in relation to a background on which that change could be charted; at which point it becomes clear that we are no longer managing to conceive of a change to *that background matrix*. Anything that alters is, *ipso facto*, something that presupposes, rather than something that comprises, the basic spatio-temporal matrix.[56] The temptation to think that that background can change (in the sense identified) can perhaps in part be traced back to the distinction between the two elements of constancy I have identified as holding across moments of experience: the

---

[55] Wittgenstein himself is not, of course, talking of a spatio-temporal background, but generally can be taken to be suggesting the idea of a background that is only relatively stable (possibly subject to change, albeit imperceptible—Wittgenstein, *On Certainty*, 1969, §99), against which merely empirical facts are distinguished. The relation between the kind of changeable background Wittgenstein leaves us with (see Ch. 6 above) and the kind of invariance introduced here will be addressed further in Ch. 8.

[56] This is essentially only a reformulation of the Kantian thought (First Analogy) that all change that can be anything for us must be experienced as an alteration of some underlying substance, such that a change in that substance is not a possible object of experience. But where Kant talks of substance, we are making a claim only about a neutral spatio-temporal matrix, for reasons that will emerge below.

It might be helpful to note that the point here is structurally similar to one that Quine famously makes regarding determinacy of meaning and ontological relativity (see, in particular, his comparison with spatial position and velocity, in Quine, 'Ontological Relativity'; 1969*b*: 48–50). For Quine, in the semantic realm, we find fixity resulting from the absence of internal resources to generate an infinite regress of translations. Translation is indeterminate; what fixes the meaning and reference of a language is the choice of a background language into which to translate it. But eventually we come to rest with our home language, where no further language is available for us to regress into. Here questions of translation just do not apply; nor, therefore, do questions of determinacy. We just acquiesce: a kind of absolute is generated, just by the fact that for lack of sufficient internal resources translation no longer makes sense, and so has come to an end. In a similar way, it is being pointed out here that change presupposes a background matrix, such that when we reach that matrix, there are no longer the resources available for change to it to make sense.

presupposition of a constant spatio-temporal matrix across different moments of one and the same domain of presentation, and the necessity of some experiences remaining constant for there to be experience of change. While the former must remain invariant throughout the domain of presentation, the latter can vary: items that were constant through one change then themselves changing while some other content is held constant. To the extent that these two sorts of constancy are conflated, the fact that the latter elements of constancy are not invariant might lead to the thought that the former, too, is not.

It is important to note a further feature of the relation between these two sorts of constancy across moments of experience. The single spatio-temporal matrix that remains invariant across different moments of one and the same domain of presentation is itself, for the reasons that we have already seen, not a sensory modality, and so is in itself not observable. By contrast, the experienced content that remains constant across a change constitutive of temporal duration must be observable. It is this difference that explains why both are necessary. The one, which is observable, and by virtue of being observable, presupposes the other; yet the presupposed, not being observable, will not do on its own.

With this we reach the conclusion that any heterogeneous domain of presentation, however rudimentary it may be, presupposes an invariant spatio-temporal matrix, one which serves as an abiding substratum underlying all change that can be experienced within that domain of presentation; a substratum in relation to which all experienced contents are rendered commensurable, while it is itself not a possible object of observation. The broad convergence of this conclusion with Kant's contention that experience necessarily involves a unified objective world is evident. As such it has anti-sceptical promise. This, as well as a comparison with the course of Kant's argument, is something I will turn to below. First, though, it is important to clarify the position reached here by noting a crucial point of divergence from Kant, one that emerges most specifically from a comparison with the conclusion that Kant draws in the First Analogy. It is particularly important for what follows to bring out the way in which, initial appearances notwithstanding, the conclusion here is in fact no weaker than the appropriate conclusion of Kant's parallel argument.

5.1. Kant on Substance

The argument in this chapter so far is largely aligned with the gist of Kant's argument in the First Analogy. Kant recognizes that if all we had was bare succession of contents, there would be no continuity of consciousness, no way of plotting the contents in relation to one another so as to experience that there were (say) two of them. Each would be a world unto itself. For experience as we know it (i.e. as heterogeneous) to be possible, it must be possible to have a synthetic unity of perceptions (i.e. to plot them in relation to one another), and for that to be possible they must all be plotted as so many items on one unvarying background matrix, or substratum. And, as we have also just seen, a change in that background matrix or substratum cannot itself be experienced, or even be conceived of. Kant identifies that substratum with time,[57] whereas we have recognized it to be the spatio-temporal structure, but that difference does not matter for now. (It results merely from the narrow definition of space that Kant gives, which has the consequence that while all events are in time, not all are in space. With the more generic notion of space that has been at work in the above, this limitation no longer holds.[58]) The relevant point of divergence comes when Kant argues that since that matrix is not itself an object of perception, there must be something that, so to speak, *fills it*: something that stands in for it, rendering it a perceptible permanent matrix. Thus:

Only through the permanent does existence in different parts of the time-series acquire a magnitude which can be entitled duration. For in bare succession existence is always vanishing and recommencing, and never has the least magnitude. Without the permanent there is therefore no time-relation. Now time cannot be perceived in itself; the permanent in the appearances is therefore the substratum of all determination of time, and, as likewise follows, is also the condition of the possibility of all synthetic unity of perceptions, that is, of experience. All existence and all change in time have thus to be viewed as simply a mode of the existence of that which remains and persists. In all appearances the permanent is the object itself, that is, substance as phenomenon; everything, on the other hand, which changes or can change belongs only to the way in which substance or substances exist, and therefore to their determinations.[59]

---

[57] Thus, the opening sentence: 'All appearances are in time; and in it alone, as substratum (as permanent form of inner intuition), can either coexistence or succession be represented' (*Critique*, B224). He goes on in the course of the same paragraph to elide the use of the term 'substratum' so that it becomes synonymous with substance, as the permanent that fills time. It is, for reasons that will become clear shortly, the latter sense that then dominates the rest of the discussion. (See next quoted paragraph for an example of this latter use of the term.)

[58] But for an appreciation of the elegance of Kant's parsimonious starting-point in the Analogies, see e.g. Strawson (1966: 123–4).

[59] *Critique*, A183–4/B226–7. See also, for example:

Now time itself cannot be perceived. Consequently there must be found in the objects of perception, that is, in the appearances, the substratum, which represents time in general; and all change or coexistence must, in being apprehended, be perceived in this substratum, and through relation of the appearances to it. But the substratum of all that is real, that is, of all that belongs to the existence of things, is *substance*; and all that belongs to existence can be thought only as a determination of substance. Consequently the permanent, in relation to which alone all time-relations of appearances can be determined, is substance in the [field of] appearances, that is, the real in appearance, and as the substrate of all change remains ever the same. And as it is thus unchangeable in its existence, its quantity in nature can be neither increased nor diminished. (A182/B225)

A Compulsion to Objectivity 259

The idea is that what fills time, or, in terms of the present discussion, the *spatio*-temporal structure, can and must inherit the permanence of that structure, thereby delivering something akin to the traditional notion of substance. Kant here in effect runs together the two kinds of constancy identified above: of perceivable content across any two moments of experience, and of an unperceivable spatio-temporal matrix. He appears to take the necessary invariance of the latter to dictate an invariance of the former.

That Kant's argument for this conclusion regarding substance involves a *non sequitur* has perhaps been most succinctly pointed out by Bennett.[60] Put in terms of the present discussion, from the fact that across any perceived difference or change there must be some perceptible content that is held constant, it cannot validly be inferred that there is some content that is constant across all such change. But the identification merely of a *non sequitur* in Kant's argument could establish only that Kant draws too strong a conclusion, not that there is anything wrong with the conclusion itself. We might then be content to withdraw to a suitably weaker conclusion for this argument, as both Bennett and Strawson do, while leaving it open to think that the stronger conclusion may yet—at least in principle—be substantiated in some other way. In fact, however, it is not merely that the argument does not license Kant's conclusion, but that no other argument could either; his conclusion that there is something—indeed, *whether perceptible or not*—that is invarient across all change (other than the spatio-temporal structure) is in fact impossible.

To bring this out it is necessary first to be clearer about the nature of this conclusion. It is important that what Kant has in mind here is not straightforwardly the traditional notion of substance, i.e. as something transcendent to the empirical world and which is very probably not a possible object of experience. Any claim to there being substance in that sense would involve precisely the sort of metaphysical excess that Kant regards as uncritical and unlicensed. Rather, Kant is concerned with 'substance as phenomenon', or 'substance in the [field of] appearance', i.e. as something within the empirically real world. And the essential invariance of substance in question is to be conceived of as transcendental: that is, it is essential because it is a precondition of our experience. There is, of course, nothing to preclude a metaphysically conceived essential invariance, allowing that something that is standardly

---

[60] 'This is a non-sequitur. If all happenings are alterations, then throughout any happening there is something which remains in existence; but this does not entail that there is something which remains in existence throughout every happening. (The sun is always shining somewhere; but there is no place at which the sun always shines.)' (Bennett 1966: 199–200). As Bennett makes clear (1966: 200), this mistake is distinct from the further mistake Kant makes, of assuming that from the existence of substance any quantitative conservation law can be inferred. While Strawson (1966: 129) is less clear about this latter distinction between the two mistakes, his gloss is closer to the present differentiation between the two kinds of constancy at work (see also 1966: 130–1).

observable might yet be invariant—a permanent substance—because of some external assurance, say, at the limit, that God had made it so. And in that case, if God were to change his mind and withdraw permanence from that object, its transience would unproblematically be a possible object of experience for us. But such metaphysically sustained invariance is of little interest here, and would be of no interest to Kant, of course, if only because it leaves too much in the lap of the gods to be able to provide us with the epistemic assurances we want. He is interested only in a claim to the status of substance that is transcendentally (i.e. internally) rather than transcendently grounded.[61]

Two further points remain to be clarified: one addresses the issue of plurality, and leads on to the other, of observability. Turning to the first, the question is whether such phenomenal substance, that which seamlessly fills space and time, is to be thought of as comprising a single substance, or a plurality of such substances, existing side by side, each filling time, and jointly filling space and time. Since Kant defines substance as that which exists throughout time,[62] rather than throughout space and time, there is in principle scope to appeal to a plurality of coexisting substances, all extended throughout time. And in the First Analogy Kant seems unclear which way to go on this: for the most part he seems to have in mind there being a single substance, but he also clearly leaves open the possibility of there being a plurality of substances (see e.g. A184/B227). Interestingly, however, Kant later returned to the issue with a clearer recognition that what is in question is a single extended substance.[63] In any event it is not difficult to see that a plurality of substances will not do here.

Such coexisting substances would either have to be conceived of as spatially discontinuous with one another, or as continuous. As spatially discontinuous, it would appear possible that they might all be qualitatively identical, and still leave room for being regarded as distinct from one another. But this cannot work, for two reasons. First, for that to be the case there would have

---

[61] Recall that he introduces substance on the strength of the argument that it is a condition not only for the determination of time relations, but also 'of the possibility of all synthetic unity of perceptions, that is, of experience' (*Critique*, A183/B226). And he emphasizes that his proof is both possible and distinctive because it is transcendental rather than metaphysical:

> Yet as it never occurred to anyone that such propositions are valid only in relation to possible experience, and can therefore be proved only through a deduction of the possibility of experience, we need not be surprised that though the above principle is always postulated as lying at the basis of experience (for in empirical knowledge the need for it is *felt*), it has never itself been proved. (A184–5/B228)

[62] 'We can therefore give an appearance the title "substance" just for the reason that we presuppose its existence throughout all time' (A185/B228).

[63] See *Opus Postumum* (*OP*), 21.216–22.612, *passim*. This recognition is connected to the fact that in the context of that discussion, in contrast to that of the First Analogy, Kant calls into play the fact that it is not only bare time, but also bare space, that is not itself an object of experience.

to be some difference between the properties exhibited by substances, and the absence of those properties in the gaps between them. And that would mean that we could in principle make sense of those properties no longer obtaining, ceasing to obtain, as they do in the gaps between substances, and so could in principle countenance (conceive of, and possibly experience) the demise of such a substance. This would count against these being substances in the transcendental sense—that is, such as could not be conceived of as possibly going out of existence.[64] To this it might be responded that the empty gaps between substances, with which they are contrasted, cannot themselves be experienced, and so it could not make sense to plot the envisaged coming and going of substances in experience in relation to them. This, however, leads on to the second and perhaps more telling objection to this construal. Since empty space and time are not themselves possible objects of experience, there could not in fact be any individuation—and *a fortiori* could not be any experience—of a basic plurality of substances in experience as spatially discontinuous: they would have to be construed as seamlessly filling space and time.[65] There is thus no scope for Kant to hold that substances in experience—transcendentally necessitated phenomenal substances—might be spatially discontinuous. Consequently, there is also no scope to think that substances might be different despite qualitative similarity. Given the impossibility of their spatial discontinuity, if all have the same characteristics, then there would be no sense in holding that what we had were different substances, rather than different regions of one and the same substance.

We are then forced to the other option. For the permanent that fills space and time without discontinuity to count as a plurality of substances, there would have to be some specifiable difference between them. Different substances will have different essential characteristics. But then, for any such substance candidate, it is difficult to see why its properties should be permanent features of our experience. Just as on this view it is acknowledged that across the spatial axis one substance is delimited where another coexisting substance begins, the same would in principle seem to be possible across the temporal axis. One purported substance could terminate at a point in time, and be replaced with another. As long as there was enough continuity of other contents, possibly thought of as other substances, there would be nothing to preclude experience of the termination of one set of properties and

---

[64] Here one might distinguish between two sorts of transcendental necessity. The one is that the object is such that a change in it cannot be an object of experience because we cannot even construe the object as so changing. The other is that although we can so construe it, any such change would result in the termination of experience, and so for that reason the change in question would not be a possible object of experience. But we have already seen—the *non sequitur* objection—that there are no grounds for the latter claim. It is therefore only the former that remains relevant.   [65] Kant seems to have a similar argument in mind at *OP* 21.218–19.

their replacement by another. Substances in this sense would be qualitatively distinct from one another, and so would be plotted in relation to a common background matrix, with which none was identical, and given which each could be conceived of, and possibly be experienced, as giving way to some other. Such qualitatively distinct objects could not then lay claim to the transcendentally necessitated assurance of permanence that is in question. There might, of course, be such objects that are thought of as metaphysically assured of permanence. But even if some objects had the permanence of substance thus conferred on them as a matter of metaphysics, there is nothing about them or the structure of experience to preclude the possible experience of their demise subsequent to a possible withdrawal of that status.

It would seem, then, that either way, it cannot be that the permanent which fills space and time is conceived of as a plurality of discrete substances. And, as indicated, Kant too came to recognize that the claim had to be that there was simply one phenomenal substance that seamlessly filled, or stood in for, the unified spatio-temporal structure, thereby rendering it a possible object of experience. Thus:

It amounts to a whole, which (as a self-subsistent cosmic whole) is internally self-moving and serves as the basis of all other movable matter. Independently, it forms a cosmic whole from a single material . . . The ground for this assertion is: Intuitions in space and time are mere forms, and, lacking something which renders them knowable for the senses, furnish no real objects whatsoever to make possible an existence in general . . .[66]

What is in question here, then, has come down to whether there can be such a single phenomenal substance filling all of space and time. And it is at this point that the issue of observability becomes problematic, in a way that it perhaps was not as long as a plurality of substances was entertained. The question is whether such a single phenomenal substance could be observable. Kant appears to waver. The argument-strategy in the First Analogy, as the paragraphs quoted above indicate, readily suggests that it should be. Kant appears precisely to introduce substance as the permanent substratum or substrate on the grounds that it makes possible the perception of change and of temporal succession, in a way that the bare spatio-temporal framework—which is itself not perceptible—cannot do on its own. This readily suggests that that which fills time, and inherits the permanence of that structure, is being thought of as in principle perceptible. But Kant is right to waver, and this had better not be what he is arguing. This combination, whereby

---

[66] *OP* 21.217. Similarly, he talks of 'a particular world-material, which penetrates all bodies and moves them internally, but which is itself also a self-unifying whole' (21.222); or of its being 'everywhere homogeneous and unique' (21.228), 'a universally distributed, all-penetrating world-material' (21.229). See also, for example, 22.554 n.

something could both inherit the permanence of the spatio-temporal structure and yet (at least in principle) be observable, is not possible.

The problem with this combination has already been brought out by the discussion above, in showing why the background spatio-temporal matrix must be neutral. If, for the reasons given, the background matrix cannot comprise a sensory matrix, then it cannot be experienced as having its own distinctive sensory content, and in consequence cannot be observable itself (as distinct from being furnished with observable contents). We can make the same point clearer by putting the implication, from the form of invariance in question to unobservability, the other way round. In so far as something is observable, it cannot be the single unified and constant background matrix without which the unity of experience would be disrupted. For in so far as it is observable, it would have to be such as can be experienced as itself having sensory attributes. If those sensory attributes are thought to pertain to more than one sensory modality, then these have to be kept distinct from one another, and so the conclusion immediately follows that this is not itself the constant background matrix relative to which all such variation can be experienced. But even if those sensory attributes are thought to pertain to only one sensory modality, it is still necessary that they be registered as such, if the observability in question is to be maintained. And to be registered as such, that type of sensory content must be kept distinct from all other types of sensory content, and that means plotting the sensory modality in question alongside all others. The point can equally well be brought out by noting that, to be recognized as such, there must be some sense given to the possibility of distinguishing that sensory modality from its absence. And for that to be possible either the absence must be made sense of by contrast with (and the possible intrusion of) content from a different sensory modality, or the possible absence of that sensory content has to be understood as the possible extrusion of *all* sensory content from a certain locus (the zeroth locus).

Whichever way we take it, then, there is a presupposition of a background matrix which is itself not identical with anything that can itself be experienced as having observable attributes. Thus any object or structure, however permanent, in so far as it is observable, presupposes that background matrix but cannot simply 'fill it', or be isomorphic with it. Rather, *qua* observable, its content will have a specifiable address within that matrix. Yet anything that has a specifiable locus in that way, by virtue of having a specifiable content, could in principle come to occupy a different locus, by having a different content.[67] Anything which is observable, therefore, cannot have the invariance of that background matrix, which alone cannot be allocated a locus, and so cannot even be conceived of as changing.

---

[67] This was the root of the problem with the attempt to construe a plurality of phenomenal substances.

Kant would thus be wrong to assume that there could be an observable substratum that inherits the permanence of the unobservable spatio-temporal structure that it fills—that is, that the two kinds of constancy identified above can coincide. What precludes this, and what Kant fails to note clearly, is the relation between the invariance of the background spatio-temporal matrix and observability. Basically, whatever in our experience is invariant in that way cannot be observable; or conversely, if it is observable, then it cannot have that essential invariance.

Interestingly, this point about the necessary unobservability of that which is necessarily invariant in experience can in fact be brought out in terms more obviously internal to Kant's own discussion in the First Critique. Kant rightly insists that any perceptible change requires that there be some relatively abiding content bridging the change. An absolute change, in which nothing remained constant, would not be a possible object of experience. Such a change would fragment the unity of experienced time, and of consciousness. It is here that Kant commits the *non sequitur*, thinking that the unity of time must be preserved by a matching unity of substance, not realizing that an overlapping patchwork of perceptible contents would do the preservation job just as well. But in fact Kant might have realized that his own line of thought suggested that *only that* could do the job. This can perhaps be most clearly seen by attending to his awareness that there could not be an experience of an absolute beginning or end.[68] The reason has to do with the fact that such an experience would require experience of a preceding or succeeding time. Focusing for simplicity on the case of an absolute beginning, there are two possibilities: either the preceding time is empty, or it is not.

If the preceding time is empty, then since bare time is not a possible object of experience, there can be no experience of the moment preceding the absolute beginning, and so no experience as of the sudden emergence of content into a hitherto empty spatio-temporal matrix. The relevant point here is that for that experience there would have to be a contrast between the content of experience before and after the advent, which the empty time before the new beginning obviously precludes. But the same line of thinking can be extended. Just as a new beginning would not be a possible object of perception, for lack of the appropriate contrast, so too would substance—as that which has neither beginning nor end and so to speak seamlessly fills the spatio-temporal framework—not be a possible object of perception. For substance to have a perceptible quality such as to render it observable by us, we must at least be able to contrast it with some other perceptible content. (On analogy to the time before the absolute beginning not being empty.) But once that contrast is given, there is nothing inconceivable about experiencing the demise of either

---

[68] *Critique*, A188/B231. See also A186/B229.

content given the other.⁶⁹ Transcendental permanence thus, again, gives way in the face of observability.

It might be thought that Kant could hope to avoid this conclusion by arguing that the contrast is within a plurality of (obviously coexisting) *substances*, each with different perceptible contents, such that each is ensured its perceptible content by way of contrast with the others. But as we have seen, while in the First Analogy Kant is unsure whether or not to countenance a plurality of substances, it seems clear that such appeal to a plurality of coexisting substances cannot help here. Such a move again immediately brings into play the tension between observability and invariance noted above, now threatening the claim of each to be a substance—at least in the transcendental (as opposed to metaphysical) sense. If there are such coexisting candidate substances, it is difficult to see what threat would be posed to the unity of experience by any one of them (perhaps by the grace of God) going out of existence. Hence the relevance of the focus on the fact that that invariance that is essential to our experience, rather than incidental to it, precludes its observability.

All this would seem to establish that phenomenal or transcendental substance cannot be both permanent and observable. It remains, then, to consider the possibility of an *unobservable* phenomenal substance. Certainly, Kant is not opposed to the idea of upholding the permanence of phenomenal substance without the observability claim.⁷⁰ Even in the First Analogy he seems to lean in this direction. The unobservability of substance indeed seems to be implicit in what he says, for example, in disposing of the second possible way in which one might try to conceive of an absolute beginning:

> If we assume that something absolutely begins to be, we must have a point of time in which it was not. But to what are we to attach this point, if not to that which already exists? For a preceding empty time is not an object of perception. But if we connect the coming to be with things which previously existed, and which persist in existence up to the moment of this coming to be, this latter must simply be *a determination of what is permanent in that which precedes it*.⁷¹

The permanent substance would turn out not to be that which had 'come to be', which is observable, but rather that which underlies the observable, as the unifying substratum behind the changing appearances. (And so we have not managed to conceive of experiencing an advent of substance, merely again of its alteration.) The same conception seems implicit elsewhere in the First

---

⁶⁹ Assuming that the remaining content is not thereby rendered a homogeneous domain of presentation.

⁷⁰ Given the Kantian transcendental sense of 'phenomenal', it should be clear that it would be inappropriate to worry about how something *phenomenal* could turn out to be unobservable. In just the same way causality is known to obtain in the phenomenal world, even though it is not observable.   ⁷¹ *Critique*, A188/B231; my italics.

Analogy, when Kant distinguishes substance from that which can change, and the latter includes 'accidents', or 'determinations', or substance, or 'the way in which substance or substances exist' (A184/B227). The extent of these latter characterizations strongly suggests that substance will underlie the observable, rather than being observable itself. And the observability of substance is something that Kant quite explicitly gives up on later. Thus, in the *Opus Postumum* again, *along with the recognition that there can be only one phenomenal substance,* there is also the recognition that that substance is not observable:

> Although this primary material with the property which we must ascribe to it of being primordially moving, is merely present in thought, it is not a hypothetical thing. Nor is it an object of experience; for then it would belong to physics. It has reality, however, and its existence can be postulated, because without the assumption of such a world-material and its moving forces, space would be no sense-object, and experience of it—whether affirmative or negative—would not take place. We consider such a formless primary material, penetrating all spaces (and whose reality can only be confirmed by reason) as nothing more than all-penetrating moving forces, distributed in space. Its actuality can be postulated prior to experience (i.e. *a priori*) for the sake of possible experience.[72]

The trouble with this (more traditional-sounding) view of substance can be brought out in two ways. First, as was noted above, Kant explicitly introduced the notion of substance as the permanent in appearances, which would make good the fact that bare time—and the same goes for the bare spatio-temporal structure—cannot be perceived.[73] So if it turns out that substance, the permanent in appearances, cannot itself be perceived either, then it is difficult to see how it can play the role that Kant thought necessitated its introduction, namely that of making possible time relations, and the synthetic unity of perceptions. To the extent, then, that this is the view of substance, Kant's argument for it cannot work, or at least cannot work as straightforwardly as we might have thought and as the First Analogy most readily suggests. The idea would rather have to be that substance, like bare space and time, is after all not an observable object either, but that unlike bare space and time it

---

[72] *OP* 21.219. The point is one that he repeats several times, a fact that might most appropriately be taken to indicate discomfort with it, were it not for the generally repetitive state of the manuscript of the *Opus Postumum*. In any event, here too Kant is still clearly tempted by the observability claim, and uneasy about giving it up. Thus he says, immediately after the passage just quoted: 'No *transition* can be experienced from the full, *via the void*, to the full [again]. For that would amount to a perception of nonbeing as an object present to the senses. Consequently, every space in relation to our outer senses is filled with matter' (21.220). This most readily suggests that that matter is observable. And later he uses a similar argument to establish this material as 'an object of experience in space' (22.551). But he then goes on immediately to appear to contradict this by saying that it is 'not demonstrable as an object of experience', then adding again that it 'must, nevertheless, be postulated as an object of possible experience' (22.552).

[73] This strategy is at work as much in the *Opus Postumum* as in the First Analogy.

somehow has the power to render observable content. To that extent it might be thought to be 'indirectly observable'. But, as we will see shortly, this idea is far from straightforward, and Kant himself seems to have struggled with it.[74]

This brings us to the second problem. If substance in the field of appearance, 'the real in appearance',[75] is to be construed as itself strictly *unobservable*, it is difficult to see how it can avoid simply collapsing into the permanent spatio-temporal field itself. Kant talks as if that field is filled with an object,[76] or objects, of which it is true that their states might change, that is, their attributes (determinations) come into and go out of existence, and this counts as an alteration of the underlying object(s); but that underlying object can only alter, and cannot itself go out of existence (or undergo what Bennett calls an 'existence-change'[77]). So the waves in the sea might go out of existence, for example, but this is merely an alteration of the sea which abides throughout the change; the sea itself might then go out of existence ... the question is where this process stops. If that which alters but does not itself change is supposed to be a possible object of experience for us, then the process must stop at something observable; and given what we have seen, that is to say that it cannot stop at transcendental substance itself, since such substance would not be observable. But if we allow that the object of the change in question is not something we might experience—that is, we have an observable alteration of something unobservable, rather than an alteration of something observable—then, of course, the process threatens to go on until we have nothing left but the bare spatio-temporal structure; in which case that which alters but cannot itself change is nothing other than that framework.

Clearly, if anything is to be left of the idea of substance as the permanent that exists in space and time, the process must stop before *that*, at some object(s) in space and time. Any such candidate object must have properties other than its spatio-temporal ones—otherwise there will be no distinction between the place it is at and empty space—and some of those properties must be such that cannot change. But what would it be for those properties to be unobservable? It cannot be the property of being, say, impenetrable (or relatively so) in a way that empty space is not. Anything with that property would not be unobservable (and just for that reason, as we have seen, would not be such as could not conceivably be experienced to change). The property would have to be something like a dispositional property, not observable in itself, but behind the impenetrability, visual appearance, and all the other observable determinations that might come into and go out of existence. And indeed it seems that this is just what Kant came to endorse after accepting the unobservability

---

[74] It is this discomfort that perhaps underlies his tension regarding the observability claim.
[75] *Critique*, A182/B225.
[76] Cf. the statement of the principle of permanence of substance in the A edition, A182.
[77] Bennett (1966: 187 ff.).

of substance.[78] But if substance is *nothing more than* some such dispositional property or set of properties, nothing other than moving forces distributed throughout space, then they would seem ungrounded in anything to do with the constitution of an object filling space. Strictly speaking, there is no difference between saying that those 'agitating forces' are properties of an *object* all of whose other properties might change, and saying that they are brute properties of a *spatio-temporal nexus* all of whose other properties might change. And it is not at all clear that such ungrounded dispositional properties still make any sense.[79] To say that this is all that the idea of unobservable substance in the field of appearance can come to is thus to accept in all but the form of words that it comes to nothing at all.[80]

To sum up this discussion: Anything that is observable cannot have the essential invariance required of a transcendental substance; yet if it is in principle not observable, it cannot be distinguished coherently from the bare spatio-temporal matrix. Either way, then, there is no scope for a transcendental notion of substance as that which fills space and time of the sort that Kant envisages as necessary.

What we have seen so far goes along with the Kantian conclusion that the unity of the heterogeneous domain of presentation—or in Kantian terms the unity of consciousness—requires that there be something permanent and unchanged throughout that domain. We thus agree that 'Permanence is ... a necessary condition under which alone appearances are determinable as things or objects in a possible experience.'[81] But there is reason to think not only that Kant is wrong in his purported proof that this invariant element is phenomenal substance (i.e. the *non sequitur* charge), but that he is mistaken even in thinking that it *could* be. The significance of this mistake will be more salient later, in the light of what is said about the commitment to an ontological base.

6. CONCLUSION

The argument set out above constitutes a transcendental argument to show that any experience, just in so far as it comprises two or more distinguishable

---

[78] Thus he talks, for example, of this permanent substance or matter as 'nothing more than all-penetrating moving forces, distributed in space' (21.219; see also 21.551), or as 'continuously and boundlessly distributed and *constantly self-agitating*' (22.551; my italics). He is here trying to articulate a notion of substance as purely dispositional; he refers to it as 'caloric', while insisting (21.228, 21.233, 22.550, 22.612) that the feeling of warmth must not play a role in our conception of it: i.e. that it be construed as a dispositional base devoid of observable properties.

[79] On this, see Blackburn (1990).

[80] Of course, this is not to say that we cannot make sense of dispositional properties of ordinary material objects. [81] *Critique*, A189/B232.

qualities, presupposes a spatial and temporal dimension, constituting a spatio-temporal matrix that is necessarily invariant throughout the domain. It is by establishing this basic dependence of subjective apprehension of content on a unified objective domain that is independent of individual moments of awareness that the argument promises an answer to the sceptic who thinks, specifically, to doubt the unity of a temporally and spatially extended external world. The fact that we are dealing with a generic spatial structure rather than specifically with that of our physical space does not denigrate its claim to objectivity: it merely pegs the argument at the appropriate level of generality.

It is important to be clear about what is and what is not being claimed for the argument. In particular, it should be clear that it cannot be taken as a refutation of the possibility of a form of experience—such as may be had by some rudimentary life form—for which there are only so many kaleidoscopic experiences, without any conception or awareness of a unified spatio-temporally extended domain onto which they can all be plotted. An argument designed to exclude a priori the possibility of such a rudimentary form of experience would clearly be too strong. The argument here is intended only to show that once there is experience of a heterogeneous domain, then whether or not the bearer of the experience is cognizant of it, or indeed has the capacity to cognize it, there is already the presupposition of a unified spatio-temporal world external to—i.e. independent of—particular states of awareness and subjectively registered contents, so that it is—even at that early stage—already too late for solipsistic scepticism about the external world to be (consistently) entertained.[82]

We can leave the argument of this chapter here. It should be clear, however, that it could be carried further. In particular it is important to note that while the argument here departs from Kant's conclusion regarding phenomenal substance as an invariant filling of the spatio-temporal matrix, there is nothing to preclude picking up a Kantian line of argument at the far end of the First Analogy, so to speak. (In particular, there is room to follow Kant in developing a case for the spatio-temporal world in our experience being necessarily causally structured.) Such further development can be left aside for now. The aim here has been to show merely how we can get this far by way of a reconstruction that stands to answer the solipsistic sceptic, and at the same time maximally avoids some of the strictly doctrinal aspects of transcendental psychology that emerged as problematic in Part I.

---

[82] It is, in terms of the see-saw analogy (see above, p. 44), already too late to doubt that the far side of it exists. Of course, there might still be room, for all that we have seen, for doubts about the specific denizens of that external world. The point so far is *only* that there is no room for *solipsistic* scepticism.

The question of what is involved in some forms of life being able to articulate these presuppositions whereas others cannot is strictly for natural science to answer. (The significance of this claim will be clearer in the light of what is said about natural science in Ch. 9.)

The salient respects in which this argument has indeed avoided some of the naïvely assumed claims of transcendental psychology—claims that turned out to be optional and ungrounded, and thereby weakened the standing of the arguments in which they played a part—should perhaps be made clear. First, there is nothing in the reconstructed argument by way of an assumption of transcendental structures of the mind. That is, there is no story such as Kant's about sensibility and understanding as two faculties with their respective a priori furnishings; or such as the empiricists' about how 'stacked' faculties could enable a mind starting out as a *tabula rasa* to get up to speed. Indeed the question to which those stories are answers—namely, how must the mind be if it is to become equipped with content?—is left altogether to one side. That space and time are necessary features of experience, and thus can be known a priori, is derived without any appeal to the structure of the mind, and *a fortiori* without any talk of there being a priori *furnishings* of the mind. Secondly, there is no longer any trace of the assumption so forcefully questioned by James, of a passive faculty whose sensible atoms must be united by self-conscious acts of judgement made from outside the stream of consciousness. Finally, nothing has turned on a commitment to psychological atomism, either premised or as a consequence of a particular transcendental psychology, which in general terms was common to both empiricists and Kant, or indeed on the alternative commitment to psychological holism, which in James and Bergson was seen to threaten (the most persuasive construals of) the transcendental arguments Kant developed, in the Transcendental Deduction in particular. What we have seen in fact is that starting from a point more primitive than can allow for the question of atomism or holism even to be posed, we can move to the necessity of being able to attend to contents individually, a feature which can readily be taken to encourage—although it does not entail—the view that contents are apprehended by the mind atomistically. The latter addresses an issue that not only need not be settled for present purposes, but that need not even be raised; the former is a feature to which both the atomist and the holist are committed, and that can serve well enough to drive some of the arguments that reconstruct ground covered in the Transcendental Deduction.

In all these ways the argument developed here tries to bypass some of the psychological assumptions that were seen to be at the root of subject-driven scepticism, and to provide an alternative way of grasping the interdependence between subjective contents and objective unity, and their anti-sceptical import. Another way of putting it is to say that the argument aims to start from premisses more rudimentary than Kant's, and see how the essential moves of the Transcendental Deduction can still be made. This is the point we have reached, and at which it is possible to rejoin Kant.

Now this strategy, an attempt to answer solipsistic scepticism without interference from transcendental psychology, is, of course, familiar from

Strawson's reconstructive approach to Kant. Strawson expunges both transcendental psychology and transcendental idealism (which he takes to be intimately bound up with that psychology). The result is a reconstruction that can be regarded as having a simple *modus ponens* structure, perfectly compatible with uncompromising naturalism or realism. And, for all that we have seen, exactly the same may apply here. If there is to be a simple heterogeneous experience, then there must be a permanent spatio-temporal order; from which, given the undeniability of the antecedent, we can infer that there is an abiding spatio-temporal structure. In the absence of any form of transcendental idealism, this inference is not merely to an empirically real structure, transcendentally necessary but ideal: it is simply an inference to *the way the world itself* is—happily so for us, given that it is a necessary condition of our form of experience.

The weakness of this robust realist construal of the argument has also been noted above. First, in the absence of the (apparent) safeguards provided by transcendental psychology, experience is as unstable as the brute happenings in the world that might disrupt the unity of the spatio-temporal domain, thereby denying the consequent.[83] More significantly though, given that all sorts of empirical construals (e.g. illusions) are possible, the realist argument can work only if it establishes that the required spatio-temporal order is not some such imposition on our part, and it is difficult to see how this could be established. Rather than eliminating illusion, Kant chose to consolidate it. Again, it is the appeal to transcendental psychology that is supposed to make good on this, assuring an ineliminable construal of an empirical order.[84] Now, as we also saw, it is not clear that the appeal to transcendental psychology could really produce a safeguard on either of these points, and for reasons that themselves provide grounds for rejecting such speculative psychological hypotheses: namely, that the constraints imposed by the transcendental workings of the mind are themselves only as resilient as whatever (unknown) brute forces sustain them. But it nevertheless seems prima facie right—although probably, despite what was said earlier, not very worrying to the robust realist—that without transcendental psychology (or an appeal to transcendent metaphysical guarantors) there can be no such assurances. In fact, however, I believe that there can be: that the line of argument here is such that, even in the absence of transcendental psychology or other metaphysical appeals, it provides what is required to safeguard the resilience of our grasp of the objective order of things.

---

[83] This will perhaps appear to be of reduced significance in the present context, given how rudimentary the construal of the consequent is on the argument as set out so far: it may seem obvious that there is no need for experience to be so resilient as to withstand the disruption not of objects in the external world, but of the unity of the spatio-temporal domain itself.

[84] See Ch. 2, pp. 91–3, 172–3, and *passim*.

The case for this will emerge in the course of the next chapter. It will involve a retreat from the above unqualified realist construal of the argument (as a simple *modus ponens* inference to reality) to a central insight of transcendental idealism. While a defence of the interdependence of subjectivity and objectivity without transcendental psychology is familiar and in good Strawsonian tradition, the attempt to sustain the central insight of transcendental idealism without transcendental psychology may seem more demanding.[85]

[85] The central insight in question does not itself constitute a form of transcendental idealism. And the troubling cost of transcendental idealism—namely, that we cannot know the world as it is in itself—will turn out to have been a naïve conclusion, one that a sufficiently critical treatment of the underlying insight no longer entails.

8

A Defence of Transcendental Arguments

TRANSCENDENTAL arguments standardly attempt to argue from some undeniable facts about experience, or the psychological realm, to conclusions about how the world beyond that merely psychological domain must be. Such arguments attempt—as we might put it—to cross the appearance–reality gap: to cover the distance between our beliefs and the world they are about, or between how things seem to us and how they really are.[1] Clearly, so construed, transcendental arguments hold out the promise of significant anti-sceptical mileage: they start from premisses drawn from the domain paradigmatically held to be beyond doubt, and end up with conclusions firmly within the domain paradigmatically held (by the sceptic) to be beyond knowledge. But transcendental arguments, on this standard construal, face two salient problems. There is, first, the problem of the *inference to reality*. Secondly, there is the problem of the *universality of inference*. The first concerns the spectre of idealism: the worry that in fact no argument is going to enable us to break out of the domain of how things appear to us, to bridge the gap between appearances and reality. The second is the relativist worry that, however persuasive the inference might seem, and however undeniable the conclusion, that argument might not always and in all places seem so persuasive, nor might there be some other leading to just that set of conclusions.

Of these two problems the second is of broader scope, and most of this chapter will be directed at it (taking in the other along the way). To this extent, just as the preceding chapter addressed the problems of Part I, so the present chapter addresses the problem we were left with at the end of Part II. It is important, however, first to address the first of the two problems identified, to appreciate that it is not easily sidestepped.

---

[1] These two formulations are not necessarily equivalent. For one thing, the world that our beliefs are about may be distinguished from the world of things as they really are. Crossing the appearance–reality gap in the one sense will then not be the same as crossing it in the other. This will obviously be of importance in the Kantian context of discussion that follows.

1. INFERENCE TO REALITY

This problem arose clearly at the end of the previous chapter, in relation to a robust realist construal of the transcendental arguments in question, of the sort that Strawson might favour; a construal that avoids encroachment from either transcendental psychology or transcendental idealism. Of the two problems that were outlined there, the more basic concerned the difficulty of any transcendental argument actually delivering a truth about how the world is. Even if we have an argument showing that for some undeniable p to be the case, q must also be the case, how can we tell between q being the case, and our being so deluded as to have it appear to us to be the case?

In his early paper on transcendental arguments Stroud expresses this idealist objection thus:

> Kant thought that he could argue from the necessary conditions of thought and experience to the falsity of 'problematic idealism' and so to the actual existence of the external world of material objects, and not merely to the fact that we believe there is such a world, or that as far as we can tell there is.
>
> An examination of some recent attempts to argue in analogous fashion suggests that, without invoking a verification principle which automatically renders superfluous any indirect argument, the most that could be proved by a consideration of the necessary conditions of language is that, for example, we must *believe* that there are material objects and other minds if we are to be able to speak meaningfully at all.[2]

Stroud is here precisely articulating the objection that for any conclusion of a transcendental argument, the sceptic can claim that it follows only that for the undisputed premiss to be possible it must seem to us that the disputed proposition q is true—we will believe it to be the case—but that is compatible with its not being the case. The sceptical response to transcendental arguments thus amounts to saying that we cannot cross the chasm between how things seem to us, or the contents of our representations and beliefs, and how things actually are in the world—which is precisely the chasm that paradigmatic transcendental arguments were supposed to carry us across.

But in the absence of further amplification any such criticism in the context of Kant's use of transcendental arguments must appear confusing. Kant's *starting*-point is in effect an acknowledgement of the force of that very objection. In the face of this problem Kant can be seen to have offered what might be thought of as a strategy of sophisticated capitulation. If the appearance–reality gap is thought of as that between how things appear to us, and how they are in themselves (i.e. the phenomenal–noumenal gap), then, Kant concedes, we indeed cannot cross it. But, given transcendental idealism, that still

---

[2] Stroud (1968: 256).

leaves room for a perfectly adequate sense in which that gap can be traversed: from beliefs, to the external world they are about. Thus, in one sense—the transcendental sense—of 'representation' and 'how things appear or seem to us', Kant would accept that transcendental arguments cannot take us beyond representations and how things seem to us, to knowledge of the way of the world. But in the empirical sense of those terms Kant would emphatically deny that we cannot get beyond representations to knowledge of an independent world. That is just what transcendental idealism is supposed to leave room for, and how it is supposed to accommodate valid transcendental arguments in the face of the threat of empirical idealism. That is the central point linking Kant's transcendental idealism to the validity of his transcendental arguments: without transcendental idealism, there would seem to be no available sense in which transcendental arguments can be said to take us beyond belief, beyond appearances, and yet that is precisely what they need to do. Given that this is the case, coming to terms with the problem of the inference to reality would require attending to the precise relation between transcendental arguments and transcendental idealism. But for the most part, the assessment of transcendental arguments has proceeded without attention to that relation.

However, Stroud's concern in that early paper was not specifically with the way in which transcendental arguments work in Kant, as he has recently made clear, and he acknowledges that when it comes to Kant his commitment to transcendental idealism might provide a way of making his transcendental arguments work. But since he reasonably enough shares the widespread misgivings about transcendental idealism, the question then remains what can be said to defend transcendental arguments from the idealist objection without transcendental idealism. Stroud remains pessimistic about whether, shorn of transcendental idealism, we can uphold the Kantian strategy, since that involves inferring from psychological premises to conclusions that are now, without transcendental idealism, not psychological in any sense.[3]

Now anyone averse to transcendental idealism might attempt an extension of Kant's sophisticated capitulation: that is, while conceding to the sceptic that there is perhaps no scope at all for transcendental arguments to move from beliefs to conclusions about the facts those beliefs are about, they can insist that transcendental arguments can nevertheless still serve an anti-sceptical purpose. It may, in this vein, be maintained that transcendental arguments should simply not be aimed at refuting the epistemic sceptic, but rather the doxastic sceptic. As such, they do not stand to be impugned by the acknowledgement that such arguments do not in any sense carry us beyond belief-contents. The salient question is whether and to what extent transcendental

---

[3] Stroud (1999: 11–12). He is nevertheless concerned to see what can be salvaged by way of a weaker construal of transcendental arguments.

arguments that thus avoid the inference to reality are still strong enough to be of interest, or has capitulation now gone too far.

This strategy has recently been attempted by Robert Stern.[4] Stern is concerned to identify one way in which, without appeal to transcendental idealism, and while accepting that without it the sceptical objection concerning the inference to reality cannot be met, we can nevertheless uphold the Kantian anti-sceptical use of transcendental arguments. This requires a revision in the conception of what Kant's transcendental arguments are targeted at. Essentially, the contention is that Kant's transcendental arguments work entirely on the 'near side', within the realm of how things appear to us. Of course, in a sense, this is what Kant thought too. But for Kant, as we have seen, transcendental arguments do nevertheless manage to take us across the divide between empirical appearances and empirical reality. Without transcendental idealism there is no such room to manœuvre (no 'depth of field') within the domain of appearances. So Stern cannot conceive of transcendental arguments as concerned to answer the *epistemic* sceptic—taken as the sceptic about our knowledge of an external world—in any sense.[5] Rather he views them as concerned only with the furnishings of our belief-set, asking not which of these beliefs gets the world right, but rather which beliefs are justified, which we have reason to hold by our own norms of justification. Transcendental arguments, so conceived, do not need to escape the psychological realm, conceived now as the domain of what Kant would call empirical appearances.

Stern talks of truth-directed, in contrast to belief-directed, transcendental arguments. And he holds that this maps onto a distinction between epistemic and justificatory sceptics, such that truth-directed transcendental arguments are concerned to answer the epistemic sceptic, and belief-directed transcendental arguments are concerned to answer the justificatory sceptic. He concedes that belief-directed transcendental arguments cannot answer the epistemic sceptic,[6] but thinks that they can answer the justificatory sceptic: one who merely asks to be shown that we are, in terms internal to our doxastic norms, justified in believing *p*.

---

[4] Stern (1999); an earlier version of this section appears in that volume as a response to Stern's paper. For other such attempts, see e.g. Rorty (1970), Strawson (1985), Stroud (1994).

[5] Stern identifies the epistemic sceptic merely as one 'who claims that we fail to know anything (global scepticism), or to have some sort of knowledge in particular ... where knowledge is held to require *certainty*' (1999: 48). So set up such a sceptic denies that we can know that *p*, without specifying what *p* might be about. But it must be understood that the epistemic sceptic that is left aside is only one whose disputed propositions concern the external world, rather than our beliefs. An epistemic sceptic about whether we can know what we believe would clearly still be relevant to Stern, and to Stern's Kant. So it is not quite right to say that on this reconstruction there is no concern with any form of epistemic scepticism.

[6] Again, assuming that the epistemic sceptic is concerned with more than knowledge of the contents of our belief-set.

Consider a rather different sort of sceptic, who does not ask to be shown that our grounds for believing *p* are conclusive, but who merely asks to be shown that in believing *p*, we can give grounds that *by our own lights* we are entitled to appeal to in this context, in accordance with our doxastic norms, to make the belief reasonable (if not certain). (p. 52)

Just as it stands this would seem to render justificatory scepticism too weak. Stern considers that this justificatory scepticism does have some bite, in that the conception of justification that it trades off, although internal, still leaves room for claims 'that we often believe what we ought not to believe, because no appropriate doxastic norm covering the belief can be found' (p. 52). The trouble is that it is not at all clear that this is the case: in every case of genuinely mistaken (minimally considered) belief there precisely are grounds that the believers can give which, by their own lights, they are entitled to appeal to in this context to make the belief reasonable (if not certain). The mistaken believers—be it hallucinating drug-users or devout adherents of some religion (or both at once)—typically do have what, by their own lights, they consider to be an appropriate doxastic norm covering the belief. As it stands, then, the strictly perspectival notion of internal justification at work seems too weak for a form of scepticism based on it to have any bite, or—what comes to the same thing—for the abundance of easy answers to such 'sceptical challenges' to carry any real anti-sceptical weight.

Clearly more needs to be said about what such 'internal' justification of beliefs amounts to. Rather than developing a discussion of this thorny issue, Stern at this point adverts to Sosa's characterization of what he (Sosa) calls 'reflective justification'. In this form justification by definition derives from the (correct) application of our deepest logical and intellectual standards and procedures (p. 52). Stern subsequently relies on this formulation without further specification, taking coherence to be among those standards: 'the test of coherence is one of our "deepest logical and intellectual standards and procedures"' (p. 57; see also 61 ff.).[7] On this view of justification, as Sosa points out, a belief can be justified even if it gets the world completely wrong. To put it crudely, justification is a question of internal rather than external fit.

Terminologically, casting the contrast as between 'epistemic' and 'justificatory' scepticism may be puzzling: the terms do not suggest that the two forms of scepticism should be entirely distinct. Epistemic scepticism is, after all, not unconcerned with justificatory problems. Scepticism about justification would seem prima facie to be a threat to—and a target of—both belief- and truth-directed arguments, rather than being the preserve of belief-directed arguments

---

[7] Sosa himself, in the paragraphs alluded to by Stern, indicates that for the notion of justification at work to have more substance, further specification would be needed of what those standards and procedures were. That coherence is one such norm is already explicit in Sosa's initial specification.

alone. Instead of contrasting justificatory and epistemic scepticism, it would be more perspicuous to present the contrast as between *doxastic* and epistemic scepticism. It is the sceptic about the justification *specifically* of beliefs, i.e. the doxastic sceptic, who is the proper target here, as distinct from the sceptic about the justification of knowledge-claims, the epistemic sceptic. It is only because *that* is the operative contrast that the notion of justification in play can so readily be construed in terms entirely internal to constraints of our doxastic norms. Barring idealism, such justification would be manifestly inappropriate for the justification of anything beyond beliefs.

Stern's contention, then, is that if the concern were with the epistemic sceptic, we would have to construe transcendental arguments as truth-directed, but we can instead withdraw to a belief-directed construal which is still effective against a different target, namely the doxastic sceptic, the sceptic who doubts that our beliefs are (internally) justified. The result is a defence of transcendental arguments on coherentist grounds. Transcendental arguments establish that certain disputed beliefs are nevertheless justified, on the grounds that doubting or denying them would result in a belief-set that was less coherent overall, since the beliefs in question are presuppositions of, or at least are required for upholding, other beliefs that we cannot doubt.[8]

Now there are two possible claims here. The one is that there can be a weakened and yet still fruitful construal of transcendental arguments along these lines. The other possible claim is that the Kantian use of transcendental arguments can be claimed to be of this sort. The former is something that can be left aside for now, to be addressed in the first instance indirectly by the attempt to examine the second, bolder claim. Stern in fact seems inclined to present this coherentist construal of transcendental arguments, directed at the doxastic ('justificatory') sceptic rather than the epistemic sceptic, as an accurate identification of what Kant was actually doing and who he was responding to in his employment of transcendental arguments. Although he concentrates in particular on the Second Analogy, it is clear that the aim is to provide a general strategy for understanding the anti-sceptical use of Kant's transcendental arguments. In viewing Kant in this way Stern affiliates himself with and relies on philosophers in the British Idealist tradition, such as Ewing and Blanshard. I am not primarily concerned here with the merits of this view as Kantian exegesis. It is worth noting, however, that if it is so taken, then Kant must be judged to have been simply confused in insisting on the connection between (what we call) his transcendental arguments and transcendental idealism. The latter was then not needed at all for what he was doing. Of

---

[8] I take the notion of presupposition to be a particularly strong relation of *requirement* by one belief or belief-set of another. While the notion of 'requirement' that Stern uses might accommodate weaker relations, it seems that the relation of presupposition is suitably strong to make the most out of Stern's internal justification in terms of coherence.

greater interest, however, is the question whether this can be adequate as a reconstruction of what Kant should have said, what his purposes in these arguments should have been.

It seems to me that a reconstruction along these lines of Kant's or indeed Kantian transcendental arguments is unlikely to be philosophically satisfactory. There is, first, a general problem which can be brought out as follows: Most of these transcendental arguments conclude with the vindication of beliefs about the external world, about an order of things that holds independently of that belief-set. In other words, they are beliefs that themselves presuppose that we successfully bridge the appearance–reality gap, or *at least* that we are justified in believing that we do. The question is, how can we expect the justification for the disputed beliefs to survive the admission that their central presupposition might not be met? We can put the point in the following way: If the fact that a belief q is presupposed by a significant section of our belief-set is enough to justify that belief, then the same must go for any further belief r that the belief q presupposes in turn. But one such further belief, at least in the case of the central transcendental arguments, is the belief that we successfully cross the appearance–reality gap. So by the same token we have licence to take that belief too to be justified. But if it is so taken, then how can we still accept the sceptical objection to the effect that it is not justified? Or the other way round: how can it be taken, stably, as justified, if we also accept the idealist objection to the effect that it is not? And if we accept the sceptic's objection that despite internal justification on grounds of the coherence of our belief-set, belief r might not be fully justified, then surely the justification of our belief in the disputed proposition q that presupposes it (e.g. that there is a causal order in the external world, or that there are other minds) must also be shaken. This can also be seen to follow more directly: if belief in the disputed proposition q is internally justified in virtue of its being a presupposition of other beliefs that we cannot give up, but at the same time it is acknowledged that q might not be true, that we cannot establish that it is, then that must stand to shake our conviction that it is satisfactorily justified.

Stern seems to respond to this kind of worry with a simple reaffirmation that internal justification is sufficient to sustain belief, and should continue to be so sufficient even in the face of the recognition that that justification is not truth-conducive:

> Some, of course, will be dissatisfied with the apparent modesty of this position, and insist that to be complete, the appeal to purely internal standards of justification must be grounded in a demonstration that these standards are truth-conducive, in such a way that if we take the belief that p to be justified by some norm, it is certain or more than likely to be true. The familiar difficulty with this project, however, is that once this external conception is brought in, the sceptic will find it too easy to dispute any such truth-claim against which our justificatory norms can be gauged. In my view,

the better approach is to admit that this external metajustification is unavailable, but to deny that our norms are thereby robbed of their justificatory capacity, in so far as they seem to offer the best guide to truth from where we are. (p. 59)

But, dangers of relativization aside (I will return to those), the point is that internal fit (coherence) not being *robbed* of its justificatory capacity is one thing: its retaining *sufficient* justificatory capacity to sustain belief even in the face of the knowledge that such justification alone has no bearing on the truth of the belief is quite another.[9]

The above worry arises essentially because of the tension between accepting a strictly coherentist account of *justification*, but not a coherence account of *truth*. The combination of them is inherently unstable. Is coherentist justification of beliefs enough? If it is not, then the weaker belief-directed construal of transcendental arguments will not work against the doxastic sceptic any more than it does against the epistemic sceptic. If, on the other hand, it is enough, then we are justified in believing that we successfully cross the appearance–reality divide; and if we indeed believe that, then why not expect the justification of our beliefs to be a matter also of how that world is, rather than merely of internal justification? There is then no longer any reason to believe that internal justification is all that is relevant. In a nutshell: if in realist mode we have not endorsed coherentism about belief justification, we might seem driven to it; but once we have retreated to coherentism about justification, there is no longer any reason available for remaining confined to it.

There are, it seems, only two options available to Stern by way of avoiding this problem (given his commitment to internal justification). One is to accept a coherence theory of truth as well as of justification. But that is just to accept idealism, indeed empirical idealism. There would be little point in construing transcendental arguments so weakly in order to avoid transcendental idealism, if the result was a commitment to a form of even more tendentious idealism. The other option is to contend—as Stern seems to[10]—that although truth might be conceived of as correspondence, nevertheless the only relevant consideration when it comes to justification *of beliefs* is internal coherence. Quite apart from the problem with this just noted, it is in any case difficult to see how this hybrid of positions could be independently motivated, let alone established a priori so as to enable it to serve as the basis for transcendental arguments. One might indeed think that Stern's position here reveals the weakness of its provenance. To the extent that it is

---

[9] Note, incidentally, the tension between claiming that purely internal standards of justification are not *truth-conducive*, while also claiming (in the same paragraph) that they 'seem to offer the best *guide to truth* from where we are'. This puts a lot of weight on the words 'seem to' in the latter phrase; more perhaps than is intended. The fact of this tension may help to point to the underlying problem. [10] Stern (1999: 58–9).

gleaned from the context of British Idealism, it might always have seemed risky to trust it to deliver a viable defence of transcendental arguments that avoided a commitment to idealism.[11]

A second worry under this heading is whether Kant's specific transcendental arguments can work once construed so that their aim is to secure internally justified beliefs, rather than truths about the world. We can concentrate here, as Stern does, in particular on Kant's Second Analogy. On Stern's view (again, relying on Ewing), this argument establishes only that if we are to be in a position to apply any sort of temporal determination to two states (A and B), and thus judge that events occur, then 'we must merely *believe* that A caused B' (p. 51), or, as he puts it later, our belief in causal determination 'is required, in order for us to take a sequence of representations α–β to be evidence for the event A–B, and not some other event B–A, or no event at all' (p. 56) ('where "A" and "B" stand for states and parts of things, and "α" and "β" stand for representations which are respectively *of* A and B'; p. 50). Now the mere *belief* in a necessary connection certainly seems, on the surface, to be weaker than Kant's assertion of 'a rule in accordance with which the appearances [i.e. empirically real objects] in their succession, that is, as they happen, are determined by the preceding state',[12] which is the statement Stern takes himself to be interpreting. But Stern concludes:

Ewing's suggestion that without the causal principle, 'we could have no sort of coherent system of judgements about events in time' seems to me an excellent summation of Kant's transcendental argument in the Second Analogy, which is designed to show how just such a role [namely, rendering our belief-set coherent] is played by the conception of causality it is intended to justify. (p. 57)

This clearly seems, as do other comments, to attribute this coherentist argument to Kant. But note that the summation given here is ambiguous about the conclusion of the argument: does 'without the causal principle' mean without believing it to hold, as Stern thinks, or without its *applying*? Only this ambiguity, I suggest, allows Stern to conflate the coherentist view with Kant's. But, again leaving aside the question of its viability as an interpretation of Kant's meaning, the question is whether it will do as a viable *reconstruction* of that argument.

It seems that it will not. The crux of the argument is as follows. Experiences are always successive, whether they be of coexisting states of affairs or of successive ones (i.e. of an event, an objective succession of states). So the mere

---

[11] The British Idealists, of course, had no qualms about combining a coherence theory of justification with a coherence theory of truth—as is, not surprisingly, amply clear even from the few sentences Stern quotes (1999: 54–5). The problem arises only when Stern uses the coherence account of justification but tries to prise it apart from their idealism.

[12] *Critique*, A195/B240.

fact of experiences being successive is no guide to whether or not the experienced states of affairs themselves occur in succession. The distinguishing mark between an experience of an event and of coexisting states of affairs is that in the experience of an event, the succession of perceptions must be irreversible. This irreversibility could be secured most simply by appeal to there being two successive states that provide the content of our experiences. Given that the one state comes after the other, it follows that, all other things being equal, the order of the perceptions is itself thereby fixed and irreversible.[13] But the trouble is that this works by simply assuming realism, that there are occurrences out there that dictate the irreversibility of our perceptions of them.[14] And, of course, the sceptic's point is precisely that we cannot simply help ourselves to such realism, that for all we know what appear to be independent items are mere projections of ours. A way of putting Kant's concern is to ask, how can anyone who is duly critical about the possibility of crossing the appearance–reality gap nevertheless explain the fact that we seem to experience events: where else would the irreversibility of perceptions come from? And it is here that we can take him to answer that the only other way of explaining this is if our experienced world is so construed as to render it impossible for one of the experienced items to occur except after the other. The irreversibility of those items would then dictate the irreversibility of the succession of perceptions of them. But the irreversibility of those items constitutes a rule-governed regularity that counts as a form of causal order. And so the external-world sceptic, specifically, is committed to holding that for the succession of perceptions to constitute the experience of successive states, i.e. for experience to present itself as experience of events, a causal ordering of those states must be presupposed.

Importantly, however, for the causal order thus to determine the irreversibility of the order of perceptions, it cannot be merely a matter of belief; it must be a factual order that imposes itself on belief. It must be something that is presented to us with the constraining force of a discovered, not merely an invented, order. In Kant's terms, while transcendentally it can be merely an order that we ourselves synthesize, to be effective it must be synthesized as an empirical reality that impinges upon us. It must be presented as a reality external to our belief-set, and which can exert an influence upon it. For our belief-set to be as it is, appeal to goings-on external to it must be possible.

---

[13] This is essentially the way that Strawson (1966) reconstructs the argument, and it results in his famous accusation that Kant is committing 'a *non sequitur* of numbing grossness' (1966: 137). The order of the perceptions is necessary, in the sense of its being inconceivable that they be reversed, but that does not require the assumption of any causal (or other) necessity holding between the items perceived: nothing more than their brute temporal succession is required.

[14] This objection to the Lovejoy–Strawson criticism is essentially made by Allison (1983: 232–4).

Now if that is what Kant's transcendental argument in the Second Analogy shows to be required, then Stern's suggested reconstruction is too weak for it to work. The reconstructed argument merely established a belief in a causal order to be justified on the grounds that it is presupposed by, and so coheres with, the rest of the belief-set; in fact the argument shows that we need the belief to be *upheld by the facts*. In a nutshell, what we need is not a *belief* in a rule-governed ordering, but an *experience* of one.

This same requirement that we bridge the appearance–reality gap characterizes the working of other of Kant's arguments. First, it might help to broaden the frame to take in more of the Kantian story. The following consists of a protracted transcendental argument of which the above is only a part: if there is to be unity of consciousness, experience must be temporally structured; if experience is to be temporally structured, it must include experience of change; if there is to be experience of change, then there must be experience of events; if there is to be experience of events, then there must be experience of substance(s) altering in accordance with objective causal laws. Looking at this wider canvas offers a clear reminder that the point of Kant's transcendental arguments is not that they license certain beliefs in virtue of the fact that those beliefs render the rest of our belief-set more coherent, but rather that they identify certain features that must obtain in the world beyond our belief-set if we are *to have any belief-set at all*. Similarly, the Kantian argument to the effect that experience is essentially spatial can be construed as arguing that if we are to experience objects as distinct from us, they must be located as being elsewhere, which means that experience must be spatially structured.[15] It would be wrong to think that this can be reconstructed as an argument to the effect merely that our belief-set must include the belief that the world is spatially structured. The point is rather that in our experience of it, it must *be* spatially structured. That is how it must be presented to us. Similarly with the case of the First Analogy: the conclusion is not simply that we should accept the belief in the existence of substance as justified *because it fits with our other beliefs*. Rather, the conclusion is ontological: our experience must be of objects such that the belief in substance is justified *by reference to the way that domain of objects holds together in our experience of it*.

Stern hopes both to avoid the problematic inference to reality, by not attempting to cross the appearance–reality line, and to do without any problematic resort to idealism. The trouble is that this combination leaves us with a form of confinement to beliefs, to the near side of the appearance–reality divide, that is too austere, or 'contracted', to capture the force of Kant's central arguments. In all of these, for the arguments to work, they must take us beyond our belief-sets, to something that impinges on us in experience, to facts

---

[15] See Allison (1983: 82 ff.) and Ch. 2, Sect. 1, above.

corresponding to whatever beliefs we may form about them. This in itself is obviously not to say that there is no scope for transcendental arguments of this weaker sort. But it would seem that transcendental arguments that aim more modestly at doxastic rather than epistemic scepticism, rendering beliefs justified by internal coherence within a belief-set, regardless of whether those beliefs are backed up by impinging facts in the world, are unlikely to be able adequately to reconstruct the insights of Kant's central transcendental arguments.

Of course, if transcendental arguments generally, or at any rate the Kantian ones that Stern hopes to reconstruct, are said essentially to involve a move across the appearance–reality line, then we need to address the sceptic's objection to any such inference to reality. Kant's transcendental idealism, as we have seen, is supposed to meet the objection by *conceding* that indeed we cannot cross that line, to get beyond how things seem to us, while nevertheless allowing that within the domain of transcendental appearances there is room for a distinction between empirical appearances and empirical reality, which is the line that transcendental arguments can allow us to cross. This gives him the space within appearances to talk of there being a domain of empirical facts, transcendentally structured by us, but empirically discovered, which can impinge on us, and to which our true beliefs can correspond.[16]

We have seen so far how important the inference to reality is to core transcendental arguments, and that the sceptical doubt about the validity of that inference cannot simply be sidestepped by avoiding the inference altogether. In this context transcendental idealism has emerged as seemingly the only way of safeguarding a form of that inference. This is not meant in any way as an endorsement of transcendental idealism. The point has been merely to show the force of the conditional: that Kant's central transcendental arguments, if they are to deliver what they promise, do seem to require underpinning by transcendental idealism. And to this extent it would seem that if we reject transcendental idealism, we must also forsake that use of transcendental arguments. This is of interest, since transcendental idealism is extremely dubious, and the transcendental arguments extremely attractive. It is not at all clear how, between the tug of the one conviction and the pull of the other, we could end up with a stable accommodation of either.

It is important to be clear here that what goes for Kant's central transcendental arguments also goes for the kind of Kantian arguments developed in the previous chapter. There too the conclusion was ontological: that even the most rudimentary (heterogeneous) form of experience presupposes an invariant spatio-temporal matrix. Again, the conclusion of the arguments was

---

[16] In other words, in contrast to Walker's contention (Walker 1989*a*, ch. 4) it seems that Kant can, indeed should, be construed as holding a correspondence theory of truth at the empirical level.

not merely that we are justified in believing there to be some invariant spatio-temporal matrix because this belief coheres well with our other beliefs, but rather that the domain encountered in experience must be so structured. To this extent, then, it would anyway not be an option in the present context to avoid the problem facing transcendental arguments that attempt the inference to reality by convenient resort to a form of transcendental argument that does not attempt that inference.

2. UNIVERSALITY OF INFERENCE

So much by way of emphasizing the significance of the first objection to transcendental arguments, the inference to reality. The second objection, concerning the universality of inference, is more general. It applies to any transcendental argument: as much to Kantian transcendental arguments that do attempt the inference to reality, whether with or without transcendental idealism, as to the various weaker forms of transcendental arguments that have been put forward.[17] In turning to this objection we are addressing the central problem identified in Part II. We are also, *ipso facto*, specifically addressing the problem with allowing universality to the transcendental arguments developed in the previous chapter (assuming, for the sake of argument, that we cannot fault them internally).

Given what was said in Part II, the conclusions of any such arguments threaten to be only apparently universally necessary. The question is whether the modes of reasoning and the conclusions reached are merely historically or culturally indexed universalizations, such that however unimaginable it might be for those whose horizons are suitably set, there is nothing to preclude different universalizations equally well anchored elsewhere. In terms of the distinction made in Chapter 6, the question is whether transcendental arguments employ modes of reasoning, and establish conclusions, that represent transcendental constraints, or merely transcendental features—presuppositions only of the set of orientations that currently determines the horizons of what we can conceive of: presuppositions which take on an air of strict universality only when, in uncritical mode, we take them not to be indexed in this way. Of course, that being the case would not altogether impugn the value of such arguments. If historically indexed transcendental arguments are the most that we can hope for, there is clearly still some value in uncovering by means of them those features that are currently genuinely presuppositional to our

---

[17] Stern's construal is one instance of this. For others, see n. 4 above.

orientation.[18] But in fact I think that there is no need to domesticate the yield of transcendental arguments in this way: we can go further in defence of the resilience of such arguments. Moreover, the proposed way of doing so will cast new light on how we might resolve the first problem, regarding the inference to reality.

This problem of the universality of transcendental arguments is, of course, not new.[19] The problem has been posed in terms of conceptual schemes, or belief-systems: the thought being that in different schemes or systems there would be room for different arguments, to different conclusions, such that the validity of those conclusions, far from being universal, was always only indexed to, and so dependent on the persistence of, that scheme or system. Now we have seen reasons for doubting whether the notion of conceptual schemes is either legitimate or necessary for sustaining the relevant relativist pressure. And, similarly, talk of belief-systems, at least if that is taken to indicate any strictly propositional articulation of beliefs, is also too much a piece of philosophical artifice to be necessary for the understanding of the source of relativist pressure, as the considerations drawn from the later Wittgenstein were seen to show. All we need is the epistemic duality identified in Chapter 5, which can be sustained without appeal to philosophical props, merely in terms of what Strawson calls Wittgenstein's 'social naturalism'.[20] Our ordinary practices, the routine engagements and interactions that constitute our form of life, have certain structural presuppositions—Wittgenstein, as Strawson notes, talks of a certain frame of reference,[21] a scaffolding,[22] a background,[23] a substratum[24]—which constitute the matrix in relation to which things can be judged to be true or false, justified or not, but which itself cannot be assessed for correctness. This background matrix comprises those transcendental elements that are presuppositional to our routine engagements. We can envisage transcendental arguments moving back from the mundane practices to the identification of those conditions of their possibility. Such transcendental

---

[18] The weaker construal that Strawson (1985) accords transcendental arguments would seem at first to conform to this. Having accepted that they cannot cross the appearance–reality line, but rather only describe 'the connections between the major structural elements of our conceptual scheme' (1985: 22), he goes on to acknowledge that these cannot be claimed to be universal, but might nevertheless be valuable: 'even if they do not succeed in establishing such tight or rigid connections as they initially promise, they do at least indicate or bring out conceptual connections, even if only of a looser kind; and . . . establish the connections between the major structural features or elements of our conceptual scheme' (p. 23). This might indeed, as he goes on to suggest, be a valuable task for descriptive metaphysics. In fact, however, a little later (pp. 25–7) Strawson very explicitly denies that we need to drop the assumption that there is something fixed and unalterable about our belief-system, which transcendental arguments stand to identify. I will return to this below.

[19] See e.g. Körner (1967); Stroud (1968: 251–2); Strawson (1985: 27); Harrison (1989). For references to early discussion of this in post-Kantian German Idealism, see Franks (1999: 111–45).

[20] Strawson (1985: 24).   [21] Wittgenstein, *On Certainty* (1969, §83).
[22] Ibid., §211.   [23] Ibid., §94.   [24] Ibid., §162.

arguments might then seem to lay claim to universality. But in so far as the orientation within the variety of empirical practices that comprises a form of life itself determines, rather than being determined by, that presuppositional scaffolding, this is enough to sustain the epistemic duality between the way the fundamental structure of the world is uncritically taken to be—an order imposed on us—and the way it is critically recognized to be—an order imposed by our own undertakings.[25] Critically understood, all transcendental arguments ever give us are context-dependent transcendental features. As practices vary, so might the presupposed scaffolding or framework which, within the confinement of a given set of practices, presents itself as a set of universal constraints identified by transcendental arguments.

This brings us back to the question of the extent of such relativism. In Chapter 5 it seemed to emerge as altogether unconstrained, such that there are no assured universal framework features, presuppositions that are invariant across all possible forms of experience. This conclusion is not generally accepted, and is one the present chapter aims to resist. The motivation for the resistance is clear: in the present context, specifically, without rejecting it there is no hope for the universality of transcendental arguments. However, the justificatory grounds for the rejection are less clear.

Strawson, for example, in his defence of a weaker naturalist construal of transcendental arguments, accepts Wittgenstein's 'social naturalism', that it is 'our learning, from childhood up, an activity, a practice, a social practice' that is the source of the presupposed framework;[26] and he also accepts, as connected to this, the fact that the framework is 'up to a point at least' dynamically conceived, such that—presumably as social practices mutate—what were framework elements beyond question might lose that transcendental status and 'assume the character of a hypothesis to be questioned and perhaps falsified'.[27] This readily goes along with relativization of propositions of the framework or scaffolding—identified here as transcendental features—to the alterable form of life to which they are indexed as its presuppositions. And indeed, as was noted above,[28] at one point Strawson seems to go along with this conclusion, and accept that there might be value in transcendental arguments even if they offer no more than insights into temporally indexed conceptual connections within our 'conceptual scheme'. They might serve to identify certain structures as presuppositions of some basic capacity at a given point, while recognizing that the fact that the point is located in a dynamic system means that what then seem undeniably to be necessary conditions, might not in fact be anything more than sufficient conditions to which alternatives might become available. Given the dynamism of the system, the inconceivability of

---

[25] See p. 174 above and *passim*. [26] Strawson (1985: 19). [27] 1985: 18.
[28] See n. 18.

alternative enabling conditions is not sufficient to rule out the possibility of such alternatives.[29]

In fact, however, Strawson does not simply accept such relativization. While the dynamic nature of the presupposed framework or scaffolding was introduced as dynamic 'up to a point at least' (p. 18), a few pages later it is taken to be dynamic *only up to a point*. Thus: 'some things which at some time, or in some context or relation, may have the status of framework features, beyond question or test, may at another time, or in another context or relation, become open to question or even be rejected; *others are fixed and unalterable*' (p. 25; my italics). And he goes on to develop the point that the admission of a 'dynamic element in the collective belief-system' should not lead to the denial that there is anything fixed and unalterable, and so on to a historicist conception of the role of transcendental arguments. There is, he claims, no reason to see, with the likes of Collingwood, metaphysical truths as relativized to historical periods; 'no reason why metaphysics should submit tamely to historicist pressure of this kind' (pp. 26–7). However, the grounds for this apparent limitation on the extent of the dynamic element in Wittgenstein's framework propositions, and consequently on the relativization of transcendental arguments, remain insufficiently clear.

The explication Strawson offers seems to be that while the human world-view is subject to change, it remains a human one: the very idea of its undergoing historical change but still remaining a human world-view is taken to imply something of a constant underlying conception in virtue of which it remains a human world-view, something central to it that is not subject to alteration. This invites the thought that whereas Wittgenstein's conception of a dynamic form of life, and the metaphor of the relatively stable riverbed, are most readily taken, and have been taken here, to mean only that throughout any changes in our form of life there are some things that stand fast, Strawson ends up with the stronger interpretation: there are some things that stand fast throughout all change. And it is, he claims, only because of Wittgenstein's aversion to systematic treatment of issues that he refrained from specifying which were these aspects of our world-view that could be counted upon to be so central to our 'human or natural commitment' (p. 27) as to be invariant across all scientific revolutions or social change. Whether this is a satisfactory interpretation of Wittgenstein is obviously not to the point here. That it might be is, perhaps, suggested by Wittgenstein's use of the phrase 'not subject to alteration or only to an imperceptible one'[30] (although the phrase could be taken to lend support either way here). But one might also doubt that it is, or should be, Wittgenstein's considered view, given the centrality to his later thought of family resemblance relations as undercutting precisely such

---

[29] Strawson (1985: 23).   [30] *On Certainty* (1969, §99).

essentialist claims. For any given candidate identification of some such constant or core conception, surely there would arise the possibility that it was not essential, and seemed necessary only because of the failure of imagination of those locked into that particular picture. Our conception of the human worldview might be such that we cannot entertain the idea of *it* changing without us thereby conceiving of it remaining unchanged in certain key respects. But, as Strawson himself noted earlier, the fact that certain core elements of the human world-view seem to us now to be necessary is no indication that there will not in time be alternatives to them. Inconceivability does not seem to be a reliable guide to impossibility.[31]

Indeed, this seems to be the point Wittgenstein is getting at when, in the context of developing the metaphor of the relatively stable riverbed underlying the flowing waters, he gives the example of logic as a science that might at one time seem to be clearly part of the fixed riverbed, and yet at another time might not.[32] Moreover, the particular examples that Strawson gives of such supposedly constant conceptions do not clearly seem to be such as could not be displaced by alternatives. He mentions the conception of the world of physical objects, spatio-temporally located, including among them human observers capable of action, belief, and epistemic engagement with themselves and the world around them. This could be developed further, he suggests, if we were 'to engage in the connective metaphysical task of exhibiting the relations and interdependences of the elements of the general structure'.[33] But the question is why the results of such descriptive metaphysics, of the sort that Strawson has engaged in elsewhere, should be taken to be anything more than the way things seem from within a particular context, a specific developmental stage of human beings, to which there might well be alternatives, even if they are not clearly conceivable to us now. Bergson, for one, attempts to outline an alternative to the conception of spatio-temporally situated physical objects some of which represent and acquire knowledge of others. As far as he is concerned, Strawson would be seen as describing a persistent feature of our world-view, but one which has for too long blinded us to the possibility of valuable alternatives. At the other end of the scale, temperamentally at any rate, eliminative materialism might serve to raise doubts about whether the conception of discrete psychological agents, epistemically related to one another only interpretatively, could not be surpassed once folk psychological models of the mind were no longer in play. This seems enough to motivate the thought that the kind of features that Strawson takes to hold fast might do so only relatively: they might

---

[31] Except in a restricted sense: As long as something is inconceivable to me (or us) it will constrain what it is possible for me (us) to undertake as a cognitively mediated action. But it is no guide to what can *happen* to me (us) and, consequently, is not even a guide to fixed contours of the conceivable.   [32] *On Certainty* (1969, §98).

[33] Strawson (1985: 27).

not apply to all human world-views, let alone to all forms of experience.[34] To this extent, then, Strawson does not seem to have addressed effectively the threat to the universality of transcendental arguments.

It might, however, be thought that there is a deeper point underlying Strawson's contention that the very idea of alteration in the human world-view carries with it the commitment to there being something about that world-view that remains constant, in relation to which we can conceive of *it* changing. This point is best brought out by means of a distinction between two kinds of constancy, analogous to that drawn in the previous chapter for the perceptual case. There is, first, the constancy of content required for any experienced change in content: that is, for the alteration in cognitive content to be registered. Secondly, there is the constancy of a conceptual, or to put it more generally, a normative space, in relation to which various shifts in normatively governed practices can be rendered possible, whether or not the transition from the one to the other is registered. The former sense of constancy is what I have been addressing so far. And Strawson certainly seems to be right that for us to conceive of a change occurring in the conception of x, in the sense of being able to register or experience such a change, there must remain something unaltered across the change, in virtue of which it is possible to say that it remains *that* conception, x (whether x be the human world-view, experience, logic, or anything else), that has undergone alteration. And it is of that sort of constancy that it is right to say that while there must be something that is constant across any such change in the content of a conception, it need not be the same thing that is constant across all such change in that conception. The deeper underlying point relates to the second sense of constancy.

We can bring out this second sense of constancy by looking at an example. We might consider that logic as it is at one locus might not be the same as it is at another. There might indeed at different loci be conceptions of logic between which there is nothing in common that can be detected from the perspective of those loci. That it is *logic* that is being contrasted will, of course, then not be detectable from these loci. Such relativism still makes sense, as we saw in Chapter 5,[35] because for there to be meaningful disagreement between two loci, it is not necessary that the difference in question be detectable by the parties to the disagreement. All that is needed is, as we might put it, that

---

[34] We might choose to stipulate that any form of experience that departed from these characteristics would no longer count as a specifically human world-view. But claiming that our own biological descendants would not be human if they did not share certain favoured elements of our world-view clearly brings out the desperation of the move. The more general problem with such indexing of structures to sub-groups within which they apply universally is that upholding such relativized universal claims without specifying what counts as a legitimate principle of relativization seems like just a contorted way of denying universality altogether.

[35] See pp. 186–7, 192–3 above.

A Defence of Transcendental Arguments   291

there be some matrix in relation to which the normative practices of the parties can be calibrated. That is enough to render a possible disagreement between two loci that cannot be detected, or at least cannot be accurately delineated, from either. The background matrix will in the case envisaged contain a set of loci between which family resemblance holds, such that each can be recognized by its immediate neighbours as engaging in logic, but given the intransitivity of familiarity (or of translation), we can still allow that there might be loci so unfamiliar to each other that that recognition fails to hold between them. We can still say, however, that although what logic seems to consist of essentially from within any one locus might be no more than the shadow of necessity cast by the familiar practices that shape the horizons in that vicinity, nevertheless there is, underlying that parochial identification to which there are alternatives, a single conception that is common to all loci, and to which there can be no alternatives. This is the conception comprising possibly nothing more than the disjunctive specification of the conceptions of logic at the relevant family of loci. There can be no alternatives to this framework, since any candidate alternative is simply taken up as another possibility within it (as another disjunct, as we might put it).

Now what goes for the example of logic goes equally for any other conception or normative practice. And if the combination of such practices constitutes a world-view, or form of life, then at the limit we have to say of world-views just what we have said about the constitutive practices. Coherently to say that world-views, or forms of life, or the form of experience, might change, seems to require accepting that however far removed alternative set-ups might be from the way things are here and now, and even if indeed there were no remaining common elements between how things are here, in one locus, and how they are in another, nevertheless these set-ups must be placed within a common set of coordinates. There must be a common normative matrix, offering sufficient connectedness between its parts for it to be possible to make sense of the statement that what is meant by x here is not the same as what is meant by it there, or that whereas x is a notion that has a grip here, it no longer has a grip there. Metaphorically, there must be sufficient connectedness to allow our thought the externalist content needed for it to travel from here to there.

Now it might be considered that that background matrix—again on analogy with the matrix presupposed by perceptual change—itself cannot change. This would constitute the deeper point of constancy alluded to in connection with Strawson. The idea would be that it is that fundamental matrix, rather than any identifications made from specific loci within it, that is picked out by the basic conception of a form of life as that which stands fast despite all local variation. That is, there might not be anything in common between what is identified at any of the particular loci as being essential to, and so as invariant across, any form of life—those features might indeed all be only apparently necessary, identifications that do not survive critical reflection; but the background matrix that encompasses all those loci itself constitutes the form of life to which there can be no alternatives, since it subsumes any candidate alternative as merely another locus within it. We can perhaps capture this by saying that there is ultimately only empirical relativism, on the backdrop of a single common form of life. Something of this sort seems indeed to be the assumption of some Wittgensteinians. The idea is that empirical relativism in Wittgenstein serves only to bring out, to make manifest, the shape of that background matrix, to exhibit those fixed grammatical constraints on the array of normative practices that can be accommodated.

This would clearly be significant, because if this kind of constancy holds, then we will have established that there is a domain immune from relativist pressure, the contours of which are universally binding. And this will go some way towards showing there to be, in principle, scope to uphold the universality of transcendental arguments. We will have shown that at least the argument from relativism against that possibility can be answered: an elusive necessary condition for the universality of transcendental arguments will thus have been met.[36]

In fact, however, the assumption of constancy is a problematic addition here. Allowing, as we have, that there is just one form of life, that no alternatives to it are possible, is not tantamount to saying that that form of life is invariant, that it remains constant. That there are no alternatives to it does not mean that there is any limit to the alternatives for it, or subsumed within it.[37] The two claims are distinct, and the immediately relevant point here is that the one does not entail the other. The fact that every alteration in normative practice is mappable onto a unified matrix—that all normative practices bear a relation of connectedness to one another—does not seem in itself to determine that there is a limit to what could change. To put it differently, there being no habitable loci that fall outside the framework does not of itself imply that there is a fixed array of loci within it. So the question is whether this extra claim of constancy is simply the result of a confused transition from singularity to invariance—or are there independent reasons for upholding not only the singularity of the encompassing form of life, but also its constancy?

It should be recalled, first, how difficult it is to uphold this constancy claim within a thoroughly naturalized, or post-metaphysical, orientation. A

[36] There would still remain the question whether any localized transcendental arguments could ever reach the relevant conclusions about that presupposed domain, let alone whether there would be any telling that they had (or—worse—which of them had). This is something to which I will return briefly, in addressing the issue of whether there are some truths that cannot be said.

[37] The distinction between *alternatives to* and *alternative for* us is introduced by B. Williams (1981a).

metaphysically unadorned naturalism[38] would seem to allow for brute changes in the physical world generally and at the biological level in particular, such as could extend normative structures in previously uncharted ways. Even if we have no capacity to conceive of what those normative innovations might be, even if what we can conceive of is always couched in terms limited to current options, it would nevertheless still seem open to gesture ostensively to the range of available normative structures and practices and then conceive that biology might come to sustain things that are very different from *all this*. The new options thereby introduced would, just to the extent that they differed meaningfully from earlier ones, not constitute alternatives to the existing form of life. We still preserve the singularity and interconnectedness of the unifying structure on the background of which different loci can be calibrated. But we seem to face the prospect of new loci within that structure, and which are not such as to be definable in terms of previously existing normative structures located elsewhere on the matrix. The prospect is of a genuine innovation, such that the background structure that constitutes the form of life stands to be stretched and changed in shape, so to speak, by the sheer force of biological change. The unified and interconnected background matrix thus retains its singularity and the connectedness between its various addresses, but is not invariant.

We could, of course, contain this prospect by imposing a metaphysical picture. One such picture would be a construal of the physical world, and of the biological domain in particular, such that there was a metaphysical limit on the extent to which it could undergo change. Although mutations would be accommodated, they would be possible only within the restrictions imposed by some conception of metaphysical form, which can be variously imputed, as in Plato or Aristotle, for example. World-driven change to normative structures would then be internal to, and so could not threaten, the constant normative framework sustained by that invariant metaphysical form. A different metaphysical picture would go the other way, as in traditional idealism, or immaterialism, contending that there was no material world independent of our individuations of it at all, of the sort that might undergo brute shifts eventuating in normative innovation. It may appear that, rather than appealing to metaphysical form, it claims that there is nothing on which such form might need to be imposed. But this, of course, immediately invites the response that although there might then be nothing material the vagaries of which need to be curbed by appeal to metaphysical form, that is not to say that there is no remaining possible source of capricious innovation. There is after all, for the traditional idealist, still the immaterial substance of the world; and there is no obvious reason why this, just as much as the physical or biological world,

---

[38] We will in fact see later that such a position is not as metaphysically unadorned as it takes itself to be.

should not be thought capable of brute 'mutations' that stand to sustain normative innovation. Precluding such promiscuity on the part of those free spirits would then once again need to advert to some immutable form that restricted the scope for variation. Either way, then, whether on the traditional materialist or immaterialist positions, constancy of normative structure stands to be sustained only by way of an appeal to a metaphysically real form that is imposed on the scope for empirical variation.

In the absence of these importations, that is within a genuinely post-metaphysical or naturalist view, there would seem to be no grounds for upholding the constancy claim. To that extent, then, it would appear that short of the confused inference from singularity, there is no way of introducing the kind of constancy that is in question.

That is why I concluded earlier, in discussing the later Wittgenstein,[39] that there is in fact no scope for anything over and above the transcendental features operative within local horizons. In a post-metaphysical setting of the sort that the later Wittgenstein seems to endorse, there would appear not to be any way of curbing the variation that can occur within the background matrix onto which all local normative practices are plotted. (Arguably, this is just the point that Wittgenstein is getting at in allowing that any part of the riverbed can shift, however imperceptibly.) So far, then, the scope for preserving universality of normative structure, and so the prospect of solving the problem of universality in relation to transcendental arguments, does not seem good. The weaker sense of constancy identified is available but insufficient; the stronger sense is sufficient but unavailable.

However, it can be argued that the latter is not after all forced upon us; that despite appearances there is still room to preserve something of the constancy of the basic normative framework. One way of bringing out the space that accommodates the neglected option still distinctly involves metaphysical commitment, and to this extent is not compatible with a strictly naturalist or post-metaphysical orientation. It follows on immediately from the two metaphysical alternatives just outlined. Both of those positions introduced some ontological domain independent of the normative framework, which in principle stands to exert an influence on that structure. To this extent, the constancy of that structure could be assured only by the imposition of an invariant form on the independent underlying domain, whether that base be material or immaterial. Thus it is only because both the immaterialist and the materialist are realists about some domain[40] that they require appeal to some metaphysical form to restrict the scope for brute changes to that domain. Now if the imposition of such metaphysical form is excessive, the obvious

[39] See Ch. 6. [40] For more on this claim, see Sacks (1989: 44 and *passim*).

response is to deny that there is any such independent underlying base. In effect this is to apply to both the materialist and the immaterialist just the strategy that the immaterialist, on our construal, applied to the materialist. The immaterialist as we construed him tried to avoid the materialist's imposition of metaphysical form by denying the existence of the material base that would have necessitated recourse to such form: only to find that they had themselves introduced another such base that required similar constraints. The idealist response I am now considering simply extends the same strategy to deny the existence of *any* underlying ontological base.

We can for a moment put to one side the question of the tenability of this position. Trivially, in the absence of any ontological base, there would be no room to talk of a metaphysical form imposed *on it*. More significantly, though, it can be argued that there would no longer be any threat to the constancy of the background normative framework, so that any further appeal to non-empirical constraints would no longer be called for. To the extent that there is no ontological base underlying, and possibly impacting on, our normative structures—our form of life—the threat that the vagaries of the one will result in genuine innovations in the other no longer arises. This is not to say that there would be no room left for social change, for shifts in normative practices. It is also not to say—given what was said earlier about the intransitivity of familiarity—that all normative set-ups would be as readily recognizable from all others as they are in their immediate vicinity. But it does mean that all change would have to be internally generated, in terms of already available options. While the basic normative matrix (the grammar) that constitutes our form of life can obviously allow for historical shifts from one locus to another, these would essentially always be only the waning of some normative set-ups, and the waxing of others, all of which were given at the outset. Whatever, say, logic might come to denote in some remote time and place, that possibility would already be given now; the locus in question—even if uninhabited—would already be on the map. There could be no additions of new loci, previously not encompassed within the framework that constitutes our form of life; no shift in normative practices that was not internal to the existing framework. The reason is simple: in the absence of an independent ontological base, there is no scope left for any expansion of the normative framework due to external influence. And if this is so, then it follows that the basic form of life is indeed not only singular, it is also constant. And again, if this kind of constancy holds, then we have a framework the fixed contours of which are universally binding.

However attractive this conclusion, it must be evident that the position that sustains it is not tenable. It would, barring some further qualification, seem to amount to nihilism, the ontological claim that nothing exists independently of our normative structures. Some might doubt whether the position is even coherent; whether there could be a normative framework that did not draw its structure from some ontological base. (It is, however, arguable that that would result only from being too firmly in the grip of a particular realist paradigm.) In any event it is clear that the position is extreme enough for there to have to be some independent argument for it. To introduce it merely as a way of holding on to the invariance of our normative framework would seem simply like a roundabout way of showing how forbiddingly high the price of that constancy is. Rather than offering a way of resisting relativist pressure and so securing universality of our normative framework, it would readily seem to constitute a *reductio* of that hope. Moreover, although the position does promise to secure constancy of normative structure without having to appeal to any order imposed by metaphysical form, this in no way leaves it acceptable to a naturalist or post-metaphysical orientation. It still clearly makes metaphysical claims of its own, indeed ones that fly squarely in the face of all empirical evidence.

Certainly, this extreme form of idealism cannot be pinned comfortably onto the later Wittgenstein. The minimal form of idealism identified in Wittgenstein in Chapter 6 was of interest precisely because it was compatible with a post-metaphysical or naturalist outlook. According to that position, the way in which the world is individuated in our experience of it is ultimately an expression of prevailing human interests and practices. But those human interests and practices are typically conceived of by Wittgenstein as worldly, fully enmeshed in the material machinations of the natural world. And on this view there is nothing to preclude world-driven instability of transcendental features, such that none has the universal validity which it might seem to have within its local horizons. Now, as was mentioned earlier, some take the view that there is no such threat of contingency in the later Wittgenstein; that there is indeed a constancy to the form of life, an invariant grammar, of the sort that I have been considering. What we have seen now is that although there is a form of idealism on which that conclusion can be sustained, it is not a position that would be acceptable to anyone committed to an interpretation of Wittgenstein, or to anyone committed more generally to a post-metaphysical stance. To that extent it cannot serve as a solution to the problem at hand. There is, however, another way of preserving the constancy or universality of the basic normative framework along the lines just indicated, while prising it apart from any metaphysical commitment, and which to that extent is more attractive in the context of the present discussion. Without wishing to take a stand on whether this is implicit in the later Wittgenstein, or indeed is even suggested by the texts, it does seem to be at least congenial to that position.

3. THE INSIGHT IN TRANSCENDENTAL IDEALISM

It is important to emphasize here, at the outset, that securing the scope for normative objectivity is merely one strength of a conception that we have independent reasons to endorse. This will, I hope, become clearer as the discussion progresses.

The problem of universality was seen to arise with the scope for relativism sustained by the epistemic duality between the uncritical and the critical reception of the order of things. That duality came into play as central to transcendental idealism, and remains crucially operative in the later Wittgensteinian position. And, as we have also seen, it is that same duality that then results in the collapse of what suggested themselves as transcendental constraints into mere transcendental features. In fact, however, it is not the case that solving the problem of universality necessarily requires closing the gap opened by that duality. An alternative is to take it that the root of the problem is not that the epistemic duality is operative, but that the extent of it is not properly appreciated. The suggestion is accordingly to curb relativism not by eliminating the duality in question, but by pushing it further than we have so far.[41]

What has been allowed for so far is only that a certain compulsion may come into play such that the order that we ourselves, behind our cognitive backs, have imposed on the world is then uncritically read off the world and taken at face value, as an order imposed on us by the world. I will refer to that compulsion as a *fictional force*, by which I mean a propulsion to belief that does not survive critical reflection on its evidential base.[42] At this point we are still accepting at face value the existence of a world as some ontologically basic substratum; it is only the particular individuations of it that are indexed to our practices, such that it might be cut up differently from within different imposing practices. But the epistemic duality can be extended, to be applied not merely to the order of things, but to the very notion that there is some ontological base to be ordered. Even with regard to the latter there

---

[41] It is worth noting that this strategy preserves one of the central strategic characteristics of transcendental idealism. It was pointed out above that Kant's transcendental idealism can be seen as fighting off the worrying form of idealism not by direct refutation—establishing the truth of the realist alternative—but by recourse to further idealism. In a similar manner the current strategy sets out to find, so to speak, the antidote in the poison itself.

[42] Where fictional force sustains conviction, there is obviously room for critical reflection to undermine that conviction. In certain cases such conviction, properly delimited, can count as knowledge. Indeed, as we will see below, central types of knowledge may be thought to be of this type. To this extent, then, critical reflection stands to undermine knowledge too. For central discussion of this possibility, see B. Williams (1985, esp. p. 148 and ch. 9, pp. 167 ff.) and A. W. Moore (1991a).

might be scope to distinguish a fictional force that is operative in uncritical mode and stands to be uncovered by critical reflection. In uncritical mode we simply accept that there is an ontological base to the world. It seems impossible even coherently to think otherwise. But, as we saw in the previous chapter, even the most basic heterogeneous experience is such as to presuppose a unified objective domain that is independent of individual states of awareness. Given that that is the case, there would seem to be room to suggest that what is taken in uncritical mode as sufficient evidence of an objective domain underlying and juxtaposed to subjective experience might be critically recognized as evidence of nothing more than a feature necessitated by the structure of experience.[43]

Before we can fully appraise the way in which this option promises a solution specifically to the problem of universality, by securing constancy of the basic normative framework, more obviously needs to be said by way of clarifying what it involves. We can start by saying what it does not involve. In particular, it needs to be distinguished from the idealist (or nihilist) option outlined towards the end of the previous section, with which it stands readily to be conflated. The point is not to claim that what is taken to exist independently of the structure of experience does not do so in fact, and is merely a projection of ours. That is precisely to make an ontological claim, and the position at hand should not be construed as making any such claim. Indeed, that is its central point. The point is not to run a discussion along the lines of ontological claims and counter-claims; assertions of independence versus corresponding assertions of dependence. The point is rather to align all such assertions and counter-assertions on one side as falling within an uncritical stance, to be contrasted with the critical stance on the other side. On the critical stance, having come to appreciate that all individuation is an expression of our interests and practices, and further that the very notion of some invariant substrate that gets to be articulated is itself an expression of the structure of our experience, it seems unwarranted still to allow such individuation or such an underlying substratum to pass as something merely given to and discovered by us. It can for present purposes be allowed that there could be such an ontological base, and indeed that the order we detect in it might in fact also be the way it is articulated in itself. What we come to realize, though, is that any assertions to that effect are always going to appear to be blind to the very conditions of experience in which they are made. Once revealed, those conditions turn out to be such that the grounds for the assertions cannot count as evidence for their truth, since those grounds would obtain regardless. Critical

---

[43] The possibility of regarding this, on the contrary, as the basis for a simple *modus ponens* inference, to the effect that there must therefore be some such ontological base, emerges on this view as a snare which should be regarded from a safe distance. On this, see pp. 310–11.

A Defence of Transcendental Arguments

awareness of those conditions would then seem to undermine the conviction that such assertions carry when taken at face value (their fictional force). In a fully critical context there would be no room for such assertions, or indeed for their negations.

We can further clarify the position at hand by distinguishing it from verificationism. There is no tenuous link stipulated here between scope for verification and a criterion for either meaning or truth. The claim is altogether more banal. If the evidence for a proposition is such that that evidence would obtain whether or not that proposition were true, then it must surely follow—without taking any steps towards impugning either the assumption that the proposition in question is meaningful, or that it has a truth-value[44]—that the assertion of that proposition cannot be sustained within the framework of a critical enquiry. Any proposition resting on that sort of evidential base is thereby revealed to fall outside the boundaries of critical enquiry. And the claim is that the assumption of an objective domain antecedent to subjective experience and imposing upon it is precisely of that sort. Of course, at the empirical level there is the experience of discovering a reality that constitutes an independent order. But the simple acceptance that there is such a discovery does not survive the critical insight that the structure of experience is such as to compel confrontation with an objective order at the empirical level regardless.

To avoid irrelevant objection at this point it is important to note that the epistemic duality is not in play here in quite the same way as before, when it applied merely to ontological individuations. Those were seen to be such that, regarded uncritically, they seem to be discoveries of a brutely given order, whereas, critically understood, they were revealed to be our own constructs. The point here is not to suggest, analogously, that perhaps rather than there being a brutely given ontological base, the appearance of one is merely a construct of ours, where that is taken to mean something that we project onto the world. Apart from the problem in talking here of projecting an ontological base 'onto the world', which could perhaps be regarded as a mere semantic infelicity that should not be given too much weight, there is the more worrying response that it assumes that we are the sorts of beings that have the capacity to project, to create such appearances, and that would itself seem to presuppose an ontological base (namely, that which we were made of such that we had those projecting powers). The better way of putting the point, however, is to say that the appearance of an ontological base given antecedent to experience and brutely imposing upon it is itself critically recognized to be a construal that is in accordance with an imposed form; a form imposed not by *us* but by the very structure of experience.

---

[44] But for non-verificationist doubts about the coherence of the propositions in question, see Sacks (1989, ch. 7).

We can now state in more positive terms what the position in question involves. In a thoroughly critical philosophical framework, ground-level appeal to an ontological base will have been expunged, having been recognized as involving an acceptance of appearances that does not withstand critical insight into their provenance. The fully critical account starts instead from that aspect of the structure of experience that sets up empirical experience in such a way as to make the appeal to a brutely impinging ontological base seem so obvious at the level of ordinary experience. Experience is so structured as to point us to begin explanation by simple appeal to an ontological base, while in fact it is not the uncritically accepted ostended point, but the pointer itself, that is the proper point from which to begin explanation. Thus the *obvious* starting-point for philosophical explanation is so obvious only because it remains uncritical; whereas the critically validated starting-point is one that recognizes that the structure of experience points us further than we should go. This need to resist being duped into following the pointer to reality instead of stopping at the pointer itself involves the sort of restraint in the face of fictional force (itself sustained in part by habit and custom) that is typical of the move to a critical explanatory stance. Something of this need is captured nicely by Wittgenstein, when he writes that: 'It is so difficult to find the beginning. Or better: it is difficult to begin at the beginning. And not to try to go further back.'[45] This restraint is just what is involved in the retreat from ontological commitment that accompanies the move from uncritical acceptance to critical explanation of empirical appearances. For the time being we can make do with this brief statement—it will suffice for the purpose of addressing the issue of universality. (A more detailed characterization of the position will be provided later.)

Given the extended application of the epistemic duality, it follows that within a fully critical position an ontological base of any sort would not be acceptable currency. Any resort to an ontological base would involve putting critical understanding on hold at least to an extent; it would indicate a degree of pre-reflective engagement with a context to the extent of taking at face value the appearance of discoveries within it. Once we become critically aware of the inbuilt pointer to reality, of the fact that experience anyway requires the construal of a permanent objective domain which is readily thought of as an ontological base, we recognize that it is inappropriate in a fully critical enquiry simply to go on endorsing the existence of some such base as our starting-point. This can be aligned with the familiar claim about what Kant should have held in his transcendental idealism. The basic claim is that the appeal to ontological bases is always internal—internal to the horizons set by the context in which we are immersed, to the uncritical engagement with a

---

[45] *On Certainty* (1969, §471).

A Defence of Transcendental Arguments

practice. This might be correlated as an analogue to the claim Kant makes—availing himself in a way that we have not of the notion of categorial or conceptual schemes—that *existence* is one of the categories. Given that claim, Kant should have drawn the conclusion that there is no room to assert within a duly critical philosophical stance that there is a way the world is in itself. To make the point simply, in a way that bypasses much of the Kantian machinery: if the categories are taken to determine (in part) the basic structure of our experience, and existence is one of them, then as long as we are critically aware of the provenance of that concept, we cannot have any justification for applying it to how things are independently of our application of that categorial framework.[46]

Now if it is accepted that existence-claims are always confined to a pre-reflective stance, and that the critical stance no longer allows any explanation grounded in the assumption of an ontological base, then it is easy to see how the solution to the problem of universality, along the same lines outlined towards the end of the previous section, is readily available as long as we maintain the commitment to a fully critical stance. There is now no unrealistic nihilist ontological claim to the effect that nothing exists independently of our normative structures. It is rather that the notion that there might be some such ontological base, the vagaries and mutations of which would indeed stand to render unstable the apparent fixity of our normative structures, is recognized to be one that should not be brought into play within a properly critical enquiry. The very fact that that worry arises, where it does arise, can be seen as a sign that we have not yet reached an adequately critical starting-point to enquiry. Once we come to hold back from uncritically following the pointer that would have us commence explanation from an underlying ontological base, there is no longer the space for the worry that the basic background normative form of life might alter under influence external to it. There can, as I said, still be change, but that can now amount only to moves generated internally to normative space, and as was pointed out that can consist only

---

[46] Of course, the thing in itself has long seemed to be an alien element in Kant's critical philosophy, and spurred on much of the post-Kantian German Idealist tradition. The trouble, as the discussion below will further bring out, is that within Kant's system the thing in itself is both necessary and illegitimate. As Kant's contemporary Friedrich Jacobi succinctly put it, he needed the assumption of things in themselves to enter into the Kantian system, but with that assumption he was unable to remain in it. (Jacobi's nicely honed comment is often taken to express something more, or at least other, than it was meant to. For one thing, his concern is not that the commitment to the thing in itself is a residue that gets in the way of a thoroughgoing idealism, but rather on the contrary that it fails as a last-ditch attempt by Kant to defend himself against the charge of nihilism. See Beiser 1987, esp. 122–6, for discussion of the context of Jacobi's original remark.) The present discussion is an attempt to bring out clearly a valid insight underlying the Kantian transcendental idealist position, given which the embarrassing commitment to a thing in itself no longer threatens; but neither does the accusation of nihilism.

of the actualization of already given possibilities (metaphorically, the population of previously uninhabited loci). As we might put it, all change internal to the given normative framework will be *combinatorial*—a function of available moves—and to that extent deals only with possibilities already given. In the absence of external intervention, there is no scope for innovation in the sense of radically new normative possibilities. Thus when philosophical explanation is fully critical, and takes its beginning from the right place, we come to see that the framework normative structure is indeed guaranteed to be not only singular, but also constant. And given this constancy, we have what we were after: a normative framework, a form of life, the contours of which are universally binding. It is only when and in so far as we are insufficiently critical that it can seem otherwise.

This seems clearly to capture an essential general feature of Kant's transcendental idealism. The strongest promise of transcendental idealism surely lies in the hope that by accepting that we only ever know the world as it appears to us, we can secure the scope for knowledge to lay claim to universality and necessity, for knowledge of how those appearances must be. What has been identified above promises just this. We have a position that recognizes that ontological individuation, and indeed the conception of there being an ontological base, is internal to the context of experience—what Kant would refer to as being merely empirically real—and cannot be applied outside that context; and one that also manages *thereby* to sustain the universality of the basic framework to which local normative and individuative structures must conform.

I noted earlier[47] that the epistemic duality between what is uncritically registered as a discovered order, and then critically revealed to be of our own making, involves a shift characteristic of the Copernican turn that underlies transcendental idealism, whether that turn is construed in transcendental or naturalized form. And the naturalized form of this Copernican turn was seen to comprise a structure that threatens unconstrained relativism,[48] which is not blocked by the way in which it still leaves room for a weak form of ('naturalized') transcendental idealism.[49] It is of interest, therefore, that the attempt immediately above to *extend* the application of the epistemic duality between critical and uncritical levels of understanding seems to recapture a central insight of the more full-blown form of transcendental idealism. Although this insight is not specifically idealist in itself, nevertheless it does much to explain and pick up on the point of Kant's claim specifically to *critical* idealism. For the sake of clarity it is worth bringing out the contrast with Kant's transcendental idealism in a slightly schematic way.

[47] p. 174.   [48] Ch. 5.   [49] Ch. 6.

The central insight behind transcendental idealism is sustained here without having to endorse several of Kant's more problematic commitments. First, whereas the position here avoids the need for any assumption of a thing in itself, Kant seems compelled, however uncomfortably, to accept—for reasons that I will allude to shortly—that there is a thing in itself. Secondly, there is no assumption here of a fixed egological subject the workings of which are captured by Kant's transcendental psychology. Thirdly, and precisely because transcendental psychology has been jettisoned, we do not have to exclude the realistic scope for variance in the way different subjects, in different local contexts, might construe their world. I will return to this last point shortly. The most immediately significant of these factors, strategically at least, is probably the second, that the central insight of transcendental idealism has been upheld here in generic form without the need to engage in anything like transcendental psychology. Since it is generally the highly dubious, and metaphysical, speculations that comprise Kant's transcendental psychology that have led to the rejection of transcendental idealism, it is important that an attempt to salvage an important insight from that position is no longer saddled with that unacceptable doctrine.

To clarify the possibility, and its relation to Kant's position, it is worth commenting first on the relation between Kant's commitment to the thing in itself on the one hand, and to transcendental psychology on the other. Basically, given one of the two commitments, it does not matter which, the other follows naturally. If we go along with the ready assumption that there is a pre-given ontological base, a way the world is in itself, it makes sense to think that the only way in which we can avoid scepticism is by allowing that it is not of that world that we have knowledge, but of the way in which it is necessarily construed in our experience. And since the necessity of that construal cannot be pinned on the world, on pain of the very sceptical threat that we are trying to avoid, the only alternative would be to locate its source in the way of the human mind. Conversely, as long as there is an assumption about the transcendental workings of the human subject, such that it casts its fixed form onto the world, the assumption that there is a pre-given domain, the world as it is prior to that imposition, is difficult to resist. The two commitments thus readily go hand in hand—indeed, as we will see immediately, there is a still closer link, of entailment, between them. But this whole set-up is optional, and the details of the transcendental psychological make-up as Kant sets it out are surely fanciful. It is vital that in stripping away this fanciful story, as Strawson does, we should not also have stripped away the valuable critical insight underlying Kant's transcendental idealism, which should be allowed to survive its demise.

The contrast with what has just been said about Kant's position puts this insight in a clearer perspective. The primary problem with the weaker form of transcendental idealism that traded only in transcendental features was that it left room for unconstrained relativism. The Kantian form of transcendental idealism stood to restrict that relativism by appealing to a form of transcendental psychology, which supposedly *guarantees* that all human beings will construct empirical reality in basically the same way. But fancifulness aside, there is the basic question why the transcendental psychology identified should be *invariant*; why the inconceivability of alternatives to Kant's model of the mind—assuming, for the sake of argument, that alternatives are indeed inconceivable—should be taken to imply the impossibility of there being any. It would seem that to safeguard the constancy of the transcendental psychology in question Kant would have to appeal to some underpinning metaphysical structure, and yet that is precisely the kind of uncritical excursion into metaphysics that transcendental idealism was supposed to help us to avoid. But the need for that transcendental psychology to curb relativism arises in the first place only because there is still room for assuming a level of reality underlying empirical individuations, a brute (and mutable) ontological base which is such as can bring about new and previously uncharted changes in our normative and individuative apparatus. It is thus only because Kant left room for the thing in itself that he had to appeal to transcendental psychology. Indeed, the relativism of the weaker form of transcendental idealism discussed earlier (in Chapters 5–6) ultimately arose precisely because, although that position was not developed by reference to the workings of a pre-given ontological base, it still left room for such an assumption while at the same time giving up the commitment to transcendental psychology. The position at hand leads us to give up unequivocally on both: properly understood, the truth underlying Kant's transcendental idealism *leaves no room* for the thing in itself and so no need for any form of transcendental psychology. Both of these are welcome consequences. That the resulting position, neither allowing for a thing in itself nor adverting to any form of transcendental psychology, no longer counts as a form of idealism is neither here nor there. The central underlying point is that by pushing the epistemic duality characteristic of the critical turn to its proper extent, the constancy of the framework normative structures—and hence their universality—is secured. We might capture this insight by saying that in a thoroughly critical framework of enquiry there can indeed be room for no more than transcendental features, but that those in fact—contrary to what seemed to threaten earlier—turn out to be sufficient. There are universal transcendental features with regard to which there is no scope for change. Consequently, the absence of transcendental constraints no longer matters. Or rather, the distinction between the two, once we reach genuinely universal transcendental features, loses its point.

It is important, however, that the constancy of normative and individuative structure thereby secured within a critical system should not be overstated. (This relates back to the third point of difference with Kant's transcendental idealism.) The exclusion of relativist pressure should not be construed too strongly. In fact the line between what is and is not immune from relativism now falls in just the right place. It is possible that what seem to be universal structures from within a given context will turn out not to be, that alternatives to those structures are available elsewhere. We might not, from a given location on the normative map, have immediate access to all other relevant locations. And with time, as possibilities that were at one time remote from a given context become more salient, conceivabilities and universalizations might change. There is, then, no reason to be confident that what we today identify as universally valid conclusions of transcendental arguments are indeed such, rather than locally indexed universalizations to which alternatives are possible. What does follow, however, is that there is a fixed and universally valid background normative framework, in relation to which all local normative set-ups are plotted. What we have eliminated is the worry that there might be alternatives to, or modifications of, that basic framework. The normative structures constitutive of that framework will comprise the unchanging transcendental features that our transcendental arguments are aimed at. We might in fact only ever have reached locally indexed, and so in principle transient, transcendental features. But we have established at least that there are transcendental features that are not transient, and there is scope for thinking that with a sufficiently broad-ranging base we might reach, or at least approximate to, those universal features. We can put this by saying that we are looking for those features, the obtaining of which is now established, that are globally rather than locally indexed; anchored to the entire background framework, and not to any partial set of normative practices within it to the exclusion of others that inhabit other loci on the grid.

This readily suggests the value of cognitive tourism, so to speak, of just the sort that the later Wittgenstein engaged in and recommended; the attempt to transcend local normative horizons by taking in other ways of going on. It also gives credence to the notion of an open discourse, leading to convergence at the end of the day. By transcending various local set-ups, there is hope that we will converge on the appreciation of the single normative structure that serves as the background on which all those local set-ups are calibrated. There is now scope to consider open discourse to result in ascent to a common global framework, and hence in convergence on universal normative structures. The idea of such convergence is precisely what motivates Habermas's and pragmatist appeals to the eventual terminus of open discussion. It is of interest in this context to note that for those appeals to carry any weight there must be some reason to think that there is a *propensity* for such convergence, rather than merely for the stand-off between opposing traditions. One way of securing that propensity would be to assume a metaphysical form underlying empirical appearances. In the absence of that, a post-metaphysical or naturalist orientation, as we saw, seems to threaten us with the prospect of the relativist stand-off. Naturalistic realism would not leave any room for precluding unconstrained relativism. It would seem that an altogether welcome way out of the quandary is to allow that the pragmatist and specifically the Habermasian appeal to convergence may be supplemented by the present conception of a comprehensively critical, and in consequence strictly post-metaphysical, route to sustaining an invariant universal form. From what has been said it will be seen that that form is such that it is known a priori both to apply to, and to be such as could be independently converged upon by, all parties to the discussion, without imposition from one locality to the extent of denying the basic (reflectively endorsed) commitments of another. Any claim to universality that does not meet those criteria is known a priori—from the very nature of the invariant encompassing normative structure in question—*not* to be anything more than a locally indexed pretender. This, then, is a response to the relativist threat that seemed to confront the intersubjective paradigm in our earlier discussion. But perhaps more important is the negative point. It would seem that *without* this conception there is no reason—at least in a post-metaphysical orientation—to expect convergence (unless as the result of brute force) 'at the end of the day'.[50]

---

[50] By way of bringing this out it is worth considering Taylor's attempt to secure assurance of the resilience of our normative orientation, by means of what he calls 'supersession arguments' (e.g. Taylor 1999: 161–3). The idea is to show that later stages supersede earlier developments, such that there is a one-way rational path from the earlier orientation to the later. What secures this is not only a line of argument, but an actual historical transition from one stage to the later, such that at the later stage a return to the initial orientation is no longer a real option. Taylor is clear that this irreversibility means that certain possibilities that were foreclosed by the actual trajectory history has taken might have been valuable, and perhaps in the judgement of some more valuable than the one that history actually took. In this sense there is no illusion of necessity, or strict universality, of the normative order. But there is a sense that, among the various normative orientations there might have been, what historical contingencies have singled out as the actual one is at least resilient, and binding, in the sense that there is no going back. There remain struggles and conflicts between alternatives, choices to be made between seemingly incompatible values held at different loci, but the idea is that, once made, the sheer weight of history bestows rational irreversibility on that choice.

It should be noted, however, that this kind of defence of our actual progression, whereby what seems like progress to us is rationally consolidated by the force of history, remains fragile since the rational irreversibility is in fact indexed to how things are at a given point in history. Consequently, it cannot be immune to—resilient in the face of—world-driven shifts of orientation (including with regard to judgements we_{now} make about what is irrational). Taylor mentions, but does not give due weight to, possibilities such as the Taliban reaching Chicago. Given the possibility of brute world-driven shifts, there is no real rational irreversibility to be had. What is rendered rationally irreversible at a certain stage of history is ultimately only as secure as its contingent historical nesting.

Taylor would probably agree with this, contending simply that this is all we can have. The point for now is only to note how weak this is as an attempt to secure objectivity of normative structure. The move that Taylor advocates is, essentially, also put forward by Brandom (1999: 179–82): here too correctness of normative structure is constitutively indexed to a context of judgement, and might change. This similarity is just what one should expect where, without the critical turn advocated here, and in the context of a naturalized Hegelianism, due weight is given to the historical process.

Once we start at the critically validated beginning, rather than at the apparent starting-point, we are in a position to recognize the constancy of the basic normative map, such that while local normative horizons might come to be stretched and altered by the encounter with other remote localities, there is no scope for the background normative structure as a whole to be stretched by brute ontology-driven innovation. Consequently, in being stretched, those various local horizons are each expanding in a process which, if continued sufficiently, could only ever terminate in convergence: at the limit, once all local normative set-ups are encompassed, they will have limned the contours of a normative structure to which critical thought reveals that there cannot be alternatives.[51] It is at this stage that transcendental features of experience come into play which cannot be superseded. The invariant background matrix that these features pertain to can be thought of as the invariant form of life, a fixed grammar, of the sort that seemed to fit with the interpretation of the later Wittgenstein. With this, then, we have a way in which that Wittgensteinian claim can be upheld without introducing a metaphysical, and in particular an idealist, doctrine.[52]

It is significant to note that this basic background normative structure, the invariant form of life that sustains and is delineated by genuinely universal transcendental features, plays the same role as the basic invariant spatio-temporal matrix established by the arguments of the previous chapter. Indeed, that perceptual matrix can be seen as constituting one part of the single background cognitive matrix that is being addressed here. Now it emerged that that background perceptual matrix is itself not a possible object of perception; and the question is whether that characteristic too should not be generalized now, to the effect that the basic background framework is not itself an object of cognitive experience. Something of this sort will be familiar from straightforwardly Wittgensteinian considerations. That the invariant form of life in question is closely related to, and in the context of Wittgensteinian thought can be traced as a descendant of, the *Tractarian* notion of logical form, will be clear. And in the light of this it will not be surprising to have it suggested that perhaps, like the latter, the underlying and invariant form of life we have reached is such that the truth about it cannot be *said*. In the case of logical form the truths about it are such that cannot meaningfully be negated; yet any descriptive proposition can be negated—whatever can be said can also meaningfully be denied. And it might be thought that linguistic inexpressibility followed here for the more widely construed normative framework as well,

---

[51] Indeed, that structure is normative just in the minimal but significant sense that it comprises a set of practices to which there can be no alternatives.

[52] Any form of idealism we might attribute to the later Wittgenstein would either be too strong to fit the post-metaphysical orientation, or too weak to secure an invariant form of life. By contrast the position outlined secures that invariance in a manner thoroughly congenial to a post-metaphysical orientation.

because the framework in question has no alternatives to it, whereas any contentful proposition used in a description of it can be negated. Whether or not this follows can, however, be left open for now. Similarly, we should leave room for the suggestion that we could not identify those limits on what is a possibility for us *as limits*, and so cannot delineate the contours of that basic framework, since identifying any limit requires thinking it from both sides, which is just what we cannot do in this case.[53] Again, this may be the case, but whether or not we can directly identify those genuinely universal transcendental features as capturing our limits is not the issue.

It is sufficient simply that there are those fixed transcendental features, sayable or not, such as to secure that all localities will in the long run be led by gradual reflective assimilation of alternatives to converge. (And the fact of such converging universalization would itself be indirect evidence that what was converged upon expresses—whether through *saying* or *showing*—those universal and invariant limits.) We are left to engage in cognitive investigation, to move around exploring alternatives to local normative set-ups; where things go dark for us they might not for others, where they go dark now they might not always continue do so. We continue to expand our local horizons in the knowledge now that there will in principle be a stage at which we reach points that go dark because there really is no further space to look into at those points. There we will have come up against the limits of which the invariant transcendental features of our normative framework are expressive, such that inconceivability there is indeed a guide to impossibility, and it is at those features that our transcendental arguments are aimed.

So much, then, for the outline of a solution to the problem of the universality of inference. Looking back now to the specific transcendental arguments developed in the preceding chapter, the above, of course, appropriately raises the question whether they identify merely locally indexed universalizations such as might be superseded in the course of time, or rather successfully articulate—or at least come up against—genuinely universal transcendental features of the sort they were aiming for. And it should now be clear that we should not expect a swift answer to that question; it is enough to have shown that there is an answer that stands to emerge in due course. Obviously, it was important that we did not start from some clearly localized model of the mind, to which alternatives are readily available, but rather from some minimal and rudimentary conception of experience to which we cannot conceive of alternatives. Nevertheless, it remains the case that, however wide their arc, we are still going only by our own (local) lights; and so it remains possible that the conclusions reached do not have the strict universality that the inconceivability to us$_{now}$ of alternatives to them would seem to suggest. But while we might

---

[53] Wittgenstein, *Tractatus*, 5.61.

well not be in a position to tell when our transcendental arguments have delivered up such conclusions, we do now know that there are conclusions to transcendental arguments that approach universalizations to which no alternatives are possible; and that is enough. With that in place there is every reason to engage in such arguments while entrusting their ultimate evaluation, in the spirit of open-ended enquiry, to other, more encompassing vantage-points. Indeed it can quite readily seem that this is as much as an adequate solution to the problem of universality should offer: the shape of the solution that has emerged is what is to be expected. Any stronger result, a solution that did not leave room for such fallibility, would clearly seem too strong.

Finally, it is worth indicating how the approach to the problem of universality in this section bears upon the problem, of the inference to reality, addressed in Section 1 above. The discussion of the insight underlying transcendental idealism has so far been taken in two steps: first, the appropriate extension of the epistemic duality, and secondly, the invariance of the basic normative structures that is secured in consequence of this critical turn. We can leave the latter aside for present purposes. While it is this consequence that secures the possibility of universality for transcendental arguments generally, and so also specifically for those transcendental arguments that are designed to span the gap between appearances and reality, this assurance obviously does not in itself (i.e. without a verificationist premiss) solve the specific problem of the legitimacy of the inference to reality. However, the first and primary element of the insight underlying transcendental idealism does render a solution to that problem, and again in a way that is typical of the transcendental idealist solution.

If a fully critical outlook abstains from all commitment to an ontological base, then all assumptions of existence are left confined to the pre-reflective stance of ordinary empirical engagement. At the latter level the question of the inference to reality would indeed seem insoluble. But philosophical enquiry does not properly belong at that level, and the fact that sceptical problems arise when it is conducted there should be regarded as indicative of that.[54] Confined to the critical level we come to realize that our experience is so structured as to allow and indeed to require us to pass beyond our individual thoughts, or at least such individual mental contents as there might be, to establish contact with an extra-mental objective world; but we also come to realize that that objective world should not be regarded in critical mode as anything more than an empirical reality, required for experience. From the critical level, the presentation of an ontological base at the empirical and pre-reflective level is recognized as having the status of appearance: it is presented

---

[54] On the sceptic as a troubleshooter, see Kant, *Critique*, A377 ('The sceptical idealist . . . is a benefactor of human reason'); and, differences in detail aside, Stroud (1984*b*) and Sacks (1989: 87–92).

as a discovered realm, which in a sense it is, but is critically realized to merit only the status of a structuring feature of experience. As such the empirically given division between the psychological realm and the imposing reality external to it also, from the critical perspective, merits only phenomenal status. It is internal to what Kant would refer to as transcendental appearance. Transcendental arguments that involve an inference to reality are then seen to take us only across the line between empirical appearances and empirical reality; they do not involve attempting to move beyond how things must seem to us, to how things ultimately are in a quite independent ontological base (at the critical level there remains no room for any such base). That is the move that seemed impossible, and within a sufficiently critical framework of enquiry we can see that transcendental arguments properly construed no longer involve crossing that line. Again, then, we have here the benefits of the transcendental idealist solution, without any need to introduce Kant's transcendental psychology; and correlatively, without any need to leave a residual uncritical commitment to the way the world is in itself.

This insight underlying transcendental idealism, devoid of the offending elements of the Kantian position, is what was promised at the end of the preceding chapter. Turning again specifically to the conclusions of the arguments of the previous chapter, and to the inference to reality involved, it is now clear why the naïve realist construal of that argument as a simple *modus ponens* inference to reality without further qualification was to be rejected, and why the problems it faced were altogether appropriate. That construal attempts to cross a line that in a sufficiently critical context of enquiry would not be there to be crossed. The realism involved is, in other words, just that: *naïve*, uncritical, taken in by appearances, in a way that is bound to give rise to sceptical problems. We have seen why that is so, and more importantly why the alternative does not require retreat to Kant's unacceptable form of transcendental idealism.

This chapter has revealed in outline the nature and significance of the insight identified as underlying transcendental idealism. Regarding transcendental arguments, that insight stands to solve both the main problems facing them: that of the universality of inference, and of the inference to reality. We have in fact also seen how the insight in question seems to make room for an absolute conception of the order of things that does not turn on the usual assumption that such a conception involves a commitment to what exists anyway, to an independent ontological realm (which we normally manage to approach only from within the confinement to one partial perspectival take or another).[55]

[55] A. W. Moore (1997) offers what is, to my knowledge, by far the most sustained treatment of the notion of an absolute conception understood along those lines. (See also B. Williams 1978 for an early and formative discussion.) I discuss Moore's treatment in detail, in the light of the present construal of an absolute conception, in Sacks (1999).

That assumption appears to take as basic the very distinction between subjective contents and an independent reality that the extension of the epistemic duality has revealed as uncritical. It is of interest that without that uncritical realist dichotomy the prospect of an absolute conception of the order of things remains possible. The assumption of that which exists anyway, of an independent ontological base, has turned out not to be a presupposition of there being an absolute conception of the order of things.

In view of this it is perhaps worth saying something more, in conclusion, about the characteristics of the position based on that insight.

9

Conclusion: Objectivity, Insight, and the Place of Fictional Force

TRADITIONALLY, securing a handle on objectivity or the possibility of an absolute conception of the world has been regarded as part and parcel of a strictly realist outlook. A clear statement of this all too natural alignment can, for example, be found in one of its most determined advocates. Thomas Nagel thus writes:

However often we may try to step outside of ourselves, something will have to stay behind the lens, something in us will determine the resulting picture, and this will give grounds for doubt that we are really getting any closer to reality.

The idea of objectivity thus seems to undermine itself. The aim is to form a conception of reality which includes ourselves and our view of things among its objects, but it seems that whatever forms the conception will not be included by it. It seems to follow that the most objective view we can achieve will have to rest on an unexamined subjective base, and that since we can never abandon our own point of view, but can only alter it, the idea that we are coming closer to the reality outside it with each successive step has no foundation.[1]

The basic idea is that we can secure an escape from relativism to full objectivity—to an absolute conception of the world—only if we can cover the distance between the way the world appears to us and the way it is in itself ('the great gap between the grounds of our beliefs about the world and the contents of those beliefs'[2]).

As long as this is the structuring picture, it seems clear that the subject-driven scepticism outlined in Part I will remain pertinent. Such scepticism will not, however, be exhaustive of the problems facing it. Resolution of the basic problem cannot be simply a matter of securing the right model of the mind, since the problem arises even from the mere fact of having to approach the objective domain from a subjective point of view that would have, *per impossibile*, to be transcended. And that difficulty seems to stand, whatever the model of the mind that occupies the subjective point of view might be. That indeed is the insight Bergson was responding to in his attempt to

---

[1] Nagel (1986: 68).   [2] 1986: 69.

displace the traditional subject–object polarity that Nagel, representatively, takes as still basic to the epistemic endeavour.

And with that polarity in place, it would indeed seem, as Nagel points out, that there are three possibilities by way of a response to the problem: meeting the problem head-on with some hitherto unthought-of bridge across 'the great gap' (the 'heroic' response); conceding that subjectivity cannot be eliminated, and we wrongly or at least without licence assume our belief-sets to have secured a handle on the way of the objective realm (sceptical responses); and conceding that while that gap indeed cannot be traversed effectively, there is a weaker construal of the gap, sustaining a weaker but still sufficient sense of objectivity, that can be traversed unproblematically as Kant attempts to show (reductive response).[3] The second two are clearly seen as capitulations in the face of the failure of the first and optimal approach. Nagel's commitment was firmly, and remains, to this heroic agenda.[4]

It is in relation to this orientation that the position that has emerged here stands out in sharpest relief. If the structuring ontological picture is the subject–object polarity as Nagel takes it to be, then indeed objectivity—whether about the external world, logic, or rationality—must optimally be construed realistically, and anything short of that would be an undeniable compromise. The discussion in the preceding chapter would accordingly fall in with a form of reductionist compromise. In fact, though, that discussion differs in attempting to steer clear not merely of a realist response, but also of the commitment to such a response being either optimal or indeed even relevant. And what was taken to secure this was, essentially, the fact that the subject–object polarity no longer suggests itself as the basic structure from which the epistemic endeavour should take its beginnings. The assumption of such a dichotomy from which to begin explanation does not survive the extension of the epistemic duality (between an order as it is immediately presented and as it is critically appraised) in view of what was seen, in Chapter 7, about the structure of even the most primitive heterogeneous domain of presentation. The basic ontological starting-point turns out, in the light of that, to have been the result of naïvely following the pointer to reality that is fundamental to the structure of experience, rather than stopping at the pointer itself. Once that critical turn has been taken, Nagel's structuring picture—the prevailing picture—seems not only optional, but damagingly pre-reflective. And with

---

[3] 1986: 68.

[4] The same agenda is maintained in Nagel (1997). On p. 9, referring back to the earlier work, he repeats his distinction between realist, sceptical, and reductionist responses to the challenge, and his firm commitment to the realist approach. Nevertheless, there seem to be traces of two contrasting routes to objectivity here, his primary realist route, and the kind of critical route developed above (contrast, for instance, p. 9 with pp. 20–4). There is no recognition of the way in which the two routes are in fact in tension, the ontological realism of the one undermining the constancy of the presupposed backdrop that results with the other.

314   *Conceptions of Objectivity*

that picture displaced, far from seeming like the optimal response to the problem of construing objectivity, or the possibility of an absolute conception, such metaphysical realism as Nagel represents now seems like a naïve commitment that was indeed incompatible with a properly resilient objectivity. On the alternative explored here, instead of such realism seeming optimal, we can take it that what fully critical insight into objectivity really suggests as primary is the promise of expunging in the context of critical enquiry any commitment to there being an ontological base.

Now this alternative clearly involves a separation of levels: all ontological assumptions are germane to one, but are left behind when we reach the other. In this the position falls in with a long tradition, extending from Kant through Carnap to Quine, or Wittgenstein, that sees our realist commitment (ontological talk) as strictly internal. But the distinction between levels has invariably relied on a metaphor or set of metaphors that resist satisfactory unpacking. In Kant, the distinction between the empirical and the transcendental levels proved particularly troubling, sufficient to motivate many to abandon Kant's transcendental idealism on those grounds. Naturalized Kantians, such as Carnap, Quine, and arguably (the later) Wittgenstein, drew the distinction differently, but still not always unproblematically, as Davidson's criticism of the very idea of a conceptual scheme brought out. Furthermore, the naturalized way of talking of ontological commitment as being internal to conceptual schemes or—avoiding the problems with the latter concept—to our practices, seems to leave us with precisely the relativism that Kant's appeal to transcendental constraints stood to preclude. This is because venturing into discussion at the transcendental level is avoided, thereby seemingly leaving open the clear possibility of a reality, some thing in itself, for ever beyond our empirical individuations, but the vicissitudes of which stand to pull conceptual schemes, practices, normative structures, this way and that. True, there can be no assertion that there is any such thing in itself: that would be the projection of just one more internal picture; but then so too would any corresponding denial. In contrast, the way of distinguishing between two levels of explanation involved in the present discussions avoids much of this trouble.

First, the distinction between levels here avoids the need to draw a distinction between empirical as opposed to transcendental enquiry, or truths of one sort as opposed to another; or to employ any questionable philosophical artifice such as the appeal to conceptual schemes involves. The distinction between levels is drawn innocuously, in terms of a separation between that level or context of enquiry in which critical insight is to a specifiable extent held in abeyance, and the other in which it is applied fully. The former level comprises our ordinary engaged stance in the world; the other, at which there is no restraining of critical insight, comprises the fully reflective level appropriate for philosophical activity. (If someone were to call the former 'empirical' and the latter 'transcendental', that would be unobjectionable as long as it was made clear that nothing more than that was being attributed to the Kantian terminology.) And it is not only that we have here a way of drawing a distinction between levels of understanding that is conceptually unproblematic, to the point of seeming trivial. It is also undeniable that in practice the shift from uncritical participative mode to critical reflection is easily realized. Whether or not a reflective stance could ever be critical to the extent of effectively rooting out *all* uncritical commitment is doubtful, and not only for merely pragmatic reasons. But the fact is that we now have the prospect not only of talking coherently of there being a second level, but also of talking coherently at that level. There is no longer the sense, explicitly acknowledged in naturalized Kantians like Carnap and Quine and Wittgenstein, and arguably applicable to Kant as well, even though he failed to recognize it, that we can only ever coherently talk internally to the empirical level (or to a conceptual scheme, a language, or a language game), and cannot transcend that level to describe its contours from the outside. The latter hope, the cartographer's dream, may still not be accommodated, but that turns out not to matter: what does matter is that the very ordinariness of the distinction drawn between levels now at least allows unproblematic assent from one to the next.

Secondly, with that assent we are no longer left, as Kant and his naturalized successors were, with the residual possibility of a thing in itself, on which a secure grip cannot be assured, and which threatens the stability of what seem to be objective structures. That would happen only if there was one model of objectivity at work across the two levels of enquiry. Instead, what we are left with is a clear separation of two levels of enquiry *and corresponding to them two distinct conceptions of objectivity*. At the one level, the ordinary, mundane, everyday level, the structure of experience, whereby the subject is confronted with an independent object domain, is taken at face value, as evidence of confrontation with an ontological bedrock. That sets up the subject–object dichotomy as basic, and we are then immediately committed to conceiving of objectivity in terms of crossing the line between the two (whether it is conceived of as a Cartesian chasm or not): leaving behind any merely subjective point of view and limning the contours of reality as it is in itself. If that is then carried over to the second level, then we have to say that even if all individuation is internal to the first level, we are still left to countenance as relevant at that level the possibility of some underlying ontological base, the world as it is in itself. This is, of course, just what Kant does allow, and what naturalized Kantians do not seem effectively to disallow.[5] But in fact that conception of objectivity should not travel with us from the uncritical to the

---

[5] Appeals to verificationism count, unproblematically in my view, as ineffective ways of disallowing external questions.

critical level of enquiry. If what has been said is right, then at that level, given the appropriate application of the epistemic duality to the subject–object structure of experience itself, that distinction can no longer be taken at face value as the starting-point for philosophical enquiry. Rather, a degree of fictional force has been identified. Consequently, at this critical level the suggestion of a residual commitment to an ontological base, some thing in itself, seems— as I have put it—to be wrongly to follow in the direction in which the structure of experience points us, rather than stopping at the pointer itself. Stopping where it is then appropriate to stop, and hence in the absence of the uncritical assumption of an ontological base, a different model of objectivity emerges, one that discards the picture of reality as imposing on the possible range of subjective variation, and thereby secures the possibility of universal structures to which there ultimately cannot be alternatives.[6] This is the model of objectivity with which we are left to operate at the critical level, with the other model—of the sort that Nagel favoured—revealed as essentially confined to the first level.

Now while the distinction of levels here differs favourably from Kant's, it also importantly retains an interesting parallel with the Kantian strategy. Seemingly out of place in the Fourth Paralogism, Kant sets out the strategic claim to the effect that if we start by adopting a transcendental realist framework, we end up collapsing into empirical idealism, which constitutes an unacceptable form of scepticism. The mistake of traditional metaphysicians was not in failing to answer scepticism, but in unwittingly setting out from within a framework that could not fail to lead them into that sceptical predicament. By contrast, knowledge of the external world can be secured if we don't misconstrue the sense in which it is external, as we are bound to do if we start from the way things are presented at the empirical level. If we take the transcendental turn, and start from within a transcendental idealist framework, and consequently recognize the external world as transcendental appearance, we can sustain a stable form of empirical realism: we can have knowledge of the world as it is objectively, independently of empirical appearances.[7]

---

[6] In view of its etymology, the term 'objectivity' may seem inappropriate for this alternative conception. There is, however, no other readily available philosophical term of art for that which is not merely first-personally indexed, and which holds out the prospect of universal, absolute truths. Besides, the fact that there is no other readily available term, and that this term as it is commonly used carries etymological reference to the first-level conception based on the subject–object dichotomy, perhaps constitutes an altogether appropriate indication of a genealogical link between the two levels of enquiry, to which I will return shortly.

It is worth noting that in any case the use of 'objectivity' and 'objective reality' has a varied history, and its current use is relatively recent. (Thus in Descartes's resort to the scholastic distinction between objective and formal reality (Third Meditation), talk of the 'objective' reality of an idea means something which we would probably describe as 'subjective': to us that meaning of 'objective' is almost lost since the term, as Kenny puts it, 'has come by a quirk of history to be synonymous with "extra-mental existence"'; Kenny 1968: 132.)

[7] See *Critique*, Fourth Paralogism (A366–80).

Conclusion 317

It is that same strategy, but stripped of the problematic embellishments, that fits the present case. We have two levels of enquiry, and a distinctive model of objectivity corresponding to each. At the ordinary empirical level of engagement with the world we find ourselves working with what we might refer to as the ontological model of objectivity which, short of dogmatic metaphysical or religious appeal, results in scepticism of one form or another. The real problem is not the failure to solve the sceptical problems, but the exclusive adoption of the first-level framework for objectivity, which could not fail to lead to those problems. By contrast, again, we are able to secure objectivity unproblematically if we don't misconstrue the relevant sense of objectivity, as we are bound to do if we remain confined to the way things are presented at the empirical level, but take our stand instead within the second and pervasively critical level of enquiry.

At that level of understanding two things were taken to happen. First, we come to regard critically the conception of objectivity at work at the first level and, as in Kant, the external world is then recognized as having the status merely of transcendental appearance (the independence of objects experienced at the uncritical level is, in a critical context, not regarded as evidence of anything more than a necessarily imposed structure); and being a species of appearance, there is no deep chasm that needs to be bridged in securing a grip on it. But something else seemed to happen too, something that effectively extends the same strategy. If that chasm still remained, not indeed between us and empirical objects but between the world as it appears to us and as it is in itself, this would still seem to leave us, as Kant's system does, with the problem of not being able to secure genuinely objective knowledge. This is the price Kant pays for securing knowledge of empirical reality. (As I have pointed out, the price is in fact higher than Kant thinks, since the residual ontological base stands to threaten the stability of even our seemingly necessary construals of empirical reality.) But on the view presented, that price is merely the result of still adhering to the ontological model of objectivity, derived from the level of enquiry that presents itself so immediately as our starting-point. Taking our start instead squarely from within the critical context of enquiry, we reached the second conception of objectivity. And that critical or non-ontological conception of objectivity allows for the universality of normative and perceptual structure underlying whatever variety the contingent play of empirical constructions at the uncritical level might—particularly in the absence of metaphysical assurances—have left room for.

In a nutshell, the common underlying strategy is this: the ontological starting-point immediately but uncritically arrived at in our everyday engagement with the world results in scepticism; and we do better to start theorizing instead from a position more critical of everyday appearances, which effectively secures objectivity precisely by displacing the full-blooded realism that seemed pre-reflectively obvious.

But on the present depiction of the relation between the uncritical everyday level and the critical reflective level, it is not simply, as it might seem to be in Kant's Copernican Revolution, a theoretically driven turn away from one theoretical orientation to a different starting position that proves less problematic, as if the turn is analogous to the scientist's rejection of one theoretical framework in favour of a more explanatory paradigm. The relation between the two levels is more involved than that. To bring this out we should turn in more detail to the characterization of the distinction between the two levels of enquiry in terms of the role left in them for fictional force. We saw that from the second, critical level, it seems that the mundane, everyday theorizing about the world—at which level the subject–object structure of experience is taken at face value, the confrontation with an objective realm is seen as evidence of an ontological base, with the consequent Cartesian conception of objectivity—depends on a degree of fictional force. And that fictional force is, as we might put it, *opaque*: it works, and indeed works most effectively, because it remains undetected. We are, so to speak, taken in by the structure of experience, rather than critically taking it in. But alerting ourselves to the fictional force that that structure exerts is obviously not tantamount to eliminating it. And, as we have seen, that structure seems indeed to be an essential characteristic of experience. What we can hope for at the critical level, then, is not that we might eliminate that structure (which is what someone like Bergson hoped to do) or the fictional force that it exerts. Rather, what we can do is eliminate the opacity; render the fictional force at work *transparent*. We can put the point by saying that we are dealing here with a necessary fiction, but that that does not mean that we cannot, at a reflective level, recognize it as such and thereby take a critical distance from the influence it stands to exert. Rendered transparent, the fictional force is seen as a propulsion towards transcendence, built in to the nature of experience, which we do well not to take at face value. If we do, we are left with objectivity as transcendence, and all the consequent epistemological problems, instead of the alternative conception of objectivity that emerges once the commitment to an ontological base is critically displaced.

Put in these terms, the close relationship between the two levels of enquiry is evident. Rather than alternative hypotheses, between which the choice is made on the basis of how each individually copes with the one explanatory task facing both, there is a direct link between the two. The uncritical stage does not merely play a facilitating role as a precursor: it is presuppositional to the critical stage. Without it we would not have either the psychological or the theoretical scope to recognize the contours of the alternative conception of objectivity that emerges once the commitment to an ontological base has been surpassed. Given that experience is essentially so structured as to present the subject with an independent object domain, there is no room simply to discard the uncritical conception of objectivity: the very structure of experience introduces it. The only two options then are to adhere exclusively to it, or to render transparent the fictional force with which we are pointed to ontological grounds, and so take our critical distance from it. And it is only the latter reflection on the uncritical order of things that makes the critical turn possible in the first place. Without feeling the force of that first-order pull, and recognizing the fictional force involved in it, the critical conception of objectivity would not only be quite unmotivated: we would not even have the conceptual space in which comprehendingly to articulate it. In this, that fictional force is as necessary theoretically to our critical conception of objectivity as it is in practice to our having experience in the first place. There is no way of moving straight to the second, critical level of enquiry, eliminating the transition to it from the first, uncritical level.

The nature of the close relation between the two levels of enquiry can perhaps helpfully be brought out further with the help of Plato's simile of the cave.[8] Plato, famously, invites an ontological ascent: from appearance to reality—from shadows, to puppets, to humans and the human world, and finally (supposedly) to the Forms. This can be taken as the paradigm of uncritically following the pointer to reality. The search for objectivity, for that which is universal, is here run together with the pursuit of the ultimate ontological reality. This precisely conforms to the first model of objectivity that characterizes the ordinary, uncritical level of enquiry at which the fictional force of the structure of experience remains opaque. As this extended simile might well have brought home to Plato, running the search for universality together with the search for ontologically transcendent grounds is bound to result in an unhappy regress.[9] There is never a stable terminus, because at every given putative resting-point that we might arrive at there is always the further question, the further pointer to the reality needed to explain the grounding of the properties obtaining at the point in question. These can be seen as precisely the sort of problematic consequences that follow as long as the fictional force inherent in the structure of experience remains concealed. What we approach as a given ontological base seems under closer scrutiny to lose that status. We can then either regard it as an ordering of some further ontological base, and so set out on the uncritical regress of pointers to reality; or, alternatively, we can take the critical turn and recognize the fictional force involved in ontological commitment. With that recognition it becomes obvious that there is no point in

---

[8] *Republic*, VII: 514–17.

[9] Indeed the regress is familiar: it is the same regress that arises whenever the search is on for ultimate ontological grounding (God, substance, etc.). On this, see Blackburn (1990). (The same problem, of course, is familiar in its most simple form from early mythology, in the form of questions about what supports the tortoise that supports Atlas, who supports the world on his back.)

repeating the mistake, looking for discovery of some further ontological realm, onto which the detected order is transposed. Rather, ontological commitment, the apparent discovery of an ontological base, is taken as nothing more than conviction sustained by cognitive immersion within the horizons of the necessary structure of experience. With this epistemic duality in play, with the fictional force rendered transparent (but not ineffectual), we can appreciate the deceptiveness underlying our basic commitment to an ontological base.

Once this critical turn has been taken, a different construal of the cave simile suggests itself. Of primary importance, then, is not the ostended point, the promised ontological terminus, but rather the ostensive mechanism itself. And with the appreciation of this an inversion of Plato's priorities results, replacing the ontological hierarchy with another. In an ontological order, clearly the Forms will be located at the top, and mere artefacts (puppets, shadows) at the bottom, as Plato insists. In an ordering by transparency of fictional force, however, quite the opposite order emerges: the make-believe that straddles the line between imposed and discovered order is at its most obvious, and so is least likely to take us in, in the case of artefacts; it is at its most opaque, and so least likely to be recognized, in the case of core ontological commitments. Artefacts thus are the paradigms that bring to the surface and wear openly what remains hidden throughout the lower stages of the hierarchy. It is precisely with such appearances, where the make-believe involved is manifest, that we are brought to recognize the illusion, the abeyance of critical insight, the suspension of disbelief involved in ontological commitment. These cases allow us to stop and observe the pointer to reality at work, rather than simply observing the end-result itself.

The point can be put by saying that on the critical view the inversion of Plato's cave simile comes to this: properly understood, the result of expunging all hidden fictional force is a clearer view not of reality, as Plato contends, but of the mechanism that drives us to talk of reality. Indeed, on this view, what goes for artefacts generally goes all the more clearly for art, and for representational art in particular. Rather than seeing such art, as Plato did, as a lower form of activity because it deals with mere appearances, it stands to be recognized as revealing something that the epistemological efforts of science do not. It is not that representational art, such as sustains make-believe, derives its value in so far as it mirrors reality, but rather that it makes explicit the deceptiveness at work in our pre-reflective ontological attitude.[10] The result is an appreciation of the intimate connection between ontological commitment

---

[10] To put it slightly differently: make-believe can be thought to appeal to us not because it models reality, but rather because reality in ordinary experience matches the deceptiveness of it.

and the capacity for deception, and in particular for self-deception. And where this is allowed, it is recognized that ontology, in essentially relying on fictional force, has no place in a critical context of enquiry. And it is at that point, and to that extent, that the conception of objectivity shorn of association with ontological underpinnings emerges as the critical notion that can do the required work.

What we have, then, are two hierarchies, both of which can be said to aim at insight: one appropriate to the first, uncritical level of enquiry, the other ushered in once the critical turn has been taken and we realize the fictional force at work in ontological commitment. Plato's ontological hierarchy is the natural result of associating the search for objectivity with ontological commitment; the other is the natural propaedeutic to a conception of objectivity that is duly critical in expunging the opaque fictional force inherent in ontological commitment. It is only with the second that we turn away from ontological claims to a persistently critical insight into the scope for objectivity or universality.

It is important to recognize, at this point, having clarified the distinction between the two levels and the associated conceptions of objectivity, just how extensive the first, uncritical level of enquiry is. Put in relation to Kant, it is just as inclusive as Kant's empirical reality, in the sense that it encompasses any discipline concerned with enquiry into what Kant considers to be empirical reality.[11] Put more generally, and perhaps more helpfully, the distinction between those endeavours that reside at the uncritical level of enquiry and those that occupy the critical level of explanation is precisely isomorphic with, and can in fact equally be presented as, the distinction between naturalist and non-naturalist areas of enquiry. This entails, but is not exhausted by, the claim that the demarcation is such that the natural sciences fall on one side, and philosophical explanation on the other.

That the distinction between naturalist and non-naturalist disciplines, corresponding to the distinction between levels of enquiry, is wider than that between natural science and philosophy is obvious. Nevertheless, it is worth saying something about this, however briefly. On the one hand, naturalist explanation will include more than natural science. On the other, and more interestingly, what is excluded by naturalist explanation will include more than philosophy. This is so in at least two ways. For one thing, not all science is naturalistic. And when it comes to the pure sciences, logic, for example, or mathematics, they too are not confined to, or indeed properly located within, the first level of enquiry. There is no reason why such sciences should not survive into the critical stage, without any trace left of objectivity construed

---

[11] This formulation allows for the fact that the distinction here is in terms of levels of enquiry, and not, as in Kant, of domains of fact enquired into.

as limning the structure of some ontological base. And, indeed, taken as nested within that framework we are left with the apparent room for contingency, for ontological shifts resulting in mutated logical or mathematical forms. The only hope for objectivity as the strict universality those pure sciences require is, in terms of the present discussion, to escape that uncritical level of enquiry. (This does mean that such strict universality will not be available in the natural sciences.) Secondly, apart from philosophy and the non-natural sciences, there are other spheres of human creative activity that might, without undue distortion, be thought of as areas of enquiry: in particular, representational art. The difference between natural science and representational art is well served here. Both are after all representational. Both might be said to aim at insight into the nature of things. But the conception of what the natural sciences are supposed to be true to means that they are essentially bound to the ontological conception of objectivity, whereas the representational arts not only can survive beyond that level of enquiry, but indeed the reflective insights they are typically after can, as we have seen, precisely serve to facilitate the transition from it to the critical level. It might be thought, in fact, that representational art reaches critical maturity only when it is released from subservience to the uncritical ontological level of enquiry. In view of this, it should be clear that it is entirely fitting, and so a strength of the taxonomy, that it would have such art and philosophy end up together in the same rubric.

But, of course, for present purposes the alignment specifically of natural sciences with the uncritical ontological attitude, as opposed to philosophy as occupying the critical level of enquiry, is most salient. Natural science remains wholly internal to the first level of enquiry, at which the subject–object dichotomy and the consequent ontological conception of objectivity are prevalent. For the natural scientist, enquiry into truth just is a matter of securing representations of the way of an independent ontological realm. The productivity of that mode of explanation is both valuable and unsurprising. It is perfectly well suited to our ordinary pre-reflective theoretical engagement with the world, the orientation we occupy when without question we orientate ourselves epistemically within the horizons of the subject–object dichotomy. But that is not incompatible with recognizing that, ironically, for all its rigorous endeavours to strip away appearances and reach the underlying reality, it remains an uncritical mode of enquiry. We might say that from the perspective of sufficiently critical philosophy, the scientific image is merely the manifest image.[12] It takes at face value what critical reflection reveals as the

---

[12] More metaphorically, we may say that the structure of experience sets the stage within which natural science is entirely appropriate, but that level of enquiry works precisely by being blind to the fact that it is a stage set that fixes its horizons.

fictional force inherent to the structure of experience, resulting in the unchecked impetus towards ontological transcendence. Natural science, on this view, is akin to religion in not stopping short at the pointer itself, but rather following its lead. Both, despite all the differences between them, are alike in this one respect, that they engage in uncritical (and internally unchecked) ontological commitment. By contrast, once the fictional force at work is rendered transparent, natural science can be kept in its proper place, as a rigorous enquiry internal to the engaged theoretical stance, and at the same time we then arrive at the second, non-ontological conception of objectivity appropriate to critical enquiry. The Kantian echoes of this way of stopping natural science from overstepping its proper boundaries, forcing due humility on it, should be clear.

At this point, having seen the separation of natural science and critical understanding into distinct levels of enquiry, it is perhaps easier to appreciate why the possibility of random biological mutations, or other such 'leaps', is simply irrelevant as a threat to the objectivity of canons of reason and logic. The worry is of a general type: namely, that whatever objectivity and universality there is to such normative structures is ultimately rendered fragile by world-driven shifts. If such structures are grounded in biological necessity, then they would seem to be subject to the whims of naturally occurring mutations; if they are grounded in God's will, then they would seem to be subject at any stage to possible divine revision.[13] We can now see that the apparent problem indicates merely a confusion of levels. The confusion consists in not recognizing that the ontological explanations applicable at the lower level are *confined* to it. Such explanations hold only in relation to the empirical investigation of the object-world presented in experience, at which level the fictional force continues to operate opaquely. Ontological commitment essentially rests on that opaque fictional force, and so cannot consistently be applied in a context of enquiry in which all such uncritical force has been revealed.[14] Yet it is at the latter level that philosophical investigation into the scope of universal normative structure should be conducted. When it is, we recognize that there is no danger of brute socio-historical or biological shifts that fundamentally localize the scope of transcendental arguments, or

---

[13] On the similarity between religion and biology in this respect, see Conant (1991: 109–10).

[14] It is tempting, but misleading, to compare the case to that of a character or object in a fictional context being taken to have some impact outside the scope of that fiction. This would be misleading because it wrongly suggests that the problem is that the item in question, like the fictional character, is recognized from outside the scope of the fiction not to exist. That would only obscure the relevant and significantly more radical point, namely, the blanket inapplicability of ontological commitment (whether by affirmation or denial) outside the scope of the fictional force. It is, however, worth noting that the notion of the *scope* of a fiction operator is helpful and could be developed further to good effect.

of normative structure generally. It is only if we depart from critical–reflective mode that we again make ontology our starting-point—biology (or the material world generally) is allowed in the driving seat, so to speak—and the simple possibility of mutations accordingly seems dangerous. To put the point differently, the apparent problem results from confusing those canons of objectivity adequate only for the natural sciences, with those appropriate to philosophy and the pure sciences.[15]

It is now time, by way of conclusion, to situate the above distinction between levels within the broader sweep of our discussion. Starting with nothing more than the most rudimentary heterogeneous domain of presentation, we have seen that it will be internally structured to present an independent background matrix, in relation to which all change is plotted, but which itself cannot change. We have seen too that this amounts to starting explanation not from taking the subject–object dichotomy as basic, but rather one (*explanatory*) step back from that, seeing how the basis of that dichotomy would itself emerge as part of the internally presented structure of a rudimentary domain of presentation that did not include that dichotomy as part of its external characterization. We can now appreciate that there are two directions in which we can go from this point, corresponding to the two levels of enquiry identified. Confined to the internally presented order, we find ourselves at the first, uncritical level of enquiry. Here the subject–object dichotomy is taken at face value, and explanation proceeds to a description of that independent objective domain with which we are confronted in experience. It is here that the ontological paradigm rules, resulting in the ontological commitment to independent objects, substances, a causal order, etc. And it is here too that the natural sciences belong, as an investigation of that ontological order. The other direction takes its distance from the internally presented order of empirical experience, and focuses on the subject–object dichotomy as itself part of the internally generated order. It then becomes clear that it is only by remaining blind to that insight that the pointer to an independent objective world inherent in the subject–object dichotomy, and so commitment to an ontological base, will be followed. This is the critical level of enquiry, at which the ontological commitment made at the first level is seen as essentially uncritical, resting on an opacity of fictional force.

As long as we remain confined to the internally presented structure of the domain of presentation, to the empirically registered order of things, and so too to the level of uncritical theoretical explanation, objectivity is construed

---

[15] We might also put the point by saying that we mistake ontological talk confined to the scope of a fiction operator, for ontological commitment not so confined.

ontologically, which is the dominant conception from Plato to Nagel.[16] And as long as that is the conception, attempts at a secure crossing from a subjective to an objective order will remain prone to subject-driven and world-driven sceptical problems. Radical contingency, shifts and mutations dragging the world and us this way or that, remain ineliminable. Moreover, the explanatory value of the appeal to an ontological base remains unstable, for the reasons we have seen, and the search for completion of the explanatory account can only lead to an infinite ontological regress.

Once we take leave of the internally presented structure, the subject–object dichotomy is displaced from its foundational status, and the commitment to an ontological base drops away. We are then left with a conception of objectivity as universality without ontology that is resistant to both the subject-driven scepticism of Part I, and the world-driven scepticism of Part II.

It may be thought that the present discussion has perhaps nevertheless not managed to avoid ontological commitment altogether at the critical level. That is, it might be thought that even once philosophical explanation starts, as it should, not from the ontological talk that emerges at the level of the uncritical naturalistic attitude to the subject–object dichotomy, but rather sees that too as an emerging structural feature, we will nevertheless still be taking our philosophical beginnings from an ontologically minimal commitment: surely at the very least we are committed to our starting-point in a rudimentary heterogeneous domain of presentation. But in fact there is, strictly speaking, no room to take the presence of a simple heterogeneous domain of presentation as an ontological commitment at all. That would be to import to the critical level the ontological talk that has no place at this level of enquiry. That is, it is important to be clear how the non-ontological model of objectivity that comes into play at the critical level of enquiry applies back to the starting-point of that enquiry, and so precludes a conception of it that is still ontological (even if only with reference to a base significantly more rudimentary than that of the uncritical level of enquiry).

At the same time, it is important not to let this obscure the point made earlier. Given the alternative notion of objectivity available at the level of philosophical enquiry it is tempting, but nevertheless wrong, to think that we could simply discard altogether all reference to the uncritical level of experience and internal theorizing about it, when it came to philosophy. Not to appreciate this is to fail to allow for the full importance of fictional force, not only to our experience, but also to our intellectual undertakings. Experience requires

---

[16] It is worth noting that this prevailing ontological conception does not require that reality be construed as bare (physical or material) nature. A view according to which reality is in itself conceptually structured, for example, would—at least without further explicit attention to the issue—still readily fall in with that standard conception of objectivity, consequently facing all the problems pointed out here.

an internal structure in terms of subject and object: that is just what the transcendental arguments sufficed to establish, if they establish anything at all. But so too does our theoretical understanding. If all reference to the level of experience and explanation internal to the fictional scope were eliminated, the depth of field, so to speak, needed to pose the relevant problems would not be there. Without reference to structures operative at that level, there would not be anything recognizable as experience, let alone anything like the problem of objectivity. It is only once we have sufficient structure to explain the emergence of subjects that the question of whether universal or objective normative structures constrain them even makes sense. And we cannot secure the emergence of subjects without something that is set up as an ontological base distinct from and juxtaposed to the contents of their experience. And it is only the disappointing promise of that ontological base that puts the problem of objectivity so saliently on the agenda. It is thus opaque fictional force that gets both experience and the relevant theoretical concerns off the ground in the first place. While the answer to the problem of objectivity can be presented only by leaving that uncritical level of theoretical enquiry, the question itself could not be posed without entering into it in the first place. What has emerged here is thus not only how a sufficiently critical level of enquiry may avoid the standard sceptical problems to do with objectivity, but also how that critical account cannot stand on its own, shorn of the uncritical contribution made from the lower, engaged theoretical stance. There is an ineliminable fictional contribution both to experience and to our theoretical agenda. We cannot simply set about eradicating altogether the role of fictional force.

The bearing of this on our Enlightenment ideals is worth commenting on. The eradication of all fiction from our cognitive structure, which the adherence to Enlightenment ideals would favour, turns out not to be possible. But something of the proper place of fictional force in relation to those ideals has emerged. Even if fictional force is not altogether eliminable, there might still be scope for a level of theorizing at which no unnoticed fictional force survives. And that is just what the distinction between levels of enquiry here leaves us. We have secured a conception of objectivity at a level of critical enquiry that is compatible with the Enlightenment commitment to transparency and the absence of opaque fictional force.[17] Almost as important, however, is the

---

[17] Ironically, the displacement of the theoretical status of the subject–object dichotomy that this non-ontological conception involves seems to echo Bergson's misgivings about that status, and his belief that absolute knowledge required displacing it (see Ch. 3, Sect. 4, esp. pp. 134 ff. above). The irony is in the fact that Bergson hardly intended to uphold the Enlightenment ideals (and his popularity at the time was certainly in part fuelled by the recognition of this). The impact of his work was, if anything, as a challenge to those ideals. But that orientation was determined by Bergson's positive metaphysical doctrines, in particular his claim for intuition as a means of delivering absolute knowledge rather than representational distortions, to which there is no parallel here.

fact that the standard conception of objectivity advocated by natural science, and to that extent natural science itself, turns out not to be fully compatible with those Enlightenment ideals. What the scientific paradigm overlooks, but philosophical enquiry underscores, is precisely the fictional force involved in ontological commitment.

References

ALLISON, H. (1983), *Kant's Transcendental Idealism: An Interpretation and Defense* (New Haven: Yale University Press).
AMERIKS, K. (1982), *Kant's Theory of Mind* (Oxford: Clarendon Press).
ARISTOTLE, *Physics*.
AYERS, M. (1993), *Locke: Epistemology and Ontology* (London: Routledge).
BEISER, F. C. (1987), *The Fate of Reason: German Philosophy from Kant to Fichte* (Cambridge, Mass.: Harvard University Press).
BENNETT, J. (1966), *Kant's Analytic* (Cambridge: Cambridge University Press).
—— (1971), *Locke, Berkeley, Hume* (Oxford: Clarendon Press).
BERGSON, H. (1910), *Time and Free Will* (1889), trans. F. Pogson (London: Allen & Unwin).
—— (1911a), *Creative Evolution* (1907), trans. A. Mitchell (London: Macmillan).
—— (1911b), *Matter and Memory* (1896), trans. N. M. Paul and W. S. Palmer (London: Allen & Unwin).
—— (1992a), 'An Introduction to Metaphysics' (1903); repr. in Bergson (1992c).
—— (1992b), 'Philosophical Intuition' (1911), in Bergson (1992c).
—— (1992c), *The Creative Mind* (1934), trans. M. L. Andison (New York: Citadel Press; first pub. 1946).
BIERI, P., HORSTMANN, R.-P., and KRÜGER, L. (eds.) (1979), *Transcendental Arguments in Science* (Dordrecht: Reidel).
BLACKBURN, S. (1990), 'Filling in Space', *Analysis*, 50/2: 62–5.
BOGHOSSIAN, P. (1989), 'Content and Self-Knowledge', *Philosophical Topics*, 17/1: 5–26.
—— (1997), 'What the Externalist Can Know A Priori', *Proceedings of the Aristotelian Society*, 96: 161–75.
BOLTON, D. (1982), 'Life-Form and Idealism', in G. Vesey (ed.), *Idealism Past and Present*, Royal Institute of Philosophy Lecture Series, 13 (Cambridge: Cambridge University Press).
BRANDOM, R. B. (1999), 'Some Pragmatist Themes in Hegel's Idealism: Negotiation and Administration in Hegel's Account of the Structure and Content of Conceptual Norms', *European Journal of Philosophy*, 7/2: 164–89.
BRENTANO, F. (1973), *Psychology from an Empirical Standpoint* (1874), ed. L. L. McAlister, trans. A. C. Rancurello, D. B. Terrell, and L. L. McAlister (London: Routledge).
BROOK, A. (1994), *Kant and the Mind* (Cambridge: Cambridge University Press).
BRUECKNER, A. (1983), 'Transcendental Arguments I', *Nous*, 17: 551–75.
—— (1986), 'Brains in a Vat', *Journal of Philosophy*, 83: 148–67.
—— (1996), 'Modest Transcendental Arguments', *Philosophical Perspectives*, 10: 265–80.
BURGE, T. (1979), 'Individualism and the Mental', in P. A. French, T. E. Uehling, and H. K. Wettstein (eds.), *Midwest Studies in Philosophy*, iv: *Studies in Metaphysics* (Minneapolis: University of Minnesota Press).

BURGE, T. (1982), 'Other Bodies', in A. Woodfield (ed.), *Thought and Object* (Oxford: Clarendon Press).
—— (1986), 'Cartesian Error and Perception', in Pettit and McDowell (1986).
—— (1989), 'Individuation and Causation in Psychology', *Pacific Philosophical Quarterly*, 70/4: 303–22.
—— (1994), 'Individualism and Self-Knowledge', in Cassam (1994); first pub. in *Journal of Philosophy*, 85/11 (1988), 649–63.
BURNYEAT, M. (1982), 'Idealism and Greek Philosophy: What Descartes Saw and Berkeley Missed', *Philosophical Review*, 90: 3–40.
CARNAP, R. (1937), *The Logical Structure of the World* (London: Routledge & Kegan Paul).
—— (1956), *Meaning and Necessity* (Chicago: University of Chicago Press).
CARRITHERS, M., COLLINS, S., and LUKES, S. (eds.) (1985), *The Category of the Person: Anthropology, Philosophy, History* (Cambridge: Cambridge University Press).
CARRUTHERS, P. (1992*a*), *The Animals Issue* (Cambridge: Cambridge University Press).
—— (1992*b*), 'Consciousness and Concepts', *Proceedings of the Aristotelian Society*, suppl. vol. 66: 41–59.
CASSAM, Q. (1987), 'Transcendental Arguments, Transcendental Synthesis, and Transcendental Idealism', *Philosophical Quarterly*, 37: 355–78.
—— (1989), 'Kant and Reductionism', *Review of Metaphysics*, 43/1: 72–106.
—— (ed.) (1994), *Self-Knowledge* (Oxford: Oxford University Press).
—— (1997), *Self and World* (Oxford: Clarendon Press).
CLARK, M. (1990), *Nietzsche on Truth and Philosophy* (Cambridge: Cambridge University Press).
CONANT, J. (1991), 'The Search for Logically Alien Thought: Descartes, Kant, Frege, and the *Tractatus*', *Philosophical Topics*, 20/1: 101–66.
CUMMINS, R. (1978), 'The Missing Shade of Blue', *Philosophical Review*, 87: 548–65.
DAVIDSON, D. (1984*a*), 'On the Very Idea of a Conceptual Scheme', in Davidson (1984*b*).
—— (1984*b*), *Inquiries into Truth and Interpretation* (Oxford: Oxford University Press).
—— (1994), 'Knowing One's Own Mind', in Cassam (1994); first pub. in *Proceedings and Addresses of the American Philosophical Association*, 60 (1987), 441–58.
DENNETT, D. (1987), 'Cognitive Wheels: The Frame Problem of AI', in Pylyshyn (1987); first pub. in C. Hookway (ed.), *Mind, Machines and Evolution* (Cambridge: Cambridge University Press, 1984).
—— (1991), *Consciousness Explained* (London: Penguin).
DESCARTES, R. (1975), *Meditations on First Philosophy*, in *The Philosophical Works of Descartes*, trans. E. S. Haldane and G. R. T. Ross (Cambridge: Cambridge University Press).
DETEL, W. (1996), 'Foucault on Power and the Will to Knowledge', *European Journal of Philosophy*, 4/3: 296–327.
DEWS, P. (1993), 'Subjectivity vs. Intersubjectivity', Paper delivered to a conference on the First Person, King's College, London, May.
—— (1995), 'Intersubjectivity and the Status of the Subject: Jürgen Habermas and Dieter Henrich in Debate', in *The Limits of Disenchantment: Essays on Contemporary European Philosophy* (Cambridge: Polity Press).
DRETSKE, F. (1995), *Naturalizing the Mind* (Cambridge, Mass.: MIT Press).

DURKHEIM, E. (1976), *Elementary Form of Religious Life* (London: Allen & Unwin).
—— and MAUSS, M. (1963), *Primitive Classification* (London: Cohen & West).
EVANS, G. (1982), *The Varieties of Reference*, ed. J. McDowell (Oxford: Clarendon Press).
—— (1985a), 'Things without the Mind', in Evans, *Collected Papers* (Oxford: Clarendon Press, 1985); also in Z. van Straaten (ed.), *Philosophical Subjects: Essays Presented to P. F. Strawson* (Oxford: Clarendon Press, 1980).
—— (1985b), 'Molyneux's Question', in *Collected Papers* (Oxford: Clarendon Press).
FODOR, J. A. (1979), *The Language of Thought* (Cambridge, Mass.: Harvard University Press).
—— (1987), *Psychosemantics* (Cambridge, Mass.: MIT Press).
—— (1995), *The Elm and the Expert* (Cambridge, Mass.: MIT Press).
FOGELIN, R. (1984), 'Hume and the Missing Shade of Blue', *Philosophy and Phenomenological Research*, 45: 263–72.
FORBES, G. (1995), 'Realism and Skepticism: Brains in a Vat Revisited', *Journal of Philosophy*, 92: 205–22.
FORRAI, G. (1996), 'Internal Realism, Metaphysical Realism, and Brains in a Vat', *Dialectica*, 50/4: 259–74.
FÖRSTER, E. (1989a), 'How are Transcendental Arguments Possible?', in Schaper and Vossenkuhl (1989).
—— (ed.) (1989b), *Kant's Transcendental Deductions: The Three Critiques and the Opus Postumum* (Stanford, Calif.: Stanford University Press).
FOUCAULT, M. (1967), *Madness and Civilization: A History of Insanity in the Age of Reason*, trans. R. Howard (London: Tavistock).
—— (1970), *The Order of Things: An Archaeology of the Human Sciences* (London: Tavistock).
—— (1972), *The Archaeology of Knowledge*, trans. A. Sheridan-Smith (London: Tavistock).
—— (1973), *The Birth of the Clinic: An Archaeology of Medical Perception*, trans. A. Sheridan-Smith (London: Tavistock).
—— (1988), 'Confinement, Psychiatry, Prison', in L. D. Kritzman (ed.), *Politics, Philosophy, Culture: Interviews and Other Writings, 1977–1984* (London: Routledge).
FRANKS, P. (1999), 'Transcendental Arguments, Reason and Skepticism: Contemporary Debates and the Origins of Post-Kantianism', in R. Stern (ed.), *Transcendental Arguments* (Oxford: Oxford University Press).
GADAMER, H.-G. (1994), *Truth and Method*, trans. J. Weinsheimer and D. G. Marshall (New York: Continuum).
GARDNER, S. (1999), *Kant and the Critique of Pure Reason* (London: Routledge).
GELLNER, E. (1985), *Relativism and the Social Sciences* (Cambridge: Cambridge University Press).
—— (1992), *Reason and Culture: The Historic Role of Rationality and Rationalism* (Oxford: Blackwell).
GOODMAN, N. (1978), *Ways of Worldmaking* (Hassocks: Harvester).
GRAM, M. (1971), 'Transcendental Arguments', *Nous*, 5: 15–26.
—— (1974), 'Must Transcendental Arguments be Spurious?', *Kant-Studien*, 65: 304–17.

GUYER, P. (1987), *Kant and the Claims of Knowledge* (Cambridge: Cambridge University Press).
—— (ed.) (1992), *The Cambridge Companion to Kant* (Cambridge: Cambridge University Press).
HABERMAS, J. (1985), *The Philosophical Discourse of Modernity*, trans. Frederick Lawrence (Oxford: Polity Press).
—— (1987), *The Theory of Communicative Action*, trans. Thomas McCarthy, i and ii (Boston: Beacon Press).
—— (1989), *The New Conservatism* (Cambridge: Polity Press).
—— (1992), *Postmetaphysical Thinking* (Cambridge: Polity Press).
HACKER, P. M. S. (1996a), 'On Davidson's Idea of a Conceptual Scheme', *Philosophical Quarterly*, 46/184: 289–307.
—— (1996b), *Wittgenstein's Place in Twentieth Century Philosophy* (Oxford: Blackwell).
HARRISON, R. (1970), 'Strawson on Outer Objects', *Philosophical Quarterly*, 20: 213–21.
—— (1974), *On What There Must Be* (Oxford: Clarendon Press).
—— (1982), 'Transcendental Arguments and Idealism', in G. Vesey (ed.), *Idealism Past and Present* (Cambridge: Cambridge University Press).
—— (1989), 'Atemporal Necessities of Thought; or, How not to Bury Philosophy by History', in Schaper and Vossenkuhl (1989).
HAWTHORNE, G. (1987), *Enlightenment and Despair* (Cambridge: Cambridge University Press).
HENRICH, D. (1992), 'The Origins of the Theory of the Subject', in Honneth *et al.* (1992).
HINTIKKA, J. (1972), 'Transcendental Arguments: Genuine and Spurious', *Nous*, 6: 274–81.
HOERL, C. (1998), 'The Perception of Time and the Notion of a Point of View', *European Journal of Philosophy*, 6/2: 156–71.
HOLLIS, M. (1985), 'Of Masks and Men', in Carrithers *et al.* (1985).
—— and LUKES, S. (eds.) (1982), *Rationality and Relativism* (Oxford: Blackwell).
HONNETH, A. (1991), *The Critique of Power* (Cambridge, Mass.: MIT Press).
—— (1995a), 'Decentered Autonomy: The Subject after the Fall', in *The Fragmented World of the Social: Essays in Social and Political Philosophy* (Albany: State University of New York Press).
—— (1995b), *The Struggle for Recognition: The Moral Grammar of Social Conflicts* (Cambridge: Polity Press).
—— MCCARTHY, T., OFFE, C., and WELLMER, A. (eds.) (1992), *Philosophical Interventions in the Unfinished Project of Enlightenment* (Cambridge, Mass.: MIT Press).
HOOKWAY, C. (1990), *Scepticism* (London: Routledge).
HORSTMANN, R.-P. (1989), 'Transcendental Idealism and the Representation of Space', in Schaper and Vossenkuhl (1989).
HUME, D. (1975), *Enquiries concerning Human Understanding and concerning the Principles of Morals*, ed. L. A. Selby-Bigge, 3rd edn. rev. P. H. Nidditch (Oxford: Clarendon Press).
—— (1978), *A Treatise of Human Nature*, ed. L. A. Selby-Bigge, rev. P. H. Nidditch (Oxford: Clarendon Press).

HUSSERL, E. (1997), *Cartesian Meditations*, trans. D. Cairns (Dordrecht: Kluwer).
HYLTON, P. (1990), *Russell, Idealism, and the Emergence of Analytic Philosophy* (Oxford: Oxford University Press).
JAMES, W. (1909a), 'The Philosophy of Bergson', *Hibbert Journal*, 7: 562–77; repr. abridged in James (1909b).
—— (1909b), *A Pluralistic Universe*, Hibbert Lectures on the Present Situation in Philosophy, Manchester College (New York: Longmans, Green).
—— (1910), 'Bradley or Bergson', *Journal of Philosophy, Psychology and Scientific Methods*, 7: 29–33.
——(1976), *Essays on Radical Empiricism* (Cambridge, Mass.: Harvard University Press).
—— (1981), *Principles of Psychology* (Cambridge, Mass.: Harvard University Press).
KANT, I. (1929), *Critique of Pure Reason*, trans. N. Kemp Smith (London: Macmillan).
—— (1950), *Prolegomena to Any Future Metaphysics* (Indianapolis: Bobbs-Merrill).
—— (1993), *Opus Postumum*, ed. and trans. E. Förster and M. Rosen (Cambridge: Cambridge University Press).
KEMP SMITH, N. (1962), *A Commentary to Kant's 'Critique of Pure Reason'*, 2nd edn. (New York: Humanities Press).
KENNY, A. (1968), *Descartes: A Study of his Philosophy* (New York: Random House).
KITCHER, P. (1990), *Kant's Transcendental Psychology* (Oxford: Oxford University Press).
KÖRNER, S. (1967), 'The Impossibility of Transcendental Deductions', *Monist*, 51/3: 317–31.
KRIPKE, S. (1982), *Wittgenstein on Rules and Private Language* (Oxford: Blackwell).
KYMLICKA, W. (1989), *Liberalism, Community and Culture* (Oxford: Clarendon Press).
LACEY, A. R. (1989), *Bergson* (London: Routledge).
LEAR, J. (1982), 'Leaving the World Alone', *Journal of Philosophy*, 79: 382–403.
—— (1984), 'The Disappearing "We" ', *Proceedings of the Aristotelian Society*, suppl. vol. 58: 219–42.
—— (1986), 'Transcendental Anthropology', in Pettit and McDowell (1986).
LOCKE, J. (1975), *Essay concerning Human Understanding*, ed. P. Nidditch (Oxford: Clarendon Press).
MCCARTHY, T. (1992), 'Philosophy and Social Practice: Avoiding the Ethnocentric Predicament', in Honneth *et al.* (1992).
MCDOWELL, J. (1986), 'Singular Thought and the Extent of Inner Space', in Pettit and McDowell (1986).
—— (1994), *Mind and World* (Cambridge, Mass.: Harvard University Press).
MCGINN, C. (1990), *The Problem of Consciousness* (Oxford: Blackwell).
MACINTYRE, A. (1981), *After Virtue* (London: Duckworth).
—— (1985), 'Relativism, Power and Philosophy', *Proceedings and Addresses of the American Philosophical Association*, 59: 5–22.
MAUSS, M. (1985), 'A Category of the Human Mind: The Notion of Person; the Notion of Self', in Carrithers *et al.* (1985).
MEAD, G. H. (1934), *Mind, Self and Society*, ed. and introd. C. W. Morris (Chicago: University of Chicago Press).
MILLIKAN, R. (1993), *White Queen Psychology and Other Essays for Alice* (Cambridge, Mass.: MIT Press).

MOORE, A. W. (1991), 'Can Reflection Destroy Knowledge?', *Ratio*, 4: 97–107.
—— (1992), 'Human Finitude, Ineffability, Idealism, Contingency', *Nous*, 26/4: 427–46.
—— (1997), *Points of View* (Oxford: Clarendon Press).
MOORE, G. E. (1939), 'Proof of an External World', Annual Philosophical Lecture, British Academy, 1939; *Proceedings of the British Academy*, 25: 273–300; repr. in Moore (1959).
—— (1959), *Philosophical Papers* (London: Allen & Unwin).
MORREALL, J. (1982), 'Hume's Missing Shade of Blue', *Philosophy and Phenomenological Research*, 42: 407–15.
MYERS, G. E. (1986), *William James: His Life and Thought* (New Haven: Yale University Press).
NAGEL, T. (1974), 'What is it Like to be a Bat?', *Philosophical Review*, 83: 435–50; repr. in *Mortal Questions* (Cambridge: Cambridge University Press, 1979).
—— (1986), *The View from Nowhere* (New York: Oxford University Press).
—— (1997), *The Last Word* (New York: Oxford University Press).
NIETZSCHE, F. (1973), *Beyond Good and Evil*, trans. R. J. Hollingdale (Harmondsworth: Penguin).
—— (1974), *The Gay Science*, trans. W. Kaufmann (New York: Random House).
—— (1994), *On the Genealogy of Morals*, trans. C. Diethe, ed. K. Ansell-Pearson (Cambridge: Cambridge University Press).
O'BRIEN, L. (1995), 'The Problem of Self-Identification', *Proceedings of the Aristotelian Society*, 95: 235–51.
—— (1996), 'Solipsism and Self-Reference', *European Journal of Philosophy*, 4/2: 175–94.
PATON, H. J. (1936), *Kant's Metaphysic of Experience*, 2 vols. (London: Allen & Unwin).
PEACOCKE, C. (1983), *Sense and Content: Experience, Thought, and their Relations* (Oxford: Clarendon Press).
—— (1992), *A Study of Concepts* (Cambridge, Mass.: MIT Press).
PERRY, J. (1993), 'The Problem of the Essential Indexical', in *The Problem of the Essential Indexical and Other Essays* (Oxford: Oxford University Press).
PERRY, R. B. (1935), *The Thought and Character of William James*, 2 vols. (Boston: Little, Brown).
PETTIT, P. (1993), *The Common Mind: An Essay on Psychology, Society and Politics* (Oxford: Oxford University Press).
—— and MCDOWELL, J. (eds.) (1986), *Subject, Thought and Context* (Oxford: Clarendon Press).
PIPPIN, R. (1982), *Kant's Theory of Form: An Essay on the Critique of Pure Reason* (New Haven: Yale University Press).
—— (1991), *Modernism as a Philosophical Problem* (Oxford: Blackwell).
—— (1997), *Idealism as Modernism: Hegelian Variations* (Cambridge: Cambridge University Press).
POWELL, C. T. (1990), *Kant's Theory of Self-Consciousness* (Oxford: Clarendon Press).
PRUDOVSKY, G. (1995), 'Arguments from Conceivability', *Ratio*, 8 (Apr.), 63–9.

PUTNAM, H. (1975), 'The Meaning of "Meaning" ', in *Mind, Language and Reality: Philosophical Papers*, ii (Cambridge: Cambridge University Press); first pub. in K. Gunderson (ed.), *Language, Mind and Knowledge*, Minnesota Studies in the Philosophy of Science, vii (Minneapolis: University of Minnesota Press).

—— (1981), *Reason, Truth and History* (Cambridge: Cambridge University Press).

PUTNAM, R. A. (ed.) (1997), *The Cambridge Companion to William James* (Cambridge: Cambridge University Press).

PYLYSHYN, Z. (ed.) (1987), *The Robot's Dilemma: The Frame Problem in Artificial Intelligence* (Norwood, NJ: Ablex).

QUINE, W. (1953a), *From a Logical Point of View* (Cambridge, Mass.: Harvard University Press).

—— (1953b) 'On What There Is', in Quine (1953a).

—— (1960), *Word and Object* (Cambridge, Mass.: MIT Press).

—— (1969a), 'Existence and Quantification', in Quine (1969c).

—— (1969b), 'Ontological Relativity', in Quine (1969c).

——(1969c), *Ontological Relativity and Other Essays* (New York: Columbia University Press).

—— (1969d), 'Speaking of Objects', in Quine (1969c).

ROMANOS, G. D. (1984), *Quine and Analytic Philosophy* (Cambridge, Mass.: MIT Press).

RORTY, R. (1970), 'Strawson's Objectivity Argument', *Review of Metaphysics*, 24: 207–44.

—— (1971), 'Verificationism and Transcendental Arguments', *Nous*, 5: 3–14.

—— (1980), *Philosophy and the Mirror of Nature* (Oxford: Blackwell).

—— (1982), *Consequences of Pragmatism* (Brighton: Harvester).

—— (1989), *Contingency, Irony and Solidarity* (Cambridge: Cambridge University Press).

—— (1991), 'The Priority of Democracy to Philosophy', in *Objectivity, Relativism and Truth*, Philosophical Papers, i (Cambridge: Cambridge University Press).

ROSENTHAL, D. (1991), 'Two Concepts of Consciousness', in D. Rosenthal (ed.), *The Nature of Mind* (Oxford: Oxford University Press).

RUSSELL, B. (1914), 'The Philosophy of Bergson'; repr. with reply by H. Wildon Carr (Cambridge: Bowes & Bowes); first pub. in *Monist*, 22 (1912), 321–47.

RUSSOW, L.-M. (1980), 'Simple Ideas and Resemblance', *Philosophical Quarterly*, 30: 342–50.

SACKS, M. (1989), *The World we Found* (London: Duckworth).

—— (1990), 'Through a Glass Darkly: Vagueness in the Metaphysics of the Analytic Tradition', in D. Bell and N. Cooper (eds.), *The Analytic Tradition* (Oxford: Blackwell).

—— (1992), 'Review of Putnam's *The Many Faces of Realism*', *Mind*, 101 (Jan.), 191–5.

—— (1999), 'Transcendental Idealism: Between Reproof and Celebration', Critical Notice, *International Journal of Philosophical Studies*, 7/3: 373–402.

SCHAPER, E. (1972), 'Arguing Transcendentally', *Kant-Studien*, 63: 101–16.

—— and VOSSENKUHL, W. (eds.) (1989), *Reading Kant: New Perspectives on Transcendental Arguments and Critical Philosophy* (Oxford: Blackwell).

SCHWYZER, H. (1990), *The Unity of Understanding: A Study in Kantian Problems* (Oxford: Clarendon Press).
SEARLE, J. (1992), *The Rediscovery of the Mind* (Cambridge, Mass.: MIT Press).
SHOEMAKER, S. (1984), 'Functionalism and Qualia', in *Identity, Cause, and Mind: Philosophical Essays* (Cambridge: Cambridge University Press).
SORABJI, R. (1983), *Time, Creation and Continuum: Theories in Antiquity and the Early Middle Ages* (London: Duckworth).
SOSA, E. (1988), 'Beyond Scepticism, to the Best of our Knowledge', *Mind*, 97: 153–88.
STERN, R. (1990), *Hegel, Kant and the Structure of the Object* (London: Routledge).
—— (1993), 'James and Bradley on Understanding', *Philosophy*, 68: 193–209.
—— (1999), 'On Kant's Response to Hume: The Second Analogy as Transcendental Argument', in Stern (ed.), *Transcendental Arguments* (Oxford: Oxford University Press).
STRAWSON, P. F. (1966), *The Bounds of Sense* (London: Methuen).
—— (1985), *Skepticism and Naturalism: Some Varieties* (London: Methuen).
—— (1990), *Individuals* (first pub. 1959; repr. London: Routledge).
STROUD, B. (1968), 'Transcendental Arguments', *Journal of Philosophy*, 65/9: 241–56.
—— (1977), *Hume* (London: Routledge).
—— (1984a), *The Significance of Philosophical Scepticism* (Oxford: Oxford University Press).
—— (1984b), 'Skepticism and the Possibility of Knowledge', *Journal of Philosophy*, 81/10: 545–51.
—— (1994), 'Kantian Argument, Conceptual Capacities, and Invulnerability', in P. Parrini (ed.), *Kant and Contemporary Epistemology* (Dordrecht: Kluwer).
—— (1999), 'The Goal of Transcendental Arguments', in R. Stern (ed.), *Transcendental Arguments* (Oxford: Oxford University Press).
TAYLOR, C. (1985a), *Philosophy and the Human Sciences*, Philosophical Papers, i and ii (Cambridge: Cambridge University Press).
—— (1985b), 'Foucault on Freedom and Truth', in Taylor (1985a).
—— (1989), *Sources of the Self* (Cambridge: Cambridge University Press).
—— (1991), 'Rorty in the Epistemological Tradition', in A. Malachowski (ed.), *Reading Rorty* (Oxford: Blackwell).
—— (1992), 'Inwardness and the Culture of Modernity', in Honneth *et al.* (1992).
—— (1995), *Philosophical Arguments* (Cambridge, Mass.: Harvard University Press).
—— (1999), 'Comment on Jürgen Habermas' "From Kant to Hegel and Back Again"', *European Journal of Philosophy*, 7/2: 158–63.
TUGENDHAT, E. (1986), *Self-Consciousness and Self-Determination*, trans. P. Stern (Cambridge, Mass.: MIT Press).
WALKER, R. C. S. (1978), *Kant* (London: Routledge).
—— (1989a), *The Coherence Theory of Truth* (London: Routledge).
—— (1989b), 'Transcendental Arguments and Scepticism', in Schaper and Vossenkuhl (1989).
WALZER, M. (1983), *Spheres of Justice: A Defence of Pluralism and Equality* (Oxford: Blackwell).

WEISKRANTZ, L. (1986), *Blindsight* (Oxford: Oxford University Press).

WELLMER, A. (1991), 'The Dialectic of Modernism and Postmodernism: The Critique of Reason since Adorno', in *The Persistence of Modernity: Essays on Aesthetics, Ethics, and Postmodernism*, trans. D. Midgley (Cambridge, Mass.: MIT Press).

WIGGERHAUS, R. (1994), *The Frankfurt School: Its History, Theories and Political Significance*, trans. M. Robertson (Cambridge: Polity Press).

WILKERSON, T. E. (1970), 'Transcendental Arguments', *Philosophical Quarterly*, 20: 200–12.

WILLIAMS, B. (1978), *Descartes: The Project of Pure Enquiry* (Harmondsworth: Penguin).

—— (1981a), 'The Truth in Relativism', in *Moral Luck* (Cambridge: Cambridge University Press).

—— (1981b), 'Wittgenstein and Idealism', in *Moral Luck* (Cambridge: Cambridge University Press).

—— (1985), *Ethics and the Limits of Philosophy* (London: Fontana Paperbacks).

WILLIAMS, W. H. (1992), 'Is Hume's Shade of Blue a Red Herring?', *Synthese*, 92: 83–99.

WITTGENSTEIN, L. (1952), *Philosophical Investigations* (Oxford: Blackwell).

—— (1961), *Tractatus Logico-Philosophicus*, trans. D. F. Pears and B. F. McGuiness (London: Routledge & Kegan Paul).

—— (1969), *On Certainty* (Oxford: Blackwell).

WRIGHT, C. (1994), 'Putnam's Proofs that we are not Brains in a Vat', in P. Clark and B. Hale (eds.), *Reading Putnam* (Oxford: Blackwell).

—— (1996), 'Human Nature?', *European Journal of Philosophy*, 4: 235–54.

—— SMITH, B. and McDONALD, C. (eds.) (1998), *Knowing our Own Minds* (Oxford: Oxford University Press).

YABLO, S. (1993), 'Is Conceivability a Guide to Possibility?', *Philosophy and Phenomenological Research*, 53/1: 1–42.

Index

absolute change 264
absolute conception 130, 310–11, 312, 314
absolute knowledge 130, 134, 136, 137, 138, 139, 326 n.
Adorno, T. 174
Allison, H. 37 n. 117, 48 n. 10, 49 n. 14, 50, 54, 55 n. 22, 55 n. 23, 58 n. 24, 68 n. 42, 74 n. 58, 199 n. 6, 239 n. 32, 241 n. 36, 282 n. 14, 283 n.
Analogies 75 n. 59, 84, 116, 258 n. 58
 First Analogy 84, 105 n., 240 n., 256 n. 56, 257, 260, 262, 265, 266, 269, 283
 Second Analogy 87 n. 80, 92 n. 87, 278, 281–3
analytic tradition 146–9, 153–7, 161, 162, 164–7, 168 n. 46, 175 n. 9
animal perception 77 n. 62
appearance:
 pure 56
 and reality 17, 83, 89, 91, 124, 319
 transcendental 17, 309–10
appearance-reality gap 273, 274, 279, 282–4, 286 n. 18
apprehension 116–17, 233
Aristotle 237 n. 30, 293
 Aristotelian form 167, 169
 Aristotle's immanent platonism 167
 representational art 320, 322
artefacts 320
association of ideas, 40, 59, 65–8
 associationism 61, 65, 71, 101
atomism:
 perceptual 77–9, 86, 93, 111, 113–15, 120, 133, 239
 psychological 11, 12, 20, 25–8, 30–1, 39–40, 45–7, 54–6, 59, 65–6, 68–9, 71, 76–9, 84, 93–7, 104, 112, 114–15, 119, 121, 129, 131–2, 221–2, 228, 270
 sensory 76, 77, 78
attention 116–17
Ayers, M. 11 n. 17, 12 n. 21

behaviourism 161, 177
Beiser, F. C. 301 n.

Bennett, J. 75 n. 60, 82 n. 69, 90, 91 n. 83, 259, 267
Bergson, H. 27, 129–42, 216 n. 46, 221, 270, 289, 312, 318, 326 n.
 knowledge by analysis 131–2, 140
 knowledge by intuition 131–41, 326 n.
 see also philosophical intuition
biology (biological structure) 160, 167, 168, 293, 323–4
Blackburn, S. 268 n. 79, 319 n. 9
Blanshard, B. 278
blindness (cognitive, epistemic) 15, 17, 44
blindsight 223 n. 4
Boghossian, P. 159 n. 25
Bolton, D. 207–8
brain 103, 109, 123, 170, 172, 244 n. 42
 in a vat 92 n. 86
Brandom, R. B. 306 n.
Brentano, F. 96
British Idealism 278, 281
Brueckner, A. 92 n. 86
Burge, T. 148 n. 7, 158–9, 161, 162 n. 33

caloric 268 n. 78
Carnap, R. 175, 176, 177, 314–15
Carruthers, P. 223 n. 4, 227 n. 12
Cassam, Q. 235 n. 26
Categories 60, 63, 64, 73–5, 81, 83, 88, 124, 301
causality (causal law) 13, 40, 43, 57, 64, 87 n. 80, 90, 92, 113, 124, 269, 282, 324
charity 185–6
co-existence 39
 see also spatial contiguity
cogito 99
Collingwood, R. G. 288
combination 60, 68, 76
 see also synthesis
commensurability (incommensurability) 237, 244–5, 249–51, 253, 255
communitarianism 154, 155 n. 18, 163, 164
Conant, J. 323 n. 13
conceptions of objectivity 315–27
 ontological conception 317–22, 324–7
 non-ontological conception 317–23, 325, 326

Index

concepts, conceptualization 59–64, 67–8, 69, 71–81, 115, 133, 137, 140, 224, 229
  concept application 63, 67–8, 69, 74, 77, 81, 83, 115, 133
  conceptual experience 232–3
  formal and material 160
  pure concepts of the understanding 64, 83; *see also* Categories
conceptual scheme (framework) 176–87, 188–90, 192, 286, 287, 301, 314–15
consciousness 80–3, 86, 105, 110, 223
  abrupt qualitative change 105–6
  gaps in 105–6
  threshold of 97
contiguity, *see* temporal; spatial
convergence 147, 149, 157 n. 23, 305–8
Copernican Revolution (turn) 147, 169, 198, 302, 318
  see also naturalized Copernican turn
critical vs. naturalistic validation of belief 41
critical reflection 174, 194, 217, 297–8, 322
critical (reflective) and uncritical (pre-reflective) stances 298–302, 309–10, 314–19, 321–6
Critical Theory 151, 174
Cummins, R. 22 n. 62

Davidson, D. 159, 178–87, 189–90, 193 n. 43, 314
deception 320
defeatism 41, 43
Dennett, D. 16
Descartes, R. 7–9, 69, 88, 94, 99, 117 n. 69, 137, 141, 316 n. 6
  Cartesian dichotomy 135, 145
  Cartesian extension 136
  Cartesian framework 127
  Cartesian individual (individualism) 142, 146, 147, 161, 201 n. 11
  objective and formal reality 316 n. 6
Detel, W. 194 n. 45
Dewey, J. 175 n. 9
Dews, P. 151 n. 13, 152 n. 15
difference in simultaneity 241–5, 247, 250, 254
dispositional property 267–8
distinctions of reason 27
domains of presentation 228–57
  heterogeneous 229, 232–41, 243, 251–4, 255, 257, 268, 313, 324, 325
  heterogeneous at a moment 241–54
  homogeneous 229–40, 252, 253, 265 n. 69
  internal structure of 235, 324–5
  presented domain 229

domain of temporally extended presentation 253, 254
dream, even less than 223
Durkheim, E. 174, 175 n. 7

egological subject (self) 146–68, 169, 172 n., 196, 198, 303
eliminative materialism 289
empirical:
  appearances 56, 88 n. 81, 136, 137, 276, 284, 310, 316
  constraints 174, 214–15
  idealism 91, 171, 201, 205, 208, 275, 280, 316
  realism 18, 88, 136, 138, 173, 176, 316
  reality (world) 17, 18, 57, 58, 69, 88–92, 127, 138, 139, 165, 177, 199, 202, 235 n. 27, 271, 276, 282, 284, 302, 304, 309, 310, 317, 321
  relativism 215–16, 292
empiricism (empiricists) 19, 95, 101, 108, 111–12, 129, 131, 132, 140, 183, 221, 270
  radical empiricism 128, 221
Enlightenment 19, 20, 41, 43, 58, 90, 147, 149, 150, 151, 152, 154, 155, 163, 168, 326–7
epistemic condition 50, 52, 53, 56
epistemic duality 174, 176, 187–91, 194, 195–7, 286–7, 297, 299, 300, 302, 304, 309, 311, 313, 316, 320
Evans, G. 61 n. 29, 241 n. 35
Ewing, A. C. 278, 281
existence-change 267
experience, (always) successive 84–5, 115–17
experience of succession 86–7
experience of temporal duration 253
experience, as of objects 170–1, 172
experiences 222–8
  components of 224–8
  individual 224–6
  momentary 229 n. 16, 234–5, 236
  non-conscious 223 n. 4
externalism 159, 160, 161, 165

faculties 48, 59, 64, 74, 113, 114–15, 121–2, 136, 147, 221, 270
  stacked 63–4, 270
faith 18, 19, 41, 43, 57, 90, 163
fallibilism 172, 175 n. 8
family resemblance 288, 290
fear of reality 175 n. 8
fiction 151, 217, 326
fiction operator (scope of) 323 n. 14, 324 n.

fictional character 323 n. 14
fictional force 174, 188, 194, 297–300, 316, 318–27
  necessary role of 318–19, 325–6
  opaque 318–21, 323–4, 326
  transparent 318–20, 323, 326
first-person authority 159, 161
fixed grammatical constraints 292
Fodor, J. 24, 25, 36, 160 n. 31
Fogelin, R. 22 n. 62, 27 n. 85
Forbes, G. 92 n. 86
foreground-background structure 116, 229–32, 234, 237, 239, 243, 256
form of experience 171, 192, 213, 235, 290, 291
form(s) of life 171, 190, 191, 195, 201, 205, 207, 211, 212, 287, 291–2, 295–6, 301–2
  dynamic 288
  invariant 307
Forrai, G. 92 n. 86
Foucault, M. 148 n. 4, 174, 175 n. 7, 189, 194, 195, 196 n. 51
Fourth Paralogism 91 n. 85, 316
frame of reference 286
frame problem 16
framework limitations 212, 287
Franks, P. 286 n. 19
Frege, G. 100 n. 22
Freud, S. 148
fringes 34, 109, 110

Gadamer, H.-G. 162
Gardner, S. 54 n. 19, 58 n. 24
German Idealism 207, 286 n. 19, 301 n.
global first-person plural 201, 205, 208–9, 211, 212, 217
  globally indexed 305
God 136, 249, 260, 319 n. 9, 323
God's-eye view point 130
Goodman, N. 126 n. 92

Habermas, J. 151, 152 n. 15, 153, 155 n. 20, 164, 166 n. 43, 218, 305–6
Hacker, P. 166 n. 42, 182 n. 23
Harrison, R. 286 n. 19
Hegel 147, 148, 149, 154 n. 17, 161
  Hegelian 151, 173, 205 n. 22
  naturalized Hegelianism 161, 162, 174, 175 n. 9, 306 n.
Henrich, D. 148 n. 5
heterogeneity 118
  cross-modal h. at a time 248–9
  see also domains of presentation, heterogeneous

Hoerl, C. 229 n. 16
holism 11, 27, 97 n. 12, 103 n., 110, 112, 119, 176, 270
homogeneous domains of presentation, see domains of presentation
homogeneous experiences 233
Honneth, A. 148, 151, 152 n. 14
horizons of significance 163, 196
Horkheimer, M. 174
Horstmann, R.-P. 207
human life-world 208
Hume, D. 13, 14, 19, 20–42, 43, 44, 45, 54, 56, 58, 59, 61, 65, 66, 69, 70, 71, 79, 80, 85, 87, 88, 94, 97 n. 12, 99, 100 n. 24, 108, 125 n. 87, 246 n. 45
Husserl, E. 125 n. 86
Hylton, P. 165 n. 38

ideal speech situation 153, 164
ideas, complex and simple 10–14, 21–8, 58–9
illusion 271
imagination 29, 59
immortality 234
impressions:
  and ideas 21–30, 32, 59
  simple and complex 61–3
inconceivability, a guide to impossibility 308
inconceivability, no guide to impossibility 173, 213, 217, 289
indexical 158
individualism 8, 157 n. 23, 160 n. 31
inference to the best explanation 172
inference to reality 272, 273, 274–85, 309–10
innate ideas 9–10, 12, 22–4, 27, 28, 29, 42, 94, 97 n. 12, 137, 221
intellectual intuition 136 n. 120
intentional object 125
internal questions 178, 195
internal realist 218 n.
internalist 205
intersubjective:
  construction 152, 163
  model of the subject 150–3, 168
  paradigm 156–7, 164, 306
  recognition 149, 151–2, 156
  structure 156
intuitions 77, 223 n. 3
  see also Bergson, knowledge by intuition; philosophical intuition
intransitivity of familiarity 192–3, 291
  see also translation, intransitivity of

Jacobi, F. 301 n. 47
James, W. 27, 34, 46, 47, 79, 84, 93, 94–129, 130 n. 101, 132, 133, 134, 136 n. 118, 139, 140 n. 132, 141, 166, 210–11, 216, 221, 228 n. 14, 229 n. 16, 270
judgement 19, 60, 62, 69, 81, 82, 121, 123
  accusatives of 74, 83
  acts (acts of) 68, 73, 74, 77, 78, 79, 93, 113, 115, 121, 122, 124, 270
  faculty of 75, 114, 133, 221
  forms of 60 n. 27
  inter- and intra-perceptual 81–3
  logical functions of 109
  past tense 83, 124
  present tense 82
  self-conscious 113

Kant, I. 17, 18, 19, 30, 36, 37, 39, 41, 43–93, 94, 100, 104, 107, 108, 109, 111, 114, 118, 123, 124, 126, 127, 129, 131, 132, 136–8, 141, 150, 171 n., 173, 181, 188, 194, 198–207, 210 n. 36, 211 n. 40, 215, 217 n. 48, 222–3, 228, 233 n., 235, 237, 241 n. 36, 256 n. 56, 257–9, 262, 264–7, 270–1, 274–84, 297, 300–4, 309 n., 313–17, 321
  Kantian 31, 94, 136, 239 n. 32, 240
  naturalized Kantianism 174, 175, 176, 177, 183, 184, 195, 196, 314, 315
Kemp-Smith, N. 55 n. 21, 84 n. 75, 116
Kenny, A. 316 n. 6
Kitcher, P. 67 n. 39
Körner, S. 286 n. 19
Kripke, S. 156–7, 177 n. 13

Lacey, A. R. 135
language game 190 n. 35, 201, 204–6, 211–13, 315
Language of Thought 36, 160 n. 31
lawgiver of nature 67, 73–4
laws of nature 43, 124
Lear, J. 201, 204–8, 211 n. 40, 215 n.
Leibniz 17, 18, 137, 253
levels of enquiry 302, 309, 314–26
  empirical and transcendental 314
  see also critical (reflective) and uncritical (pre-reflective) stances
limits of language 200–1, 209–10
linguistic idealism 176
linguistic inexpressibility 307–8
linguistic turn 188
Locke, J. 10–20, 21, 24, 33, 40, 41, 43, 44, 45, 54, 56, 58, 70, 71, 94, 97 n. 12, 99
  Lockean 37

logic 191, 193, 289, 290–1, 295, 321–2, 323
logical form (space) 169, 209, 256, 307

McCarthy, T. 155 n. 20
McDowell, J. 156 n. 22, 158, 162, 165 n. 39, 166, 167
MacIntyre, A. 154 n. 16
madness 175 n. 7
make-believe 320
manifest image 322
manifold of intuition 58, 60, 62, 68, 71, 180
Marcuse, H. 174
Marx, K. 174
mathematics 321–2
matrix 231, 242–50, 290–2
  background 240, 247, 249–50, 252, 256, 258, 262, 263, 286, 290–4
  cognitive 307
  colour 28
  conceptual 186
  invariant spatio-temporal 255–7, 263, 264, 269, 285, 307
  non-sensory 249–50
  normative 291, 295
  perceptual 247, 307
  quasi-spatial 231
  spatial 50, 53, 246, 255
  temporal 252
  spatio-temporal 255
Mauss, M. 174, 175 n. 7
Mead, G. H. 151, 152, 175 n. 9
meaningful disagreement 185–7, 290–1, 293
memory 29, 35
mental state 223 n. 4
metaphysics 130, 150, 164, 166, 168, 169, 173, 195, 217, 262, 271, 293–6, 305, 316
  descriptive 286 n. 18, 289
  immanent 138
Metaphysical Deduction (of the Categories) 60, 73, 75, 81, 83, 133, 222 n. 1
metaphysical realism (realist) 169, 171–2, 178, 202–7, 210, 314
methodological solipsism 134
Millikan, R. 160 n. 29
mind-dust 94
  mind-stuff 95, 97 n. 10
missing shade of blue 22, 24, 25–6, 28–9, 32
mobility 135, 136
  see also pure duration
model of mind 7, 9, 18, 41–2, 43, 66, 114, 127, 141, 221–2, 308, 312
  Cartesian 10

Index

empiricist 10, 13, 15, 19, 20, 35, 38, 40, 44, 45, 58, 59, 61, 63, 64, 68, 70, 71
  folk psychological 289
  Hume's 37, 39, 40, 43, 64, 69
  James's 94
  Kant's 57, 69, 100, 104, 112, 113, 114, 116, 124, 129, 304
  Lockean 14, 19, 69
  rationalist 10
modus ponens inference 91, 160, 211, 271, 272, 298 n. 43, 310
monads 95, 253
Moore, A. W. 92 n. 86, 157 n. 23, 193 n. 43, 297 n. 42, 310 n.
Moore, G. E. 52 n. 16
Moreall, J. 22 n. 62
Myers, G. E. 128 n. 96

Nagel, T. 223 n. 4, 312–14, 316, 325
naïve or unqualified realism 170, 189, 200, 208, 271–2, 310
narrow content 158
natural-kind terms 158
natural world 169
naturalism 40–1, 145, 146, 165, 169, 178, 183, 184, 187, 189–90, 193, 194–6, 271, 287, 292–3, 294, 296, 305, 321, 325
  naturalized Copernican turn 172–7, 187, 188, 190, 191, 195, 196, 197, 302
  unadorned naturalism 170–2, 175
necessary connection 40
Nietzsche, F. 148
nihilism 295–6, 298, 301
non-conceptual content 61
non-empirical constraints 173
  see also transcendental constraints
normative practice 291
normative space 290, 301
normative structure (framework) 145, 146, 148, 151–7, 164–8, 169, 196–7, 296, 301–2, 305, 308, 314, 323
  universality, constancy of 293–6, 298, 301–9, 317, 323, 326
normative validity 218

object:
  bracketed 125
  of thought 125
  in the weighty sense (ontologically independent) 125, 126, 224
object domain 2345
O'Brien, L. 122 n. 74
ontological ascent 319
ontological base 268, 295–6, 297–304, 309–11, 314–20, 324–6

ontological commitment 176, 204, 238, 300, 319–27
  strictly internal 314
  suspension of disbelief involved 320
ontological dependence 199, 202, 298
ontological distinctness 53
ontological hierarchy 320
ontological independence 53, 194, 197, 298
ontological individuations 206, 210 (determinations), 211, 299, 302
ontological relativity 126, 166, 177, 185, 190, 210, 211 n. 38, 256 n. 56
ontological starting point 313, 317, 325
ontological talk 314, 325
ontology-driven innovation 307
open discourse 164, 305
open-ended enquiry 309
oracle 191, 205
organic 119, 127
ownership (of experiences) 223

paradigm (shift) 152, 153
Paton, H. J. 55 n. 21
patterns of salience 165–6, 191, 212
Peacocke, C. 61 n. 29, 160 n. 30
perceptible permanent matrix 258
perceptions 223 n. 4
Perry, J. 131 n. 104
Perry, R. B. 129 n. 99
personal consciousness 99–100, 120, 223, 225
personal identity 40, 41, 100 n. 24
perspectival:
  construal of the world 138, 310
  explanation 138
  individuation 17, 181
  structures 199
perspectives 130, 132
Pettit, P. 165 n. 39
phenomenal-noumenal gap 274
phenomenal world 88, 90, 137
phenomenologists 125
philosophical intuition 136 n. 120, 137
philosophical psychology 94
philosophical systems 139
philosophy 321–5
Plato 293, 325
  Forms 155, 167, 1679, 319–20
  naturalized platonism 162, 167
  simile of the cave 137 n. 125, 319–21
pluralism 147, 162
point of view 312
pointer to reality 300, 313, 319, 320
political philosophy 154–5

post-metaphysical orientation (setting) 150, 152, 164, 166 n. 43, 198, 204, 217–18, 292, 294, 296, 305–6, 307 n. 54
pragmatism 134, 139, 175 n. 9, 216
  pragmastists 151
pre-reflective ontological attitude 320
principles of association 20, 30, 40, 44, 59, 64, 65, 101, 104
  cause and effect 39–40
  contiguity 31, 32–9
  resemblance 31–2
problem of universality 273, 285–96, 297–8, 301, 308–10
propulsion towards transcendence 318
psychologically indivisible 236 n.
Psychologist's Fallacy 98, 101
publicity 157 n. 23
pure duration 135–41
Putnam, H. 92 n. 86, 158, 218
Pylyshyn, Z. 16 n. 42
Pyrrhonist acquiescence 218

quietude 43
qualitative state 223 n. 4
quasi-spatial structure 231, 236, 241 n. 35
Quine, W. 126 n. 92, 166, 176–9, 184, 186, 188, 189, 210–11, 256 n. 56, 314–15

Rawls, J. 218
rationality 152–7, 164–8
  rational adjudication 163 n. 36
  rational autonomy 146, 160
  rational irreversibility 306 n.
  rational thought (deliberation) 149, 150, 156, 160
reality, pre-articulated 184
reason 57, 146, 149–50, 156, 163–9, 218, 323
recognition (of perceptual or experiential content) 62–3, 72, 84, 233
  see also recognitional component
recognitional capacity 192
recognitional component (of experiences) 224–8, 233
recognitional priority 119
recurring simple ideas (mental atoms) 101–4
reflection, undermining knowledge 190 n. 36, 297 n. 42
Refutation of Idealism 44, 84, 100, 124, 228
relativism 176, 183–97, 198, 206, 215–16, 273, 287–92, 296, 297, 302, 304–6, 312, 314
  conceptual 185–7
  see also ontological relativity

religion 323
riverbed 175, 191, 192, 204, 256, 288, 289, 294
Romanos, G. D. 166 n. 42
Rorty, R. 154, 216, 276 n. 4
Rosenthal, D. 227 n. 12
rule-following 156–7, 160, 165
rules 59, 60, 156–7
  faculty of 124
Russell, B. 17
Russow, L.-M. 22 n. 62, 27 n. 85

saying/showing 308
scaffolding 286, 287, 288
sceptic, scepticism 10, 41, 43, 113–14, 118, 120–9, 134, 197, 221, 269, 273–8, 282, 303, 309–10, 316, 317, 326
  see also subject-driven scepticism; world-driven scepticism
sceptic as troubleshooter 309 n.
Schematism 75 n. 59, 84
scheme-content distinction 178–87, 188, 189, 190, 195, 196, 211, 212 n. 44
Schwyzer, H. 63 n. 31
science 19, 57, 90, 138, 140, 320
  empirical science 191
  natural science 175, 184, 321–4, 327
  pure sciences 321–2, 324
  scientific knowledge 130, 138
scientific image 322
second nature 166–7
see-saw strategy 44, 87, 118, 269 n. 82
self-ascription 85, 121, 126
  past-tense 82, 123–4
self-conscious 81–2, 92, 124, 126–7
self-conscious judgement 233 n.
self-consciousness 80, 81, 82, 85, 120, 121, 122, 149, 152, 225–8
  present continuous 122, 123
  unified over time 126
self-conscious self-identification 131
self-knowledge 140, 161
semantic externalism 158–62
  see also externalism
sense-datum experiences 225
sensibility, faculty of 48, 63–4, 72, 114, 121, 221, 270
sensory modality 92, 234, 238, 242–50, 263
  acoustic 242–3, 245
  combinatorial possibilities across 248–9, 251
  exclusionary relationships within 248
  rogue modality 251
  single-modality domain of presentation 243–4

Index

tactile 230
taste 245
visual 230, 242
shadow of necessity 213, 291
Shoemaker, S. 63 n. 31, 77 n. 61
solipsism 133, 200, 209
  solipsistic scepticism 269, 270
sound field 231
space 37–9, 45, 48–56, 241–54
  bare space 243 n.
  Euclidean 241 n. 35
  generic 241, 243, 244, 245
  physical 241 n. 35, 242
  spatial contiguity 32, 37–40, 45–6, 112
  spatial structure 33, 38–9, 50–1, 230, 236, 241, 243, 250–1, 254, 259
space and time:
  forms of 64, 88
space of reasons 166–8
spatio-temporal:
  bare spatio-temporal framework 262–8
  form 57–8
  structure 44–5, 57–8, 76, 254, 271
  world 75, 136
Stern, R. 276–85
Strawson, P. F. 49 n. 13, 68 n. 42, 75 n. 59, 90, 91 n. 83, 93, 199, 221, 224–8, 229, 233, 241 n. 35, 258 n. 58, 259, 271, 272, 274, 276 n. 4, 282 n. 13, 286–91, 303
  Strawson's sound world 230–1
stream of thought (consciousness) 44, 99, 104–10, 112–13, 119, 124–8, 132, 140 n. 132, 255 n., 270
  transitive and substantive parts 107–10
Stroud, B. 22 n. 62, 26 n. 83, 29 n. 89, 40 n. 127, 274, 275, 276 n. 4, 286 n. 19, 309 n.
structure of experience 172–3, 298, 300, 301, 313, 315, 318–20, 323
  feature necessitated by 298–9
  subject-object structure of experience 318, 326
structuring feature of experience 310
subject 141
  dialogical model 149–52
  sociological model 149, 151
  substantive subject 152
  see also egological subject
subject-driven scepticism 7, 87, 128, 145, 162, 270, 312, 325
subject-object dualism 139
subject-object dichotomy 313, 315, 322, 324, 325, 326 n.
substratum 14, 15, abiding substratum 254–7, 258, 262, 264, 265, 286

ontologically basic 297–8
  see also substance
substance 14, 15, 18, 19, 40, 84, 105, 124, 256 n. 56, 257–68
  immaterial 293
  phenomenal substance 259–62, 263 n., 265, 268, 269
  transcendental vs. metaphysical 259–60, 261, 262, 265, 267, 268
substantive kernel 125, 210
succession 36, 39, 40, 112
  perception of 33–4, 45–6
  see also experience of succession
survival 16, 65, 171
synthesis 60, 65–9, 72–5, 76, 81, 88, 113, 202, 222 n. 1
  of apprehension 67
  of reproduction 68
  rules for 73
synthetic unity of perceptions 258, 260 n. 61

tabula rasa 10, 20, 21–5, 27, 28, 30, 31, 33, 37–40, 44–7, 55, 64, 79, 270
tactile modality; *see* sensory modality
Tarski, A. 182
Taylor, C. 145 n. 2, 154 n. 16, 154 n. 17, 163, 169, 196, 306 n.
tendency, feelings of 109, 110
thing in itself 181, 204–5, 207, 274, 301 n., 303, 304, 314, 316
  see also world as it is in itself
thought:
  is in constant change 100–4, 115
  pulse of 117, 118, 119
  is sensibly continuous 104, 107, 122
time 32–9, 49, 55–6, 236–40
  bare time 239, 243 n., 252, 253
  not itself an experienced property 236–7
  temporal contiguity 32, 33–7, 39, 40
    duration 36, 117 n. 65, 252, 253
    extension 46, 236
    order 116, 124
    points 238
    relations 238–9
    structure 13, 33, 35, 36, 37, 39, 86, 124, 236–9
    succession 35, 252, 262
  transcendental status of 239
traces 34–5
Tractatus 209, 256, 307
transcendent reality 17, 18, 122 n. 75, 204–5, 208, 212
  grounds 216, 319
  order 215
  structure 211

transcendental:
  appearance 17, 88–90, 284, 316, 317
  ego, subject 122 n. 75, 202
  limits 205–6
  realism 69, 91, 136, 215, 316
  reality 18, 235 n. 27
  structure 174, 176, 213
  synthesis 113, 114, 124
Transcendental Aesthetic 48, 237 n. 29
Transcendental Analytic 48
transcendental arguments 44, 193, 217 n. 48, 221, 235, 268, 270, 273–94, 305, 308–10, 323, 326
  historically relativized 285, 288
  weaker construals 275–85
  universality of 285–6, 290, 292, 294, 305, 308–9
transcendental condition of experience 47
transcendental constraints 138, 198, 201, 203, 207, 210, 213–18, 285, 297, 304, 314
Transcendental Deduction 70 n. 44, 71, 74–9, 81, 83, 100, 118, 120, 221, 222, 228, 235, 239, 270
transcendental features 198, 210, 213–18, 285, 287, 294, 297
  universal 304–5, 307–8
transcendental idealism 18, 57, 87–93, 136, 147, 148, 169, 172–7, 178, 194 n. 46, 197, 198–210, 214–16, 274–6, 278, 280, 284–5, 297, 300–5, 310, 314, 316
  central insight in 271–2, 297–311
transcendental psychology 90–1, 113, 202, 210 n. 36, 211 n. 40, 221, 222, 228, 239, 251, 269, 270–2, 274, 303–4, 310
translation 130
  failure of 185, 187
  indeterminacy of 177
  intransitivity of 187, 193 n. 43, 291
  partial 187

unconscious mind (ideas, thought) 24, 36, 37, 97, 148
understanding:
  faculty of 48, 58, 59, 61, 63–4, 67, 83, 93, 115, 121, 270
unity of consciousness 13, 69–87, 88–9, 91–3, 96, 100 n. 24, 105–7, 109, 112–14, 118, 120–1, 123, 140, 141, 222, 224–6, 229, 235, 240, 268, 283
  across modalities 245, 251
  dissolution of 234–5
unity of the objective world 240
unowned experiences 222

verificationism 186, 274, 299, 309, 315 n.
visual field 230
visual modality, *see* sensory modality

Walker, R. C. S. 199, 284 n.
Walzer, M. 154 n. 16
Weber, M. 174
webs of interlocution 196
Weiskrantz, L. 223 n. 4
Wellmer, A. 148, 151, 155 n. 20
Williams, B. 192 n. 40–1, 200–1, 204–9, 212, 215, 292 n. 37, 297 n. 42, 310 n.
Williams, W. H. 22 n. 62, 27 n. 85
Wittgenstein, L. 139 n. 126, 155–7, 174 n. 6, 189–92, 194 n. 45, 195, 197, 198–218, 256 n. 55, 286–9, 292, 294, 296, 305, 307, 308 n., 314–15
world as it is in itself 18, 57–8, 69, 88–90, 136, 172, 176, 199–200, 202, 216, 271, 272 n., 301, 303, 310, 315, 317
world-driven scepticism 145, 146, 168, 325
world-driven shifts 323
Wright, C. 92 n. 86, 159 n. 25, 162 n. 34

Zeno 119, 129
zeroth locus 248, 263